# ELEMENTS OF ARGUMENT

# ELEMENTS OF ARGUMENT

## A Text and Reader

Annette T. Rottenberg
*University of Massachusetts at Amherst*

A Bedford Book
ST. MARTIN'S PRESS      NEW YORK

**For Alex**

*Typography:* Anna Post
*Cover design:* Richard Emery
Honoré Daumier, *Lawyers and Justice* (L. Delteil No. 1343, April 24, 1845),
    courtesy Museum of Fine Arts, Boston.

**Acknowledgments**

Susan Seidner Adler, ''Bribing Delinquents to Be Good.'' Reprinted from *Commentary*,
    October 1981, by permission; all rights reserved.
Gina Allen, ''Across the River to the Farm.'' This article first appeared in the November/
    December 1981 issue of *The Humanist* and is reprinted by permission.
Woody Allen, ''My Speech to the Graduates.'' Copyright © 1979 by The New York
    Times Company. Reprinted by permission.
Gordon Allport, ''The Nature of Prejudice.'' From the Seventeenth Claremont Reading
    Conference Yearbook, 1952. Reprinted by permission.

*(Continued on page 464)*

# Preface

Argumentation as the basis of a composition course should need no defense, especially at a time of renewed pedagogical interest in critical thinking. A course in argumentation encourages practice in close analysis, use of supporting materials, and logical organization. It encompasses all the modes of development around which composition courses are often built. It teaches students to read and to listen with more than ordinary care. Not least, argument can engage the interest of students who have been indifferent or even hostile to required writing courses. Because the subject matter of argument can be found in every human activity, from the most trivial to the most elevated, both students and teachers can choose the materials that appeal to them. And those materials need not be masterpieces of the genre, as in courses based on literature; students can exercise their critical skills on flawed arguments that allow them to enjoy a well-earned superiority.

Composition courses using the materials of argument are, of course, not new. But the traditional methods of teaching argument through mastery of the formal processes of reasoning cannot account for the complexity of arguments in practice. Even more relevant to our purposes as teachers of composition is the tenuous relationship between learning about induction and deduction, however helpful in analysis, and the actual process of student composition. E. D. Hirsch, Jr., in *The Philosophy of Composition*, wrote, "I believe, as a practical matter, that instruction in logic is a very inefficient way to give instruction in writing."[1] The challenge has been to find a method of teaching argument that assists students in defending their claims as directly and efficiently as possible, a method that reflects the way people actually go about organizing and developing claims outside the classroom.

One such method, first adapted to classroom instruction by teachers of rhetoric and speech, uses a model of argument advanced by Stephen Toulmin in *The Uses of Argument*. Toulmin was interested in producing a description of the real *process* of argument. His model was the law. "Arguments," he said, "can be compared with law-suits, and the claims we make and argue for in extra-legal contexts with claims made in the courts."[2] Toulmin's model of argument was based on three principal elements: claim, evidence, and warrant. These elements answered the questions, "What are you trying to prove?" "What have you got to go on?" "How did you get from evidence to claim?" Needless to say, Toulmin's model of argument does not guarantee a classroom of skilled arguers, but his questions about the parts of an argument and their relationship are precisely the ones that students must ask and answer in writing their own essays and analyzing those of others. They lead students naturally into the formulation and development of their claims.

My experience in supervising hundreds of teaching assistants over a number of years has shown that they also respond to the Toulmin model with enthusiasm. They appreciate its clarity and directness and the mechanism it offers for organizing a syllabus.

In this text I have adapted — and greatly simplified — some of Toulmin's concepts and terminology for freshman students. I have also introduced two elements of argument with which Toulmin is not directly concerned. Most rhetoricians consider them indispensable, however, to a discussion of what actually happens in the defense or rejection of a claim. One is motivational appeals — warrants based on appeals to the needs and values of an audience, designed to evoke emotional responses. A distinction between logic and emotion may be useful as an analytical tool, but in producing or attacking arguments human beings find it difficult, if not impossible, to make such a separation. In this text, therefore, persuasion through appeals to needs and values is treated as a legitimate element in the argumentative process.

---

[1] *The Philosophy of Composition* (Chicago: University of Chicago Press, 1977), p. 142.

[2] *The Uses of Argument* (Cambridge: Cambridge University Press, 1958), p. 7.

I have also stressed the significance of audience as a practical matter. In the rhetorical or audience-centered approach to argument, to which I subscribe in this text, success is defined as acceptance of the claim by an audience. Arguers in the real world recognize intuitively that their primary goal is not to demonstrate the purity of their logic, but to win the adherence of their audiences. To gain this adherence, students need to be reminded of the necessity for establishing themselves as credible sources for their readers.

The organization of Part I, The Structure of Argument, represents, as far as possible, the steps students take in organizing their own arguments. After the introductory overview in Chapter 1, a chapter is devoted to each of the chief elements in the argumentative process — claims, definition, support, warrants, and language. Chapter 7 treats popular fallacies; here a brief review of induction and deduction seems appropriate. Because fallacies represent errors in the reasoning process, a knowledge of induction and deduction can make clear how and why fallacies occur.

I have made every effort to provide examples, readings, and teaching strategies — including questions and writing suggestions for every reading — that are both practical and stimulating. The examples throughout, with the exception of several student dialogues, are real, not invented; they have been taken from speeches, editorial opinions, letters to the editor, advertisements, radio debates, and news reports. They reflect the liveliness and complexity that invented examples often suppress.

The readings in Part I support the discussions in several important ways. First, they illustrate the elements of argument developed in each chapter. Second, they are drawn from current publications and cover as many different subjects as possible to convince students that argument is a pervasive force in the world they live in and read about. Third, some of the essays are obviously flawed and enable students to identify the kinds of weaknesses they should avoid in their own essays. One or more essays in each chapter have been analyzed to emphasize the chapter's principle of argument.

Part II, Opposing Viewpoints, exhibits arguers in action, using both formal and informal language, debating head-on. The subjects — affirmative action, animal rights, euthanasia, immigration policy, and pornography — represent controversies which, at this writing, could hardly be more newsworthy or significant. Yet, despite their immediacy, the passions they arouse make it likely that they will continue to be controversial for a long time.

Part III offers an alphabetical arrangement of examples of good argument drawn from many sources. This mixture of old and new includes a number of classics that many teachers find invaluable in any composition course.

Finally, the appendix on writing an argumentative paper is a succinct but comprehensive guide to which students can refer throughout the semester for help in composing both the parts and the whole of every assignment. The appendix is followed by a glossary of terms and an index to authors and titles.

An instructor's manual provides additional suggestions for finding and using the enormous variety of materials available to us in a course on argument.

I hope this text will lead students to discover not only the practical and intellectual rewards of learning how to argue but the real excitement of engaging in civilized debate.

I wish to thank the reviewers who helped make this text better than it might have been without their suggestions: Lester Faigley, University of Texas at Austin; Cheryl W. Ruggiero, Virginia Polytechnic Institute; Michael Havens, University of California at Davis; Judith Kirscht, University of Michigan; Richard Katula, University of Rhode Island; Carolyn R. Miller, North Carolina State University at Raleigh; A. Leslie Harris, Georgia State University; Richard S. Hootman, University of Iowa; Donald McQuade, Queens College; and David. L. Wagner.

Above all, I owe thanks to the staff at Bedford Books, who were always discerning, patient, and generous: Charles H. Christensen, Joan Feinberg, Susan Warne, Jane Rautenberg, Nancy Lyman, Karen Henry, Carol Verburg, and Chris Rutigliano.

# *Contents*

## 3.  Definition   *54*

## 4.  Support   *75*

## PART THREE:   ANTHOLOGY   *331*

be rich, this reviewer can't help wondering why any sane person would want to be OK.

What purpose does the current grading system serve besides screening students for lazy employers or graduate-school boards and reassuring anxious parents? If the goal of higher education *is* education, let's use tests that foster learning, not competition.

It's popular to dismiss stereotypes as a generalized form of negativity; but it may be more productive to look into the reasons *why* groups attach certain labels to one another.

Although biological science can now enable some infertile women to bear children, our knowledge of embryonic mechanics may have outpaced our judgment of the risks and priorities involved.

This stirring exhortation to marchers at a civil rights rally rings out like a church bell with rhythm, imagery, joy, hope, and deep conviction. Don't just read the words — listen to the music!

A person's sexual preference is private, gays often assert, and should not be grounds for discrimination in jobs, housing, or any other arena. Leo agrees — and turns the argument back on militants seeking legal protection for their homosexuality.

If torture is the only way to squeeze life-saving information out of a kidnapper, mad bomber, or would-be assassin, shouldn't we overcome our repugnance and apply the electrodes?

When we treat freedom of expression as our own generous tolerance of other people's foolish opinions, we are forgetting that we learn most from those who tell us what we don't know or don't agree with.

PART ONE

# The Structure of Argument

# 1 *Introduction to Argument*

## THE NATURE OF ARGUMENT

A conversation overheard in the school cafeteria:

*"Hey, how come you didn't order the meat loaf special? It's pretty good today."*

*"Well, I read this book about vegetarianism, and I've decided to give up meat. The book says meat's unhealthy and vegetarians live longer."*

*"Don't be silly. Americans eat lots of meat, and we're living longer and longer."*

*"Listen, this book tells how much healthier the Danes were during World War II because they couldn't get meat."*

*"I don't believe it. A lot of these health books are written by quacks. It's pretty dumb to change your diet after reading one book."*

These people are having what most of us would call an argument, one that sounds dangerously close to a quarrel. There are, however, significant differences between the colloquial meaning of argument as a dispute or quarrel and its defintion as a process of reasoning and advancing proof, although even the exchange reported above exhibits some of the characteristics of formal argument. The kinds of arguments we deal with in this text are neither disputes nor quarrels. Often, however, they resemble ordinary discourse about controversial issues. You may, for example, overhear a conversation like this one:

*"This morning while I was trying to eat breakfast I heard an announcer describing the execution of that guy in Texas who raped and murdered a teen-aged couple. They gave him an injection, and it took him ten minutes to die. I almost lost my breakfast listening to it."*

*"Well, he deserved it. He didn't show much pity for his victims, did he?"*

*"Okay, but no matter what he did, capital punishment is really awful, barbaric. It's murder, even if the state does it."*

*"No, I'd call it justice. I don't know what else we can do to show how we feel about a cruel, pointless murder of innocent people. The punishment ought to be as terrible as we can make it."*

Each speaker is defending a value judgment about an issue that tests ideas of good and evil, right and wrong, and that cannot be decided by facts.

In another kind of argument the speaker or writer proposes a solution for a specific problem. Two men, both aged twenty, are engaged in a conversation.

*"I'm going to be broke this week after I pay my car insurance. I don't think it's fair for males under twenty to pay such high rates. I'm a good driver, much better than my older sister. Why not consider driving experience instead of age or sex?"*

*"But I always thought that guys our age had the most accidents. How do you know that driving experience is the right standard to apply?"*

*"Well, I read a report by the Highway Commission that said it's really driving experience that counts. So I think it's unfair for us to be discriminated against. The law's behind the times. They ought to change the insurance laws."*

In this case someone advocates a policy that appears to fulfill a desirable goal — making it impossible to discriminate against drivers just because they are young and male. Objections arise that the arguer must attempt to answer. In these three dialogues, as well as in all the other arguments you will read in this book, human beings are engaged in explaining and defending their own actions and beliefs and opposing those of others.

They do this for at least two reasons: to justify what they do and think both to themselves and to their opponents and, in the process, to solve problems and make decisions, especially those dependent on a consensus between conflicting views.

Most of the arguments in this book will deal with matters of public controversy, an area traditionally associated with the study of argument. As the word *public* suggests, these matters concern us as members of a community. "They are," according to one rhetorician, "the problems of war and peace, race and creed, poverty, wealth, and population, of democracy and communism. . . . Specific issues arise on which we must take decision from time to time. One day it is Suez, another Cuba. One week it is the Congo, another it is the plight of the American farmer or the railroads. . . . On these subjects the experts as well as the many take sides."[1] Today the issues are different from the issues that writer confronted more than twenty years ago. Today we are concerned about the nuclear freeze, unemployment, illegal immigration, bilingual education, gun control, homosexual rights, drug abuse, prayer in school, to name only a few.

Unlike the examples cited so far, the arguments you will read and write will not usually take the form of dialogues, but arguments are implicit dialogues. Even when our audience is unknown, we write to convince the unconvinced, to acquaint them with good reasons for changing their minds. As one definition has it, "Argumentation is the art of influencing others, through the medium of reasoned discourse, to believe or act as we wish them to believe or act."[2] This process is inherently dramatic; a good argument can create the kinds of tensions generated at sporting events. Who will win? What are the factors enabling a winner to emerge? One of the most popular and enduring situations on television is the courtroom debate, in which two lawyers (one, the defense attorney, the hero, unusually knowledgeable and persuasive; the other, the prosecuting attorney, bumbling and corrupt) confront each other before an audience of judge and jury that must render a heart-stopping verdict. Tensions are high because a life is in the balance. In the classroom the stakes are neither so intimidating nor so melodramatic, but even here a well-conducted argument can throw off sparks.

Clearly, if all of us agreed about everything, if harmony prevailed everywhere, the need for argument would disappear. But given what we know about the restless, seeking, contentious nature of human beings

---

[1] Karl R. Wallace, "Toward a Rationale for Teachers of Writing and Speaking," *English Journal*, September 1961, p. 386.

[2] J. M. O'Neill, C. Laycock, and R. L. Scale, *Argumentation and Debate* (New York: Macmillan, 1925), p. 1.

and their conflicting interests, we should not be surprised that many controversial questions, some of them as old as human civilization itself, will not be settled nor will they vanish despite the energy we devote to settling them. Unresolved, they are submerged for a while and then reappear, sometimes in another form, sometimes virtually unchanged. Capital punishment is one such stubborn problem; abortion is another. Nevertheless, we value the argumentative process because it is indispensable to the preservation of a free society. In *Areopagitica*, his great defense of free speech, John Milton, the seventeenth-century poet, wrote, "I cannot praise a fugitive and cloistered virtue, unexercised and unbreathed, that never sallies out and sees her adversary." How can we know the truth, he asked, unless there is a "free and open encounter" between all ideas? "Give me the liberty to know, to utter, and to argue freely, according to conscience, above all liberties."

## WHY STUDY ARGUMENT?

Perhaps the question has already occurred to you: Why *study* argument? Since you've engaged in some form of the argumentative process all your life, is there anything to be learned that experience hasn't taught you? We think there is. If you've ever felt frustration in trying to decide what is wrong with an argument, either your own or someone else's, you might have wondered if there were rules to help in the analysis. If you've ever been dissatisfied with your attempt to prove a case, you might have wondered how good arguers, the ones who succeed in convincing people, construct their cases. Good arguers do, in fact, know and follow rules. Studying and practicing these rules can provide you with some of the same skills.

You will find yourself using these skills in a variety of situations, not only in arguing important public issues. You will use them, for example, in your academic career. Whatever your major field of study — the humanities, the social sciences, the physical sciences, business — you will be required to defend views about materials you have read and studied.

— **Humanities.** Why have some of the greatest novels resisted translation into great films?

— **Social Science.** What is the evidence that upward social mobility continues to be a positive force in American life?

— **Physical Science.** What will be the effect on world climate of the increasing atmospheric content of carbon dioxide?

— **Business.** Are the new tax laws beneficial or disadvantageous to the real estate investor?

For all these assignments, different as they may be, you would use the same kinds of analysis, research techniques, and evaluation. The conventions or rules for reporting results might differ from one field of study to another, but for the most part the rules for defining terms, evaluating evidence, and arriving at conclusions cross disciplinary lines. Many employers, not surprisingly, are aware of this. One sheriff in Arizona advertised for an assistant with a degree in philosophy. He had discovered, he said, that the methods used by philosophers to solve problems were remarkably similar to the methods used in law enforcement.

Whether or not you are interested in serving as a sheriff's assistant, you will encounter situations in the workplace that call for the same analytical and argumentative skills employed by philosophers and law enforcement personnel. Almost everywhere — in the smallest businesses as well as the largest corporations — a worker who can articulate his or her views clearly and forcefully has an important advantage in gaining access to positions of greater interest and challenge. Even when they are primarily informative, the memorandums, reports, instructions, questions, and explantions that issue from offices and factories obey the rules of argumentative discourse.

You may not anticipate doing the kind of writing or speaking at your job that you will practice in your academic work. It is probably true that in some careers, writing constitutes a negligible part of a person's duties. But outside the office, the studio, and the salesroom, you will be called on to exhibit argumentative skills as a citizen, as a member of a community, and as a consumer of leisure. In these capacities you can contribute to decision making if you are knowledgeable and prepared. By writing or speaking to the appropriate authorities, you can argue for a change in the meal ticket plan at your school or the release of pornographic films at the neighborhood theater or against a change in automobile insurance rates. Most of us are painfully aware of opportunities we lost because we were uncertain of how to proceed, even in matters that affected us deeply.

A course in argumentation offers another invaluable dividend: It can help you to cope with the bewildering confusion of voices in the world around you. It can give you tools for distinguishing between what is true and what is false, what is valid and what is invalid, in the claims of politicians, promoters of causes, newscasters, advertisers, salespeople, teachers, parents and siblings, employers and employees, neighbors, friends, and lovers, any of whom may be engaged at some time in attempting to persuade you to accept a belief or adopt a course of action. It can even offer strategies for arguing with yourself about a personal dilemma.

We can, in fact, defend the study of argumentation for the same reasons that we defend universal education despite its high cost and sometimes controversial results. In a democracy, widespread literacy ultimately benefits all the members of the society, not only those who are the immediate beneficiaries of the education, because only an informed citizenry can make responsible choices. One distinguished writer explains that "democracy depends on a citizenry that can reason for themselves, on men who know whether a case has been proved, or at least made probable."[3]

So far we have treated argument as an essentially pragmatic activity that benefits the individual. But choosing argument over force or evasion has clear moral benefits for society as well. Argument is a civilizing influence, the very basis of democratic order. In totalitarian countries, coercion, which may express itself in a number of reprehensible forms — censorship, imprisonment, exile, torture, or execution — is a favored means of removing opposition to establishment "truth." In free societies, argument and debate remain the preeminent means of arriving at consensus.

Of course, rational discourse in a democracy can and does break down. Confrontations with police at nuclear power plants, shouting and heckling at a meeting to prevent a speaker from being heard, student sit-ins in college administrators' offices — such actions have become common in recent years. The demands of the demonstrators are often passionately and sincerely held, and the protesters sometimes succeed through force or intimidation in influencing policy changes. When this happens, however, we cannot be sure that the changes are justified. History and experience teach us that reason, to a far greater degree than other methods of persuasion, ultimately determines the rightness or wrongness of our actions.

A piece of folk wisdom sums up the superiority of reasoned argument as a vehicle of persuasion: "A man convinced against his will is of the same opinion still." Those who accept a position after engaging in a dialogue offering good reasons on both sides will think and act with greater willingness and conviction than those who have been coerced or denied the privilege of participating in the decision.

## WHY WRITE?

If we agree that studying argumentation provides important critical tools, one last question remains: Why *write*? Isn't it possible to learn the rules by reading and talking about the qualities of good and bad argu-

---

[3] Wayne C. Booth, "Boring from Within: The Art of the Freshman Essay," adapted from a speech delivered to the Illinois Council of College Teachers of English in May 1963.

ments? Not quite. All writers, both experienced and inexperienced, will probably confess that looking at what they have written, even after long thought, can produce a startled disclaimer: But that isn't what I meant to say! They know that more analysis and more hard thinking are in order. Writers are also aware that words on paper have an authority and a permanency that invite more than casual deliberation. It is one thing to make an assertion, to express an idea or a strong feeling in conversation, and perhaps even to deny it later; it is quite another to write out an extended defense of your own position or an attack on someone else's that will be read and perhaps criticized by people unsympathetic to your views.

Students are often told that they must become better thinkers if they are to become better writers. It works the other way, too. In the effort to produce a clear and convincing argument, a writer matures as a thinker and a critic. The very process of writing calls for skills that make us better thinkers. An authority on language, the British etymologist Eric Partridge, put it this way.

> Good — that is, clear, effective, entirely adequate — speaking and writing will ease and smooth the passage of general thought and the conveyance of a particular thought or impression in statement or question or command. Bad speaking and writing do just the opposite and, worse, set up doubt and ambiguity.[4]

In sum, writing argumentative essays tests and enlarges important mental abilities — developing and organizing ideas, evaluating evidence, observing logical consistency, expressing ourselves clearly and economically — that we need to exercise all our lives in our various social roles, whether or not we continue to write after college.

## THE TERMS OF ARGUMENT

One definition of argument, emphasizing audience, has been given earlier: "Argumentation is the art of influencing others, through the medium of reasoned discourse, to believe or act as we wish them to believe or act." A distinction is sometimes made between argument and persuasion. Argument, according to most authorities, gives primary importance to logical appeals. Persuasion introduces the element of ethical and emotional appeals. The difference is one of emphasis. In real-life arguments about social policy, the distinction is hard to measure. In this

---

[4] "Speaking of Books: Degraded Language," *New York Times Book Review*, September 18, 1966, p. 2.

book we use the term *argument* to represent forms of discourse that attempt to convince readers or listeners to accept a claim, whether acceptance is based on logical or emotional appeals or, as is usually the case, on both. The following brief definition includes other elements: *An argument is a statement or statements offering support for a claim.*

An argument is composed of at least three parts: the claim, the support, and the warrant.*

## The Claim

The claim (also called a *proposition*) answers the question "What are you trying to prove?" It may appear as the thesis statement of your essay, although in some arguments it may not be stated directly. There are three principal kinds of claim (discussed more fully in Chapter 2): claims of fact, of value, and of policy. (The three dialogues at the beginning of this chapter represent these three kinds of claim respectively.) *Claims of fact* attempt to prove that a condition exists or will exist, that something is or will be true. They are based on facts or data that the audience will accept:

Capital punishment is not a deterrent to crime.

Horse racing is the most dangerous sport.

California will experience colder, stormier weather for the next ten years.

All these claims must be supported by data. Although the last example is an inference or an educated guess about the future, a reader will probably find the prediction credible if the data seem authoritative.

*Claims of value* attempt to prove that some things are more or less desirable than others. They express approval or disapproval of standards of taste and morality. Advertisements and reviews of cultural events are one common source of value claims, but such claims emerge whenever people argue about what is good or bad, beautiful or ugly.

One look and Crane [writing paper] says you have a tasteful writing style.

*Tannhäuser* provides a splendid viewing as well as listening experience.

Football is one of the most dehumanizing experiences a person can face. — Dave Meggyesy

Ending a patient's life intentionally is absolutely forbidden on moral grounds. — Presidential Commission on Medical Ethics, 1983

---

*Some of the terms and analyses used in this text are adapted from Stephen Toulmin's *The Uses of Argument* (Cambridge: Cambridge University Press, 1958).

*Claims of policy* assert that specific policies should be instituted as solutions to problems. The expression *should, must*, or *ought to* usually appears in the statement.

> Prisons should be abolished because they are crime-manufacturing concerns.

> Our first step must be to immediately establish and advertise drastic policies designed to bring our own population under control. — Paul Ehrlich, biologist

> The New York City Board of Education should make sure that qualified women appear on any new list [of candidates for Chancellor of Education].

Policy claims call for analysis of both fact and value.

## The Support

Support consists of the materials used by the arguer to convince an audience that his or her claim is sound. These materials include *evidence* and *motivational appeals*. The evidence or data consist of facts, statistics, and testimony from experts. The motivational appeals are the ones that the arguer makes to the values and attitudes of the audience to win support for the claim. The word *motivational* points out that these appeals are the reasons that move an audience to accept a belief or adopt a course of action. For example, in his argument advocating population control, Ehrlich first offered statistical evidence to prove the magnitude of the population explosion. But he also made a strong appeal to the generosity of his audience to persuade them to sacrifice their own immediate interests to those of future generations.

## The Warrant

The warrant is an inference or an assumption, a belief or principle that is taken for granted. In commercial transactions a warrant is a guarantee of reliability; in argument the warrant guarantees the soundness of the relationship between the support and the claim. It allows the reader to make the connection between the support and the claim.

Warrants or assumptions underlie all the claims we make. They may be stated or unstated. If the arguer believes that the audience shares his assumption, he may feel it unnecessary to express it. But if she thinks that the audience is doubtful or hostile, she may decide to state the assumption in order to emphasize its importance or argue for its validity.

This is how the warrant works. In the dialogue beginning this chapter, one speaker made the claim that vegetarianism was more healthful than a diet containing meat. As support he offered the evidence that the authors of a book he had read recommended vegetarianism for greater health and longer life. He did not state his warrant — that the authors of the book were trustworthy guides to theories of healthful diet. In outline form the argument looks like this:

CLAIM: Adoption of a vegetarian diet leads to healthier and longer life.

SUPPORT: The authors of *Becoming a Vegetarian Family* say so.

WARRANT: The authors of *Becoming a Vegetarian Family* are reliable sources of information on diet.

A writer or speaker may also need to offer support for the warrant. In the case cited above, the second speaker is reluctant to accept the unstated warrant, suggesting that the authors may be quacks. The first speaker will need to provide support for the assumption that the authors are trustworthy, perhaps by introducing proof of their credentials in science and medicine. Notice that although the second speaker accepts the evidence, he cannot agree that the claim has been proved unless he also accepts the warrant. If he fails to accept the warrant — that is, if he refuses to believe that the authors are credible sources of information about diet — then the evidence cannot support the claim.

The following example demonstrates how a different kind of warrant can lead an audience to accept a claim.

CLAIM: Laws making marijuana illegal should be repealed.

SUPPORT: People should have the right to use any substance they wish.

WARRANT: No laws should prevent citizens from exercising their rights.

The support does not consist of evidence that marijuana is harmless. The reader who agrees with the principle that nothing should prevent people from exercising their rights, including the right to use any substance, will probably consider harmfulness irrelevant. In accepting the warrant, the reader agrees with the claim.

One more element of argument remains to be considered — *definition*. Definition, of course, is important in all forms of exposition, but it can be crucial in argument. For this reason we've devoted a whole chapter to it in this text. Many of the controversial questions you will encounter in your reading about public affairs are primarily arguments about the definitions of terms. Such terms as *abortion, pornography, equality, poverty,* and *insanity* must be defined before useful public policies about them can be formulated.

## THE AUDIENCE

All arguments are composed with an audience in mind. We have already pointed out that an argument is an implicit dialogue or exchange. Often the writer of an argument about a public issue is responding to another writer or speaker who had made a claim that needs to be supported or opposed. In writing your own arguments, you should assume that there is a reader who may or may not agree with you. Throughout this book, we will continue to refer to ways of reaching such a reader.

Speechmakers are usually better informed than writers about their audience. Some writers, however, are familiar with the specific persons or groups who will read their arguments; advertising copywriters are a conspicuous example. They discover their audiences through sophisticated polling and marketing techniques and direct their messages to a well-targeted group of prospective buyers. Other professionals may be required to submit reports to convince a specific and clearly defined audience of certain beliefs or courses of action. An engineer may be asked by an environmental interest group to defend his plans for the building of a sewage treatment plant. A town planner may be called on to tell the town council why she believes that rent control will not work. A sales manager may find it necessary to explain to his superior why a new product should be launched in the Midwest rather than the South.

In such cases the writer asks some or all of the following questions about the audience:

— Why has this audience requested this report? What do they want to get out of it?
— How much do they already know about the subject?
— Are they divided or agreed on the subject?
— What is their emotional involvement with the issues?

### Assessing Credibility

Providing abundant evidence and making logical connections between the parts of an argument may not be enough to win agreement from an audience. In fact, success in convincing an audience is almost always inseparable from the writer's credibility, or the audience's belief in the writer's trustworthiness. Aristotle, the Greek philosopher who wrote

13

a treatise on argument that has influenced its study and practice for more than two thousand years, considered credibility — what he called *ethos* — the most important element in the arguer's ability to persuade the audience to accept his or her claim.

Aristotle named "intelligence, character, and good will" as the attributes that produce credibility. Today we might describe these qualities somewhat differently, but the criteria for judging a writer's credibility remain essentially the same. First, the writer must convince the audience that he is knowledgeable, that he is as well informed as possible about the subject. Second, he must persuade his audience that he is not only truthful in the presentation of his evidence but also morally upright and dependable. Third, he must show that, as an arguer with good intentions, he has considered the interests and needs of others as well as his own.

As an example in which the credibility of the arguer is at stake, consider a wealthy Sierra Club member who lives on ten acres of a magnificent oceanside estate and who appears before a community planning board to argue against future development of the area. His claim is that more building will destroy the delicate ecological balance of the area. The board, acting in the interests of all the citizens of the community, will ask themselves: Has the arguer proved that his information about environmental impact is complete and accurate? Has he demonstrated that he sincerely desires to preserve the wilderness, not merely his own privacy and space? And has he also made clear that he has considered the needs and desires of those who might want to live in a housing development by the ocean? If the answers to all these questions are yes, then the board will hear the arguer with respect, and the arguer will have begun to establish his credibility.

A reputation for intelligence, character, and goodwill is not often won overnight. And it can be lost more quickly than it is won. Once a writer or speaker has betrayed an audience's belief in her character or judgment, she may find it difficult to convince an audience to accept subsequent claims, no matter how sound her data and reasoning are. "We give no credit to a liar," said Cicero, "even when he speaks the truth."

Political life is full of examples of lost and squandered credibility. After it was discovered that President Lyndon Johnson had deceived the American public about U.S. conduct in the Vietnam War, he could not regain his popularity. After Senator Edward Kennedy failed to persuade the public that he had behaved honorably at Chappaquiddick, his influence and power in the Democratic party declined. After President Gerald Ford pardoned former President Richard Nixon for his complicity in the Watergate scandal, Ford was no longer a serious candidate for reelection.

We can see the practical consequences when an audience realizes that an arguer has been guilty of a deception — misusing facts and authority, suppressing evidence, distorting statistics, violating the rules of logic. But suppose the arguer is successful in concealing his or her manipulation of the data and can persuade an uninformed audience to take the action or adopt the idea that he or she recommends. Even supposing that the argument promotes a "good" cause, is the arguer justified in using evasive or misleading tactics?

The answer is no. To encourage another person to make a decision on the basis of incomplete or dishonestly used data is profoundly unethical. It indicates lack of respect for the rights of others — their right to know at least as much as you do about the subject, to be allowed to judge and compare, to disagree with you if they challenge your own interests. If the moral implications are still not clear, try to imagine yourself not as the perpetrator of the lie but as the victim.

There is a danger in measuring success wholly by the degree to which audiences accept our arguments. Both as writers and readers, we must be able to respect the claim, or proposition, and what it tries to demonstrate. Toulmin has said: "To conclude that a proposition is true, it is not enough to know that this man or that finds it 'credible': the proposition itself must be *worthy* of credence."[5]

## Acquiring Credibility

You may wonder how you can acquire credibility. You are not yet an expert in many of the subjects you will deal with in assignments, although you are knowledgeable about many other things, including your cultural and social activities. But there are several ways in which you can create confidence by your treatment of topics derived from academic disciplines, such as politics, psychology, economics, sociology, and art, on which most assignments will be based.

First, you can submit evidence of careful research, demonstrating that you have been conscientious in finding the best authorities, giving credit, and attempting to arrive at the truth. Second, you can adopt a thoughtful and judicious tone that reflects a desire to be fair in your conclusion. Tone expresses the attitude of the writer toward his or her subject. When the writer feels strongly about the subject and adopts a belligerent or complaining tone, for example, he or she forgets that readers who feel differently may find the tone disagreeable and unconvincing.

---

[5] *An Examination of the Place of Reason in Ethics* (Cambridge: Cambridge University Press, 1964), p. 71.

In the following excerpt a student expresses his feelings about standard grading, that is, grading by letter or number on a scale that applies to a whole group.

> You go to school to learn, not to earn grades. To be educated, that's what they tell you. "He's educated, he graduated Magna Cum Laude." What makes a Magna Cum Laude man so much better than a man that graduates with a C? They are both still educated, aren't they? No one has a right to call someone less educated because they got a C instead of an A. Let's take both men and put them in front of a car. Each car has something wrong with it. Each man must fix his broken car. Our C man goes right to work while our Magna Cum Laude man hasn't got the slightest idea where to begin. Who's more educated now?

Probably a reader who disagreed with the claim — that standard grading should not be used — would find the tone, if not the evidence itself, unpersuasive. The writer sounds as if he is defending his own ability to do something that an honors graduate can't do while ignoring the acknowledged purposes of standard grading in academic subjects. He sounds, moreover, as if he's angry because someone has done him an injury. Compare the preceding passage to the following one, written by a student on the same subject.

> Grades are the play money in a university Monopoly game. As long as the tokens are offered, the temptation will be largely irresistible to play for them. Students are so busy taking notes, doing tests, and getting tokens that they have forgotten to ask: Of what worth is all this? Or perhaps they ask and the grade is their answer.
>
> One certainly learns something in the passive lecture-note-read-note-test process: how to do it all more efficiently next time (in the hope of eventually owning Boardwalk and Park Place). As Marshall McLuhan has said, we learn what we do. In this process most students come to view learning as studying and remembering what other people have learned. They assume that knowledge is logically and for practical reasons divided up into discrete pieces called "disciplines" and that the highest knowledge is achieved by specializing in a discipline. By getting good grades in a lot of disciplines they conclude they have learned a lot. They have indeed, and it is too bad.[6]

Most readers would consider this writer more credible, in part because he has adopted a tone that seems moderate and impersonal. That is, he does not convey the impression that he is interested only in defending his own grades. Notice also that the language of this passage suggests a higher level of learning and research.

---

[6] Roy E. Terry in "Does Standard Grading Encourage Excessive Competitiveness?" *Change*, September 1974, p. 45.

Sometimes, of course, an expression of anger or even outrage is appropriate and morally justified. But if readers do not share your sense of outrage, you must try to reach them through a more moderate approach. In his autobiography, Benjamin Franklin recounted his attempts to acquire the habit of temperate language in argument:

> Retaining . . . the habit of expressing myself in terms of modest diffidence; . . . never using, when I advanced anything that may possibly be disputed, the words *"certainly, undoubtedly,"* or any others that give the air of positiveness to an opinion; but rather say, I conceive or apprehend a thing to be so and so; it appears to me, *I should think it is so or so*, for such and such reasons; or *I imagine it to be so*; or *it is so, if I am not mistaken*. This habit, I believe, has been of great advantage to me when I have had occasion to inculcate my opinions, and persuade men into measures that I have been from time to time engaged in promoting.[7]

This is not to say that the writer must hedge his or her opinions or confess uncertainty at every point. Franklin suggests that the writer must recognize that other opinions may also have validity and that, although the writer may disagree, he or she respects the other opinions. Such an attitude will also dispose the reader to be more generous in evaluating the writer's argument.

A final method of establishing credibility is to produce a clean, literate, well-organized paper, with evidence of care in writing and proofreading. Such a paper will help persuade the reader to take your efforts seriously.


## SAMPLE ANALYSIS


# *The Declaration of Independence*

### THOMAS JEFFERSON


When in the course of human events, it becomes necessary for one    1
people to dissolve the political bands which have connected them with another, and to assume among the Powers of the earth, the separate and equal station to which the Laws of Nature and Nature's God entitle

---

[7] *The Autobiography of Benjamin Franklin* (New York: Pocket Library, 1954), pp. 22–23.

them, a decent respect to the opinions of mankind requires that they should declare the causes which impel them to the separation.

We hold these truths to be self-evident, that all men are created 2 equal, that they are endowed by their Creator with certain unalienable Rights, that among these are Life, Liberty and the pursuit of Happiness.

That to secure these rights, Governments are instituted among 3 Men, deriving their just powers from the consent of the governed.

That whenever any Form of Government becomes destructive of 4 these ends, it is the Right of the People to alter or to abolish it, and to institute a new Government laying its foundation on such principles and organizing its powers in such form, as to them shall seem most likely to effect their Safety and Happiness. Prudence, indeed, will dictate that Governments long established should not be changed for light and transient causes; and accordingly all experience hath shown that mankind are more disposed to suffer, while evils are sufferable, than to right themselves by abolishing the forms to which they are accustomed. But when a long train of abuses and usurpations pursuing invariably the same Object evinces a design to reduce them under absolute Despotism, it is their right, it is their duty, to throw off such government, and to provide new Guards for their future security.

Such has been the patient sufferance of these Colonies; and such is 5 now the necessity which constrains them to alter their former Systems of Government. The history of the present King of Great Britain is a history of repeated injuries and usurpations, all having in direct object the establishment of an absolute Tyranny over these States. To prove this, let Facts be submitted to a candid world.

He has refused his Assent to laws, the most wholesome and neces- 6 sary for the public good.

He has forbidden his Governors to pass Laws of immediate and 7 pressing importance, unless suspended in their operation till his Assent should be obtained; and when so suspended, he has utterly neglected to attend to them.

He has refused to pass other Laws for the accommodation of large 8 districts of people, unless those people would relinquish the right of Representation in the Legislature, a right inestimable to them and formidable to tyrants only.

He has called together legislative bodies at places unusual, uncom- 9 fortable, and distant from the depository of their Public Records, for the sole purpose of fatiguing them into compliance with his measures.

He has dissolved Representative Houses repeatedly, for opposing 10 with manly firmness his invasions on the rights of the people.

He has refused for a long time, after such dissolutions, to cause oth- 11 ers to be elected; whereby the Legislative Powers, incapable of Annihilation, have returned to the People at large for their exercise; the State remaining in the mean time exposed to all the danger of invasion from without, and convulsions within.

He has endeavored to prevent the population of these States; for 12 that purpose obstructing the Laws of Naturalization of Foreigners; refusing to pass others to encourage their migration hither, and raising the conditions of new Appropriations of Lands.

He has obstructed the Administration of Justice, by refusing his As- 13 sent to Laws for establishing Judiciary Powers.

He has made Judges dependent on his Will alone, for the tenure of 14 their offices, and the amount and payment of their salaries.

He has erected a multitude of New Offices, and sent hither swarms 15 of Officers to harass our People, and eat out their substance.

He has kept among us, in time of peace, Standing Armies without 16 the consent of our Legislature.

He has affected to render the Military independent of and superior 17 to the Civil Power.

He has combined with others to subject us to jurisdictions foreign to 18 our constitution, and unacknowledged by our laws; giving his Assent to their acts of pretended Legislation:

For quartering large bodies of armed troops among us: 19

For protecting them, by a mock Trial, from Punishment for any 20 Murders which they should commit on the Inhabitants of these States:

For cutting off our Trade with all parts of the world: 21

For imposing Taxes on us without our Consent: 22

For depriving us in many cases, of the benefits of Trial by Jury: 23

For transporting us beyond Seas to be tried for pretended offenses: 24

For abolishing the free System of English Laws in a Neighbouring 25 Province, establishing therein an Arbitrary government, and enlarging its boundaries so as to render it at once an example and fit instrument for introducing the same absolute rule into these Colonies:

For taking away our Charters, abolishing our most valuable Laws, 26 and altering fundamentally the Forms of our Governments:

For suspending our own legislatures, and declaring themselves in- 27 vested with Power to legislate for us in all cases whatsoever.

He has abdicated Government here, by declaring us out of his Pro- 28 tection and waging War against us.

He has plundered our seas, ravaged our Coasts, burnt our towns and 29 destroyed the Lives of our people.

He is at this time transporting large Armies of foreign Mercenaries 30 to compleat the works of death, desolation and tyranny, already begun with circumstances of Cruelty & perfidy scarcely paralleled in the most barbarous ages, and totally unworthy the Head of a civilized nation.

He has constrained our fellow Citizens taken Captive on the high 31
Seas to bear Arms against their Country, to become the executioners of
their friends and Brethren, or to fall themselves by their Hands.

He has excited domestic insurrections amongst us, and has endeav- 32
ored to bring on the inhabitants of our frontiers, the merciless Indian
Savages, whose known rule of warfare is an undistinguished destruction
of all ages, sexes and conditions.

In every stage of these Oppressions We Have Petitioned for Redress 33
in the most humble terms. Our repeated petitions have been answered
only by repeated injury. A Prince, whose character is thus marked by
every act which may define a Tyrant, is unfit to be the ruler of a free
People.

Not have We been wanting in attention to our British brethren. We 34
have warned them from time to time of attempts by their legislature to
extend an unwarrantable jurisdiction over us. We have reminded them
of the circumstances of our emigration and settlement here. We have appealed to their native justice and magnanimity and we have conjured
them by the ties of our common kindred to disavow these usurpations,
which would inevitably interrupt our connections and correspondence.
They too have been deaf to the voice of justice and of consanguinity. We
must, therefore, acquiesce in the necessity, which denounces our Separation, and hold them, as we hold the rest of mankind, Enemies in War, in
Peace Friends.

We, therefore, the Representatives of the United States of America, 35
in General Congress, Assembled, appealing to the Supreme Judge of the
world for the rectitude of our intentions, do, in the Name, and by Au-
thority of the good People of these Colonies, solemnly publish and declare, That these United Colonies are, and of Right ought to be, Free and
Independent States; that they are Absolved from all Allegiance to the
British Crown, and that all political connection between them and the
State of Great Britain, is and ought to be totally dissolved; and that as
Free and Independent States, they have full power to levy War, conclude
Peace, contract Alliances, establish Commerce, and to do all other Acts
and Things which Independent States may of right do. And for the sup-
port of this Declaration, with a firm reliance on the protection of Divine
Providence, we mutually pledge to each other our lives, our Fortunes and
our sacred Honor.

## ANALYSIS

*Claim:* What is Jefferson trying to prove? *The American colonies are
justified in declaring their independence from British rule.* Jefferson and
his fellow signers might have issued a simple statement such as appears
in the last paragraph, announcing the freedom and independence of

these United Colonies. Instead, however, they chose to justify their right to do so.

*Support:* What does Jefferson have to go on? The Declaration of Independence bases its claim on two kinds of support: *factual evidence* and *motivational appeals* or appeals to the values of the audience.

*Factual Evidence:* Jefferson presents a long list of specific acts of tyranny by George III, beginning with ''He has refused his Assent to Laws, the most wholesome and necessary for the public good.'' This list constitutes more than half the text. Notice how Jefferson introduces these grievances: ''The history of the present King of Great Britain is a history of repeated injuries and usurpations, all having in direct object the establishment of an absolute Tyranny over these States. *To prove this, let Facts be submitted to a candid World*'' (italics added). Jefferson hopes that a recital of these specific acts will convince an honest audience that the United Colonies have indeed been the victims of an intolerable tyranny.

*Appeal to Values:* Jefferson also invokes the moral values underlying the formation of a democratic state. These values are referred to throughout. In the second and third paragraphs he speaks of equality, ''Life, Liberty, and the pursuit of Happiness,'' ''Just powers,'' ''Consent of the governed,'' and safety. In the last paragraph he refers to freedom and independence. Jefferson believes that the people who read his appeal will, or should, share these fundamental values. Audience acceptance of these values constitutes the most important part of the support. Some historians have called the specific acts of oppression cited by Jefferson trivial, inconsequential, or distorted. Clearly, however, Jefferson felt that the list of specific grievances was vital to definition of the abstract terms in which values are always expressed.

*Warrant:* How does Jefferson get from support to claim? *People have a right to revolution in order to free themselves from oppression.* This warrant is explicit: ''But when a long train of abuses and usurpations pursuing invariably the same Object evinces a design to reduce them under absolute Despotism, it is their right, it is their duty, to throw off such government, and to provide new Guards for their future security.'' Some members of Jefferson's audience, especially those whom he accuses of oppressive acts, will reject the principle that any subject people have earned the right to revolt. But Jefferson believes that the decent opinion of mankind will accept this assumption. Many of his readers will also be aware that the warrant is supported by seventeenth century political philosophy which defines government as a social compact between the government and the governed.

If Jefferson's readers do, in fact, accept the warrant and if they also

**21**

believe in the accuracy of the factual evidence and share his moral values, then they will conclude that his claim has been proved, that Jefferson has justified the right of the colonies to separate themselves from Great Britain.

*Audience:* The Declaration of Independence is addressed to several audiences: to the American colonists; to the British people; to the British Parliament; to the British king, George III; and to mankind or a universal audience.

Not all the American colonists were convinced by Jefferson's argument. Large numbers remained loyal to the King and for various reasons opposed an independent nation. In the next to the last paragraph, Jefferson refers to previous addresses to the British people. Not surprisingly, most of the British citizenry as well as the King also rejected the claims of the Declaration. But the universal audience, the decent opinion of mankind, found Jefferson's argument overwhelmingly persuasive. Many of the liberal reform movements of the eighteenth and nineteenth centuries were inspired by the Declaration. In basing his claim on universal principles of justice and equality, Jefferson was certainly aware that he was addressing future generations.

## Discussion Questions

1. From the following list of claims, select the ones you consider most controversial. Tell why they are difficult to resolve. Are the underlying assumptions controversial? Is support hard to find or disputed? Can you think of circumstances under which some of these claims might be resolved?
   a. Congress should endorse the right-to-life amendment.
   b. Solar power can supply 20 percent of the energy needs now satisfied by fossil and nuclear power.
   c. Homosexuals should have the same job rights as heterosexuals.
   d. Rapists should be treated as mentally ill rather than depraved.
   e. Whale hunting should be banned by international law.
   f. Violence on television produces violent behavior in children who watch more than four hours a day.
   g. Both creationism and evolutionary theory should be taught in the public schools.
   h. Mentally defective men and women should be sterilized or otherwise prevented from producing children.
   i. History will pronounce Reggie Jackson a greater all-round baseball player than Joe DiMaggio.
   j. Bilingual instruction should not be permitted in the public schools.
   k. Some forms of cancer are caused by a virus.

     l. Dogs are smarter than horses.

    m. Hitler is still alive in Argentina and planned the Falkland Islands invasion.

    n. The federal government should impose a drinking age of twenty-one.

    o. The United States should proceed with unilateral disarmament.

    p. Security precautions at airports are out of proportion to the dangers of terrorism.

2. Report on an argument you have heard recently. Identify the parts of that argument — claim, support, warrant — as they are defined in this chapter. What were the strengths and weaknesses in the argument you heard?

## Writing Suggestions

1. Choose one of the more controversial claims in the previous list and explain the reasons it is controversial. Is support lacking or in doubt? Are the warrants unacceptable to many people? Try to go as deeply as you can, exploring, if possible, systems of belief, traditions, societal customs. You may confine your discussion to personal experience with the problem in your community or group. If there has been a change over the years in the public attitude toward the claim, offer what you think may be an explanation for the change.

2. Write your own argument for or against the value of standard grading in college.

3. Discuss an occasion when a controversy arose that the opponents could not settle. Describe the problem and tell why you think the disagreement was not settled.

# 2    *Claims*

Claims, or propositions, represent answers to the question: "What are you trying to prove?" Although they are the conclusions of your arguments, they often appear as thesis statements. Claims can be classified as *claims of fact, claims of value,* and *claims of policy.*

## CLAIMS OF FACT

Claims of fact assert that something is or will be true. Their support consists of facts—statistics, examples, and testimony. One dictionary defines a fact as "something said to have occurred or supposed to be true." A fact possesses a high degree of public acceptance. That is, most of us can agree on what we call a fact because we assume that it has been or can be verified by responsible observers.

Many facts are not matters for argument: Our own senses can confirm them, and other observers will agree about them. We can agree that a certain number of students were in the classroom at a particular time, that lions make a louder sound than kittens, and that apples are sweeter than potatoes.

We can also agree about information that most of us can rarely confirm for ourselves — information in reference books, such as atlases, almanacs and telephone directories; data from scientific resources about the physical world; and happenings reported in the media. We can agree on the reliability of such information because we trust the observers who report it.

The factual map is constantly being redrawn, however, by new data in such fields as history and science that cause us to reevaluate our conclusions. For example, the discovery of the Dead Sea Scrolls in 1947 revealed that some books of the Bible — *Isaiah*, for one — were far older than we had thought. Researchers at New York Hospital – Cornell Medical Center say that many symptoms previously thought inevitable in the aging process are now believed to be treatable and reversible symptoms of depression.[1]

In your conversations with other students you probably generate claims of fact every day, some of which can be verified without much effort, others of which are more difficult to substantiate.

> CLAIM: Most of the students in this class come from towns within fifty miles of Boston.

To prove this the arguer would need only to ask the students in the class where they come from.

> CLAIM: Students who take their courses Pass/Fail make lower grades than those who take them for specific grades.

In this case the arguer would need to have access to student records showing the specific grades given by instructors. (In most schools the instructor awards a letter grade, which is then recorded as a Pass or a Fail if the student has elected this option.)

> CLAIM: The Red Sox will win the pennant this year.

This claim is different from the others because it is an opinion about what will happen in the future. But it can be verified (in the future) and is therefore classified as a claim of fact.

More complex factual claims about political and scientific matters remain controversial because proof on which all or most observers will agree is difficult or impossible to obtain.

> CLAIM: The nuclear arsenal of the Soviet Union exceeds that of the United States.

[1] *New York Times*, February 20, 1983, Sec. 22, p. 4.

CLAIM: The recently discovered diaries of Adolf Hitler are authentic.

Not all claims are so neatly stated or make such unambiguous assertions. Because we recognize that there are exceptions to most generalizations, we often qualify our claims with words such as *generally, usually, probably, as a rule.* It would not be true to state flatly, for example, "College graduates earn more than high school graduates." This statement is generally true, but we know that some high school graduates who are electricians or city bus drivers or sanitation workers earn more than college graduates who are schoolteachers or nurses or social workers. In making such a claim, therefore, the writer should qualify it with a word that limits the claim.

To support a claim of fact, the writer needs to produce sufficient and appropriate data, that is, examples, statistics, and testimony from reliable sources. Provided this requirement is met, the task of establishing a factual claim would seem to be relatively straightforward. But, as you have probably already discovered in ordinary conversation, finding convincing support for factual claims can pose a number of problems. Whenever you try to establish a claim of fact, you will need to ask at least three questions about the material you plan to use: What are sufficient and appropriate data? Who are the reliable authorities? and Have I made clear whether my statements are facts or inferences?

## Sufficient and Appropriate Data

The amount and kind of data for a particular argument depend on the importance and complexity of the subject. The more controversial the subject, the more facts and testimony you will need to supply. Consider the claim "The nuclear arsenal of the Soviet Union is greater than that of the United States." If you want to prove the truth of this claim, obviously you will have to provide a larger quantity of data than for a claim that says, "By following three steps, you can train your dog to sit and heel in fifteen minutes." In examining your facts and opinions, an alert reader will want to know if they are accurate, recent, and typical of other facts and opinions that you have not mentioned.

The reader will also look for testimony from more than one authority, although there may be cases where only one or two experts, because they have achieved a unique breakthrough in their field, will be sufficient. These cases would probably occur most frequently in the physical sciences. The Nobel Prize winners James Watson and Francis Crick, who first discovered the structure of the DNA molecule, are an example of such experts. In the case of the so-called Hitler diaries, however, which surfaced in 1983, at least a dozen experts — journalists, historians, bibliographers who could verify the age of the paper and the ink — were needed to establish that they were forgeries.

## Reliable Authorities

Not all those who pronounce themselves experts are trustworthy. Your own experience has probably taught you that you cannot always believe the reports of an event by a single witness. The witness may be poorly trained to make accurate observations — about the size of a crowd, the speed of a vehicle, his distance from an object. Or his own physical conditions — illness, intoxication, disability — may prevent him from seeing or hearing or smelling accurately. The circumstances under which he observes the event — darkness, confusion, noise — may also impair his observation. In addition, the witness may be biased for or against the outcome of the event, as in a hotly contested baseball game, where the observer sees the play that he wants to see. You will find the problems associated with the biases of witnesses to be relevant to your work as a reader and writer of argumentative essays.

You will undoubtedly want to quote authors in some of your arguments. In most cases you will not be familiar with the authors. But there are guidelines for determining their reliability: the rank or title of the experts, their publications if they have been accepted by other experts, their association with reputable universities, research centers, and think tanks. For example, for a paper on euthanasia, you might decide to quote from an article by Paul Ramsey, identified as the Harrington Spear Paine Professor of Religion at Princeton University. For a paper on prison reform you might want to use material supplied by Tom Murton, a professional penologist, formerly superintendent in the Arkansas prison system, now professor of criminology at the University of Minnesota. Most readers of your arguments would agree that these authors have impressive credentials in their fields.

What if several respectable sources are in conflict? What if the experts disagree? After a preliminary investigation of a controversial subject, you may decide that you have sufficient material to support your claim. But if you read further, you may discover that other material presented by equally qualified experts contradicts your original claim. In such circumstances you will find it impossible to make a definitive claim.

## Facts or Inferences

We have defined a fact as a statement that can be verified. An inference is "a statement about the unknown on the basis of the known."[2] As you and your classmates wait in your classroom on the first day of the semester, a middle-aged woman wearing a tweed jacket and a corduroy skirt appears and stands in front of the room. You don't know who this woman is. However, based on what you do know about the appearance of many college teachers and the fact that teachers usually stand in front of the classroom, you may *infer* that this woman is your teacher. You will probably be right. But you cannot be certain until you have more information. Perhaps you will find out that this woman has come from the department office to tell you that your teacher is sick and cannot meet the class today.

The difference between facts and inferences is important to you as the writer of an argument because an inference is an interpretation of a fact or facts. You have probably come across a statement such as the following in a newspaper or magazine: "Excessive television viewing has caused the steady decline in the reading ability of children and teenagers." Presented this way, the statement is clearly intended to be read as a factual claim that has been or can be proved. But it is an inference. The facts, which can and have been verified, are (1) the reading ability of children and teenagers has declined and (2) the average child views television for six or more hours a day. (Whether this amount of time is "excessive" is also an opinion.) The cause-effect relation between the two facts is an *interpretation* or an opinion of the investigator, who has examined both the reading scores and the amount of time spent in front of the television set and *inferred* that one is the cause of the other. The causes of the decline in reading scores are probably more complex than the original statement indicates. Since we can seldom or never create laboratory conditions for testing the influence of television separate from other influences in the family and the community, any statement about the connection between reading scores and television viewing can only be a guess.

By definition, no inference can ever do more than suggest probabilities. Of course, some inferences are much more reliable than others and afford high probability. Almost all claims in science are based on infer-

---

[2]S. I. Hayakawa, *Language in Thought and Action* (New York: Harcourt, Brace, Jovanovich, 1978), p. 35.

ences, interpretations of data on which most scientists agree. Paleontologists find a few ancient bones from which they make inferences about an animal that might have been alive millions of years ago. We can never be absolutely certain that the reconstruction of the dinosaur in the museum is an exact copy of the animal it is supposed to represent, but the probability is fairly high because no other interpretation works so well to explain all the observable data — the existence of the bones in a particular place, their age, their relation to other fossils, and their resemblance to the bones of existing animals with which the paleontologist is familiar.

Inferences are profoundly important, and most arguments could not proceed very far without them. But an inference is not a fact. The writer of an argument must make it clear when he or she offers an inference, an interpretation or an opinion, that it is not a fact.

## Defending a Claim of Fact

Here is a summary of the guidelines that should help you to defend a factual claim. (We'll say more about support of factual claims in Chapter 4.)

1. Be sure that the claim — what you are trying to prove — is clearly stated, preferably at the beginning of your paper.
2. Define terms that may be controversial or ambiguous. For example, in trying to prove that "radicals" had captured the student government, you would have to define "radicals," distinguishing them from "liberals" or members of other ideological groups, so that your readers would understand exactly what you meant.
3. As far as possible, make sure that your evidence — facts and opinions, or interpretations of the facts — fulfills the appropriate criteria. The data should be sufficient, accurate, recent, typical; the authorities should be reliable.
4. Make it clear when conclusions about the data are inferences or interpretations, not facts. For example, you might write, "The series of lectures, 'Modern Architecture,' sponsored by our fraternity, was a failure because the students at this college aren't interested in discussions of art." What proof could you offer that this *was* the reason, that your statement was a *fact*? Perhaps there were other reasons that you haven't considered.
5. Arrange your evidence in order to emphasize what is most important. Place it at the beginning or the end and devote more space to it.

**SAMPLE ANALYSIS: CLAIM OF FACT**

# What a Cigarette Packs in Radiation

## MARK S. BOGUSKI

To the Editor:

1　An Oct. 17 letter from Prof. W. D. Walker addressed the subject of the relative risk of low-level radiation exposure associated with commercial nuclear energy, as compared with exposure from various other sources.

2　Although the issues are complex, as pointed out by Gerald Delcioppo in a letter published Oct. 24, I am basically in agreement with Dr. Walker, and I would like to bring to the attention of your readers a specific example of relative risk.

3　Two radioactive isotopes, polonium-210 and lead-210, are highly concentrated in particles in cigarette smoke. The major source of polonium is the phosphate fertilizer used in growing tobacco. In a person smoking one and one-half packs of cigarettes per day, the annual radiation dose is equivalent to that of 300 X-ray films of the chest.

4　In contrast a person standing for 25 hours directly downwind of the Three Mile Island nuclear power plant following the accident received the equivalent of one chest X-ray.

5　Although these facts are well known (and apparently well documented) in the medical/scientific literature (see Correspondence, *New England Journal of Medicine*, vol. 307, pp. 309–313, 1982), they have received surprisingly little attention in the popular press.

6　Caution and experience dictate that we remain vigilantly mindful of the potential hazards of nuclear power generation. But perhaps a little more emphasis should be placed on the real and present dangers of cigarette smoking, which, according to the U.S. Surgeon General, will kill 129,000 Americans in 1982 and cause significant disability in many times this number.

Mark S. Boguski

---

The writer is in the medical scientist training program at Washington University.

ANALYSIS

This letter provides data to prove that the radiation dosage associated with cigarette smoking is greater than that associated with nuclear power. Four aspects of this factual claim are noteworthy. First, the claim offers a rebuttal of commonly held beliefs about the dangers of certain kinds of radiation. Many factual claims originate in just this way — as answers to previous claims. Second, the author, as a medical scientist in training at a reputable university, apparently has expert knowledge of the scientific data he reports. He is careful to name the sources of his data. Third, the data he supplies take the form of comparative statistics. Such a use of numbers is obviously essential in comparing some things, such as more and less dangerous sources of radiation dosage. Finally, the author is making this claim to promote a change in our attitudes toward cigarette smoking. Many readers would find the information new and disturbing, a result the author clearly wanted to achieve. This use of factual claims as a first step in calling for changes in attitude and behavior is a familiar and often effective argumentative strategy.

## CLAIMS OF VALUE

Unlike claims of fact, which attempt to prove that something is true and which can be validated by reference to the data, claims of value make a judgment. They express approval or disapproval. They attempt to prove that some action, belief, or condition is right or wrong, good or bad, beautiful or ugly, worthwhile or undesirable.

CLAIM: Democracy is superior to any other form of government.

CLAIM: Killing animals for sport is wrong.

CLAIM: The Sam Rayburn building in Washington is an aesthetic failure.

CLAIM: Chess is a more intellectual pastime than bridge.

Some claims of value are simply expressions of taste, of likes and dislikes, preferences and prejudices. The Latin proverb "De gustibus non est disputandum" says that we cannot dispute about tastes. If you express a preference for chocolate over vanilla, your listener can only express agreement or disagreement. But he or she cannot refer to an outside authority or produce data or appeal to your moral sense to convince you that your preference is wrong.

Many opinions can be defended or attacked, however, and we will be concerned with these. Controversies about works of art—about the aesthetic value of books, paintings, sculpture, architecture, dance, drama, and movies—rage fiercely among critics and lay people alike. Contrary to popular belief, one value judgment is not as good as another. This becomes apparent when expressions of preference are phrased not merely as matters of personal taste but as matters that can be settled by reference to standards. Almost all movie critics agreed that *E.T.* and *Tootsie* were superior films. They also agreed that *A Tomato Ate My Sister*, a horror film, was terrible. The fact that critics of films agree so often on what is good and bad indicates that their choices are based on agreement about certain criteria that filmmakers have or have not met.

Such judgments are found in all the arts. Hearing someone praise the singing of a popular vocalist, Sheila Jordan, you might ask why she is so well regarded. You expect Sheila Jordan's fan to say more than "I like Sheila Jordan" or "Man, she's great." You expect the fan to give reasons to support his claim. "She's unique," he says. He shows you a short review from a widely read newspaper that says, "Her singing is filled with fascinating phrasings, twists, and turns, and she's been compared with Billie Holiday for her emotional intensity. . . . She can be so heart-wrenching that conversations stop cold." Her fan agrees with the criteria for judging a singer listed by the author of the review: uniqueness, fascinating phrasings, emotional intensity.

You may or may not agree that these are the only standards or even the significant ones for judging a singer. But the establishment of standards itself offers material for a discussion or an argument. You may argue about the relevance of the criteria, or, agreeing on the criteria, you may argue about the success of the singer in meeting them. Perhaps you prefer cool singers to intense ones. Or perhaps, even if you choose intensity over coolness, you don't think Sheila Jordan can be described as "expressive." And in arguments about criteria, differences in experience and preparation acquire importance. You would probably take for granted that a writer with formal musical training who has listened carefully to dozens of singers over a period of years, who has read a good deal of musical criticism and discussed musical matters with other knowledgeable people would be a more reliable critic than someone who lacked these qualifications.

In moral judgments as well, judgments about right or wrong, good or evil, some opinions are to be preferred to others. In general you would listen more willingly to and be more likely to accept the judgments of people who are known to lead honest and decent lives than of people who have committed crimes or otherwise violated your notions of good behavior.

Although you and your reader may share many values, among them a belief in democracy, a respect for learning, and a desire for peace, you may also disagree, even profoundly, about other values. The subject of divorce, for example, despite its prevalence in our society, can produce a conflict between differing moral standards. Some people may insist on adherence to absolute standards, arguing that the values they hold are based on religious precepts derived from God and Scripture and that some things are always right or wrong. Since marriage is sacred, divorce is forbidden, they may say, whether or not the conditions of society change. Other people may argue that their values are based on the changing needs of societies in different places and at different times. Since marriage is an institution created by human beings at a particular time in history to serve particular social needs, they may say, it can also be dissolved when other social needs arise. The same opposition of moral values might occur in discussions of abortion or suicide.

As a writer you cannot always know what system of value judgments is held by your reader. Yet in regard to some human activities, it ought to be possible to find a rule or rules on which almost all readers might agree. One such rule was expressed by the nineteenth-century German philosopher Immanuel Kant: "Man and, in general, every rational being exists as an end in itself and not merely as a means to be arbitrarily used by this or that will."[3] Translated into more contemporary language, Kant's prescription urges us not to subject any creature to a condition that it has not freely chosen. We cannot use other creatures for our own purposes without their consent. (Some philosophers would extend this rule to the treatment of animals by human beings.) This standard of judgment has, in fact, been invoked in recent years against medical experimentation without consent on human beings in prisons and hospitals and against sterilizing poor or mentally defective women without their understanding the decision.

Just as your friend might not have been able to convince you that Sheila Jordan is an accomplished vocalist, you will not always be able to persuade those with whom you disagree that your values are superior to theirs and that they should therefore change their attitudes. Nor would you want to compromise your values or pretend that they were different to win an argument. What you can and should do, however, is give *good reasons* why you think one thing is better than another. As a child, when you asked why it was wrong to take your brother's toys, you may have been told by an exasperated parent, "Because I say so." Some adults still

---

[3] *Kant Selections*, edited by Theodore Meyer Greene (New York: Scribner's, 1957), p. 308.

give such answers in defending their judgments, but such answers are not arguments and do nothing to win the agreement of others.

Standards for making moral judgments can be formulated, but a majority preference is not enough to confer moral value. If in a certain neighborhood, most of the young men decide to harass a few homosexuals, that consensus does not make their action right. In formulating value claims, you should be prepared to ask and answer questions about the way in which your value claims and those of others have been arrived at. Lionel Ruby, an American philosopher, sums it up in these words: "The law of rationality tells us that we ought to justify our beliefs by evidence and reasons, instead of asserting them dogmatically."[4]

## Defending a Claim of Value

The following suggestions are a preliminary guide to the defense of a value claim. (We discuss value claims further in Chapter 4)

1. Try to make clear that the values or principles you are defending should have priority on any scale of values. Keep in mind that you and your readers may differ about their relative importance. For example, although your readers may agree with you that brilliant photography is important in a film, they may think that a well-written script is even more crucial to its success. And although they may agree that freedom of the press is a mainstay of democracy, they may regard the right to privacy as even more fundamental.
2. Suggest that adherence to the values you are defending will bring about good results in some specific situation or bad results if respect for the values is ignored. You might argue, for example, that a belief in freedom of the press will make citizens better informed and the country stronger while a failure to protect this freedom will strengthen the forces of authoritarianism.
3. Since value terms are abstract, use examples and illustrations to clarify meanings and make distinctions. Comparisons and contrasts are especially helpful. If you are using the term "heroism," can you provide examples to differentiate between "heroism" and "foolhardiness" or "exhibitionism"?
4. Use testimony of others to prove that knowledgeable or highly regarded people share your values.

---

[4] *The Art of Making Sense* (New York: Lippincott, 1968), p. 271.

SAMPLE ANALYSIS: CLAIM OF VALUE

# Creating a "Learning Society"

## MEG GREENFIELD

The best part of the report of the National Commission on Excel- 1
lence in Education got the least attention in all the posturing and gloat-
ing and unconvincing lamentation that was set off by its publication.
This was the report's suggestion that the value of learning is not contingent on any material public or private "payoff." The activity itself, pursued not just in school but rather throughout a lifetime, *is* the payoff. So
the commission strongly implies, anyway, by its insistence that the principal object of our educational reform should be the creation of a "learning society," one devoted to the joys and rewards of continuous learning, as distinct from the one-shot passing of some exam or other.

True, this admirably uncommissionlike thought appears in the 2
company of (no doubt justified) warnings about the perils we face as individuals and a nation by being such slobs about the quality of our
schooling; and it may not be quite as unqualified as I would like and
therefore have made it sound. But the thought is there. And — naturally — it was widely disregarded by the Axgrinders International when
they took up the report. We were at once back to our usual national
mode of discussing what is wanted from education: to keep ahead of the
international competition, to maintain a strong defense, to get good jobs
and keep them. We were also back in a cross fire of I-told-you-so's: the
people who are against permissiveness felt vindicated, as, of course, did
the people who are for the expenditure of more money, as did those (I
am one) who do not find it inconsistent to hold both positions. In the
melee, the part about the intrinsic value of learning got lost. It always
does — when anyone is eccentric enough to bring it up at all, that is.

I realize that there is a sense in which we have a real emergency in 3
the schools, that there are classrooms in various places full of teen-agers
who can't read or write and teachers who aren't a whole lot better, that
we are at an increasing competitive disadvantage in many areas and that
some of what is being taught is so junky and unimportant that it's prob-

Meg Greenfield has written editorials for *Reporter* magazine, the *Washington Post*,
and *Newsweek*. In 1978 she won a Pulitzer Prize for her editorials in the *Washington Post*.

ably no tragedy that it is not being learned. All this, God knows, needs work. My complaint is that the values we bring to the effort to right the situation are precisely the ones that got us in trouble in the first place and are only likely to perpetuate our grief.

Education as an "investment," education as a way to beat the Russians and best the Japanese, education as a way to get ahead of the fellow down the street—it is true that generations of Americans have been brought together culturally by the great force of our public schools and that millions of them have rightly seen their schooling as a one-way ticket out of economic and social privation. But you really do not generate the educational values that count when you stress only these external, comparative advantages. People do not become educated or liberated so much as they become opportunistic in relation to such schooling. And anyway, on the great national-security issues, when was the last time you heard of a youngster doing his homework because he wanted to be better than the Russians in geometry?

You give a child nothing, I think, when you give him this joyless, driven concept of the meaning of learning. But alas, there are plenty among us who think this is just fine. Following the great cackles of the political antipermissiveness crowd when this report was released, I was struck again by how much such people, who claim to be champions of education, implicitly view education as a disagreeable thing. It is invariably discussed by them—and with relish—as something between a medicine and a punishment that must be administered to its unwilling little subjects for their own good no matter how they howl. *It is not supposed to be fun,* they admonish, and children cannot be expected to like it—what ever happened to our moral fiber, and so forth.

Interestingly, this same conception of schooling as something essentially unpleasant that is ultimately vindicated by its benefits seems to animate our occasional bursts of enthusiasm for intellectual pursuits. It is all there in the historic news photos of the quiz contestant Charles Van Doren, earphoned up in his "isolation booth" back in the late '50s, before the program's scam was revealed. I remember thinking the revelation, when it came, was no cruel national disillusion (as the wisdom of the time ran), but rather the most useful thing that could have happened. For the real scam had been the game itself and the idolization of the contestant for trained-seal tricks of memory. It was a mockery of the life of the mind which it pretended to exalt, and the implication of all the adulatory comment was really: look how lucrative this boring, longhair stuff can be. I was glad when the program and its "hero" crashed.

I am bound to say I sense something comparable in certain of those projects we hear about now for making infants preternaturally well informed—a physics instructor at seven months, an art critic at two, that sort of thing. Not all of it, but some of its strikes me as having nothing to do with teaching a child the joy of learning — of giving him that incomparable and invaluable gift. I see baby quiz-show winners, victims of the same fundamentally anti-intellectual values, people who want to acquire, to please, to show off — not to discover, to learn, to be surprised.

Schooling needs to be saved from these "friends" — the punishers, the opportunists and the exploiters who profess an undying devotion to the old-fashioned virtues and the life of the mind. But it will of course not be saved by the purveyors of "fun" whose idea of making education enjoyable is to gut it and teach things not worth knowing. There is a difference — night and day — between this kind of "fun" and the joy of learning, and everyone who has ever had one great teacher of a serious subject knows what it is. So do those kids in a handful of slum schools notoriously programmed to fail who instead thrive because they are in the care of people who know what teaching is about. If we could acquire, come to honor, this great value, if we could truly aspire to become a "learning society," the rest — the competitive and material benefits — would follow. But we keep trying to do it the other way around.

## ANALYSIS

Greenfield argues that the real value of education in America has been ignored or misundertood, even by professional educators. At the end of the first paragraph she states her case: "the principal object of our educational reform should be the creation of a 'learning society,' one devoted to the joys and rewards of continuous learning, as distinct from the one-shot passing of some exam or other." She does not, however, offer a plan for producing such a society. Her purpose is less ambitious — to develop the claim that learning for the joy of learning is superior to education for other reasons: "to keep ahead of the international competition, to maintain a strong defense, to get good jobs and keep them." The education goals that count, she says, cannot be fostered when we appeal to "external, comparative advantages."

Her argumentative strategy is primarily negative. Most of the article is an attack on the goals and values of those who favor "external, comparative advantages" rather than the activity of learning itself pursued "throughout a lifetime." But her attack on these opposing views is modified by several concessions that acknowledge the difficulty of promoting joyful education in our schools and persuade readers of her attempt to be fair.

As this well-written article demonstrates, claims of value can be hard to prove. Can the "joy of learning" be defined? If readers have never experienced it, how does the writer persuade them that such learning is superior to learning as an "investment"? We notice that the arguments against learning for external rewards — in Greenfield's attacks on quiz show contestants and superbabies — are enlivened by examples and details. Perhaps a greater part of her article should have been devoted to examples or details that dramatize for readers the positive joy of learning that she herself has apparently been lucky enough to experience.

## CLAIMS OF POLICY

Claims of policy argue that certain conditions should exist. As the name suggests, they advocate adoption of policies or courses of action because problems have arisen that call for solution. Almost always *should* or *ought to* or *must* is expressed or implied in the claim.

CLAIM: Voluntary prayer should be permitted in public schools.

CLAIM: A dress code should be introduced for all public high schools.

CLAIM: A law should permit sixteen-year-olds and parents to "divorce" each other in cases of extreme incompatibility.

CLAIM: Mandatory jail terms should be imposed for drunk driving violations.

In defending such claims of policy you may find that you must first convince your audience that a problem exists. This will require that, as part of your longer argument, you make a factual claim, offering data to prove that present conditions are unsatisfactory. You may also find it necessary to refer to the values that support your claim. Then you will be ready to introduce your policy, to persuade your audience that the solution you propose will solve the problem.

We will examine a policy claim in which all these parts are at work. The claim can be stated as follows: "The time required for an undergraduate degree should be extended to five years." Immediate agreement with this policy among student readers would certainly not be universal. Some students would not recognize a problem. They would say, "The college curriculum we have now is fine. There's no need for a change. Besides, we don't want to spend more time in school." First, then, the arguer would have to persuade a skeptical audience that there is a problem, that four years of college are no longer enough because the stock of knowledge in almost all fields of study continues to increase. The arguer would provide data to show how many more choices in history, literature, and science students have now compared to the choices in those fields a generation ago. She would also find it necessary to emphasize the value of greater knowledge and more schooling compared to the value of other goods the audience cherishes, such as earlier independence. Finally, the arguer would offer a plan for putting her policy into effect. Her plan would have to take into consideration initial psychological resistance, revision of the curriculum, the costs of more instruction, and the costs of lost production in the work force. Most important, she would point out the benefits for both individuals and society if this policy were adopted.

In this example, we assumed that the reader would disagree that a problem existed. In many cases, however, the reader may agree that there is a problem but disagree with the arguer about the way of solving it. Most of us, no doubt, will agree that we want to reduce or eliminate the following problems: misbehavior and vandalism in schools, drunk driving, crime on the streets, child abuse, pornography, pollution. But how shall we go about solving those problems? What public policy will give us well-behaved, diligent students who never destroy school property? Safe streets where no one is ever robbed or assaulted? Loving homes where no child is ever mistreated? Some members of society would choose to introduce rules or laws that punish infractions so severely that wrongdoers would be unwilling or unable to repeat their offenses. Other members of society would prefer policies that attempt to rehabilitate or reeducate offenders through training, therapy, counseling, and new opportunities.

## Defending a Claim of Policy

The following steps will help you organize arguments for a claim of policy.

1. Make your proposal clear. The terms in the proposal should be precisely defined.
2. If necessary, establish that there is a need for a change. If changes have been ignored or resisted, there may be good or at least understandable reasons why this is so. (It is often wrongly assumed that people cling to cultural practices long after their significance and necessity have eroded. But rational human beings do not continue to observe practices unless those practices serve a purpose. The fact that you and I may see no value or purpose in the activities of another is irrelevant.)
3. Consider the opposing arguments. You may want to state the opposing arguments in a brief paragraph in order to answer them in the body of your argument.

4. Devote the major part of your essay to proving that your proposal is an answer to the opposing arguments and that there are distinct benefits for your readers in adopting your proposal.
5. Support your proposal with solid data, but don't neglect the moral considerations and the common-sense reasons, which may be even more persuasive.

## SAMPLE ANALYSIS: CLAIM OF POLICY

# So That Nobody Has to Go to School If They Don't Want To

### ROGER SIPHER

A decline in standardized test scores is but the most recent indicator that American education is in trouble.

One reason for the crisis is that present mandatory-attendance laws force many to attend school who have no wish to be there. Such children have little desire to learn and are so antagonistic to school that neither they nor more highly motivated students receive the quality education that is the birthright of every American.

The solution to this problem is simple: Abolish compulsory-attendance laws and allow only those who are committed to getting an education to attend.

This will not end public education. Contrary to conventional belief, legislators enacted compulsory-attendance laws to legalize what already existed. William Landes and Lewis Solomon, economists, found little evidence that mandatory-attendance laws increased the number of children in school. They found, too, that school systems have never effectively enforced such laws, usually because of the expense involved.

There is no contradiction between the assertion that compulsory attendance has had little effect on the number of children attending school and the argument that repeal would be a positive step toward improving education. Most parents want a high school education for their children. Unfortunately, compulsory attendance hampers the ability of public

Roger Sipher is associate professor of history at the State University of New York at Cortland.

school officials to enforce legitimate educational and disciplinary policies and thereby make the education a good one.

Private schools have no such problem. They can fail or dismiss stu- 6 dents, knowing such students can attend public school. Without compulsory attendance, public schools would be freer to oust students whose academic or personal behavior undermines the educational mission of the institution.

Has not the noble experiment of a formal education for everyone 7 failed? While we pay homage to the homily, "You can lead a horse to water buy you can't make him drink," we have pretended it is not true in education.

Ask high school teachers if recalcitrant students learn anything of 8 value. Ask teachers if these students do any homework. Ask if the threat of low grades motivates them. Quite the contrary, these students know they will be passed from grade to grade until they are old enough to quit or until, as is more likely, they receive a high school diploma. At the point when students could legally quit, most choose to remain since they know they are likely to be allowed to graduate whether they do acceptable work or not.

Abolition of archaic attendance laws would produce enormous divi- 9 dends.

First, it would alert everyone that school is a serious place where one 10 goes to learn. Schools are neither day-care centers nor indoor street corners. Young people who resist learning should stay away; indeed, an end to compulsory schooling would require them to stay away.

Second, students opposed to learning would not be able to pollute 11 the educational atmosphere for those who want to learn. Teachers could stop policing recalcitrant students and start educating.

Third, grades would show what they are supposed to: how well a 12 student is learning. Parents could again read report cards and know if their children were making progress.

Fourth, public esteem for schools would increase. People would 13 stop regarding them as way stations for adolescents and start thinking of them as institutions for educating America's youth.

Fifth, elementary schools would change because students would 14 find out early that they had better learn something or risk flunking out later. Elementary teachers would no longer have to pass their failures on to junior high and high school.

Sixth, the cost of enforcing compulsory education would be elimi- 15 nated. Despite enforcement efforts, nearly 15 percent of the school-age children in our largest cities are almost permanently absent from school.

Communities could use these savings to support institutions to deal 16 with young people not in school. If, in the long run, these institutions prove more costly, at least we would not confuse their mission with that of schools.

Schools should be for education. At present, they are only tangen- 17 tially so. They have attempted to serve an all-encompassing social function, trying to be all things to all people. In the process they have failed miserably at what they were originally formed to accomplish.

## ANALYSIS

Roger Sipher's article offers a straightforward solution to a distressing educational problem. Following a clear and familiar pattern of organization, the author begins by referring to the problem and the need for change that has induced him to present this solution. He seems sure that his readers will recognize the disciplinary problems arising from compulsory attendance, and he therefore alludes to them but omits any specific mention of them. Instead he concentrates on the unfortunate educational consequences of compulsory attendance. In the third paragraph he states his thesis directly: "Abolish compulsory-attendance laws and allow only those who are committed to getting an education to attend."

Sipher is no doubt aware that his proposal will strike many readers as a radical departure from conventional solutions, perhaps more damaging than the problem itself. He moves at once to dispel the fear that public education will suffer if mandatory attendance laws are repealed. He offers as proof a study by two economists who conclude that compulsory attendance has little effect on the actual number of students who attend school. But in this part of the discussion Sipher is guilty of a seeming contradiction. The reader may ask, "If compulsory attendance laws make little difference — that is, if students attend in the same numbers regardless of the laws — why is it necessary to abolish them?" Later in the essay Sipher points out that in some large cities almost 15 percent of school-age children are permanently absent. If they are absent, they cannot be the ones who are "polluting the educational atmosphere." Apparently, then, the author is referring to a small number of students uninterested in learning who continue to come to school because they are compelled to do so.

In the middle section Sipher elaborates on the difficulties of teaching those who are uninterested in learning. The use of the imperative mode, of speaking directly to the reader — "Ask high school teachers if recalcitrant students learn anything of value" — is effective. Here, too, however, some readers may want to know if Sipher is aware of the alternative educational programs introduced into many city schools for reaching unwilling students or whether he knows about them but regards them as unsuccessful.

The strongest part of the argument appears in the last third of the essay, where the author lists six advantages that will follow the repeal of compulsory attendance laws. He also seems to recognize that some readers will have another question: "What will become of the young people who are required to leave school?" His answer — "institutions" — is vague. But since the burden of his proposal is to offer ways of improving the quality of education, Sipher may consider that he is justified in declining to answer this question more fully.

The strengths of Sipher's argument are the clear, direct organization, the readable language, and the listing of the specific dividends that would follow implementation of his proposal. Equally important is the novelty of the proposal, which will outrage some readers and delight others. In either case the proposal will arouse attention and initiate discussion.

However, the orginality of the solution may also constitute a weakness. The more original the solution to a problem, the more likely it is to encounter initial resistance. Sipher's argument is too short to answer the many questions his readers might have about possible disadvantages. This argument, in other words, should be considered an introduction to any attempt to solve the problem, a limitation of which Sipher was probably aware.

READINGS FOR ANALYSIS

# Gun Control: Historically Ineffective, Imprudent, and Coercive

## BRUCE POWELL MAJORS

With the recent handgun shootings of prominent individuals, most notably Ronald Reagan and John Lennon, the cries from many quarters for some form of national handgun prohibition have reached a crescendo. Here in the District, the D.C. police have instituted a "voluntary surrender" poster campaign aimed at the many D.C. residents who are resisting the District's gun control laws. Let's look at the history behind the current events. 1

Gun control is not a new idea. The first government restrictions on handgun ownership in the United States were implemented in the post–Civil War South as part of the Black Codes — a body of laws designed to keep blacks in legally mandated serfdom. Don B. Kates, Jr., Professor of Law at St. Louis University and editor of *Restricting Handguns: The Liberal Skeptics Speak Out*, writes: "Meaningful black access to self-defense weapons occurred only in the mid 1870s when the cheap, off-brand revolver began to be sold in the South in large numbers. The Klan recognized in the mere existence of these a threat to its previous virtual monopoly of violence. . . . Instead of formal legislation, Mississippi, Florida, and the rest of the Deep South simply continued to enforce the pre-emancipation statutes forbidding blacks to possess arms. Mississippi formalized the custom by enacting the first registration law for gun retailers in 1906." 2

Other elements undesirable to the status quo in the late 1800s were used to foment support for gun ownership restrictions. Poor whites became almost as threatening as blacks in the South during the push for agrarian reform in the late 1800s. Businessmen became staunch supporters of gun control laws in order to disarm "labor agitators." Immigrants and "anarchists," often used synonymously during the late 1800s and early 1900s, soon followed as new bogeymen for the gun control movement to disarm. 3

---

Bruce Majors is a graduate student in philosophy at Catholic University of America.

In 1911 New York State passed the Sullivan Law, which made own-  4
ership of a handgun illegal without a police permit. This became the
"model" gun law for the rest of the nation. So-called "progressives"
joined the gun control bandwagon after 1920 when it became apparent
that their pet solution to crime, alcohol prohibition, was not working.

Today, most American gun owners would be surprised to hear that  5
there are "no controls." In fact, there are more than 20,000 statutes at
the state, federal, and local levels which in some way restrict or regulate
the acquisition, ownership, or carrying of firearms. In 1968, the federal
Gun Control Act was passed banning mail order gun sales and firearm
imports, and requiring identification, supplementary information, and
"penalty of perjury" forms for all retail sales. (The 1968 act was heavily
lobbied *for* by domestic arms manufacturers as a way of impeding competition from imports. It is a classic example of special interest legislation
camouflaged by a "noble cause.") The 1968 act is enforced by the Bureau of Alcohol, Tobacco and Firearms (BATF), which, with an annual
budget of $160 million, interprets the law and regularly conducts raids
to confiscate firearms from peaceful citizens.

Organizations such as Handgun Control, Inc., are pushing for fed-  6
eral legislation outlawing private ownership of handguns with a one year
mandatory *prison sentence* for violators. Vocal support for such gun control laws comes from the gun manufacturers. Since 1968, Smith and
Wesson; Remington Arms Co.; Colt's Inc.; Savage Arms; Sturm, Ruger
& Co.; and other major arms manufacturers have gone on record as endorsing some form of national handgun prohibition, mostly aimed at
their low-priced competition, the "Saturday Night Specials." The *most*
vocal support for gun control comes from an articulate, largely white,
upper class establishment. Many gun control proponents, well protected
in *their* police patrolled neighborhoods, hold the same blind, undying
faith in the ability of a few good people (themselves) to use government
to successfully organize our lives for us. As Professor Kates pointed out,
"The position of all too many who would ban guns is indistinguishable
from Archie Bunker's views on legalizing pot and homosexuality: 'I
don't like it and I don't like those who do — so it ought to be illegal.'"

There is no empirical evidence that supports the contention that  7
gun control laws reduce crime or the number of firearms related deaths.
Kates reports, "Hawaii, Michigan, Missouri, New Jersey, New York,
North Carolina and Puerto Rico have laws that prohibit their residents
from purchasing or possessing a handgun without a discretionary police
permit. As these laws have been in effect for twenty-five to sixty-five
years in each state, any violence reductive effect should be apparent in
these jurisdictions' crime statistics. Six different criminological studies
have compared the per capita homicide and other violent crime rates of

these jurisdictions in various years to those of states that allow handguns. The conclusion of each study is that taken together, the handgun prohibiting states have consistently as high or higher homicide and other violent crime rates as the handgun allowing states.'' In the District, between 1974 and 1976 the murder rate *fell* 30%. Then, in February 1977, D.C.'s law prohibiting handgun ownership went into effect. Between 1977 and 1980 the murder rate in the District *increased* 11%, from 28.0 to 31.5 per 100,000 (the national average murder rate was 9.7 per 100,000). The same thing happened in New York City when it toughened its gun control laws in August of 1980. The four cities with gun control laws — D.C., New York, Chicago, and Detroit — account for one sixth of all the murders in the United States.

Gun control doesn't stop criminals from committing crimes. Someone who will risk legal penalties to murder or rob or rape isn't going to worry about legal penalties for owning a gun. Gun control does disarm the victims of rapists, killers and thieves.                                              8

There is a legitimate concern about so-called ''crimes of passion,''             9
where people who know each other are temporarily caught up in a rage and one kills the other. There should be housing and employment, and perhaps entire neighborhoods where guns are banned or controlled by contract or land-use covenants. Such arrangements should be available to individuals as they choose, and not imposed as part of a centralized coercive process. The fact that some neighborhoods are given adequate police protection because their inhabitants are wealthy or white does not mean that all neighborhoods can afford to turn over the guns to professionals only. Leaving only criminals and the government with guns is not the solution.

## Discussion Questions

1. Is the author's claim one of fact, of value, or of policy? What, specifically, is his claim?
2. How does the history of gun control support the author's view that gun control is coercive or oppressive?
3. What is the author's response to the criticism that there are ''no controls''? Why was the 1968 federal Gun Control Act lobbied for by domestic arms manufacturers?
4. Who are the most vocal supporters of gun control today? What reasons does the author give for their support of gun control legislation?
5. How does the author respond to the argument that gun control reduces crime or death by firearms?
6. What solution does he offer for ''crimes of passion''?
7. Has the author proved, as the title of the article suggests, that gun control

is "historically ineffective, imprudent and coercive"? Do you think that he has answered all or most of the arguments raised by gun control advocates?

## Writing Suggestions

1.  Select a problem at your school and write a paper arguing for or against the existence of the problem. Support your claim with your own careful observations and those of others. (For a longer paper, you may have to look at university reports and interview officials.) If you argue for the existence of a problem, don't offer a solution; merely prove that it exists. *Examples:* adequacy of the health service, availability of study space, quiet in the dorms, availability of desired courses, quality of social life, registration for courses.
2.  Examine an advertisment consisting largely of factual material rather than pictures or slogans. Evaluate the facts by answering some or all of the following questions: Does the advertisement confuse facts with inference? Can a reader or prospective buyer determine the accuracy of the facts? Why or why not? Have credible authorities been cited in support of the data? Has the advertisment offered answers to questions a buyer might ask? If not, what other facts should the advertisement have provided?

# *Life Is an Inalienable Right*
## REUBEN GROSS

To the Editor of the *Jerusalem Post*:

Sir, — Secularists throughout Israel are undoubtedly rejoicing over 1 the thrashing of religionists in the battle over the abortion bill. Many humanists, however, may be having sober second thoughts. Permission to shed human blood, even of a not-yet viable individual, or to tear off a part of one's own body, destroys a cornerstone of humanistic and democratic civilization.

Civilization as developed in the free countries of the West rests on a 2 belief in the sanctity of human life. In 200 years there has been no improvement upon Thomas Jefferson's terse summary of that creed as set forth in the Declaration of Independence by the American Colonies. Therein he wrote, "Life (is) an inalienable right . . . endowed by the Creator." Supporters of the right of a woman to abort her potential off-

---

Reuben Gross is senior vice-president of the Union of Orthodox Jewish Congregations of America.

spring have rested their case on the claim of "ownership" by the woman of her own body and have indeed argued that the "inalienability of life" is a warranty of title by each person to his own body and to the right of disposition thereof. This is a grave error. Life was declared "inalienable" for the very opposite reason. John Locke, Jefferson's mentor in political philosophy, stated clearly what Jefferson merely hinted: that people cannot assign to a government what is not theirs, to wit, the disposition of their bodies which are the work of the Divine Creator which He entrusts to mankind as an endowment.

One need not speculate as to the consequences of displacing a belief 3 in the sancity of life by a belief in the ownership of one's person. Many are already evident in places that have adopted liberal abortion laws. Rape is no longer a heinous crime. Euthanasia is discussed seriously and is in fact practised, *sub rosa*, in the same manner that abortions were formerly handled. Medical experimentation is edging closer to the use of viable foetuses and of living persons. The legalization of abortion must inevitably produce a public callousness toward human life that will seek compensation in maudlin sympathy for animals, wild life and trees.

An abortion may not be murder, but it is the shedding of human 4 blood concerning which Tora states that one who so sheds blood deserves to have his blood shed. This was the great lesson which the Jewish people taught mankind. Should not every believer in the true and sacred quality of human life tremble at the legalization of the right to destroy it?

Reuben Gross

## Discussion Questions

1. Is Gross's claim one of fact, of value, or of policy? What is his claim?
2. What is Gross's principal objection to abortion? Find the place or places in the letter where he makes his objections explicit.
3. How does he answer the claim that a woman has a right to ownership of her body?
4. In the first paragraph Gross speaks of "human blood, even of a not-yet-viable individual." Is that a contradiction? How do you think Gross would explain his use of the word *human* to describe something that is "not yet viable"?
5. One dictionary defines *humanism* as "a philosophy that emphasizes human interests and values" and "often rejects supernaturalism." Why, then, does Gross assume that humanists may also be dismayed at the idea of abortion? How are quotations from Thomas Jefferson and John Locke meant to support his claim?
6. Does Gross feel that acceptance of abortion will lead to acceptance of other immoral practices? Use examples from his letter to explain.

# A "Right to Life"
# Unacknowledged by Nature

## MARK N. COHEN AND ROY S. MALPASS

To the Editor:

We note with some enjoyment Gerald Weissman's discussion of sea 1
urchin eggs offered in response to the testimony of biologists concerning
the moment when life begins. We think, however, that his point can be
made more forcefully.

For any biologist to argue that life begins at conception — and 2
therefore is subject to protection from that moment on — is to fly in the
face of overwhelming evidence. If there is any lesson to be learned from
looking at other organisms, it is that conception is never a guarantee of a
"right to life."

Most species produce offspring in numbers far in excess of those re- 3
quired to replace the adult population or even to permit modest population growth. These offspring are essentially turned loose to try to survive
on their own. Most fail, and indeed the long-term viability of both species and ecosystem demands that most fail.

It is characteristic of mammals, as a class of organisms, that they 4
conceive fewer offspring than do most other organisms and that they offer more parental aid to each offspring. But the price of this parental aid
is that the parent retains (and exercises) the power to terminate conceived offspring selectively. Fetuses may be aborted spontaneously
through the mother's physiological reponses to external stresses, and babies may be eliminated through selected neglect or outright infanticide.

Excess fertility combined with selective elimination of offspring ap- 5
pears to be the mechanism by which organisms (including mammals)
achieve reproductive flexibility needed to adjust to environmental fluc-
tuations.

The case is the same for human beings. Almost all known human 6
groups (there are a very few arguable cases) have the ability to produce
babies in excess of those which will actually be utilized as adults (or die
naturally). Moreover, human groups universally (or nearly so) utilize this
potential to be selective about which fertilized egg will be permitted to
mature.

Mark N. Cohen is professor of anthropology and Roy S. Malpass is professor of behavioral science at the State University of New York at Plattsburgh.

Many groups assume that such decisions are the private prerogative  7
of the mother or of the two spouses together. Other groups bound the
decision with legal rules which protect life, most commonly either from
birth or from the time — at about age two — when the infant is thought
to have demonstrated its viability and is granted full citizenship.

The important point is that societies vary widely in their rules and  8
that the rules are societal choices geared to a variety of social values rather
than grounded in biological "rules."

We in the United States have the right and duty to debate our own  9
social and legal choices, but we should recognize them as social contracts
rather than as biological "facts." A study of other cultures makes it clear
that there are no simple moral absolutes, and a study of other species
makes a mockery of arguments that biology can be used to support the
"right to life" beginning at conception.

Mark N. Cohen<br>Roy S. Malpass

## Discussion Questions

1. What is the authors' claim about abortion? Do they state it directly or indirectly? Select the sentence or sentences that make their position clear.
2. What is the basis of their claim? Compare their principles of judgment —
   religious, humanitarian, scientific, or political — to those of Gross in the
   previous letter. Summarize the differences.
3. The authors make an analogy between human beings and other forms of
   animal life. Do you find this analogy persuasive? Why or why not?
4. Explain the possible implications of this assertion: "Other groups bound
   the decision with legal rules which protect life, most commonly either from
   birth or from the time — *at about age two* — when the infant is thought to
   have demonstrated its viability and is granted full citizenship" (italics
   added).
5. Does the fact that the authors are an anthropologist and a behavioral scientist lend their argument greater force? To what audience would these credentials make a strong appeal? Would another audience consider the religious affiliations of Rabbi Gross more relevant to an argument on
   abortion?

## Writing Suggestions

1. Select a ritual with which you are familiar and argue for or against the values it represents. *Examples:* the high school prom, Christmas gift-giving, a
   fraternity initiation, a wedding, a confirmation or bar mitzvah, a funeral
   ceremony, a Fourth of July celebration.

2. Write a review of a movie, play, television program, concert, restaurant, or book. Make clear your criteria for judgment and their order of importance.

# Registration Drive

## FRANKLIN LAVIN

The pictures are among the most ridiculous you'll ever see on televi-  1
sion or in the papers. There's this 18-year-old whose criminal record consists of nothing more than teasing his sister or staying at the drive-in after curfew, and he's being hauled off to *jail* for refusing to register for the draft.

Instead of indicting, trying, and convicting the 600,000 non-regis-  2
trants as if they were chain-saw murderers, why not try a more benign, cheaper, and much more effective form of enforcement?

I have an idea for one, which I call "Registration Drive." Rather  3
than hustling young men off to jail and liberal martyrdom, the federal government should require all states simply to issue driver's licenses that expire on the holder's 18th birthday, and prohibit the states from renewing the license of anyone who refuses to register for the draft.

I hardly need to spell out the implications of the loss of a driver's li-  4
cense to the average teenage American male, rich or poor, black or white. Only a very few would subject themselves to the resulting social humiliation and lack of mobility. Anyone willing to suffer such consequences could almost be eligible for conscientious-objector status on this basis alone. The punishment would be as unpopular as driving is popular, which is exactly the right degree of severity for a crime of this kind.

Of course the main reason for the plan is not to punish but to con-  5
vince young men that they should register. The current approach doesn't do that. Out of the hundreds of thousands who refuse to register, only a handful will ever face the courts. The non-registrants simply can play the odds: 43,000 to one against an indictment, 100,000 to one against a conviction. Because none of these offenders will ever be able to repeat their crimes, jailing or fining them makes very little sense. "Protecting society," "repaying society," "rehabilitating the guilty," and all of the other justifications for normal punishment just aren't relevant in this situation — nor in many others.

Franklin Lavin is assistant director of the President's Commission on Executive Exchange.

The government's plan to deny financial aid to students failing to 6
register suffers several defects. Not all draft-age men attend college; rich
students who don't need aid can escape. A Minnesota judge also ruled
recently that the plan violates the constitution's self-incrimination
clause. That may be a concern with a jail sentence looming; if the punishment is denying a privilege (a driver's license), this standard seems ludicrous.

Some might object that the Registration Drive would be ineffective 7
for those who don't drive, whether they're rich teenagers from Manhattan or very poor ones who just can't afford a car. However, with the exception of those totally estranged from society, young men do drink in
bars or cash checks, and they need a driver's license for identification.
Besides, getting a license is an important part of the rites of male passage. Whether they own a car or not, 99.9 percent of the male teenage
population *wants* a license.

The driver's license renewal could be a model of creative punish- 8
ment for a victimless crime. The beauty of this type of penalty is that enforcement would be swift, almost without costs (states would have only
to change expiration dates on some licenses), and painless to the social
fabric. Not even the Berrigan brothers could get excited over this one.
What would they shout — "Let my people drive"?

## Discussion Questions

1. Is the author's claim one of fact, of value, or of policy? What is his claim?
2. What evidence does the author provide to support his plan's effectiveness?
3. Why does he feel the present plan of denying financial aid to college students is ineffective as a punishment?
4. In what way is a driver's license important even for those who don't drive?
   Why is the author's plan a model of "creative punishment"?

## Writing Suggestions

1. If you are against registration for the draft, write a defense of your position.
   If you favor a different punishment for registration evaders than the author's suggestion, develop a proposal for it.
2. The author characterizes his solution as "creative punishment for a victimless crime." Choose another so-called victimless crime — prostitution, va-
   grancy, marijuana use — and propose a creative punishment. Or argue that
   the crime should not be punished at all. Explain why.

## Additional Writing Suggestions:

1. Look for personal advertisements (in which men and women advertise for various kinds of companionship) in a local or national paper or magazine. (the *Village Voice*, a New York paper, is an outstanding source.) What inferences can you draw about the people who place these particular ads? About the "facts" they choose to provide? How did you come to these conclusions? You might also try to infer the reasons that many more men than women place ads.

2. "I like Colonel Sanders" is the title of an article that praises ugly architecture, shopping malls, laundromats, and other symbols of "plastic" America. The author claims that these aspects of the American scene have unique and positive values. Defend or refute his claim by pointing out what the values of these things might be, giving reasons for your own assessments.

3. A psychiatrist says that in pro football personality traits determine the positions of the players. Write an essay developing this idea and providing adequate evidence for your claim. Or make inferences about the relationship between the personalities of the players and another sport that you know well.

4. Tell whether you plan to have a small family, a large one, or none at all. Emphasize the values that govern your answer. You may want to look at the opinions of some experts who relate such choices to cultural as well as personal experience.

5. The controversy concerning seat belts and air bags in automobiles has generated a variety of proposals, one of which is mandatory use of seat belts in all the states. Make your own policy claim regarding laws about safety devices (the wearing of motorcycle helmets is another thorny subject), and defend it by using both facts and values — facts about safety, values concerning individual freedom and responsibility.

6. At least one city in the world — Reykjavik, the capital of Iceland — bans dogs from the city. Defend or attack this policy by using both facts and values to support your claim.

7. Choose a school problem and offer a solution for the problem. Assume that the existence of the problem has already been established. Make clear the advantage of your plan.

8. Choose a recommended policy — from the school newspaper or elsewhere — and argue that it will or will not work to produce beneficial changes. *Examples:* expansion of core requirements, comprehensive tests as a graduation requirement, reinstitution of a physical education requirement, removel of junk food from campus vending machines, refusal to allow Dow Chemical Co. recruiters on campus.

# 3   *Definition*

## THE PURPOSES OF DEFINITION

Definition in argument can be used in two ways: to clarify the meanings of vague or ambiguous terms, especially those in the claim; or as a method of development for the whole essay. The essay allows you to elaborate on the meaning of a broad concept or an experience that cannot be adequately defined in a shorter space.

The Roman statesman Cicero said, "Every rational discussion of anything whatsoever should begin with a definition in order to make clear what is the subject of dispute." You have probably already discovered the importance of definition in argument. If you have ever had a disagreement with your parents about using the car or drinking or dyeing your hair or going away for a weekend or staying out till three in the morning, you know that you were really arguing about the meaning of the term "adolescent freedom."

Arguments often revolve around definitions of crucial terms. For example, how does one define *democracy*? Does a democracy guarantee freedom of the press, freedom of worship, freedom of assembly, freedom of movement? In the United States, we would argue that such freedoms are essential to any definition of *democracy*. But countries in which these freedoms are nonexistent also represent themselves as democracies or governments of the people. In the words of Senator Daniel J. Moynihan, "For years now the most brutal totalitarian regimes have called themselves 'people's' or 'democratic' republics." Rulers in such governments are aware that defining their regimes as democratic may win the approval of people who would otherwise condemn them. In his formidable attack on totalitarianism, *1984*, George Orwell coined the slogans "War Is Peace" and "Slavery Is Freedom," phrases that represent the corrupt use of definition to distort reality.

But even where there is no intention to deceive, the snares of definition are difficult to avoid. How do you define *abortion*? Is it "termination of pregnancy"? Or is it "murder of an unborn child"? During a celebrated trial in 1975 of a physician who performed an abortion and was accused of manslaughter, the prosecution often used the word *baby* to refer to the fetus, but the defense referred to "the products of conception." These definitions of *fetus* reflected the differing judgments of those on opposite sides. Not only do judgments create definitions; definitions influence judgments. In the abortion trial, the definitions of *fetus* used by both sides were meant to promote either approval or disapproval of the doctor's action.

Definitions can indeed change the nature of an event or a "fact." How many farms are there in the state of New York? The answer to the question depends on the definition of *farm*. In 1979 the *New York Times* reported:

> Because of a change in the official definition of the word "farm," New York lost 20 percent of its farms on January 1, with numbers dropping from 56,000 to 45,000. . . .
>
> Before the change, a farm was defined as "any place from which $250 or more of agricultural products is sold" yearly or "any place of 10 acres or more from which $50 or more of agricultural products is sold" yearly. Now a farm is "any place from which $1000 or more of agricultural products is sold" in a year.[1]

A change in the definition of *poverty* can have similar results. Census Bureau data show that poverty has risen from 1979 to 1983 and that there are "nearly 10 million more poor people now than in 1978." But David Stockman, director of the Office of Management and Budget, argues that "if noncash benefits [Medicaid, food stamps, housing subsidies] had counted as income, the poverty rate would have been reduced

---

[1] *New York Times*, March 4, 1979, Sec. 1, p. 40.

from the official 15 percent to 9.6 percent, and the number of poor people would have dropped by more than a third, from 34.4 million to 22 million.''² The difference is wholly a matter of definition. On the one hand, poverty is defined by money income alone; on the other, by the addition of nonmoney income in the form of benefits.

## DEFINING THE TERMS IN YOUR CLAIM

In almost all your arguments you will introduce terms in your claim that require definition. A definition of poverty is crucial to any debate on the existence of poverty in the United States. The same may be true in a debate about the legality of euthanasia, or mercy killing. Are the arguers referring to passive euthanasia, that is, the withdrawal of life support systems, or to active euthanasia, in which death is hastened through the direct administration of drugs?

It is not uncommon, in fact, for arguments about controversial questions to turn into arguments about definition of terms. If, for example, you wanted to argue in favor of the regulation of religious cults, you would first have to define *cult*. In so doing, you might discover that it is not easy to distinguish clearly between conventional religions and cults. Then you would have to define *regulation*, spelling out the legal restrictions you favored so as to make them apply only to cults, not to established religions. An argument on the subject might end almost before it began if writer and reader could not agree on definitions of these terms. While clear definitions do not guarantee agreement, they ensure that all parties understand the nature of the argument.

### Defining Vague and Ambiguous Terms

You will need to define other terms in addition to those in your claim. If you use words and phrases that have two or more meanings, they may appear vague and ambiguous to your reader. In arguments of value and policy abstract terms such as *freedom*, *justice*, *patriotism*, and *equality* require clarification. Despite their vagueness, however, they are among the most important in the language because they represent the ideals that shape our laws. When conflicts arise, the courts must define these terms to establish the legality of certain practices. Is the Ku Klux Klan permitted to make disparaging public statements about ethnic and

---

²*New York Times*, November 27, 1983, Sec. E, p. 6.

racial groups? That depends on the court's definition of "free speech." Can execution for some crimes be considered "cruel and unusual punishment"? That, too, depends on the court's definition of "cruel and unusual punishment." In addition, such terms as *happiness*, *mental health*, *success*, and *creativity* often defy precise definition because they reflect the differing values within a society or a culture.

The definition of *success*, for example, varies not only among social groups but among individuals within the group. One scientist has postulated five signs by which to judge the measure of success: wealth (including health), security (confidence in retaining the wealth), reputation, performance, and contentment.[3] Consider whether all of these are necessary to your own definition of *success*. If not, which may be omitted? Do you think others should be added? Notice that one of the signs — reputation — depends on definition by the community; another — contentment — can be measured only by the individual. The assessment of performance probably owes something to both the group and the individual.

Christopher Atkins, the young actor in *Blue Lagoon* and *Dallas*, gave an interviewer an example of an externalized definition of success:

> Success to me is judged through the eyes of others. I mean, if you're walking around saying, "I own a green Porsche," you might meet somebody who says, "Hey, that's no big deal, I own a green Porsche and a house." So all of a sudden, you don't feel so successful. Really, it's in the eyes of others.[4]

So difficult is the formulation of a universally accepted measure for success that some scholars regard the concept as meaningless. Nevertheless, we continue to use the word as if it represented a definable concept because the idea of success, however defined, is important for the identity and development of the individual and the group. It is clear, however, that when crossing subcultural boundaries, even within a small group, we need to be aware of differences in the use of the word. If "contentment" — that is, the satisfaction of achieving a small personal goal — is enough, then a person lying under a palm tree subsisting on handouts from picnickers may be a success. But you should not expect all your readers to agree that these criteria are enough to define *success*.

In arguing about aesthetic matters, whose vocabulary is almost always abstract, the criteria for judgment must be revealed, either directly or indirectly, and then the abstract terms that represent the criteria must

---

[3] Gwynn Nettler, *Social Concerns* (New York: McGraw-Hill, 1976), pp. 196–197.
[4] *New York Times*, August 6, 1982, Sec. III, p. 8.

be defined. If you want to say that a film is distinguished by great acting, have you made clear what you mean by *great*? That we do not always understand or agree on the definiton of *great* is apparent, say, on the morning after the Oscar winners have been announced. Or to take a less familiar example, how would a photographer define "Indianness"? Edward S. Curtis, a nineteenth- and early-twentieth century photographer of North American Indians, tried to capture in his photographs a quality he called "primitive Indianness." But what was it? As one critic remarked, "His conception of Indianness, although never clearly defined, appears to have been based on the popular illusion that change depleted Indianness — that true Indianness was that which was unaffected by white culture."[5] The critic explains how this definition forced Curtis "to ignore the effect of white culture" and to create an unnatural environment in his studio for his Indian subjects.

Robert Sommer, an architect who is critical of the "hard" architecture of prison cells, dormitory rooms, and public facilities such as picnic tables and restrooms, explains the meaning of *hard* by setting down its characteristics: strength, resistance to human imprint, lack of permeability between inside and out. He defines the last term by giving details:

> The new postal center in Oakland, with its tiny slit windows, looks as if it were intended for urban guerilla warfare. Older buildings that still have plate glass use steel shutters and gates that can be drawn across the exterior in a matter of minutes. Some corporations are moving their data-processing machinery underground where they are less vulnerable to attack.[6]

References to other matters of taste outside the arts — food, fashions, games — also require definition of criteria if arguer and reader are to understand each other. How does the reviewer define "very good" for the restaurant to which she awards two stars? How does the wearer define Jordache jeans as "better" than Wrangler's? How does the maker define Intellivision football as "superior" to Atari football?

## METHODS FOR DEFINING TERMS

The following strategies for defining terms in an argument are by no means mutually exclusive. You may use all of them in a single argumentative essay.

---

[5] Andy Grundberg, *New York Times Book Review*, September 5, 1982, p. 10.

[6] Robert Sommer, *Tight Spaces: Hard Architecture and How to Humanize It* (Englewood Cliffs, N.J.: Prentice-Hall, 1974), p. 7.

## Dictionary Definition

Giving a dictionary definition is the simplest and most obvious way to define a term. An unabridged dictionary is the best source because it usually gives examples of the way a word can be used in a sentence; that is, it furnishes the proper context.

In many cases, the dictionary definition alone is not sufficient. It may be too broad or too narrow for your purpose. Suppose in an argument about pornography, you wanted to define the word *obscene*. *Webster's New Internaitonal Dictionary* (third edition, unabridged) gives the definition of *obscene* as "offensive to taste; foul; loathsome; disgusting." But these synonyms do not tell you what qualities make an object or an event or an action "foul," "loathsome," and "disgusting." In 1973 the Supreme Court, attempting to narrow the definition of *obscenity*, ruled that obscenity was to be determined by the community in accordance with local standards. One person's obscenity, as numerous cases have demonstrated, may be another person's art. The celebrated trials in the early twentieth century about the distribution of novels regarded as pornographic — D. H. Lawrence's *Lady Chatterley's Lover* and James Joyce's *Ulysses* — emphasized the problems of definition.

Another dictionary definition may strike you as too narrow. *Patriotism*, for example, is defined in one dictionary as "love and loyal or zealous support of one's country, especially in all matters involving other countries." Some readers may want to include an unwillingness to support government policies they consider wrong.

## Stipulation

Using stipulation, the writer specifies the meaning of a word to limit or control the argument. Someone has said, "Part of the task of keeping definitions in our civilization clear and pure is to keep a firm democratic rein on those with the power, or craving the power, to stipulate meaning." Perhaps this writer was thinking of a term like *national security*, which can be defined by a nation's leaders in such a way as to sanction persecution of citizens and reckless military adventures. Likewise, a term such as *liberation* can be appropriated by terrorist groups whose activities often lead to oppression rather than liberation.

Religion is usually defined as a belief in a supernatural power to be obeyed and worshiped. But in an article entitled "Civil Religion in America," a sociologist offers a different meaning.

> While some have argued that Christianity is the national faith, and others that church and synagogue celebrate only the generalized religion of

"the American way of life," few have realized that there actually exists alongside of and rather clearly differentiated from the churches an elaborate and well-institutionalized civil religion in America. This article argues not only that there is such a thing, but also that this religion . . . has its own seriousness and integrity and requires the same care in understanding that any other religion does.[7]

When the author adds, "This religion — there seems no other word for it — was neither sectarian nor in any specific sense Christian," he emphasizes that he is distinguishing his definition of religion from definitions that associate religion and church.

Even the word *violence*, which the dictionary defines as "physical force used so as to injure or damage" and whose meaning seems so clear and uncompromising, can be manipulated to produce a definition different from the one normally understood by most people. Some pacifists refer to conditions in which "people are deprived of choices in a systematic way" as "institutionalized quiet violence." Even where no physical force is employed, this lack of choice in the schools, in the workplace, in the black ghettos is defined as violence.[8]

In *Through the Looking Glass* Alice asked Humpty Dumpty "whether you can make words mean so many different things."

"When I use a word," Humpty Dumpty said scornfully, "it means just what I choose it to mean, neither more nor less."[9]

A writer, however, is not free to invent definitions that no one will recognize or that create rather than solve problems between writer and reader.

## Negation

To avoid confusion it is sometimes helpful to tell the reader what a term is *not*. In discussing euthanasia, a writer might say, "By euthanasia I do not mean active intervention to hasten the death of the patient."

A negative definition may be more extensive, depending on the complexity of the term and the writer's ingenuity. The ex-Communist

---

[7] Robert N. Bellah, "Civil Religion in America," *Daedalus*, Winter 1967, p. 1.

[8] Newton Garver, "What Violence Is," in *Moral Choices*, edited by James Rachels (New York: Harper and Row, 1971), pp. 248–249.

[9] Lewis Carroll, *Alice in Wonderland and Through the Looking Glass* (Grosset and Dunlap, 1948), p. 238.

Whittaker Chambers, in a foreword to a book on the spy trial of Alger Hiss, defined communism this way:

> First, let me try to say what Communism is not. It is not simply a vicious plot hatched by wicked men in a sub-cellar. It is not just the writings of Marx and Lenin, dialectical materialism, the Politburo, the labor theory of value, the theory of the general strike, the Red Army secret police, labor camps, underground conspiracy, the dictatorship of the proletariat, the technique of the coup d'etat. It is not even those chanting, bannered millions that stream periodically, like disorganized armies, through the heart of the world's capitals: Moscow, New York, Tokyo, Paris, Rome. These are expressions, but they are not what Communism is about.[10]

This, of course, is only part of the definition. Any writer beginning a definition in the negative must go on to define what the term *is*.

## Examples

One of the most effective ways of defining terms in an argument is the use of examples. Both real and hypothetical examples can bring life to abstract and ambiguous terms. The writer in the following passage defines *preferred categories* (people who are meant to benefit from affirmative action policies) by invoking specific cases:

> The absence of definitions points up one of the problems with preferred categories. . . . These preferred categories take no account of family wealth or educational advantages. A black whose father is a judge or physician deserves preferential treatment over any non-minority applicant. The latter might have fought his way out of the grinding poverty of Appalachia, or might be the first member of an Italian-American or a Polish-American family to complete high school. But no matter.[11]

*Insanity* is a word that has been used and misused to describe a variety of conditions. Even psychiatrists are in dispute about its meaning. In the following anecdote, examples narrow and refine the definition.

> Dr. Zilboorg says that present day psychiatry does not possess any satisfactory definition of mental illness or neurosis. To illustrate, he told a story: A psychiatrist was recently asked for a definition of a "well-adjusted

---

[10] *Witness* (New York: Random House, 1952), p. 8.

[11] Anthony Lombardo, "Quotas Work Both Ways," *U.S. Catholic*, February 1974, p. 39.

person'' (not even slightly peculiar). The definition: ''A person who feels in harmony with himself and who is not in conflict with his environment.'' It sounded fine, but up popped a heckler. ''Would you then consider an anti-Nazi working in the underground against Hitler a maladjusted person?'' ''Well,'' the psychiatrist hemmed, ''I withdraw the latter part of my definition.'' Dr. Zilboorg withdrew the first half for him. Many persons in perfect harmony with themselves, he pointed out, are in ''distinctly pathological states.''[12]

## Extended Definition

When we speak of an extended definition, we usually refer not only to length but also to the variety of methods for developing the definition. Let's take the word *materialism*. A dictionary entry offers the following sentence fragments as definitions: ''1. the doctrine that comfort, pleasure and wealth are the only or highest goals or values. 2. the tendency to be more concerned with material than with spiritual goals or values.'' But the term *materialism* has acquired so many additional meanings, especially emotional ones, that an extended definition serves a useful purpose in clarifying the many different ideas surrounding our understanding of the term.

Here is a much longer definition of *materialism*, which appears at the beginning of an essay entitled ''People and Things: Reflections on Materialism.''[13] The authors make a distinction between two kinds of materialism and provide an extended explanation, using contrast and examples.

> There are two contemporary usages of the term, materialism, and it is important to distinguish between them. On the one hand we can talk about *instrumental materialism*, or the use of material objects to make life longer, safer, more enjoyable. By instrumental, we mean that objects act as essential means for discovering and furthering personal values and goals of life, so that the objects are instruments used to realize and further those goals. There is little negative connotation attached to this meaning of the word, since one would think that it is perfectly sensible to use things for such purposes. While it is true that the United States is the epitome of materialism in this sense, it is also true that most people in every society aspire to reach our level of instrumental materialism.

---

[12] Quoted in *The Art of Making Sense*, p. 48.

[13] Mihaly Csikszentmihalyi and Eugene Rochberg-Halton, ''People and Things: Reflections on Materialism,'' *University of Chicago Magazine*, Spring 1978, pp. 7–8.

On the other hand the term has a more negative connotation, which might be conveyed by the phrase *terminal materialism*. This is the sense critics use when they apply the term to Americans. What they mean is that we not only use our material resources as instruments to make life more manageable, but that we reduce our ultimate goals to the possession of things. They believe that we don't just use our cars to get from place to place, but that we consider the ownership of expensive cars one of the central values in life. Terminal materialism means that the object is valued only because it indicates an end in itself, a possession. In instrumental materialism there is a sense of directionality, in which a person's goals may be furthered through the interactions with the object. A book, for example, can reveal new possibilities or widen a person's view of the world, or an old photograph can be cherished because it embodies a relationship. But in terminal materialism, there is no sense of reciprocal interaction in the relation between the object and the end. The end is valued as final, not as itself a means to further ends. And quite often it is only the status label or image associated with the object that is valued, rather than the actual object.

## THE DEFINITION ESSAY

The argumentative essay can take the form of an extended definition. An example of such an essay is the one from which we've just quoted, as well as the three essays at the end of this chapter. The definition essay is appropriate when the idea under consideration is so controversial or so heavy with historical connotations that even a paragraph or two cannot make clear exactly what the arguer wants his readers to understand. For example, if you were preparing a definition of your own patriotism, you would want to answer some or all of the following questions. You would probably use a number of methods to develop your definition: personal narrative, examples, stipulation, comparison and contrast, and cause and effect analysis.

1. **Dictionary Definition.** Is the dictionary definition the one I will elaborate on? Do I need to stipulate other meanings?
2. **Personal History.** Where did I first acquire my notions of patriotism? What was taught? How and by whom was it taught?
3. **Cultural Context.** Has my patriotic feeling changed in the last few years? Why or why not? Does my own patriotism reflect the mood of the country or the group to which I belong?
4. **Values.** What is the value of patriotism? Does it make me more humane, more civilized? Is patriotism consistent with tolerance of other systems and cultures? Is patriotism the highest duty of a citizen? Do any other values take precedence? What was the meaning

of President Kennedy's injunction: "Ask not what your country can do for you; ask rather what you can do for your country"?

5. **Behavior**. How do I express my patriotism (or lack of it)? Can it be expressed through dissent? What sacrifice, if any, would I make for my country?

## WRITING AN ESSAY OF DEFINITION

The following list suggests several important steps to be taken in writing an essay of definition.

1. Choose a term that needs definition because it is controversial or ambiguous, or because you want to offer a personal definition that differs from the accepted interpretation. Explain why an extended definition is necessary. Or choose an experience that lends itself to treatment in an extended definition. One student defined "culture shock" as she had experienced it while studying abroad in Hawaii among students of a different ethnic background.

2. Decide on the thesis — the point of view you wish to develop about the term you are defining. If you want to define "heroism," for example, you may choose to develop the idea that this quality depends on motivation and awareness of danger rather than on the specific act performed by the hero.

3. Begin by consulting the dictionary for the conventional definition, the one with which most readers will be familiar. Make clear whether you want to elaborate on the dictionary definition or take issue with it because you think it is misleading or inadequate.

4. Distinguish wherever possible between the term you are defining and other terms with which it might be confused. If you are defining "love," can you make a clear distinction between the different kinds of emotional attachments contained in the word?

5. Try to think of several methods of developing the definition — using examples, comparison and contrast, analogy, cause and effect analysis. However, you may discover that one method alone — say, a number of examples — will suffice to narrow and refine your definition. See "The Nature of Prejudice" at the end of this chapter as an example of such a development.

6. Arrange your supporting material in an order that gives emphasis to the most important ideas. The essay at the end of the chapter, "How to Tell Bad from Worse," demonstrates this kind of organization.

SAMPLE ANALYSIS

# How to Tell Bad from Worse

## MICHAEL LEVIN

The distinction between authoritarianism and totalitarianism is 1
much in the news. Despite its clumsy defense by the Reagan Administration and the obfuscation of such critics as Amnesty International, the distinction is a clear and vital one. Nero was not Stalin, and it is important to understand why.

An authoritarian regime is the rule of a strongman or clique which 2
forbids all activities that threaten its position, such as a critical press or an opposition party. It punishes resistance ruthlessly. Authoritarian rulers are typically venal and capricious; their rule encourages corruption and disaffection. There is, however, an important limit to the excesses of authoritarian regimes: they are indifferent to behavior that does not threaten their security.

By contrast, a totalitarian regime wants to control *everything* — not 3
just political power, but all aspects of its subjects' lives. As its name suggests, a totalitarian state dictates values, art and personal and economic association. In addition to an official press, the totalitarian wants an official hour for calisthenics. The authoritarian does not care who becomes a doctor, so long as doctors remain apolitical; the totalitarian determines who becomes a doctor, where doctors practice, their remuneration and, so far as he can, their attitude toward doctoring. (Totalitarians want doctors to regard their skill as For The People.)

Where the authoritarian wants obedience, the totalitarian wants 4
worship — not for himself, but for his regime. He wants the hearts and minds of his subjects. The totalitarian attacks religious and moral traditions precisely because they are independent objects of devotion.

This difference in the degree of control should be obvious. It is, 5
however, relatively superficial. At a more fundamental level, what distinguishes totalitarians from authoritarians is the *kind of justification* they claim. Only when this is appreciated does the greater menace of totalitarianism become apparent. Only then does it become clear why to-

---

Michael Levin (b. 1943) is professor of philosophy at City College of New York. He is the author of *Metaphysics and the Mind/Body Problem*.

talitarian states have given mankind a quite new idea of its own capacity for wickedness.

An authoritarian claims no legitimacy, properly speaking. He is 6 where he is by being strong enough to get and stay there. He offers, at most, stability. But the totalitarian is a utopian who, intoxicated by some scheme for perfecting the world, regards his control as *justified* by the need to force his ideal on a shortsighted populace. Marxists, those paradigm utopians, see a workers' paradise emerging once the sin of ownership is extinguished, and they see this as entitling them to use whatever means are necessary to speed the process. A little duress is OK when there is a world to win.

Utopians always have a theory of Human Nature which implies that 7 humanity as we know it is a stunted version of what it can be under their ministrations. Marxists, again, hold that people are all naturally creative, but have been "alienated" from their true selves by wage labor. As all past societies have thus deformed Human Nature, the utopian remedy is correspondingly sweeping; everything old — that is, everything — must go. The totalitarian sees his subjects as cripples, his measures as those of a dedicated surgeon. (Since what is being rectified is an abstraction — Human Nature — individuals get rather short shrift.)

A regime is totalitarian, then, if it justifies its full control as serving 8 a higher good. In the China of the 1960s engineers were instructed to contemplate Mao's thoughts and courting couples to raise each other's revolutionary consciousness. Such policies were not instituted to prevent insurrection, but to speed the coming of the New Man. Even Nazi ideology was thought by its devotees to be a blueprint for a better world.

Totalitarian states are inevitably worse than authoritarian ones, first 9 because the totalitarian sees nothing less than the human future at stake in his efforts. A Franco will execute (or imprison) all his rivals, but avoid further brutality as pointless. A Pol Pot will liquidate anyone with a European (hence "corrupt") education. If the disappearance of 8,000 Argentines is an outrage, what shall we make of the 20 million Russians that Beria eliminated?

Second, since *utopia will never arrive*, the totalitarian's "tempo- 10 rary" measures will become permanent. Worse, since the totalitarian must attribute failure to the insufficiency of his methods — the soundness of his overarching theory is a matter of faith — ever more surveillance and propaganda are inevitable. Disobedience is treated with special harshness. The authoritarian sees disobedience as a crime to be deterred; the totalitarian sees any deviation from the new order as persistent corruption in the human material he is out to mold. Indeed, since he has shown the way to utopia, backsliding must be subversive. Deviation implies reaction, against which the totalitarian is always on guard.

Lenin said it best: "A good communist is always at the same time a good Chekist." (The Cheka, or Committee against Counterrevolution, had unlimited powers of life and death.)

Worst of all, the totalitarian is driven by a reformer's zeal. Threaten 11 a tyrant and you may dissuade him; threaten a zealot and you only stiffen his resolve. As George V. Higgins put it, "There is no one as dangerous as an idealist with a machine gun."

Walter Mondale wants to know the difference between authoritar- 12 ian and totalitarian torture. There is plenty. Totalitarian cruelty is worse than its authoritarian counterpart because of its scope, and because its rationale will always expand its scope. Murder is murder, but the scale of the murder counts. By this measure, totalitarianism easily outstrips all rival systems in evil.

Totalitarianism is a new phenomenon. The idea of remaking man 13 by remaking society is — Plato's anticipations aside — scarcely two centuries old, and only the technology of this century has permitted armed prophets to attempt it. The old vocabulary for assessing governments is too narrow, and current jargon too trivial, to encompass totalitarianism. If insisting that IRA gunmen wear prison uniforms is a serious issue of "human rights," we need some other words for the Gulag.

## ANALYSIS

Michael Levin says that it is important to know the difference between authoritarianism and totalitarianism. He doesn't specify the reasons, but he obviously hopes that by the end of his article, readers will know why. If totalitarianism "easily outstrips all rival systems in evil," as he attempts to prove, then public policy and international relations will have to take this fact into account.

The author uses a familiar pattern of organization, moving from what is less important to what is more important and reserving his strongest arguments for the body and conclusion of his essay. He begins by offering a definition of *authoritarianism* in the second paragraph. With the transitional phrase "By contrast" in the third paragraph, he introduces a point-by-point contrast between the two systems of government based on the degree to which each system controls its citizens.

In the fifth paragraph, he mounts his most important argument. He calls the differences he has discussed so far "relatively superficial" and presents the really significant difference, the "kind of justification" claimed by totalitarians for their society. This justification is the achievement of a revolution in human nature, a utopian ideal. Notice that the author italicizes this difference for emphasis. The eleventh paragraph begins, "Worst of all. . . ." The reader can thus follow the organization of the essay by attending to the author's signals as he advances from less important to more important issues.

Levin develops his definitions in several ways: through comparison and contrast and use of reasons and explanations, details and examples. We have already referred to the point-by-point contrast in the first part of the essay. But the bulk of his argument is devoted to reasons for condemning the most important attribute of totalitarianism — the utopian ideal. First, it is an ideal so grand that it can be realized, if at all, only at the cost of immense human sacrifice, the suffering and death of millions. Second, since utopia will never arrive, the totalitarian regime must stay in place forever, continuing to exact obedience from its subjects until human nature is changed.

Levin's concept of the utopian ideal is not entirely original, but it is one of which many readers, confused about the essential difference between authoritarianism and totalitarianism, may not be aware. This concept is directly and forcefully argued, and it represents the principal strength of the essay.

Levin's use of details and examples is less effective because there are too few of them. He mentions people and organizations with whom he assumes his readers will be familiar — Nero, Stalin, Mao, Franco, Pol Pot, Lenin, the Nazis, the IRA — and about whom he assumes they share his feelings. He also offers examples to illustrate his general statements: "In addition to an official press, the totalitarian wants an official hour for calisthenics" (paragraph 3) and "A Pol Pot will liquidate anyone with a European (hence corrupt) education" (paragraph 9). Unfortunately, Levin does not provide enough of these details and examples to allow some readers to come to their own conclusions about the validity of his argument.

This article is appropriate for an informed audience. It appeared in *Newsweek*, whose readers would probably understand Levin's general statements and supply their own examples. When he writes, for example, "Authoritarian rulers are typically venal and capricious; their rule encourages corruption and disaffection" (paragraph 2), most readers would think of the Shah of Iran or King Farouk of Egypt. But less informed readers, without familiar examples, would be at a loss to understand exactly what Levin meant.

Despite the lack of examples, however, Levin's writing is exceptionally clear and readable. His subject requires the use of abstract terms, but he is not afraid to mix colloquial expressions with more formal language: "A little duress is OK when there is a world to win" (paragraph 6). In addition, he offers an interesting combination of long and short sentences. The short ones, such as "There is plenty," emphasize like a drumbeat the urgency of his message.

READINGS FOR ANALYSIS

# *Bribing Delinquents to Be Good*

## SUSAN SEIDNER ADLER

A child's behavior is an accurate measure of the success of any pro- 1
gram aimed at his rehabilitation. If he no longer gets into trouble, it is a
success; if he does, it is a failure. Yet since it is impossible to define, let
alone gauge, what is a successful recovery from delinquency (as opposed
to rehabilitation; "recovery" is non-specific and finds its meaning in the
eyes of the beholder) the agencies are free to define success in any way
they please. Do they consider treatment succcessful if they occasionally
turn a violent mugger into a mugger who stops short of brutalizing his
victim? The answer was unanimous: sure, sure. It is not an answer that
would satisfy most people.

Furthermore, the agencies could not define the nature of the prob- 2
lem that they were expected to solve any more than they could define
their objectives, or success. Since the response to a problem is largely determined by how it is defined — one corrects wrongdoing; one treats acting out — and since the agencies have defined their populations incorrectly, it is more than likely that the agencies have been treating them
incorrectly as well. Like it or not, the whole treatment approach was designed for the emotionally troubled, dependent-neglected children that
they had once had, and not for the anti-social children who now made
up the majority of their population. Since they were unwilling or unable
to change their approach, it was in their own interest to define all their
residents as dependent-neglecteds, and to define all forms of anti-social
behavior as emotional disorders. But such an act of definition does not
make of the definition a fact, and it does not follow that anti-social
behavior is indeed an emotional illness, or that it can be treated with
therapy.

Far from being a sickness, anti-social behavior has definite advan- 3
tages for lower-class children in terms of the values that define their own
way of life. It is not inappropriate, unacceptable, and it is not even anti-

---

Susan Seidner Adler is a portrait painter who has also worked as an editor at Thomas
Y. Crowell and Scribner's. She undertook her research on juvenile delinquency out of cu-
riosity and because she found it difficult to get "straight answers to simple questions."

social — it is simply anti-middle class, anti-white, and most often, anti-both. There is no reason to assume that because children do not accept middle-class values, they do not understand them, any more than there is reason to assume that they do not know when they are breaking the law. . . .

. . . For the problem is not that children who are defiant are sick, 4 do not understand commonly held standards of right and wrong, or do not know when they are breaking the law. The problem is that they do not want middle-class approval because middle-class values are, almost by definition, in conflict with their own. They may well take a certain pride in being delinquent. . . .

. . . If delinquency is a sickness caused by deprivation, it follows 5 that expensive privileges are the proper medicine for the disease. Or, to put it in the language of the field — disadvantaged children need advantages. Which leads to the next confusion: the agencies never doubt that they know what advantages mean. For example, they offer education as something that will profit young delinquents, even though its benefits derive from the class and cultural values that they do not defend and the children do not understand. Yet education offers nothing but disadvantages to children whose idea of success is more likely to be easy money than hard-won achievement, beating the system than working in it. The same holds true for the small amount of vocational training or job-related skills that the agencies offer. A child who knows he can steal a gold chain in a few seconds sees no need to work long hours at a menial job for what he must consider small change. Furthermore, because it is the avowed purpose of treatment to work in the best interest of the child, not to transmit values, the child cannot be faulted for knowing where his self-interest truly lies. In their well-intentioned determination to overlook guilt and focus on needs, the agencies are in fact defining and judging behavior in terms similar to those of the most sociopathic of their children, and only confusing those who have some sense of right and wrong.

## Discussion Questions

1. What does the author mean by "dependent-neglected" children?
2. How would you define "emotionally ill" children? Is it necessary to define emotional health before you can define emotional illness?
3. Are there advantages, for society or the individual, in defining the juvenile criminal as "dependent-neglected" or "emotionally ill"? Are there disadvantages? Which are greater? Be specific in your answer.
4. In what way would treatment of the emotionally ill child differ from treat-

ment of the antisocial child? What form of "treatment" does the author advocate, as far as you can tell from this excerpt? What principle underlies her view of treatment?

5. Explain what Adler means by "they do not want middle-class approval because middle-class values are, almost by definition, in conflict with their own." What middle-class values do you think the author is referring to? What are the values of the delinquent children? What are the reasons for the differences?

## Writing Suggestions

1. Do some research to discover a point of view different from that expressed by Adler. Summarize the two positions; then defend one of them.
2. Choose a middle-class value and define it, using some of the strategies outlined in this chapter.

# The Nature of Prejudice
## GORDON ALLPORT

Before I attempt to define prejudice, let us have in mind four instances that I think we all would agree are prejudice. 1

The first is the case of the Cambridge University student, who said, 2 "I despise all Americans. But," he added, a bit puzzled, "I've never met one that I didn't like."

The second is the case of another Englishman, who said to an American, "I think you're awfully unfair in your treatment of Negroes. How *do* Americans feel about Negroes?" The American replied, "Well, I suppose some Americans feel about Negroes just the way you feel about the Irish." The Englishmen said, "Oh, come now. The Negroes are human beings." 3

Then there's the incident that occasionally takes place in various parts of the world (in the West Indies, for example, I'm told). When an American walks down the street the natives conspicuously hold their noses till the American goes by. The case of odor is always interesting. Odor gets mixed up with prejudice because odor has great associative 4

---

Gordon Allport (1897–1967) was a psychologist who taught at Harvard from 1922 until his death. He was the author of numerous books, among them *Personality: A Psychological Interpretation* (1937).

power. We know that some Chinese deplore the odor of Americans. Some white people think Negroes have a distinctive smell and vice versa. An intrepid psychologist recently did an experiment; it went as follows. He brought to a gymnasium an equal number of white and colored students and had them take shower baths. When they were nice and clean he had them exercise vigorously for fifteen minutes. Then he brought his judges in, and each went to the sheeted figures and sniffed. They were to say "white" or "black," guessing at the identity of the subject. The experiment seemed to prove that when we are sweaty we all smell the same way. It's good to have experimental demonstration of the fact.

The fourth example I'd like to bring before you is a piece of writing 5 that I quote. Please ask yourselves who, in your judgment, wrote it. It's a passage about the Jews.

> The synagogue is worse than a brothel. It's a den of scoundrels. It's a criminal assembly of Jews, a place of meeting for the assassins of Christ, a den of thieves, a house of ill fame, a dwelling of iniquity. Whatever name more horrible to be found, it could never be worse than the synagogue deserves.
>
> I would say the same things about their souls. Debauchery and drunkenness have brought them to the level of lusty goat and pig. They know only one thing: to satisfy their stomachs and get drunk, kill, and beat each other up. Why should we salute them? We should have not even the slightest converse with them. They are lustful, rapacious, greedy, perfidious robbers.

Now who wrote that? Perhaps you say Hitler, or Goebbels, or one of 6 our local anti-Semites? No, it was written by Saint John Chrysostom, in the fourth century A.D. Saint John Chrysostom, as you know, gave us the first liturgy in the Christian church still used in the Orthodox churches today. From it all services of the Holy Communion derive. Episcopalians will recognize him also as the author of that exalted prayer that closes the offices of both matin and evensong in the *Book of Common Prayer*. I include this incident to show how complex the problem is. Religious people are by no means necessarily free from prejudice. In this regard be patient even with our saints.

What do these four instances have in common? You notice that all 7 of them indicate that somebody is "down" on somebody else — a feeling of rejection, or hostility. But also, in all these four instances, there is indication that the person is not "up" on his subject — not really informed about Americans, Irish, Jews or bodily odors.

So I would offer, first a slang definition of prejudice: *Prejudice is* 8 *being down on somebody you're not up on*. If you dislike slang, let me offer the same thought in the style of St. Thomas Aquinas. Thomists have defined prejudice as *thinking ill of others without sufficient warrant*.

You notice that both definitions, as well as the examples I gave, 9 specify two ingredients of prejudice. First there is some sort of faulty generalization in thinking about a group. I'll call this the process of *categorization*. Then there is the negative, rejective, or hostile ingredient, a *feeling* tone. "Being down on something" is the hostile ingredient; "that you're not up on" is the categorization ingredient; "thinking ill of others" is the hostile ingredient; "without sufficient warrant" is the faulty categorization.

Parenthetically I should say that of course there is such a thing as 10 *positive* prejudice. We can be just as prejudiced *in favor of* as we are *against*. We can be biased in favor of our children, our neighborhood or our college. Spinoza makes the distinction neatly. He says that *love prejudice* is "thinking well of others, through love, more than is right." *Hate prejudice*, he says, is "thinking ill of others, through hate, more than is right."

## Discussion Questions

1. Are there any significant differences among the examples, in length, seriousness, shock value? Explain.
2. What does the Cambridge student's remark tell about the origin of stereotyping?
3. Explain the historic background of the Englishman's feeling about the Irish.
4. What was the most convincing example of Allport's definition of prejudice? Why?
5. Does the arrangement of the examples suggest the author's attitude toward his subject? Explain.
6. Read "Stereotype Truth" on page 362. How can the conclusions in that essay be reconciled with Allport's?

## Writing Suggestions

1. Choose an abstract term and write an essay modeled on Allport's. Use examples as he does to illustrate your definition, and try to imitate his organization.
2. Write about an experience you have had with prejudice and tell what you learned as a result.

## Additional Writing Suggestions

1. Choose one of the following statements and define the italicized term. Make the context as specific as possible (for example, by referring to the Declaration of Independence or your own experience).
   a. All men are created *equal*.
   b. I believe in *God*.
   c. This school doesn't offer a *liberal education*.
   d. The marine corps needs *good men*.
   e. *The Empire Strikes Back* is a *better* picture than *Return of the Jedi*.

2. Many recent controversial movements and causes are identified by terms that have come to mean different things to different people. Choose one of the following and define it, explaining both the favorable and unfavorable connotations of the term. Use examples to clarify the meaning.
   a. women's lib
   b. Palestinian homeland
   c. affirmative action
   d. Moral Majority
   e. nuclear freeze

3. Choose two words that, like *authoritarianism* and *totalitarianism*, are sometimes confused, and define them to make their differences clear. *Examples*: envy and jealousy; sympathy and pity; cult and established church; justice and equality; liberal and radical; agnostic and atheist.

4. Define a good parent, a good teacher, a good husband or wife. Try to uncover the assumptions on which your definition is based. (For example, in defining a good teacher, students sometimes mention the ability of the teacher to maintain order. Does this mean that the teacher alone is responsible for classroom order?)

5. Define any popular form of entertainment, such as the soap opera, the western, the detective story, or the science fiction story or film. Support your definition with references to specific shows or books. *Or* define an idealized type from fiction, film, the stage, advertising, or television, describing the chief attributes of that type and the principal reasons for its popularity.

6. From your own experience write an essay describing a serious misunderstanding that arose because two people had different meanings for the term they were using.

7. Write about an important or widely used term whose meaning has changed since you first learned it. Such terms often come from the slang of particular groups: teenagers, drug users, rock music fans, musicians, athletes.

# 4 _Support_

## TYPES OF SUPPORT: EVIDENCE AND APPEALS TO NEEDS AND VALUES

All the claims you make — whether of fact, of value, or of policy — must be supported. Support for a claim represents the answer to the question, "What have you got to go on?"[1] There are two basic kinds of support in an argument: evidence and appeals to needs and values. Evidence, as one dictionary defines it, is "something that tends to prove; ground for belief." When you provide evidence, you use facts, including statistics, and opinions, or interpretations of facts, both your own and those of experts. In the following conversation, the first speaker offers facts and the opinion of an expert to convince the second speaker that robots are exceptional machines.

_"You know, robots do a lot more than work on assembly lines in factories."_

---

[1]Toulmin, _The Uses of Argument_ (Cambridge: Cambridge University Press, 1958), p. 98.

*"Like what?"*

*"They shear sheep, pick citrus fruit, and even assist in neurosurgery. And by the end of the century, every house will have a robot slave."*

*"No kidding. Who says so?"*

*"An engineer who's the head of the world's largest manufacturer of industrial robots."*

A writer often appeals to readers' needs, that is, requirements for physical and psychological survival and well-being, and values, or standards for right and wrong, good and bad. In the following conversation, the first speaker makes an appeal to the universal need for self-esteem and to the principle of helping others, a value the second speaker probably shares.

*"I think you ought to come help us at the nursing home. We need an extra hand."*

*"I'd like to, but I really don't have the time."*

*"You could give us an hour a week, couldn't you? Think how good you'd feel about helping out, and the old people would be so grateful. Some of them are very lonely."*

Although they use the same kinds of support, conversations are less rigorous than arguments addressed to larger audiences in academic or public situations. In the debates on public policy that appear in the media and in the courts, the quality of support can be crucial in settling urgent matters. The following summary of a well-known court case demonstrates the critical use of both evidence and value appeals in the support of opposing claims.

On March 30, 1981, President Ronald Reagan and three other men were shot by John W. Hinckley, Jr., a young drifter from a wealthy Colorado family. Hinckley was arrested at the scene of the shooting. In his trial the factual evidence was presented first: There were dozens of reliable witnesses who had seen the shooting at close range. Hinckley's diaries, letters, and poems revealed that he had planned the shooting to impress actress Jodie Foster. Opinions, consisting of testimony by experts, were introduced by both the defense and the prosecution. This evidence was contradictory. Defense attorneys produced several psychiatrists who defined Hinckley as insane. If this interpretation of his conduct convinced the jury, then Hinckley would be confined to a mental hospital rather than a prison. The prosecution introduced psychiatrists who interpreted Hinckley's motives and actions as those of a man who knew what he was doing and knew it was wrong. They claimed he was *not* insane by legal definition. The fact that experts can make differing conclusions about the meaning of the same information indicates that interpretations are less reliable than other kinds of support.

Finally, the defense made an appeal to the moral values of the jury. Under the law, criminals judged to be insane are not to be punished as harshly as criminals judged to be sane. The laws assume that criminals who cannot be held responsible for their actions are entitled to more compassionate treatment, confinement to a mental hospital rather than prison. The jury accepted the interpretive evidence supporting the claim of the defense, and Hinckley was pronounced not guilty by reason of insanity. Clearly the appeal to values proved to be decisive.

In your arguments you will advance your claims, not unlike a lawyer, with these same kinds of support. But before you begin, you should ask two questions: Which kind of support should I use in convincing an audience to accept my claim? and How do I decide that each item of support is valid and worthy of acceptance? This chapter presents the different types of evidence and appeals you can use to support your claim and examines the criteria by which you can evaluate the soundness of that support.

## EVIDENCE

### Factual Evidence

In Chapter 2, we defined facts as "statements possessing a high degree of public acceptance." In theory, facts can be verified by experience alone. Eating too much will make us sick; we can get from Hopkinton to Boston in a half hour by car; in the Northern Hemisphere it is colder in December than in July. The experience of any individual is limited in both time and space, so we must accept as fact thousands of assertions about the world that we ourselves can never verify. Thus we accept the report that human beings landed on the moon in 1969 because we trust those who can verify it. (Country people in Morocco, however, received the news with disbelief because they had no reason to trust the reporters of the event. They insisted on trusting their senses instead. One man said, "I can see the moon very clearly. If a man were walking around up there, wouldn't I be able to see him?")

Factual evidence appears most frequently as examples and statistics, which are a numerical form of examples.

#### EXAMPLES

Examples are the most familiar kind of factual evidence. In addition to providing support for the truth of a generalization, examples can enliven otherwise dense or monotonous prose.

In the following paragraph the writer supports the claim in the topic sentence by offering a series of specific examples. (The article claims that most airport security is useless.)

> Meanwhile, seven hijacking incidents occurred last year (twenty-one in 1980 and eleven the year before), despite the security system. Two involved the use of flammable liquids. . . . In four other cases, hijackers claimed to have flammables or explosives but turned out to be bluffing. In the only incident involving a gun, a man brushed past the security system and brandished the weapon on the plane before being wrestled to the ground. One other hijacking was aborted on the ground, and the remaining five were concluded after some expense, fright, and delay — but no injuries or deaths.[2]

Hypothetical examples, which create imaginary situations for the audience and encourage them to visualize what might happen under certain circumstances, can also be effective. The following paragraph, taken from the same article as the preceding paragraph, illustrates the use of hypothetical examples.

> But weapons can get through nonetheless. Some are simply overlooked; imagine being one of those 10,000 "screeners" staring at X-rayed baggage, day in and day out. Besides, a gun can be broken down into unrecognizable parts and reassembled past the checkpoint. A hand grenade can be hidden in an aerosol shaving-cream can or a photographer's lens case. The ingredients of a Molotov cocktail can be carried on quite openly; any bottle of, say, duty-free liquor or perfume can be emptied and refilled with gasoline. And the possibilities for bluffing should not be forgotten; once on board, anyone could claim that a bottle of water was really a Molotov cocktail, or that a paper bag contained a bomb.[3]

Claims about art, as in movie or concert or book reviews, would be boring or unintelligible without examples to illuminate them. If you claim that a movie contains "some unusual special effects," you will certainly have to describe some of the effects to convince the reader that your generalization can be trusted.

## STATISTICS

Statistics express information in numbers. Statistics may be used to express raw data, that is, factual evidence in numerical form, as in the following example.

---

[2] Patrick Brogan, "The $310 Million Paranoia Subsidy," *Harper's*, September 1982, p. 18.

[3] Ibid.

Surveys have shown that almost half of all male high school seniors —
and nearly 20% of all 9th grade boys — can be called "problem drinkers."
. . . Over 5000 teenagers are killed yearly in auto accidents due to drunken
driving.[4]

These grim numbers probably have meaning for you, partly because you
already know that alcoholism exists even among young teenagers and
partly because your own expeience enables you to evaluate the numbers.
But if you are unfamiliar with the subject, such numbers may be difficult
or impossible to understand. Statistics, therefore, are more effective in
comparisons that indicate whether a quantity is relatively large or small
and sometimes even whether a reader should interpret the result as grati-
fying or disappointing. For example, if a novice gambler were told that
for every dollar wagered in a state lottery, 50 percent goes back to the
players as prizes, would the gambler be able to conclude that the percentage is high or low? Would he be able to choose between playing the
state lottery and playing a casino game? Unless he had more information, probably not. But if he were informed that in casino games, the return to the players is over 90 percent and in slot machines and racetracks
the return is around 80 percent, the comparison would enable him to
evaluate the meaning of the 50 percent return in the state lottery and
even to make a decision about where to gamble his money.[5]

Comparative statistics are also useful for measurements over time.

Tolerance of intermarriage has been gradually increasing in recent years. In
a 1983 Gallup Poll on attitudes toward interracial marriage, 43 percent approved, 50 percent disapproved and 7 percent had no opinion. This contrasts with a 1978 Gallup Poll showing that 36 percent approved and 54
percent disapproved, and a 1968 Gallup Poll showing that only 20 percent
approved while 72 percent disapproved.[6]

Diagrams, tables, charts, and graphs can make clear the relations
among many sets of numbers. The following charts and diagrams allow
readers to grasp the information more easily than if it were presented in
paragraph form.

In a poll conducted in December 1982 voters were asked to put a
checkmark next to the one — and only one — problem they felt was most
important. The results are shown on the next page.[7]

---

[4] "The Kinds of Drugs Kids Are Getting Into" (Spring House, PA: McNeil Pharma-
ceutical, n.d.).

[5] Curt Suphee, "Lotto Baloney," *Harper's*, July 1983, p. 20

[6] *New York Times*, June 20, 1984, Sec. C, p. 7.

[7] *Public Opinion*, December 1982–January 1983, p. 31.

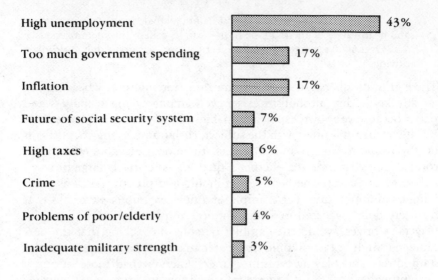

High unemployment 43%

Too much government spending 17%

Inflation 17%

Future of social security system 7%

High taxes 6%

Crime 5%

Problems of poor/elderly 4%

Inadequate military strength 3%

In poll conducted in August 1982 voters were asked to indicate the likelihood that the United States *would become* involved in a nuclear war within the next ten years. The results are indicated in the following pie chart.[8]

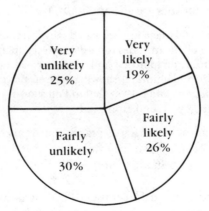

Very unlikely 25%

Very likely 19%

Fairly likely 26%

Fairly unlikely 30%

## Opinions: Interpretations of the Facts

We have seen how opinions of experts influenced the verdict in the trial of John Hinckley. Facts alone were not enough to substantiate the claim that Hinckley was guilty of attempted assassination. Both the de-

---

[8] *Public Opinion*, August–September 1982, p. 34

fense and the prosecution relied on experts — psychiatrists — to interpret the facts. Opinions or interpretations about the facts are the inferences discussed in Chapter 2. They are an indispensable source of support for your claims.

Suppose a disco for teenagers — Studio 44: A Young Adult Dance Club — has opened in your town. That is a fact. What is the significance of it? Is the disco's existence good or bad? What consequences will it have for the community? Some parents fear the idea of a disco. Others approve of discos. The importance of these interpretations is that they, not the fact itself, help people decide what actions they should take. If the community accepts the interpretation that Studio 44 is a source of delinquency, they may decide to revoke the owner's license and close the disco. As one writer puts it, "The interpretation of data becomes a struggle over power."

Opinions or interpretations of facts generally take three forms: (1) They may suggest a causal connection between two sets of data or the cause for a condition; (2) they may offer predictions about the future; (3) they may suggest solutions to a problem.

## CAUSAL CONNECTION

It is a fact that approximately two-thirds of all major crimes are committed by males between the ages of fifteen and twenty-four who are often poor and unemployed. What is the connection between the incidence of crime and the facts about the criminals? One interpretation was offered by former Vice President Hubert Humphrey, who inferred that poverty was the cause of crime. "Surely," he said, "the facts indicate that poverty, poor education, discrimination, lack of skills, and the ugliness of slums contribute to criminal behavior."[9] Other observers offer different interpretations of the same data, attributing crime by young adults to leniency by the courts: Certain research "not only debunks the myth that poverty causes crime, but it shows that the most fundamental contributing cause to rising crime is quite simply declining punishment."[10]

## PREDICTIONS ABOUT THE FUTURE

The facts are that both the United States and the Soviet Union possess 50,000 nuclear weapons and plan to build 20,000 more nuclear war-

---

[9] "Poverty Is a Major Cause of Crime," *The Causes of Crime*, edited by David L. Bender and Gary E. McCuen (Minneapolis: Greenhaven Press, 1977), p. 2.

[10] Warren T. Brooks, "The Myth That Poverty Causes Crime," in *The Causes of Crime*, p. 13.

heads in the next decade. One interpretation predicts that such an arsenal will almost certainly lead to nuclear war. A contrary interpretation predicts that such an arsenal will act as a deterrent on both sides.

## SOLUTIONS TO PROBLEMS

In an article on the prevalence of graffiti on subway cars in New York City and the lack of success in deterring the graffitists, the author concludes, nevertheless, that a solution is possible. He has observed that trucks parked in lots and garages are seldom or never painted by the graffitists because, if they are caught by the truck drivers, they are severely beaten. He infers, therefore, that swift and unpleasant punishment for the graffitists would solve the problem of the painted subway cars.[11]

For many of the subjects you discuss and write about, you will find it necessary to accept and use the opinions of experts. Based on their reading of the facts, experts express opinions on a variety of controversial subjects: whether capital punishment is a deterrent to crime; whether legalization of marijuana will lead to an increase in its use; whether children, if left untaught, will grow up honest and cooperative; whether sex education courses will result in less sexual activity and fewer illegitimate births. The interpretations of the data are often profoundly important because they influence social policy and affect our lives directly and indirectly.

For the problems mentioned above, the opinions of people recognized as authorities are more reliable than those of people who have neither thought about nor done research on the subject. But opinions may also be offered by student writers in areas in which they are knowledgeable. If you were asked, for example, to defend or refute the statement that work has advantages for teenagers, you could call on your own experience and that of your friends to support your claim. You can also draw on your experience to write convincingly about your special interests.

One opinion, however, is not as good as another. The value of any opinion depends on the quality of the evidence and the trustworthiness of the person offering it.

## EVALUATION OF EVIDENCE

Before you begin to write, you must determine whether the facts and opinions you have chosen to support your claim are sound. Can they convince your readers? A distinction between the evaluation of facts and

---

[11] Nathan Glazer, "On Subway Graffiti in New York, *Public Interest*, Winter 1979, pp. 8–9.

the evaluation of opinions is somewhat artificial because many facts are verified by expert opinion, but for our analysis we discuss them separately.

## Evaluation of Factual Evidence

### 1. Is the evidence up to date?

The importance of up-to-date information depends on the subject. If you are defending the claim that suicide is immoral, you will not need to examine new data. For many of the subjects you write about, recent research and scholarship will be important, even decisive, in proving the soundness of your data. "New" does not always mean "best," but in fields where research is ongoing — education, psychology, technology, medicine, and all the natural and physical sciences — you should be sensitive to the dates of the research.

In writing a paper a few years ago warning about the health hazards of air pollution, you would have used data referring only to outdoor pollution produced by automobile and factory emissions. But writing about air pollution today, you would have to take into account new data about indoor pollution, which has become a serious problem as a result of attempts to conserve energy. Because research studies in indoor pollution are continually being updated, recent evidence will probably be more accurate than past research.

### 2. Is the evidence sufficient?

The amount of evidence you need depends on the complexity of the subject and the length of your paper. Given the relative brevity of most of your assignments, you will need to be selective. For the claim that indoor pollution is a serious problem, one example would obviously not be enough. For a 750-to-1000-word paper, three or four examples would probably be sufficient. The choice of examples should reflect different aspects of the problem: in this case, different sources of indoor pollution — gas stoves, fireplaces, kerosene heaters, insulation — and the consequences for health.

Indoor polution is a fairly limited subject for which the evidence is clear. But more complex problems require more evidence. A common fault in argument is generalization based on insufficient evidence. In a 1000-word paper you could not adequately treat the causes of unrest in the Middle East; you could not develop workable solutions for the health care crisis; you could not predict the development of education in the next century. In choosing a subject for a brief paper, determine whether you can produce sufficient evidence to convince a reader who may not agree with you. If not, the subject may be too large for a brief paper.

### 3. Is the evidence relevant?

All the evidence should, of course, contribute to the development of your argument. Sometimes the arguer loses sight of the subject and introduces examples that are wide of the claim. In defending a national health care plan, one student offered examples of the success of health maintenance organizations, but such organizations, although subsidized by the federal government, are not the structure favored by sponsors of a national health care plan. The examples were interesting but irrelevant.

Also keep in mind that not all readers will agree on what is relevant. Is the unsavory private life of a politician relevant to his or her performance in office? If you want to prove that a politician is unfit to serve because of his or her private activities, you may first have to convince some members of the audience that private activities are relevant to public service.

### 4. Are the examples representative?

This question emphasizes your responsibility to choose examples that are typical of all the examples you do not use. Suppose you offered Vermont's experience to support your claim that passage of a bottle bill would reduce litter. Is the experience of Vermont typical of what is happening or may happen in other states? Or is Vermont, a small, mostly rural New England state, different enough from other states to make the example unrepresentative?

### 5. Are the examples consistent with the experience of the audience?

The members of your audience use their own experiences to judge the soundness of your evidence. If your examples are unfamiliar or extreme, they will probably reject your conclusion. Consider the following excerpt from a flyer distributed on a university campus by the Revolutionary Communist Party.

> What is growing up female in a capitalist society? Growing up to Laverne and Shirley and the idea that female means scatter-brained broad? Being chained to the kitchen and let out on a leash to do cheap labor? Overburdened by the hardships of trying to raise children in this putrid, degenerate society — with or without husbands?

If most members of the audience find such a characterization of female experience inconsistent with their own, they will probably question the validity of the claim.

## Evaluation of Statistics

The questions you must ask about examples also apply to statistics. Are they recent? Are they sufficient? Are they relevant? Are they typical? Are they consistent with the experience of the audience? But there are additional questions directed specifically to evaluation of statistics.

### 1. Do the statistics come from trustworthy sources?

Perhaps you have read newspaper accounts of very old people, some reported to be as old as 135, living in the Caucasus or the Andes, nourished by yogurt and hard work. But these statistics are hearsay; no birth records or other official documents existed to verify them. Now two anthropologists have concluded that the numbers were part of a rural mythology and that the ages of the people were actually within the normal range for human populations elsewhere.[12]

Hearsay statistics should be treated with the same skepticism accorded to gossip or rumor. Sampling a population to gather statistical information is a sophisticated science; you should ask whether the reporter of the statistics is qualified and likely to be free of bias. Among the generally reliable sources are polling organizations such as Gallup, Roper, and Louis Harris and agencies of the U.S. government such as the Census Bureau and the Bureau of Labor Statistics. Other qualified sources are well-known research foundations, university centers, and insurance companies that prepare actuarial tables. Statistics from underdeveloped countries are less reliable for obvious reasons: lack of funds, lack of trained statisticians, lack of communication and transportation facilities to carry out accurate censuses.

### 2. Are the terms clearly defined?

In an example in Chapter 3, the reference to "poverty" made clear that any statistics would be meaningless unless we knew exactly how "poverty" was defined by the user. "Unemployment" is another term for which statistics will be difficult to read if the definition varies from one user to another. For example, are seasonal workers "employed" or "unemployed" during the off-season? Are part-time workers "employed"? (In Russia they are "unemployed.") Are workers on government projects "employed"? (During the 1930s they were considered "employed" by the Germans and "unemployed" by the Americans.) The more abstract or controversial the term, the greater the necessity for clear definition.

---

[12] Richard B. Mazess and Sylvia H. Forman, "Longevity and Age Exaggeration in Vilcabamba, Ecuador," *Journal of Gerontology*, 1979, pp. 94–98.

### 3. Are the comparisons between comparable things?

Folk wisdom warns us that we cannot compare apples and oranges. Population statistics for the world's largest city, for example, should indicate the units being compared. Greater London is defined in one way; greater New York in another; and greater Tokyo in still another. The population numbers will mean little unless you can be sure that the same geographical units are being compared.

### 4. Has any significant information been omitted?

*The Plain Truth*, a magazine published by the World-Wide Church of God, advertises itself as follows:

> *The Plain Truth* has now topped 5,000,000 copies per issue. It is now the fastest growing magazine in the world and one of the widest circulated mass-circulation magazines on earth. Our circulation is now greater than *Newsweek*. New subscribers are coming in at the rate of around 40,000 per week.

What the magazine neglects to mention is that it is *free*. There is no subscription fee, and the magazine is widely distributed free in drugstores, supermarkets, and airports. *Newsweek* is sold on newsstands and by subscription. The comparison therefore omits significant information.

## Evaluation of Opinions

When you evaluate the reliability of opinions in subjects with which you are not familiar, you will be dealing almost exclusively with opinions of experts. Most of the following questions are directed to an evaluation of authoritative sources. But you can also ask these questions of students or of others with opinions based on their own experience and research.

### 1. Is the source of the opinion qualified to give an opinion on the subject?

The discussion on credibility in Chapter 1 pointed out that certain achievements by the interpreter of the data — publications, acceptance by colleagues — can tell us something about his or her competence. Although these standards are by no means foolproof — people of outstanding reputations have been known to falsify their data — nevertheless they offer assurance that the source is generally trustworthy. The answers to questions you must ask are not hard to find: Is the source qualified by education? Is the source associated with a reputable institution — a university or a research organization? Is the source credited with having made contributions to the field — books, articles, research studies? Suppose in writing a paper recommending relaxation of rules on prescription drugs you came across an article by Michael J. Halberstam. He is identified as follows: [13]

> Michael J. Halberstam, MD, is a practicing cardiologist, associate clinical professor of medicine at George Washington University School of Medicine, and editor-in-chief of *Modern Medicine*. He is also a member of the advisory committee of the Center for Health Policy Research at the American Enterprise Institute.[13]

These credentials would suggest to almost any reader that Halberstam is a reliable source of information about prescription drugs.

If the source is not so clearly identified, you should treat the data with caution. Such advice is especially relevant when you are dealing with popular works about such subjects as miracle diets, formulas for instant wealth, and sightings of monsters and UFOs. Do not use such data until you can verify them from other, more authoritative sources.

In addition, you should question the identity of any source listed as "spokesperson" or "reliable source" or "an unidentified authority." The mass media are especially fond of this type of attribution. Sometimes the sources are people in public life who plant stories anonymously or off the record for purposes they prefer to keep hidden.

Even where the identification is clear and genuine, you should ask if the credentials are relevant to the field in which the authority claims expertise. So specialized are areas of scientific study today that scientists in one field may not be competent to make judgments in another. William Shockley is a distinguished engineer, a Nobel Prize winner for his contribution to the invention of the electronic transistor. But when he made the claim, based on his own research, that blacks are genetically inferior to whites, geneticists accused Shockley of venturing into a field where he was unqualified to make judgments. Similarly, advertisers invite stars from the entertainment world to express opinions about products with which they are probably less familiar than members of their audience. All citizens have the right to express their views, but this does not mean that all views are equally credible or worthy of attention.

## 2. Is the source biased for or against his interpretation?

Even authorities who satisfy the criteria for expertise may be guilty of bias. Bias arises as a result of economic reward, religious affiliation,

---

[13] Michael Halberstam, "Too Many Drugs?" (Washington, DC: Center for Policy Health Research, 1979), inside cover.

political loyalty, and other interests. The expert may not be aware of the bias; even an expert can fall into the trap of ignoring evidence that contradicts his or her own intellectual preferences. A British psychologist has said:

> The search for meaning in data is bound to involve all of us in distortion to greater or lesser degree. . . . transgression consists not so much in a clear break with professional ethics, as in an unusually high-handed, extreme or self-deceptive attempt to promote one particular view of reality at the expense of all others.[14]

Before accepting the interpretation of an expert, you should ask: Is there some reason why I should suspect the motives of this particular source?

Consider, for example, an advertisement claiming that sweetened breakfast cereals are nutritious. The advertisement, placed by the manufacturer of the cereal, provides impeccable references from scientific sources to support its claims. But since you are aware of the economic interest of the company in promoting sales, you may wonder if they have reproduced only facts that favor their claims. Are there other facts that might prove the opposite? As a careful researcher you would certainly want to look further for data about the advantages and disadvantages of sugar in our diets.

It is harder to determine bias in the research done by scientists and university members even when the research is funded by companies interested in a favorable review of their products. If you discover that a respected biologist who advocates the use of sugar in baby food receives a consultant's fee from a sugar company, should you conclude that the research is slanted and that the scientist has ignored contrary evidence? Not necessarily. The truth may be that the scientist arrived at conclusions about the use of sugar legitimately through experiments that no other scientist would question. But it would probably occur to you that a critical reader might ask about the connection between the results of the research and the payment by a company that profits from the research. In this case you would be wise to read further to find confirmation or rejection of the claim by other scientists.

The most difficult evaluations concern ideological bias. Early in our lives we learn to discount the special interest that makes a small child brag, "My mother (or father) is the greatest!" Later we become aware that the claims of people who are avowed Democrats or Republicans or Marxists or Yankee fans or zealous San Franciscans or joggers must be examined somewhat more carefully than those of people who have no special commitment to a cause or a place or an activity. This is not to say that

---

[14] Liam Hudson, *The Cult of the Fact* (New York: Harper and Row, 1972), p. 125.

all partisan claims lack support. They may, in fact, be based on the best available support. But whenever special interest is apparent, there is always the danger than an argument will reflect this bias.

### 3. Has the source bolstered the claim with sufficient and appropriate evidence?

In an article attacking pornography, one author wrote, "Statistics prove that the recent proliferation of porno is directly related to the increasing number of rapes and assaults upon women."[15] But the author gave no further information — neither statistics nor proof that a cause-effect relation exists between pornography and violence against women. The critical reader will ask, "What are the numbers? Who compiled them?"

Even those who are reputed to be experts in the subjects they discuss must do more than simply allege that a claim is valid or that the data exist. They must provide facts to support their interpretations.

## When Experts Disagree

Authoritative sources can disagree. Such disagreement is probably most common in the social sciences. They are called the "soft" sciences precisely because a consensus about conclusions in these areas is more difficult to arrive at than in the natural and physical sciences. Consider the issue of merit pay for teachers. Should superior teachers be paid more? If so, how are superior teachers to be selected? This issue curently divides the educational profession. T. H. Bell, U.S. secretary of education, believes that merit pay provides incentives for the best students to become teachers and for the best teachers to remain in the profession. But William McGuire, past president of the National Education Association, believes that decisions about raises under a merit pay system would depend on "personal relationships or subservient behavior rather than good teaching."[16] Resolving this issue is complicated by the difficulty of controlling all the factors that motivate human behavior.

But even in the natural and physical sciences, where the results of experiments are far more conclusive, you may encounter serious differences of opinion. A sharp debate has emerged in recent years about the origins of "yellow rain" in Southeast Asia. What is yellow rain? On one side is the view expressed by John Deutch, dean of science at the Massa-

---

[15] Charlotte Allen, "Exploitation for Profit," *Daily Collegian* [University of Massachusetts], October 5, 1976, p. 2.

[16] *New York Times*, May 29, 1983, Sec. I, p. 1.

chusetts Institute of Technology, with which other distinguished scientists agree: "In my judgment the weight of the evidence is remarkably on the side of the conclusion that mycotoxins have been used in Southeast Asia by man." On the other side is the view of Matthew S. Meselson, a Harvard biochemist, and other equally distinguished scientists, who have advanced the theory that "the yellow rain spots cited as evidence of chemical warfare in Southeast Asia may be little more than the excrement of bees."[17]

How can you choose between authorities who disagree? If you have applied the tests discussed so far and discovered that one source is less qualified by training and experience or makes claims with little support or appears to be biased in favor of one interpretation, you will have no difficulty in rejecting that person's opinion. If conflicting sources prove, as in the case above, to be equally reliable in all respects, then continue reading other authorities to determine whether a greater number of experts support one opinion rather than another. Although numbers alone don't guarantee the truth, nonexperts have little choice but to accept the authority of the greater number until evidence to the contrary is forthcoming. Finally, if you are unable to decide between competing sources of evidence, you may conclude that the argument must remain unsettled. Such an admission is not a failure; after all, such questions are considered controversial because even the experts cannot agree, and such questions are often the most interesting to consider and argue about. This book contains a section (Part II) on several longstanding, highly controversial questions, some of them very old and still unresolved.

## APPEALS TO NEEDS AND VALUES

Good factual evidence is usually enough to convince an audience that your factual claim is sound. Using examples, statistics, and expert opinion, you can prove, for example, that women do not earn as much as men for the same work. But even good evidence may not be enough to convince your audience that unequal pay is wrong or that something should be done about it. In making value and policy claims, an appeal to the needs and values of your audience is absolutely essential to the success of your argument. If you want to persuade the audience to change their minds or adopt a course of action — in this case, to demand legalization of equal pay for equal work — you will have to show that assent to your claim will bring about what they want and care deeply about.

As a writer, you cannot always know who your audience is; it's im-

---

[17] *New York Times*, June 21, 1983, Sec. C, p. 1.

possible, for example, to predict exactly who will read a letter you write to a newspaper. Even in the classroom, you have only partial knowledge of your readers. You may not always know or be able to infer what the goals and principles of your audience are. You may not know how they feel about big government, the draft, private school education, feminism, environmental protection, homosexuality, religion, or any of the other subjects you might write about. If the audience concludes that the things you care about are very different from what they care about, if they cannot identify with your goals and principles, they may treat your argument with indifference, even hostility, and finally reject it. But you can hope that decent and reasonable people will share many of the needs and values that underlie your claims.

## Appeals to Needs

Suppose that you are trying to persuade Joan Doakes, a friend who is still undecided, to attend college. In your reading you have come across a report about the benefits of a college education written by Howard Bowen, a professor of economics at Claremont (California) Graduate School, former president of Grinnell College, and a specialist in the economics of higher education. Armed with this testimony, you write to Joan. As support for your claim that she should attend college, you offer evidence that (1) college graduates earn more throughout their lifetime than high school graduates; (2) college graduates are more active and exert greater influence in their communities than high school graduates; and (3) college graduates achieve greater success as partners in marriage and as thoughtful and caring parents.[18]

Joan writes back that she is impressed with the evidence you've provided — the statistics, the testimony of economists and psychologists — and announces that she will probably enroll in college instead of accepting a job offer.

How did you succeed with Joan Doakes? If you know your friend pretty well, the answer is not difficult. Joan has needs that can be satisfied by material success; more money will enable her to enjoy the comforts and luxuries that are important to her. She also needs the esteem of her peers and the sense of achievement that political activity and service to others will give her. Finally, she needs the rootedness to be found in close and lasting family connections.

Encouraged by your success with Joan Doakes, you write the same

---

[18] "The Residue of Academic Learning," *Chronicle of Higher Education*, November 14, 1977, p. 13.

letter to another friend, Fred Fox, who has also declined to apply for admission to college. This time, however, your argument fails. Fred, too, is impressed with your research and evidence. But college is not for him, and he repeats that he has decided not to become a student.

Why such a different response? The reason, it turns out, is that you don't know what Fred really wants. Fred Fox dreams of going to Alaska to live alone in the wilderness. Money means little to him; influence in the community is irrelevant to his goals, and at present he feels no desire to become a member of a loving family.

Perhaps if you had known Fred better, you would have offered different evidence to show that you recognized what he needed and wanted. You could have told him that Bowen's study also points out that "college-educated persons are healthier than are others," that "they also have better ability to adjust to changing times and vocations," that "going to college enhances self-discovery" and enlarges mental resources, which encourage college graduates to go on learning for the rest of their lives. This information might have persuaded Fred that college would also satisfy some of his needs.

As this example demonstrates, you have a better chance of convincing your reader to accept your claim if you know what he or she wants and what importance he or she assigns to the needs that we all share. Your reader must, in other words, see some connection between your evidence and his or her needs.

The needs to which you appealed in your letters to Joan and Fred are the requirements for physiological or psychological well-being. The most familiar classification of needs was developed by the psychologist Abraham H. Maslow in 1954.[19] These needs, said Maslow, motivate human thought and action. In satisfying our needs, we attain both long- and short-term goals. Because Maslow believed that some needs are more important than others, he arranged them in hierarchical order from the most urgent biological needs to the psychological needs that are related to our roles as members of a society.

— **Physiological Needs.** Basic bodily requirements: food and drink; health; sex

— **Safety Needs.** Security; freedom from harm; order and stability

— **Belongingness and Love Needs.** Love within a family and among friends; roots within a group or a community

— **Esteem Needs.** Material success; achievement; power, status, and recognition by others

— **Self-actualization Needs.** Fulfillment in realizing one's potential

---

[19] *Motivation and Personality* (New York: Harper and Row, 1954), pp. 80–92.

For most of your arguments you won't have to address the audience's basic physiological needs for nourishment or shelter. The desire for health, however, now receives extraordinary attention. Appeals to buy health foods, vitamin supplements, drugs, exercise and diet courses, and health books are all around us. Many of the claims are supported by little or no evidence, but readers are so eager to satisfy the need for good health that they often overlook the lack of facts or authoritative opinion. The desire for physical well-being, however, is not so simple as it seems; it is strongly related to our need for self-esteem and love.

Appeals to our needs to feel safe from harm, to be assured of order and stability in our lives are also common. Insurance companies, politicians who promise to rid our streets of crime, and companies that offer security services all appeal to this profound and nearly universal need. (We say "nearly" because some people are apparently attracted to risk and danger.) At this writing the nuclear freeze movement has attempted both to arouse fears for our safety and to suggest ways of removing the dangers that make us fearful.

The last three needs in Maslow's hierarchy are the ones you will find most challenging to appeal to in your arguments. It is clear that these needs arise out of human relationships and participation in society. Advertisers make much use of appeals to these needs.

— **Belongingness and Love Needs.**

"Gentlemen prefer Hanes."

"Whether you are young or old, the need for companionship is universal." (ad for dating service)

— **Esteem Needs.**

"Enrich your home with the distinction of an Oxford library."

"Apply your expertise to more challenges and more opportunities. Here are outstanding opportunities for challenge, achievement and growth." (Perkin-Elmer Co.)

— **Self-actualization Needs.**

"Be all that you can be." (U.S. Army)

"Are you demanding enough? Somewhere beyond the cortex is a small voice whose mere whisper can silence an army of arguments. It goes by many names: integrity, excellence, standards. And it stands alone in final judgment as to whether we have demanded enough of ourselves and, by that example, have inspired the best in those around us." (*New York Times*)

Of course, it is not only advertisers who use these appeals. We hear them from family and friends, from teachers, from employers, from editorials and letters to the editor, from people in public life.

## Appeals to Values

Needs give rise to values. If we feel the need to belong to a group, we learn to value commitment, sacrifice, and sharing. And we then respond to arguments that promise to protect our values. It is hardly surprising that values, the principles by which we judge what is good or bad, beautiful or ugly, worthwhile or undesirable, should exercise a profound influence on our behavior. Virtually all claims, even those that seem to be purely factual, contain expressed or unexpressed judgments. The scientist quoted in Chapter 2 who presented evidence that cigarette smoke contained radioactive isotopes did so not for academic reasons but because he hoped to persuade people that smoking was bad.

For our study of argument, we will speak of groups or systems of values because any single value is usually related to others. People and institutions are often defined by such systems of values. We can distinguish, for example, between those who think of themselves as traditional and those who think of themselves as modern by listing their differing values. One writer contrasts such values in this way:

> Among the values of traditionalism are: merit, accomplishment, competition, and success; self-restraint, self-discipline, and the postponement of gratification; the stability of the family; and a belief in certain moral universals. The modernist ethos scorns the pursuit of success; is egalitarian and redistributionist in emphasis; tolerates or encourages sensual gratification; values self-expression as against self-restraint; accepts alternative or deviant forms of the family; and emphasizes ethical relativism.[20]

Systems of values are neither so rigid nor so distinct from one another as this list suggests. Some people who are traditional in their advocacy of competition and success may also accept the modernist values of self-expression and alternative family structures. One editorial writer explained the popularity of the governor of New York, Mario Cuomo:

> He embodies that rare combination of an old-fashioned liberal who has traditional, conservative family values — calling for compassion for the needy and afflicted while inveighing against a lack of discipline in American life.[21]

Values, like needs, are arranged in a hierarchy; that is, some are clearly more important than others to the people who hold them. Moreover, the arrangement may shift over time or as a result of new experiences. In 1962, for example, two speech teachers prepared a list of what

---

[20] Joseph Adelson, "What Happened to the Schools," *Commentary*, March 1981, p. 37.
[21] *New York Times*, June 21, 1983, Sec. I, p. 29.

they called "Relatively Unchanging Values Shared by Most Americans."[22] Included were "puritan and pioneer standards of morality" and "perennial optimism about the future." More than twenty years later, an appeal to these values might fall on a number of deaf ears.

You should also be aware not only of changes over time but of different or competing value systems that reflect a multitude of subcultures in our country. Differences in age, sex, race, ethnic background, social environment, religion, even in the personalities and characters of its members define the groups we belong to. Such terms as "honor," "loyalty," "justice," "patriotism," "duty," "responsibility," "equality," "freedom," and "courage" will be interpreted very differently by different groups.

All of us belong to more than one group, and the values of the several groups may be in conflict. If one group to which you belong, say peers of your own age and class, is generally uninterested in and even scornful of religion, you may nevertheless hold to the values of your family and continue to place a high value on religious belief.

How can a knowledge of your readers' values enable you to make a more effective appeal? Suppose you want to argue in favor of a sex education program in the junior high school you attended. The program you support would not only give students information about contraception and venereal disease but also teach them about the pleasures of sex, the importance of small families, and alternatives to heterosexuality. If the readers of your argument are your classmates or your peers, you can be fairly sure that their agreement will be easier to obtain than that of their parents, especially if their parents think of themselves as conservative. Your peers are more likely to value experimentation, tolerance of alternative sexual practices, freedom, and novelty. Their parents are more likely to value restraint, conformity to conventional sexual practices, obedience to family rules, and foresight in planning for the future.

Knowing that your peers share your values and your goals will mean that you need not spell out the values supporting your claim; they are understood by your readers. Persuading their parents, however, who think that freedom, tolerance, and experimentation have been abused by their children, will be a far more challenging task. In one written piece you have little chance of changing their values, a result that might be achieved only over a longer period of time. So you might first attempt to reduce their hostility by suggesting that, even if a community-wide program were adopted, students would need parental permission to en-

---

[22] Edward Steele and W. Charles Redding, "The American Value System: Premises for Persuasion," *Western Speech*, Vol. 26, Spring 1962, pp. 83–91.

roll. This might convince some parents that you share their values regarding parental authority and primacy of the family. Second, you might look for other values to which the parents subscribe and to which you can make an appeal. Do they prize maturity, self-reliance, responsibility in their children? If so, you could attempt to prove, with authoritative evidence, that the sex education program would promote these qualities in students who took the course.

But familiarity with the value systems of prospective readers may also lead you to conclude that winning assent to your argument will be impossible. It would probably be fruitless to attempt to persuade a group of lifelong pacifists to endorse the use of nuclear weapons. The beliefs, attitudes, and habits that support their value systems are too fundamental to yield to one or two attempts at persuasion.

## EVALUATION OF APPEALS TO NEEDS AND VALUES

If your argument is based on an appeal to the needs and values of your audience, the following questions will help you evaluate the soundness of your appeal.

1. **Have the values been clearly defined?** If you are appealing to the patriotism of your readers, can you be sure that they agree with your definition? Does patriotism mean "Our country, right or wrong!" or does it mean dissent, even violent dissent, if we think our country is wrong? Since value terms are abstractions, you must make their meaning explicit by placing them in context and providing examples.

2. **Are the needs and values to which you appeal prominent in the reader's hierarchy at the time?** An affluent community, fearful of further erosion of quiet and open countryside, might resist an appeal to allow establishment of a high-technology firm, even though the firm would bring increased prosperity to the area.

3. **Is the evidence in your argument clearly related to the needs and values to which you appeal?** Remember that the reader must see some connection between your evidence and his or her goals. Suppose you were writing an argument to convince a group of people to vote in an upcoming election. You could provide evidence to prove that only 20 percent of the town voted in the last election. But this evidence would not motivate your audience to vote unless you could provide other evidence to show that their needs were not being served by such a low turnout.

SAMPLE ANALYSIS

# A Red Light for Scofflaws

## FRANK TRIPPETT

Law-and-order is the longest-running and probably the best-loved   1
political issue in U.S. history. Yet it is painfully apparent that millions of
Americans who would never think of themselves as lawbreakers, let alone
criminals, are taking increasing liberties with the legal codes that are designed to protect and nourish their society. Indeed, there are moments
today — amid outlaw litter, tax cheating, illicit noise and motorized anarchy — when it seem as though the scofflaw represents the wave of the
future. Harvard Sociologist David Riesman suspects that a majority of
Americans have blithely taken to committing supposedly minor derelic-
tions as a matter of course. Already, Riesman says, the ethic of U.S. society is in danger of becoming this: ''You're a fool if you obey the rules.''

Nothing could be more obvious than the evidence supporting Ries-   2
man. Scofflaws abound in amazing variety. The graffiti-prone turn public surfaces into visual rubbish. Bicyclists often ride as though two-
wheeled vehicles are exempt from all traffic laws. Litterbugs convert their
communities into trash dumps. Widespread flurries of ordinances have
failed to clear public places of high-decibel portable radios, just as earlier
laws failed to wipe out the beer-soaked hooliganism that plagues many
parks. Tobacco addicts remain hopelessly blind to signs that say NO
SMOKING. Respectably dressed pot smokers no longer bother to duck out
of public sight to pass around a joint. The flagrant use of cocaine is a fes-
tering scandal in middle- and upper-class life. And then there are (hello,
Everybody!) the jaywalkers.

The dangers of scofflawry vary wildly. The person who illegally spits   3
on the sidewalk remains disgusting, but clearly poses less risk to others
than the company that illegally buries hazardous chemical waste in an
unauthorized location. The fare beater on the subway presents less threat
to life than the landlord who ignores fire safety statutes. The most immediately and measurably dangerous scofflawry, however, also happens to
be the most visible. The culprit is the American driver, whose lawless activities today add up to a colossal public nuisance. The hazards range
from routine double parking that jams city streets to the drunk driving
that kills some 25,000 people and injures at least 650,000 others yearly.

---

Frank Trippett is a senior writer for *Time* magazine.

Illegal speeding on open highways? New surveys show that on some interstate highways 83% of all drivers are currently ignoring the federal 55 m.p.h. speed limit.

The most flagrant scofflaw of them all is the red-light runner. The 4 flouting of stop signals has got so bad in Boston that residents tell an anecdote about a cabby who insists that red lights are "just for decoration." The power of the stoplight to control traffic seems to be waning everywhere. In Los Angeles, red-light running has become perhaps the city's most common traffic violation. In New York City, going through an intersection is like Russian roulette. Admits Police Commissioner Robert J. McGuire: "Today it's a 50-50 toss-up as to whether people will stop for a red light." Meanwhile, his own police largely ignore the lawbreaking.

Red-light running has always been ranked as a minor wrong, and so 5 it may be in individual instances. When the violation becomes habitual, widespread and incessant, however, a great deal more than a traffic management problem is involved. The flouting of basic rules of the road leaves deep dents in the social mood. Innocent drivers and pedestrians pay a repetitious price in frustration, inconvenience and outrage, not to mention a justified sense of mortal peril. The significance of red-light running is magnified by its high visibility. If hypocrisy is the tribute that vice pays to virtue, then furtiveness is the true outlaw's salute to the force of law-and-order. The red-light runner, however, shows no respect whatever for the social rules, and society cannot help being harmed by any repetitious and brazen display of contempt for the fundamentals of order.

The scofflaw spirit is pervasive. It is not really surprising when 6 schools find, as some do, that children frequently enter not knowing some of the basic rules of living together. For all their differences, today's scofflaws are of a piece as a symptom of elementary social demoralization — the loss by individuals of the capacity to govern their own behavior in the interest of others.

The prospect of the collapse of public manners is not merely a mat- 7 ter of etiquette. Society's first concern will remain major crime, but a foretaste of the seriousness of incivility is suggested by what has been happening in Houston. Drivers on Houston freeways have been showing an increasing tendency to replace the rules of the road with violent outbreaks. Items from the Houston police department's new statistical category — freeway traffic violence: (1) Driver flashes high-beam lights at car that cut in front of him, whose occupants then hurl a beer can at his windshield, kick out his tail lights, slug him eight stitches' worth. (2) Dump-truck driver annoyed by delay batters trunk of stalled car ahead and its driver with steel bolt. (3) Hurrying driver of 18-wheel truck deliberately rear-ends car whose driver was trying to stay within 55 m.p.h. limit. The Houston Freeway Syndrome has fortunately not spread everywhere. But the question is: Will it?

Americans are used to thinking that law-and-order is threatened 8 mainly by stereotypical violent crime. When the foundations of U.S. law have actually been shaken, however, it has always been because ordinary law-abiding citizens took to skirting the law. Major instance: Prohibition. Recalls Donald Barr Chidsey in *On and Off the Wagon:* "Lawbreaking proved to be not painful, not even uncomfortable, but, in a mild and perfectly safe way, exhilarating." People wiped out Prohibition at last not only because of the alcohol issue but because scofflawry was seriously undermining the authority and legitimacy of government. Ironically, today's scofflaw spirit, whatever its undetermined origins, is being encouraged unwittingly by government at many levels. The failure of police to enforce certain laws is only the surface of the problem: they take their mandate from the officials and constituents they serve. Worse, most state legislatures have helped subvert popular compliance with the federal 55 m.p.h. law, some of them by enacting puny fines that trivialize transgressions. On a higher level, the Administration in Washington has dramatized its wish to nullify civil rights laws simply by opposing instead of supporting certain court-ordered desegregation rulings. With considerable justification, environmental groups, in the words of *Wilderness* magazine, accuse the Administration of "destroying environmental laws by failing to enforce them, or by enforcing them in ways that deliberately encourage noncompliance." Translation: scofflawry at the top.

The most disquieting thing about the scofflaw spirit is its extreme 9 infectiousness. Only a terminally foolish society would sit still and allow it to spread indefinitely.

## ANALYSIS

This article demonstrates the successful use of the forms of support we've discussed in this chapter — facts, expert opinion, and appeals to needs and values.

Trippett makes a policy claim that's suggested in the title: Scofflaws must be stopped. Although he doesn't offer specific recommendations, he calls for federal and local officials to enforce the laws.

First, Trippett must convince a possibly skeptical reader that a problem exists. The second, third, and fourth paragraphs are devoted to factual evidence, including statistics — specific examples that reveal the extent to which the law is everywhere being broken. These examples are both vivid and familiar. The seventh paragraph cites Houston as a frightening example of the violence that can result from "the collapse of public manners" and that may portend the wave of the future.

In addition, Trippett quotes authoritative sources who interpret this phenomenon from their different perspectives. They are a prominent sociologist, the former New York City police commissioner, a writer about the Prohibition era of sixty years ago, and the authors of a magazine devoted to environmental interests. All of these sources lend added credibility to Trippett's charges, especially since Trippett himself is not an authority on "law and order."

Most important, however, is Trippett's emphasis on the needs and values of a civilized society which are violated by the scofflawry spirit. We've pointed out that facts alone mean little unless they are offered as *proof* of something. Trippett makes clear that drunk driving, freeway traffic violence, and even the smaller crimes of illegal noise and litter threaten our needs for safety and belongingness. Most readers, including those who have been guilty of the acts described by Trippett, would also agree that these repeated violations encourage contempt for the law with dangerous consequences for some of the things a community values most — peace, order, civility.

In all its formal aspects, Trippett's essay is highly effective. His prose is readable, his examples are varied, lively, and alarming, his value appeals are universal. Nevertheless, as with any other argument that proposes a change in behavior, the real test is whether you, as audience, are persuaded, not only to insist on stricter penalties by law enforcement officials, but to modify your own habits wherever they scoff at the law.

READINGS FOR ANALYSIS

# Lotteries Cheat, Corrupt the People

## GEORGE F. WILL

On the outskirts of this city of insurance companies, there is an- 1
other, less useful, business based on an understanding of probabilities. It
is a jai alai fronton, a cavernous court where athletes play a fast game for
the entertainment of gamblers and the benefit of, among others, the
state treasury.

Half the states have legal betting in casinos, at horse or dog tracks, 2
off-track betting parlors, jai alai frontons, or in state-run lotteries. Only
Connecticut has four (the last four) kinds of gambling, and there is talk
of promoting the other two.

Not coincidentally, Connecticut is one of just seven states still 3
fiercely determined not to have an income tax. Gambling taxes yielded
$76.4 million last year, which is not a large slice of Connecticut's $2.1
billion budget, but it would be missed, and is growing.

Last year Americans legally wagered $15 billion, up 8 percent over 4
1976. Lotteries took in 24 percent more. Stiffening resistance to taxes is
encouraging states to seek revenues from gambling, and thus to encourage gambling. There are three rationalizations for this:

State-run gambling controls illegal gambling. 5

Gambling is a painless way to raise revenues. 6

Gambling is a "victimless" recreation, and thus is a matter of moral 7
indifference.

Actually, there is evidence that legal gambling increases the respect- 8
ability of gambling, and increases public interest in gambling. This creates new gamblers, some of whom move on to illegal gambling, which
generally offers better odds. And as a revenue-raising device, gambling is
severely regressive.

Gamblers are drawn disporportionately from minority and poor 9
populations that can ill-afford to gamble, that are especially susceptible
to the lure of gambling, and that especially need a government that will
not collaborate with gambling entrepreneurs, as in jai alai, and that will
not become a gambling entrepreneur through a state lottery.

A depressing number of gamblers have no margin for economic 10
losses and little understanding of the probability of losses. Between 1975

---

George F. Will is a columnist for *Newsweek* magazine.

and 1977 there was a 140 percent increase in spending to advertise lotteries — lotteries in which more than 99.9 percent of all players are losers. Such advertising is apt to be especially effective, and cruel, among people whose tribulations make them susceptible to dreams of sudden relief.

Grocery money is risked for such relief. Some grocers in Hartford's 11 poorer neighborhoods report that receipts decline during jai-alai season. Aside from the injury gamblers do to their dependents, there is a more subtle but more comprehensive injury done by gambling. It is the injury done to society's sense of elemental equities. Gambling blurs the distinction between well-earned and "ill-gotten" gains.

Gambling is debased speculation, a lust for sudden wealth that is 12 not connected with the process of making society more productive of goods and services. Government support of gambling gives a legitimating imprimatur to the pursuit of wealth without work.

"It is," said Jefferson, "the manners and spirit of a people which 13 preserves a republic in vigor." Jefferson believed in the virtue-instilling effects of agricultural labor. Andrew Jackson denounced the Bank of the United States as a "monster" because increased credit creation meant increased speculation. Martin Van Buren warned against "a craving desire . . . for sudden wealth." The early nineteenth century belief was that citizens could be distinguished by the moral worth of the way they acquired wealth; and physical labor was considered the most ennobling labor.

It is perhaps a bit late to worry about all this: the United States is a 14 developed capitalist society of a sort Jefferson would have feared if he had been able to imagine it. But those who cherish capitalism should note that the moral weakness of capitalism derives, in part, from the belief that too much wealth is allocated in "speculative" ways, capriciously, to people who earn their bread neither by the sweat of their brows nor by wrinkling their brows for socially useful purposes.

Of course, any economy produces windfalls. As a town grows, some 15 land values soar. And some investors (like many non-investors) regard stock trading as a form of roulette.

But state-sanctioned gambling institutionalizes windfalls, whets the 16 public appetite for them, and encourages the delusion that they are more frequent than they really are. Thus do states simultaneously cheat and corrupt their citizens.

## Discussion Questions

1. What is Will's claim? (Careful. The title is *not* the claim.)
2. Why, according to Will, is raising revenue through state-run gambling unfair?

3. What evidence does Will provide that state-run gambling cheats the gamblers? Do you find the evidence convincing? Why or why not?

4. In what way does gambling corrupt people? Do you think that most readers agree with Will?

5. How does Will use "expert" opinion in his article? Since the people he quotes are not experts in a technical sense, how do they support his claim?

6. What American values does Will appeal to? How popular are they?

## Writing Suggestions

1. Will concedes that "any economy produces windfalls" — that is, luck or speculation are often rewarded. Write an essay in which you argue that some, or even many, decisions in life are gambles. Develop several specific examples.

2. Who do people gamble? Since almost everyone gambles at some time, you are probably familiar with some of the reasons for the appeal of gambling. Do you think that these reasons can be described as either good or bad, or maybe both, depending perhaps on the consequences? Write an essay defending or attacking the reasons for gambling.

3. Will seeks to refute some of the "rationalizations" for state-run gambling. Choose one or more of these reasons and defend them.

# *On Belonging to Tribes*

## ANDREW OLDENQUIST

What makes some people sacrifice time and effort trying to save 1 Laker Airlines, and what makes others stay drunk on auto-assembly lines and weld Coke bottles into the rocker panels? "Some people have a sense of group loyalty and others are alienated." But *why*?

Laker Airlines was just a company, after all. But perhaps people are 2 such social animals that if our official communities and tribes don't generate in us a deep enough sense of belonging, we invent new ones. Saying we are social animals means we evolved to feel a need to belong to something larger than ourselves (because that is where our security lay), and that we are wretched and "incomplete" if we feel we belong to nothing.

Think of parents rallying to save a mediocre school from closing, 3 neighbors uniting to save a park that they scarcely noticed before, English workers marching together to save Freddie Laker's airline. They are

---

Andrew Oldenquist teaches philosophy at Ohio State University. He has written widely on the necessity for moral education in our schools.

moved by loyalties they did not even know they had, before some ancient call for tribal defense stirred deep within them. If this is so and we are by nature tribal creatures who crave to share with others a common good, then we are group egoists, collectivists as well as individualists.

When I think of what makes me a dedicated member of a social 4 group I realize that burdens and crises are more effective than benefits. Perceived threats to the common good stir us to work and sacrifice to a degree that appeals to self-interest never can. This behavior in turn reinforces our sense that the "tribe" we sacrifice for is *our* tribe.

Thus schools that make students shovel snow and bloodthirsty dic- 5 tators who hold their citizens' loyalty by provoking international crises share a common wisdom. Cause a person to believe there is something larger than himself which is *his*, a social unit in terms of which he partly defines himself and moreover which *needs* him, and his group egoism will triumph over his personal egoism every time.

This line of reasoning tells us that to make students loyal to their 6 school, require them to do chores, make minor repairs, participate in school ceremonies and "adopt" younger schoolmates. To make young people see their neighborhood as theirs, require them through the schools to visit shut-ins and help local needy and handicapped people. In this way age segregation is diminished and the elderly again become part of one's tribe. To attack and rob the elderly would be unthinkable for youth who live with or regularly help the aged. (In the movie *On Golden Pond* try to imagine the adolescent who spends a month with Henry Fonda and Katharine Hepburn saying nothing if his friends were to propose mugging an 80-year-old.)

We help produce national loyalty by expecting immigrants (and 7 their children) to learn English. It is a primary badge of tribal membership. It would be unthinkable for an immigrant to France or Mexico not to be expected to learn French or Spanish.

A year of compulsory national service for *everyone* at 18, with very 8 low pay, would, like a tribal rite of passage, tell young men and women that they belonged and were needed. It would, at the same time, virtually eliminate youth unemployment, provide an opportunity to teach skills to the unskilled, and each year cycle perhaps 20 percent of these 18-year-olds through military training. The defense budget would be reduced and the quality of those who choose the military would improve.

I don't think I am unusual in sensing that if, and only if, I perceive 9 a thing as *mine*, will I be proud when it prospers, ashamed when it deteriorates and indignant when it is threatened. I don't feel this way about, say, an iceberg: I can be neither proud nor ashamed of an iceberg unless some clever fellow persuades me that it is my iceberg and hence a possible object of loyalty. If I *am* persuaded it is mine I will be unlikely to burgle or vandalize it.

American educators, juvenile-justice professionals, urban planners 10
and social thinkers in general appear not to know what causes group loyalty; they also appear to fear it. They may think that because sense of
community creates "insiders" and "outsiders" it inevitably leads to in-
tolerance and war. These individualists do not seem to realize that the
greater problem facing American society today is not the competition of
group loyalties but their absence — alienation and not giving a damn.

What seems probable, and also hard for us Americans to grasp — es- 11
pecially during the '60s and '70s when individualism went mad — is that
young people are social animals who need the socialization process itself
to complete their natures. Just being given the security and benefits of
society is not enough. For example, we know that criminals tend to come
from families that both didn't accept them and didn't set firm rules and
limits on behavior. These are two essential functions of a tribe, our families being mini-tribes; actually, they are a single function, since if a social
group does not impose its rules on me and hold me responsible to it, I
know it does not accept me as a member. It is also worth noting that here
is something we know affects criminal behavior which has nothing to do
with money.

Perhaps human beings are born genetically primed to be socialized, 12
just as we are born genetically primed to learn a language. We are born
ready and receptive to be limited and molded by rules, ethics, ritual,
manners and tradition, and we go bad when our society — our tribe —
neglects to limit and mold us in these ways. We go bad because this is a
form of rejection. We are rejected as surely when we are not held ac-
countable, not expected to dance to the drums or walk with others on the
red hot coals, as when we are denied food or shelter.

On this view we can understand "mindless" violence that serves no 13
rational interest — frenzied vandalism, refusing to be taken alive for a
traffic citation, pushing strangers in front of subways — as rage at tribal
exclusion. It is the revenge of an innately tribal creature for not being
initiated into society and treated as a member. To be a social animal
means subjection to rules and being held personally answerable to
them in ways in which a mad dog or a virus is not.

## Discussion Questions

1. What examples does Oldenquist offer to prove that "some people have a
   sense of group loyalty"?
2. Why does he think that giving young people tasks and responsibilities will
   promote their loyalty to school and neighborhood?
3. What advantages does he see for compulsory national service?
4. Why, according to Oldenquist, are educators and other professionals afraid
   of encouraging group loyalty? What is his response to them?

5. What is the relation between criminality and the lack of socialization? What examples does the author give?

## Writing Suggestions

1. From your experience (or that of others you know), write about a situation that proves the author's contention that "burdens and crises" are more effective than benefits in creating community spirit.
2. If you disagree with the author about the advantages of compulsory national service, write a response.
3. Offer an explanation for the lack of group loyalty among some people in our society.
4. Do you think some educators and other professionals are right to be fearful of the consequences of group loyalty? Explain.

## Additonal Writing Suggestions

1. What kind of evidence would you offer to prove to a skeptic that the moon landings — or any other space ventures — have actually occurred? What objections would you anticipate?

2. A group of white people in a middle-class community who define themselves as devout Christians have organized to keep a low-income black family from joining their church. What kind of support would you offer for your claim that the black family should be welcomed into the church? Address your argument to the group of people unwilling to admit the black family.

3. In the summer of 1983, after an alarming rise in the juvenile crime rate, the mayor of Detroit instituted a curfew for young people under the age of eighteen. What kind of support can you provide for or against such a curfew?

4. "Racism [or sexism] is [not] a major problem on this campus [or home town or neighborhood]." Produce evidence to support your claim.

5. Write a full-page advertisement to solicit support for a project or cause that you believe in.

6. How do you account for the large and growing interest in science fiction films and literature? In addition to their entertainment value, are there other less obvious reasons for their popularity?

7. According to some researchers soap operas are influential in transmitting values, lifestyles, and sexual information to youthful viewers. Do you agree? If so, what values and information are being transmitted? Be specific.

8. Choose one of the following stereotypical ideas and argue that it is true or false or partly both. Discuss the reasons for the existence of the stereotype.
   a. Jocks are stupid.
   b. The country is better than the city for bringing up children.
   c. TV is justly called "the boob tube."
   d. A dog is man's best friend.
   e. Beauty contests are degrading to women.

9. Defend or refute the view that organized sports build character.

10. The philosopher Bertrand Russell said, "Most of the work that most people have to do is not in itself interesting, but even such work has certain advantages." Defend or refute this assertion. Use your own experience as support.

# 5   *Warrants*

We now come to the third part in the structure of the argument — the warrant. In the first chapter we defined the warrant as an assumption, a principle or a belief that is taken for granted and that the writer and audience must share for the writer's argument to be accepted. It answers the question, How did you get from the support to the claim? Like a commercial warranty that guarantees the performance of a product, the warrant of an argument guarantees that the support justifies the claim.

Consider the following example. The beautiful and unspoiled Eastern Shore of Maryland is being discovered by thousands of tourists, vacationers, and developers who will, according to the residents, change the landscape and the way of life, which is now based largely on fishing and farming. In a few years the Eastern Shore may become a noisy, crowded string of resorts. Mrs. Walkup, the Kent County commissioner, says,

> Catering to the wealthy puts property back on the tax rolls, but it's going to make the Eastern Shore look like the rest of the country. Everything that made our way of life so special is being eroded. We are a fragile area. The Eastern Shore is still special, but it is feeling pressure from all directions. Lots of people don't seem to appreciate the fact that God made us to need a little peace and quiet now and then.[1]

---

[1] Michael Wright, "The Changing Chesapeake," *New York Times Magazine*, July 10, 1983, p. 27.

In simplified form the argument of those opposed to development would be outlined this way:

CLAIM: Development will bring undesirable changes to the present way of life on the Eastern Shore, a life of farming and fishing, peace and quiet.

SUPPORT: Developers will build express highways, condominiums, casinos, and nightclubs.

WARRANT: A pastoral life of fishing and farming is superior to the way of life brought by expensive, fast-paced modern development.

Notice that the warrant is a broad generalization that can apply to a number of different situations. The claim is about a specific place and time.

To be convinced of the validity of this claim, you must first find that the support is true, that the developers plan to introduce drastic changes that will destroy the pastoral life of the Eastern Shore. You may, however, believe that the support is not entirely sound, that the development will be much more modest than residents fear, and that the Eastern Shore will not be seriously altered. Next, you may want to see more justification for the warrant. Is pastoral life superior to the life that will result from large-scale development? Perhaps you have always thought that a life of fishing and farming means poverty and limited opportunities for the majority of the residents. Although the superiority of a way of life is largely a matter of taste and therefore difficult to prove, Mrs. Walkup may need to produce backing for her belief that the present way of life is more desirable than one based on developing the area for new residents and summer visitors. If you find either the support or the warrant unconvincing, you cannot accept the claim.

Remember that a claim is often modified by one or more qualifiers, which limit the claim. Mrs. Walkup might have said, "Development will *probably* destroy *some aspects of* the present way of life on the Eastern Shore." Warrants can also be modified or limited by *reservations*, which remind the reader that there are conditions under which the warrants will not be relevant. Mrs. Walkup might have added, ". . . unless increased prosperity and exposure to the outside world brought by development improve some aspects of our lives."

In the argument we have just analyzed, the warrant was *stated* by those who opposed development on the Eastern Shore. But arguers will often neglect to state their warrants for one of two reasons: First, they may believe that the warrant is obvious and need not be expressed; second, they may want to conceal the warrant in the hope that the reader will overlook its weakness.

**109**

Here is an example of the first case. If someone exclaims, ''All this buying of gifts! I think people have forgotten that Christmas celebrates the birth of Christ,'' he need not state the assumption — that the buying of gifts violates what ought to be a religious celebration. Like many other warrants, it goes *unstated* by the speaker because it has been uttered so often that the hearer accepts it without questioning. From time to time, although not often enough, such warrants are examined, and some of our most fruitful conclusions emerge as a result of these reexaminations. In the case just mentioned, it might be — and has been — argued that the purchase of gifts is not a violation but an affirmation of the religious spirit of Christmas.

The second reason for refusal to state the warrant lies in the arguer's intention to disarm or deceive the reader, although the arguer may not be aware of this. For instance, failure to state the warrant is common in advertising and politics, where the desire to sell a product or an idea may outweigh the responsibility to argue explicitly. The following advertisement is famous not only for what it says but for what it does not say:

> In 1918 Leona Currie scandalized a New Jersey beach with a bathing suit cut above her knees. And to irk the establishment even more, she smoked a cigarette. Leona Currie was promptly arrested.
>
> Oh, how Leona would smile if she could see you today.
>
> You've come a long way, baby. *Virginia Slims*. The taste for today's woman.

What is the unstated warrant? The manufacturer of Virginia Slims hopes we will agree that being permitted to smoke cigarettes is a significant sign of female liberation. But many readers would insist that proving ''You've come a long way, baby'' requires more evidence than women's freedom to smoke (or wear short bathing suits). The shaky warrant weakens the claim.

Politicians, too, conceal warrants that may not survive close scrutiny. In the 1983 mayoral election in Chicago, one candidate revealed that his opponent had undergone psychiatric treatment. He did not have to state the warrant supporting his claim. He knew that many in his audience would assume that anyone who had undergone psychiatric treatment was unfit to hold public office. This same assumption contributed to the withdrawal of a vice-presidential candidate from the 1972 campaign.

## TYPES OF WARRANTS

In this section we show how arguments may be classified according to the types of warrants offered as proof. Because warrants represent the reasoning process by which we establish the relationship between support and claim, analysis of warrants enables us to see the whole argument as a sum of its parts.

Seven types of warrants will be examined. One type — authority — assumes that the source is credible. Another large category assumes that the relationship between support and claim is logical, that it can be verified independently of the source and can offer predictions. This category includes five types of warrants — generalization, sign, cause and effect, comparison, and analogy. Analogy assumes a need or value that reader and writer share. This warrant is more subjective than the others, a reflection of feelings and attitudes. The examples that follow represent the most common kinds of arguments in each classification, the ones you will use most frequently.

## Authority

Arguments from authority depend on the credibility of their sources.

> [Benjamin] Bloom maintains that most children can learn everything that is taught them with complete competence.[2]

Because Benjamin Bloom is a professor of education at the University of Chicago and a widely-respected authority on educational psychology, his statement about the educability of children carries considerable weight. Notice that Professor Bloom has qualified his claim by asserting that "most" children, but not all, can learn everything. The reader might also recognize the limits of the warrant — the authority could be mistaken, or there could be disagreement among authorities.

CLAIM: Most children can learn everything that is taught them with complete competence.

SUPPORT: Professor Bloom attests that this is so.

WARRANT: Professor Bloom's testimony is sufficient because he is an accepted authority on educational achievement.

RESERVATIONS: Unless the data for his studies were inaccurate, unless his criteria for evaluation were flawed, and so on.

## Generalization

Arguments from generalization are based on the belief that we can derive a general principle from a series of examples. But their warrants

---

[2] Michael Alper, "All Our Children Can Learn," *University of Chicago Magazine*, Summer 1982, p. 3.

are credible only if the examples are representative of the whole group being described and if there are not too many contradictory examples being ignored. In the following excerpt the author documents the tragic effects for children born "unnaturally" (outside the mother's womb) or lacking knowledge of their fathers.

> For years I've collected bits of data about certain unfortunate people in the news: Son of Sam, the Hillside strangler, the Pennsylvania shoemaker who raped and brutalized several women, a Florida man who killed at least 34 women, the man sought in connection with the Tylenol scare. All of them grew up not knowing at least one of their natural parents; most knew neither.[3]

In outline the argument takes this form:

CLAIM: People brought up without a sense of identity with their natural parents will respond to the world with rage and violence.

SUPPORT: Son of Sam, the Hillside strangler, the Pennsylvania shoemaker, the Florida murderer, the man in the Tylenol scare responded to the world with rage and violence.

WARRANT: What is true of this sample is true for others in this class.

RESERVATION: Unless this sample is too small or exceptions have been ignored.

## Sign

As their name suggests, in arguments based on sign the arguer offers an observable datum as an indicator of a condition. The warrant that a sign is convincing can be accepted only if the sign is appropriate, if it is sufficient, and if other indicators do not dispute it. We have already examined one such argument, in which the enjoyment of Virginia Slims is presented as a sign of female liberation. In the following example the warrant is stated:

> There are other signs of a gradual demoting of the professions to the level of ordinary trades and businesses. The right of lawyers and physicians to advertise, so as to reintroduce money competition and break down the "standard practices," is being granted. Architects are being allowed to act as contractors. Teachers have been unionized.[4]

Here, too, a reservation is in order.

---

[3] Lorraine Dusky, "Brave New Babies?" *Newsweek*, December 6, 1982, p. 30.
[4] Jacques Barzun, "The Professions Under Seige," *Harper's*, October 1978, p. 66.

CLAIM:     Professions are being demoted to the level of ordinary trades and businesses.

SUPPORT:    Lawyers and physicians advertise, architects act as contractors, teachers have been unionized.

WARRANT:    These business practices are signs of the demotion of the professions.

RESERVATION:    Unless these practices are not widespread.

## Cause and Effect

Causal reasoning assumes that one event or condition can bring about another. We can reason from the cause to the effect or from the effect to the cause. The following is an example of reasoning from effect (the claim) to cause (the warrant). The quotation is taken from the famous Supreme Court decision of 1954, *Brown v. Board of Education*, which mandated the desegregation of public schools throughout the United States.

> Segregation of white and colored children in public schools has a detrimental effect upon the colored children. The impact is greater when it has the sanction of the law; for the policy of separating the races is usually interpreted as denoting the inferiority of the Negro group. A sense of inferiority affects the motivation of a child to learn. Segregation with the sanction of law, therefore, has a tendency to [retard] the educational and mental development of Negro children and to deprive them of some of the benefits they would receive in a racial[ly] integrated school system.[5]

The outline of the argument would take this form:

CLAIM:    Colored children have suffered mental and emotional
(EFFECT)    damage in legally segregated schools.

SUPPORT:    They suffer from feelings of inferiority, which retard their ability to learn. They are being deprived of important social and educational benefits.

WARRANT:    Any system that requires legal segregation of children on
(CAUSE)    the basis of race will cause mental and emotional damage.

In cause-effect arguments the reasoning may be more complicated than an outline suggests. For one thing, events and conditions in the world are not always the result of single causes, nor does a cause necessar-

---

[5] *Brown v. Board of Education of Topeka*, 347 U.S. 487–496 (May 17, 1954).

ily produce a single result. It is probably more realistic to speak of chains of causes as well as chains of effects. A recent headline emphasizes this form of reasoning: "Experts Fear That Unpredictable Chain of Events Could Bring Nuclear War." The article points to the shooting of the Archduke Francis Ferdinand of Austria-Hungary in the Bosnian city of Sarajevo in 1914, which "set in motion a series of events that the world's most powerful leaders could not stop" — that is, World War I.

Or take this example. Recent polls have indicated Americans' unwillingness to "approve any bellicose activity, unless U.S. interests are seen as truly vital and are clearly defined."[6] The immediate cause of this isolationism is usually attributed to the "Vietnam syndrome," the relic of a bitter experience in an unpopular war. But this single cause, according to some students of the problem, is insufficient to explain the current mood. History, they say, reveals "decades of similar American resistance to foreign involvements."

Causes can also be either *necessary* or *sufficient*. That is, to contract tuberculosis, it is necessary to be exposed to the bacillus, but this exposure in itself may not be sufficient to bring on the disease. However, if the victim's immune system is depressed for some reason, exposure to the bacillus will be sufficient to cause the illness. Or, to take an example from law and politics: To reduce the incidence of drunk driving, it would be necessary to enact legislation that penalized the drunk driver. But that would not be sufficient unless the police and the courts were diligent in making arrests and imposing sentences.

If you are aware of the intricate relations between causes and effects, you will be cautious about proposing simple explanations or inferring simple results from some of the complex subjects you examine.

## Comparison

In some arguments we compare characteristics and circumstances in two or more cases to prove that what is true in one case ought to be true in another. Unlike the elements in analogies, which we will discuss next, the things being matched in comparisons belong to the same class. The following is a familiar argument based on a comparison of similar activities in different countries at different times. On the basis of these apparent similarities the author makes a judgment about America's future.

> Perhaps I'm wrong, but the auguries seem to me threatening. Like the bourgeoisie of pre–World War I in Europe, we are retreating into our

---

[6] *Public Opinion*, April–May 1982, p. 16.

well-furnished houses, hoping the storm, when it comes, will strike someone else, preferably the poor. Our narcissistic passion for sports and fitness reminds me of Germany in the '20s and early '30s, when the entire nation turned to hiking, sun-bathing and the worship of the body beautiful, in part so as not to see what was happening to German politics — not to speak of the family next door. The belief that gold in the garden is more important than government helped to bring France to defeat in 1940 and near civil war in the 1950s. When the middle class stops believing in government or in the future, it's all over, time truly to sew the diamonds in the lining of your coat and make a run for it.[7]

This is the argument in outline form:

CLAIM: The behavior of many middle-class Americans today threatens our future.

SUPPORT: The same kind of behavior by the Germans in the twenties and thirties and by the French in the thirties and forties led to disaster.

WARRANT: Because such behavior brought disaster to Germany and France, it will bring disaster to America.

But is this warrant believable? Are the dissimilarities between our country now and these European countries in earlier decades greater than the similarities? For example, if our present passion for sports and fitness is caused by very different social forces than those that operated in Germany in the twenties and thirties, then the comparison warrant is too weak to support the author's claim.

The following letter compares an American military operation in 1916 with the Israeli invasion of Lebanon in the summer of 1982:

> In 1916, at the direction of President Woodrow Wilson, a U.S. Army invaded Mexico to ''pursue and disperse'' Mexican guerrillas led by Pancho Villa, who had raided American border towns and killed American citizens. The excuse given by the U.S. was the overriding need to protect Americans from terrorism and banditry, in the face of the inability or unwillingness of the Mexican Government to curb Villa. Isn't this the same justification that Israel used when it moved into Lebanon?
>
> Americans should feel proud that their Government is willing to protect its citizens through military action when all else fails, whether in Mexico then or more recently in Iran. Americans can hardly condemn another country which seeks to protect its citizens in exactly the same way![8]

---

[7] Michael Korda, ''The New Pessimism,'' *Newsweek*, June 14, 1982, p. 20
[8] Herbert Adise, ''Protecting Citizens,'' *New York Times*, June 18, 1982, Sec. A, p. 30.

CLAIM: The Israelis were justified in pursuing their enemy across the border into Lebanon in 1982.

SUPPORT: The Americans justified their own pursuit of the enemy across the border into Mexico in 1916.

WARRANT: The two military actions are comparable.

Here, too, the reader would want to analyze carefully the historical data to determine the accuracy of the comparison and therefore the validity of the warrant.

## Analogy

An analogy warrant assumes a resemblance in some characteristics between dissimilar things. Analogies differ in their power to persuade. Some are explanatory; others are merely descriptive. Those that describe are less likely to be useful in a serious argument. In conversation we often liken human beings to other animals — cows, pigs, rats, chickens. Or we compare life and happiness to a variety of objects: "Life is a cabaret," "Life is just a bowl of cherries," "Happiness is a warm puppy." But such metaphorical uses are more colorful than precise. In those examples one quality is abstracted from all the others, leaving us with two objects that remain essentially dissimilar. Descriptive analogies promise immediate access to the reader, as do paintings or photographs. For this reason you may find the idea of such short cuts tempting, but descriptive analogies are seldom enough to support a claim. Consider the following example, which appears in a speech by Malcolm X, the black civil rights leader, criticizing the participation by whites in the march on Washington in 1962 for black rights and employment:

> It's just like when you've got some coffee that's too black, which means it's too strong. What do you do? You integrate it with cream, you make it weak. But if you pour too much cream in it, you won't even know you ever had coffee.[9]

This is the outline of the argument:

CLAIM: Integration of black and white people in the march on Washington weakened the black movement for rights and jobs.

SUPPORT: Putting white cream into black coffee weakens the coffee.

WARRANT: Weakening coffee with cream is analogous to weakening

---

[9] "Message to the Grass Roots," *Roots of Rebellion*, edited by Richard P. Young (New York: Harper and Row, 1970), p. 357.

the black rights movement by allowing white people to participate.

The imagery is vivid, but the analogy does not represent convincing proof. The dissimilarites between whitening coffee with cream and integrating a political movement are too great to persuade the reader of the damaging effects of integration n the march. Moreover, words like *strong* and *weak* as they apply to a civil rights movement need careful definition. To make a convincing case, the author would have to offer not imagery but facts and authoritative opinion.

The following analogy is more successful because it is explanatory rather than descriptive. Although on one side of the analogy the use is literal (breaking a piece of chalk) and on the other, figurative (the cause of war), the action of the key terms, *strain, stress,* and *break* is inherent in both processes. It might, in fact, be difficult to talk about the issue, the causes of war, without resorting to metaphorical language.

> Boulding [Kenneth Boulding, an economist from the University of Colorado] argues that the search for the causes of war is a hopeless one, because the real world is too complex for such analysis. Instead he offers a *strain-stress-break* model as a way of thinking about war. He reduces it to what he calls the Chalk Analogy: If you break a piece of chalk with your fingers, the chalk had a certain strength holding it together which was progressively overcome by the strain your fingers put on it to the point where a break occurred. "Did it break because the strain was too great," Boulding asks, "or because the strength was too little? In the literal sense, this is an almost meaningless question. The chalk broke because the strain was too great for the strength."
>
> Peace and war, he believes, can be looked at in the same way; there is always conflict between societies; but sometimes the strains of conflict become so great that the strength of their relationships and institutions can't contain them, and the conflict breaks out into war. Thus, to prevent or minimize war, there are two [sic] avenues to pursue: Either reduce the strains, or increase the strength of the system to contain them, or both.[10]

Professor Boulding's argument may be outlined like this:

CLAIM: To prevent war, we can reduce the strains on the international system, increase its strength, or both.

SUPPORT: The chalk broke under the strain of your fingers because the strain was too great for its strength.

WARRANT: The strain of your fingers and the breaking of the chalk are analogous to the strains between nations and the outbreak of war.

---

[10]Chuck Fager, "A Consumer's Guide to Peace," *Valley Advocate* (Springfield, MA), June 23, 1982, p. 7A.

But Boulding cannot base his argument on analogy alone. He, too, must provide more substantial proof that the causes of war are the result of the kinds of stresses and strains he uses in the analogy.

## Values

Warrants may also reflect needs and values, and readers accept or reject the claim to the extent that they find the warrants relevant to their own goals and standards. Mrs. Walkup and others based their opposition to development of the Eastern Shore on a value warrant: Rural life is superior to the way of life being introduced by developers. Clearly, numbers of outsiders who valued a more sophisticated way of life did not agree.

The persuasive appeal of advertisements, as we know, leans heavily on value warrants, which are often unstated. Sometimes they include almost no printed message, only the name of the product accompanied by a picture. The advertisers expect us to assume that if we use their product, we can acquire the desirable characteristics of the attractive people shown using it.

Value warrants are indispensable in arguments on public policy. In the following excerpt from a radio debate, a professor of statistics at Berkeley argues in favor of affirmative action policies to promote the hiring of women faculty. Her claim has been made earlier, but her warrant and any reservations remain unstated. This is her supporting material.

> 6.9% is very tiny proportion of the faculty. You still have to go a long ways to see a woman teaching in this university. Most all of the students go to this university and never, ever have a woman professor, a woman associate professor, even a woman assistant professor teaching them. There's a lack of role models, there's a lack of teaching, and it brings a lack of breadth into the teaching.[11]

CLAIM: The proportion of women on the Berkeley faculty should be increased.

SUPPORT: Because women are only 6.9 percent of the faculty, most students never have a woman teacher.

WARRANT: Exposure of students to women faculty is a desirable educational goal.

RESERVATION: Unless individual women faculty members are significantly less competent than men.

---

[11]Elizabeth Scott, quoted in *Affirmative Action: Not a Black and White Issue*, National Public Radio, week of April 25, 1977, p.7.

## EVALUATION OF WARRANTS

We've pointed out that the warrant underlying your claim will define the kind of argument you are making. Answering the following questions about their warrants, whether expressed or unexpressed, will help you to judge the soundness of your arguments.

1. **Authority.**
   Is the authority sufficiently respected to make a credible claim?
   Do other equally reputable authorities agree with the authority cited?
   Are there equally reputable authorities who disagree?

2. **Generalization.**
   Are sufficient examples given to convince us that a general statement is justified? That is, are the examples given representative of the whole community?
   Are there sufficient negative instances to weaken the generalization?

3. **Sign.**
   Is the sign used appropriate as an indicator?
   Is the sign sufficient to account for the claim?
   Are negative signs — that is, other indicators — available that might contradict the claim?

4. **Cause and Effect.**
   Does the cause given seem to account entirely for the effect?
   Are other possible causes equally important as explanations for the effect?
   Is it possible to prove that the stated cause produced the effect?

5. **Comparison.**
   Are the similarities between the two situations greater than the differences?
   Have all or only a few of the important characteristics been compared? Have some important dissimilarities been overlooked?

6. **Analogy.**
   Is the analogy explanatory or simply descriptive?
   Are there sufficient similarities between the two elements to make the analogy appropriate?

7. **Values.**
   Is the value one that the audience will regard as important?
   Is the value relevant to the claim?

119

## SAMPLE ANALYSIS

# *Funerals Are Good for People*

## WILLIAM M. LAMERS, JR.

While attending a medical meeting about a year ago, I ran into a  1
fellow I'd known in residency. "What are you doing here, Bill?" he
asked. "Giving a talk on the responses to death," I replied. "It will
cover the psychological value of funerals as well as — "

"Funerals!" he exclaimed. "What a waste *they* are! I've made it  2
plain to my wife that *I* don't want a funeral. Why spend all that money
on such a macabre ordeal? And why have the kids standing around wondering what it's all about?"

"Look, Jim," I said patiently, "I've seen case after case of depres-  3
sion caused by the inability of patients — young and old — to work
through their feelings after a death. I've found that people are often better off if they have a funeral to focus their feelings on. That lets them do
the emotional work necessary in response to the loss." My friend still
looked doubtful. And, as we parted company, I wondered how many
other physicians are also overlooking the psychological value of funerals.

Their value is brought home time and time again in my own prac-  4
tice. Consider the woman who called me recently after making a suicide
attempt. She was a divorcée and the mother of three sons, the youngest
of whom had died of encephalitis about two months before. She was very
much attached to her sons and highly dependent on them emotionally. The youngest had been her pet, and her grief at his loss was overwhelming.

Well-meaning friends persuaded the woman to have an immediate  5
cremation and memorial service rather than go through the pain of a funeral. As a result, within a few hours after the boy's death, his body was
cremated. Two weeks later a memorial service was held. The mother
went around smiling to show people how well she'd adjusted to the
boy's death. There was a small rock 'n' roll band and several poetry reci-
tations. It was very pleasant and happy and likely provided some beautiful memories. Yet it was all only frosting on an underbaked cake.

Within a few weeks the mother became extremely depressed. She  6
was afraid to express her true feelings from fear of offending the friends
who had planned the memorial service. She didn't want them to feel it

---

William Lamers, Jr., is a psychiatrist from California.

wasn't good enough, and she tried to cover up her tremendous unresolved grief. All that was a prelude to her suicide attempt. This woman still had doubts that her son was dead. I'm convinced that, had she gone through a formalized funeral experience and been allowed to vent her grief, her son's death would have held some finality for her. And her feelings wouldn't have healed superficially while the core still continued to fester.

I see constant evidence that the problems resulting from a serious 7 separation — through death, divorce, or other means — can have great psychological impact. If these problems remain unresolved, grave emotional trouble can result later. That's what happened to a patient I saw several years ago. She'd been married and divorced four times, each time to men at least 20 years older than she. And all were men who were gone from home most of the time — sea captains, traveling men, and the like.

She began to develop ulcers, high blood pressure, and had made 8 several suicide attempts. When referred to me, she was about to divorce her fifth husband and marry a sixth. Apparently she also went through psychiatrists as fast as husbands: I was the fourth she'd seen. In consultation she told me she couldn't remember anything before the age of 10. Two or three sessions with her brought no results. Finally, trying to get at her early childhood through the back door, I said, "Tell me about your mother and father." She told me she'd been brought up in Europe and that her father had died in the early days of World War II.

Slowly, more of the story came out. One day, her father came back 9 from the mountains — he was a guerrilla leader — to a triumphant reception in the village. Apparently he was also under strong suspicion of collaborating with the Germans. He'd been home less than an hour when some of his soldiers came and, on a ruse, took him away. Minutes later, my patient painfully recalled, she and her mother were summoned to the village square. There, with no explanation from the villagers, her father was shot before her eyes.

In that village it was the custom for villagers to file through the 10 home to view the body and express condolences. Then there would be a funeral service, a procession, and a gathering afterwards. In this instance, however, my patient and her mother were carted away to another town. No one knows what happened to the father's body, but there was no funeral. Possibly as a direct result, my patient had never been able to accept emotionally the fact of her father's death.

In my office she finally wept. The extent of her reaction indicated 11 that at last she was beginning to express the feelings that might have been more properly handled about 20 years earlier. From then on, she was gradually able to understand that, in marrying older men who were away most of the time, she'd been searching for her father. Today, she's

121

settled down considerably. But I can't help believing that a funeral, with its acknowledgement of death, would have contributed to her emotional well-being years earlier.

When a death occurs, most people feel a need to *do* something. 12 And the doing can come out in several ways — in crying, in the funeral and burial, perhaps in informing others that the death has occurred, perhaps in assuring themselves that what was seen and heard was, in fact, a true happening. The funeral makes these things easier by providing the setting in which people can begin to resolve their feelings about death.

Children, of course, are especially vulnerable to the suffering that 13 results from unresolved grief situations. So we do them a tremendous injustice when we don't let them know the facts or we lie — describing "the trip" Grandfather has gone on, for example. We need to answer their questions about death in a straightforward manner and give them the opportunity to talk about death and to express their feelings toward it. Many parents don't seem to understand this. They're not doing their children a favor by sheltering them.

A case in point is that of a 7-year-old girl whose mother brought her 14 to me shortly after the death of the father. The little girl had become despondent, and her mother couldn't understand why. As the mother explained it, she'd done everything to protect her daughter's feelings. She'd kept almost all knowledge of the death from the child and hadn't allowed her to participate in the services or the burial.

Their first visit to me occurred about a week before President John 15 F. Kennedy's assassination. Shortly after the assassination, the mother called to tell me her daughter had run away. Desperately, she asked me what to do, but I couldn't be of much help.

A few days later the girl returned home. She'd been at a friend's 16 house where for the entire weekend she'd watched the Kennedy funeral on TV — a steady, continuous ritual of mourning. When the little girl came home, she told her mother: "Everything's O.K. now. I know what happened to Daddy."

Are there any satisfactory funeral substitutes — a memorial service, 17 for example? In my opinion, there aren't. Though a memorial service is a response to loss and can be extremely satisfying for many, it's not ideal because it lacks several basic elements. First, a memorial service usually doesn't take place when feelings are most intense, which is shortly after the death. Second, members of the family aren't involved in communications, participation, and repeated exposure to the fact that death has occurred. These things force people to acknowledge the reality of loss. Finally, a memorial service doesn't include the presence of the body, which means people aren't given as great an opportunity to fix the fact of death in their minds.

.In contrast to the memorial service, which is a one-time gathering, 18 the traditional funeral as we know it in this country is a continuum of things. It includes visitations at the funeral home, usually with the remains lying in state. Frequently, there are religious services there as well as in the church, a procession to the place of burial, and committal service. Afterward, there's often a gathering of close friends and relatives. Throughout these events there's a repeated acceptance of condolences, acknowledgement of the fact of death, sharing of grief feelings, and encouragement for the future.

Since I'm so profuneral, you may wonder how I feel about those at- 19 tacks on the funeral profession in recent years. Let me make it plain that I don't own a funeral home. Some funeral directors *are* guilty of abuse and of taking advantage of the public. I contend, however, that they're in the minority and that criticism of the funeral business has been blown out of proportion. In time of need, the majority of the directors provide an effective means of helping families through a lot of turmoil.

What can we, as physicians, do to steer families of dying patients in 20 the right direction? Naturally, we can't actively impose our beliefs on others. In other words, it's unwise to steer a family toward a particular kind of funeral or service. If they prefer to have a memorial service held, then this may well be the most satisfactory for them.

On the other hand, a family that's avoiding the reality of death, try- 21 ing to seal it over without allowing normal emotional responses to come to the surface, may need guidance. In that case, we doctors have an obligation to point out the possible consequences and to make ourselves available to discuss the situation. We do patients a disservice when we oversedate or overtranquilize them so that they're unaware of what's happening or unable to experience normal feelings of grief.

In short, we should encourage the practice of something as psycho- 22 logically economical as funerals. They do a therapeutic job, and in most cases they can do it for a lot less money than we psychiatrists could.

ANALYSIS

The author's claim that funerals have a beneficial effect on people is based primarily on a *cause and effect warrant* that tells why: Formalized rituals such as funerals cause the normal feelings of grief to be released and bring about more rapid recovery from bereavement. The author supplies evidence of the effects of funerals, or lack of them, in the form of three extended examples of people he has known who, after the death of a loved one, suffered both physical and mental trauma because they did not openly express their grief through a funeral service.

These examples resemble vivid short stories calculated to rouse our sympathy for the characters. They are persuasive in part because the author is a psychiatrist. We are therefore inclined to trust not only his detailed observations of behavior but also his analyses of the causes of these people's suffering. Our confidence in the author's authority is especially necessary to the success of this particular argument. Only the last case, that of the seven-year-old girl, represents a positive proof that funerals are good for people. The other two cases are negative examples, that is, examples of individuals who did not find release from grief. However, the author obviously believes that his professional expertise enables him to make the right inferences: "But I can't help believing that a funeral, with its acknowledgement of death, would have contributed to her emotional well-being years earlier."

As we learn from the opening dialogue, the warrant underlying the author's claim needs support. The author realizes that the other doctor, who disparages funerals, may be only one of many doctors and laypeople who need to be convinced that the formalized funeral experience is psychologically desirable. For this reason the last quarter of the article is devoted to an explanation of why funerals are superior to other rituals, such as memorial services. Here, too, the writer's authority as a psychiatrist is an important part of the support for the warrant.

Finally, the argument has moral force. Dr. Lamer is interested in promoting funerals to relieve the suffering of the bereaved, a *value* he can assume his readers will share. His appeal is affirmed by an apparent willingness to sacrifice his own interests: Funerals "do a therapeutic job, and in most cases they can do it for a lot less money than we psychiatrists could." All in all, this is a convincing cause and effect argument, backed up by authority and values, for the psychological benefits provided by funerals.

READINGS FOR ANALYSIS

# No More MoonJune: Love's Out

## RICHARD STENGEL

Romantic love is a supreme fiction, marriage for love the conse- 1
quence of that fiction, and divorce the painful evidence of that initial
delusion.

The history of romantic love is the continuing ironic testimony of 2
the power of our minds to mesmerize our bodies, while romantic marriage is the most recent and least successful evolutionary stage in the history of matrimony.

Now that the Census Bureau has estimated that more than one in 3
three marriages will end in divorce, it is apparent that the solution to the
troubled state of matrimony is a return to the tradition of arranged marriages.

The sentimental sanctity of love was the invention of the Provençal 4
poets of the twelfth century, and they saw it as the exotic refinement of a
bored aristocracy. Since then, however, love has democratized itself and
is no longer the luxury of a courtly minority but the expectation of every
man and woman. Indeed, the joys of romantic love are the birthright of
every American, for the Framers of the Declaration of Independence declared "the pursuit of happiness" to be the inalienable right of all men
and women.

Love, though, is neither a right nor an instinct, but a learned form 5
of behavior; it is not a spontaneous feeling but an artificial ritual. It is a
response that we have learned from literature, and its contemporary
handmaidens, the news media.

As lovers, we are all actors — we imagine ourselves most spontane- 6
ous when we are most imitative. We learn how to love from movies, television, novels, magazines and advertisements. We learn to adore love, to
idolize love, to fall in love with love.

To most Americans, love is romantic love. It is a drive or state of 7
tension induced by our prevailing romantic myths. The lover's nourishment is the expectation of bliss. Love is a competitive and covetous
game: Competition for a mate brings out the best in an individual. To
be alone is not considered a self-imposed choice but evidence of failure
in the contest of love.

During the Industrial Revolution, arranged romantic marriages suc- 8
cumbed to individual love matches. The monotony of work and the im-

personality of the city led people to escape monotony in personal relations and retreat from impersonality to the "emotional fortress" of marriage. Urbanization caused the "privatization" of marriage so that the intimacy of wedlock became a sanctuary from a world where all intimacy was excluded.

Yet, romantic marriage was the cradle of its own demise. More and more pressure was forced on marriage to be "a haven in a heartless world." As the temptations of the outside world were becoming more varied, the standards of marital fidelity became more exigent. Opportunity multiplies, morality declines: The pressure on marriage increased geometrically. Between 1870 and 1920 the number of divorces multiplied fifteenfold. 9

In the past, when society was more structured, married partners were externally oriented, and did not have to rely exclusively on each other for emotional gratification. They could find that elsewhere. Romantic passion had always existed *outside* of marriage but it had nothing to do with wedlock. Contemporary society forces couples to depend on each other for permanence and stability, functions that were formerly provided by a large familial and social network. 10

Today, marriage has not lost its function; it suffers from a surfeit of functions. The marriage partner must not only be a lover, but a friend, a colleague, a therapist, and a tennis partner. Indeed, the standards of romantic marriage — unquestioned fidelity and undiminished passion — are merely an ideal to be approximated, not a universal precept to be obeyed. 11

Traditionally, the selection of mates has been determined by social, political and economic considerations directed either toward establishing new ties or reaffirming old ones. Every arranged marriage was the formation of a new society — a merger of a network of familial and social relationships. Marriage was a duty. Its *raison d'être* was procreation. Children were best raised in a congenial home, and a congenial home was best created by a reasonable arrangement between congenial people. Marriage was contracted according to a principle other than the self-interest of the participants, and emotional satisfaction was neither the origin nor purpose of marriage. 12

The concept of arranged marriage is based on a positive view of human nature. Its guiding principle is that marriage requires a more durable foundation than romantic love, that wisdom is more important in the choosing of a partner than passion, and that everyone can find something to "love, honor, and cherish" in anyone else. 13

Romantic love, however, is fundamentally narcissistic; we either choose someone who resembles ourself, the self we'd like to be or think we are, or we choose someone who complements us. The former is inces- 14 tuous, the latter entropic. If love means touching someone outside of ourselves, then romantic love is solipsistic while arranged marriage is altruistic.

Romantic love allows us the reverie of imagining what the other per- 15 son is like, whereas arranged marriage forces us to acknowledge truly another human being. Instead of falling in love with an ideal-image, an arranged marriage teaches us how to live with an actual individual. The myth of romantic love teaches us how to fall in love. Perhaps when marriages are arranged, we will learn *how* to love.

## Discussion Questions

1. How does the author characterize romantic love? What evidence does he offer to support his characterization? Is it adequate?
2. What, according to the author, is the origin of romantic love?
3. Why were marriages in the past apparently more successful? What reasons does the author offer for the failures of present-day marriages?
4. In what way is the concept of arranged marriages based on a positive view of human nature? Why is it superior to romantic love as a foundation for marriage?

## Writing Suggestions

1. If you disagree with the author's explanations for the failure of present-day marriage, offer your own. Try to respond to specific charges in Stengel's essay.
2. Do you agree that "everyone can find something to 'love, honor, and cherish' in anyone else"? Be specific in explaining your reasons.
3. Write a refutation of the concept of arranged marriages. Make clear your warrants about the purpose of marriage.

# *The Springsteening of Disarmament*

## MICHAEL LEVIN

A vast number of supporters of disarmament ignore or willfully mis- 1 understand the lessons of postwar Soviet-American diplomacy, perhaps because the lessons are so cheerless and the rallies, like the one in Central Park, often are so pleasant, offering camaraderie, sometimes music and always a good cause.

Michael Levin studied at Amherst College and Northwestern University Law School.

Lesson 1: The Soviet Union is content to sign human rights and arms-limitation agreements and does not mind ignoring its citizens' rights while increasing its military strength. The United States cannot verify Soviet compliance with arms agreements. Young Americans expect the Russians to uphold a disarmament pact. They are too kind. 2

Lesson 2: While the world's expanding arsenal of nuclear weapons is a distressing problem, draining funds from human needs, it is an unfortunate aspect of postwar life with which we must live and for which we must pay. Organizers of the disarmament movement correctly observe that the world's destruction could come at the touch of a button, but the buttons have gone untouched during 37 years of wars, hot and cold. If we have learned anything from living with the bomb, it is that no one in charge really wants to die. 3

We cannot "disinvent" the bomb. The blows of 750,000 "hammers" in Central Park cannot nail shut Pandora's Box. If anything keeps the world from destruction, it is the knowledge that the Russians' weapons are not better than ours, nor ours better than theirs — the aptly and chillingly termed "balance of terror." The Russians may lead the call for disarmament but they have given little evidence of intending to keep their part of the bargain. 4

With all the problems facing America today — the faltering economy, joblessness, the equal rights movement, poverty, the troubled criminal-justice system — only disarmament could draw so large a following. 5

Here are a few reasons why the crowd in Central Park last Saturday was so enormous, and why so many people participated in demonstrations in succeeding days. 6

*American idealism.* We like to be on the right side of any given issue, and nobody likes to be in favor of total destruction. Disarmament as an issue requires no sacrifice, little thought, no blood spilled in the streets, no loss of job or social esteem — in short, no risk. It's the perfect feel-good issue. 7

*It's a scene.* Who in his or her right mind would want to miss out when history is being made? You might even get on television. How many of the hundreds of thousands who attended did so because they wanted to see what hundreds of thousands of people look like? 8

*First-rate entertainment at the right price.* Bruce Springsteen and Jackson Browne do not provide free concerts at the drop of a hat, and seldom appear on the same bill. 9

*Newly discovered guilt over Hiroshima.* We conveniently forget that the Japanese attacked and declared war against the United States and that the alternative to nuclear weapons was an invasion of the Japanese islands that would have taken more than a million Japanese and American lives. And who sheds tears over Pearl Harbor? 10

*Residual guilt over Vietnam.* Many college students barely remem- 11
ber the Vietnam War. They seem to conclude from it that American mil-
itarism is necessarily a bad thing and that if we and the Russians agree
not to blow each other up, then the whole problem of military aggression will be resolved. By the way, if you ever want to receive a blank stare
from a 20-year-old, ask him about the Kremlin's adherence to the Hel-
sinki accords of 1975.

*Naïveté.* Fans of disarmament have reversed the old idea that if we 12
throw enough money at a problem, we will solve it — that is, if we don't
fund nuclear weapons, war will go away.

*Economics is too complex to be fun.* A crowd-pleasing and crowd- 13
raising issue must be reducible to extremely simple terms to accommo-
date the largest number under its wings. Disarmament lends itself to
suitable simplification: Big Bombs Are Bad.

This is not to question the intentions of those who went to the pro- 14
test in order to protest, for their hearts are in the right place. Nor should
my criticism imply that nuclear energy is desirable. Disarmament and
nuclear energy are related but hardly identical as issues. Woody Allen
once asked what would happen if 10,000 New Yorkers went to the same
restaurant on the same night and ordered the same kind of soup. Well,
75 times as many people did just about the same thing last Saturday
afternoon, but we should distinguish between those who really like the
fare and those who came for the atmosphere, especially when we weigh
claims that the demonstration represents the way Americans feel about
disarmament.

We are turning into a nation of nuclear over-reactors, a race of nice 15
guys, and you know what happens to nice guys.

## Discussion Questions

1. What is the meaning of this article's title?
2. The author claims that the advocates of nuclear disarmament are deluded.
   What evidence does he supply? Is it convincing? Why or why not?
3. On what warrants, according to the author, did the protesters base their
   decision to participate in the rally? (One, for example, is that disarmament
   is a no-risk issue.)
4. What criticism does the author make of these warrants? He says he doesn't
   question the intentions of the protesters. What *does* he question?
5. What different kinds of argumentative strategies does the author use? Can
   you find examples of the warrants discussed in this chapter — authority,
   generalization, sign, cause and effect, analogy? Does one kind of argument
   predominate?
6. What is your opinion of the author's attack on the protesters? Has he been

fair to them? Is he guilty of offering faulty warrants? Do you detect any unstated warrants?

7. What is the implication of the last sentence?

## Writing Suggestions

1. If you disagree with the author's interpretation, write an essay defending the seriousness of the disarmament demonstrators.
2. Are all the reasons given for the size of the crowd equally influential? If not, choose the ones that seem to you most important and develop them.
3. Write about another occasion when the motives of a group were not what they seemed to be.

## Additional Writing Suggestions

1. What are some of the assumptions underlying the "back-to-nature" movement? Consider food, medicine, housing, attitudes toward technology, "life-style," and any other relevant topics.

2. Is plagiarism wrong? What assumptions about education are relevant to the issue of plagiarism? (Some students defend it. What kinds of arguments do they provide?)

3. Choose an advertisement and examine the warrants on which the advertiser's claim is based.

4. "Religious beliefs are (or are not) necessary to a satisfactory life." Explain the warrants underlying your claim. Define any ambiguous terms.

5. Should students be given a direct voice in the hiring of faculty members? On what warrants about education do you base your answer?

6. Discuss the validity of the warrant in this statement from *The Watch Tower* (a publication of the Jehovah's Witnesses) about genital herpes: "The sexually loose are indeed 'receiving in themselves the full recompense, which was due for their error' (Romans 1:27)."

7. Read the following passage about suicide by the Greek philosopher Aristotle (adapted from his *Ethics*). Then defend or attack his argument, being careful to make clear both Aristotle's and your own warrants.

   Just as a murderer does not have the right to take a mother from her family or a child from her parents and simultaneously to deny society the use of a productive citizen, so the suicide, even though he or she freely chooses to be his or her own victim, does not possess the right to thus diminish the welfare of so many others.

8. In view of the increasing attention to health in general, and nutrition and exercise in particular, do you think that universities and colleges should impose physical education requirements? If so, what form should they take? If not, why not? Defend your reasons.

9. In recent years the Food and Drug Administration has been embroiled in controversies over the banning of laetrile, saccharin, and other substances that large numbers of people want to use. What principles do you think ought to guide government regulation of these substances?

10. The author of the following passage, Katherine Butler Hathaway, became a hunchback as a result of a childhood illness. Here she writes about the relationship between love and beauty from the point of view of someone who is deformed. Discuss the warrants on which the author bases her conclusion.

    I could secretly pretend that I had a lover . . . but I could never risk showing that I thought such a thing was possible for me . . . with any man. Because of my repeated encounters with the mirror and my irrepressible tendency to forget what I had seen, I had begun to force myself to believe and to remember, and especially to remember, that I would never be chosen for what I imagined to be the supreme and most intimate of all experience. I thought of sexual love as an honor that was too great and too beautiful for the body in which I was doomed to live.

# 6    *Language*

## THE POWER OF WORDS

Words play such a critical role in argument that they deserve special treatment. We have made both direct and indirect reference to language. Chapter 3 discusses definitions, and the appendix, Writing an Argumentative Essay, discusses style — the choice and arrangement of words and sentences — and shows how successful writers express arguments in language that is clear, vivid, and thoughtful. An important part of their equipment is a large and active vocabulary, but no single chapter in a book can give this to you; only reading and study can widen your range of word choices. Even in a brief chapter, however, we can point out how words influence the feelings and attitudes of an audience, both favorably and unfavorably.

One kind of language responsible for shaping attitudes and feelings is *emotive language*, language that expresses and arouses emotions. Understanding it and using it effectively is indispensable to the arguer who wants to move an audience to accept a point of view or undertake an action.

Long before you thought about writing your first argument, you learned that words had the power to affect you. Endearments and affectionate and flattering nicknames evoked good feelings about the speaker and yourself. Insulting nicknames and slurs produced dislike for the speaker and bad feelings about yourself. Perhaps you were told, "Sticks and stones may break your bones, but words will never hurt you." But even to a small child it must be clear that ugly words are as painful as sticks and stones and that the injuries are sometimes more lasting.

Nowhere is the power of words more obvious and more familiar than in advertising, where the success of a product may depend on the feelings that certain words produce in the prospective buyer. Even the names of products may have emotive significance. In recent years a new industry, composed of consultants who supply names for products, has emerged. Although most manufacturers agree that a good name won't save a poor product, they also recognize that the right name can catch the attention of the public and persuade people to buy a product at least once. According to an article in the *Wall Street Journal*, a product name not only should be memorable but should also "remind people of emotional or physical experiences." One consultant created the name Magnum for a new malt liquor from Miller Brewing Company: "The product is aimed at students, minorities, and lower-income customers." The president of the consulting firm says that Magnum "implies strength, masculinity and more bang for your buck."[1]

It is not hard to see the connection between the use of words in conversation and advertising and the use of emotive language in the more formal arguments you will be writing. Emotive language reveals your approval or disapproval, assigns praise or blame — in other words, makes a judgment about the subject. Keep in mind that unless you are writing purely factual statements, such as scientists write, you will find it hard to avoid expressing judgments. Neutrality does not come easily, even where it may be desirable, as in news stories or reports of historical events. For this reason you need to attend carefully to the statements in your argument, making sure that you have not disguised judgments as statements of fact. Of course, in attempting to prove a claim, you will not be neutral. You will be revealing your judgment about the subject, first in the selection of facts and opinions and the emphasis you give to them and second in the selection of words.

Like the choice of facts and opinions, the choice of words can be effective or ineffective in advancing your argument, moral or immoral in the honesty with which you exercise it. The following discussions offer some insights into recognizing and evaluating the use of emotive language in the arguments you read and into using such language in your own arguments where it is appropriate and avoiding it where it is not.

---

[1] *Wall Street Journal*, August 5, 1982, p. 19.

## CONNOTATION

The connotations of a word are the meanings we attach to it apart from its explicit definition. Because these added meanings derive from our feelings, connotations are one form of emotive language. For example, the word *rat* denotes or points to a kind of rodent, but the attached meanings of "selfish person," "evil-doer," "betrayer," and "traitor" reflect the feelings that have accumulated around the word.

In Chapter 3 we observed that definitions of controversial terms, such as *poverty* and *unemployment*, may vary so widely that writer and reader cannot always be sure that they are thinking of the same thing. A similar problem arises when a writer assumes that the reader shares his or her emotional response to a word. Emotive meanings originate partly in personal experience. The word *home*, defined merely as "a family's place of residence," may suggest love, warmth, and security to one person; it may suggest friction, violence, and alienation to another. The values of the groups to which we belong also influence meaning. Writers and speakers count on cultural associations when they refer to our country, our flag, and heroes and enemies we have never seen. The arguer must also be aware that some apparently neutral words trigger different responses from different groups — words such as *cult, revolution, police, beauty contest*, and *corporation*.

Various reform movements have recognized that words with unfavorable connotations have the power not only to reflect but to shape our perceptions of things. The words *Negro* and *colored* were rejected by the civil rights movement in the 1960s because they bore painful associations with slavery and discrimination. Instead the word *Black*, which was free from such associations, became the accepted designation for Afro-Americans. The women's liberation movement also insisted on changes that would bring about improved attitudes toward women. The movement condemned the use of *girl* for a female over the age of eighteen and the use in news stories of descriptive adjectives that emphasized the physical appearance of women. And the homosexual community succeeded in reintroducing the word *gay*, a word current centuries ago, as a fresh substitute for words they considered offensive.

Members of certain occupations have invented terms to confer greater respectability on their work. The work does not change, but the workers hope that public perceptions will change if janitors are called custodians, if garbage collectors are called sanitation engineers, if undertakers are called morticians, if people who sell makeup are called cosmetologists. Events considered unpleasant or unmentionable are sometimes disguised by polite terms, called *euphemisms*. Many people refuse to use the word *died* and choose *passed away* instead. Some psychologists and physicians use the phrase "negative patient care outcome" for what most of us would call "death." Even when referring to their pets, some people cannot bring themselves to say "put to death" but substitute "put to sleep" or "put down." In place of a term to describe an act of sexual intercourse, some people use "slept together" or "went to bed together" or "had an affair."

Polite words are not always so harmless. If a euphemism disguises a shameful event or condition, it is morally irresponsible to use it to mislead the reader into believing that the shameful condition does not exist. In his powerful essay "Politics and the English Language," George Orwell pointed out that politicians and reporters have sometimes used terms like "pacification" or "rectification of frontiers" to conceal acts that result in torture and death for millions of people. An example of such usage was cited by a member of Amnesty International, a group monitoring human rights violations throughout the world. He objected to a news report describing camps in which the Chinese were promoting "reeducation through labor." This term, he wrote, "makes these institutions seem like a cross between Police Athletic League and Civilian Conservation Corps camps." On the contrary, he went on, the reality of "reeducation through labor" was that the victims were confined to "rather unpleasant prison camps." The details he offered about the conditions under which people lived and worked gave substance to his claim.[2]

Perhaps the most striking examples of the way that connotations influence our perceptions of reality occur when people are asked to respond to questions of poll-takers. Sociologists and students of poll-taking know that the phrasing of a question, the choice of words, can affect the answers and even undermine the validity of the poll. In one case poll-takers first asked a selected group of people if they favored continuing the welfare system. The majority answered no. But when the poll-takers asked if they favored government aid to the poor, the majority answered yes. Although the terms "welfare" and "government aid to the poor" refer to essentially the same forms of government assistance, "welfare" has acquired for many people negative connotations of corruption and shiftless recipients.

The *New York Times* reports the result of another poll in which "a random sample of Americans were asked about their views of abortion in several different ways." The first question was phrased this way: "Do you think there should be an amendment to the Constitution prohibiting abortion, or shouldn't there be such an amendment?" The respondents were solidly opposed — 62 percent — to such an amendment. But when the question read as follows: "Do you believe there should be an amendment to the Constitution protecting the life of the unborn child,

---

[2] Letter to the *New York Times*, August 30, 1982, p. 25.

or shouldn't there be such an amendment?'' only 50 percent were in favor. ''Fully one-third of those who opposed the amendment when it was presented as 'prohibiting abortions' supported it when it was presented as 'protecting the life of the unborn child.' '' As the headline concluded, ''Wording of a Question Makes a Big Difference.''[3]

The wording of an argument is crucial. Since readers may interpret the words you use on the basis of feelings different from your own, you must support your word choices with definitions and evidence that allows readers to determine how and why you made them.

## SLANTING

Slanting, says the dictionary, is ''interpreting or presenting in line with a special interest.'' The term is almost always used in a negative sense. It means that the arguer has selected facts and words with favorable or unfavorable connotations to create the impression that no alternative view exists or can be defended. For some questions it is true that no alternative view is worthy of presentation, and emotionally charged language to defend or attack a position that is clearly right or wrong would be entirely appropriate. We aren't neutral, nor should we be, about the tragic abuse of human rights anywhere in the world or even about less serious infractions of the law such as drunk driving or vandalism, and we should use strong language to express our disapproval of these practices.

Most of your arguments, however, will concern controversial questions about which people of goodwill can argue on both sides. In such cases, your own judgments should be restrained. Slanting will suggest a prejudice — that is, a judgment made without regard to all the facts. Unfortunately, you may not always be aware of your bias or special interest; you may believe that your position is the only correct one. You may also feel the need to communicate a passionate belief about a serious problem. But if you are interested in convincing a reader to accept your belief and to act on it, you must also ask: If the reader is not sympathetic, how will he or she respond? Will he or she perceive my words as ''loaded'' — one-sided and prejudicial — and my view as slanted?

R. D. Laing, a Scottish psychiatrist, has defined prayer in this way: ''Someone is gibbering away on his knees, talking to someone who is not there.''[4] This description probably reflects a sincerely held belief. Laing also clearly intended it for an audience that already agreed with him. But

---

[3] *New York Times*, August 18, 1980, p. 15.

[4] ''The Obvious,'' in *The Dialectics of Liberation*, edited by David Cooper (Penguin Books, 1968), p. 17.

the phrases "gibbering away" and "someone who is not there" would be offensive to people for whom prayer is sacred.

The following remark by an editor of *Penthouse* appeared in a debate on women's liberation.

> I haven't noticed that there is such a thing as a rise in the women's liberation movement. It seems to me that it's a lot of minor sound and a tiny fury. There are some bitty bitty groups of some disappointed ladies who have some objective or other.[5]

An unfriendly audience would resent the use of language intended to diminish the importance of the movement: "minor sound," "tiny fury," "bitty bitty group of some disappointed ladies," "some objective or other." But even audiences sympathetic to the claim may be repelled or embarrassed by intense, colorful, obviously loaded words. In 1970, Senators Geroge McGovern and Mark Hatfield introduced an amendment to enforce America's withdrawal from the Vietnam War. A New York newspaper, violently opposed to the amendment, named it the "White Flag Amendment." An editorial called it a "bug-out scheme" designed to "sucker fence-sitting senators," "a simple and simple-minded solution" supported by "defeatists and Reds," a "cheap way out" that would reveal "the jelly content of America's spine," a "skedaddle scheme." Most readers, including those who agreed with the claim, might feel that the name-calling, slang, and exaggeration revealed a lack of dignity inappropriate to the cause they were defending. Such language is better suited to informal conversation than to serious argument.

We find slanting everywhere, not only in advertising and propaganda, where we expect to find it, but in news stories, which should be strictly neutral in their recounting of events, and in textbooks. In the field of history, for example, it is often difficult for scholars to remain impartial about significant events. Like the rest of us, they may approve or disapprove, and their choice of words will reflect their judgments.

The following passage by a distinguished Catholic historian describes the events surrounding the momentous decision by Henry VIII, king of England, to break with the Roman Catholic Church in 1534, in part because of the Pope's refusal to grant him a divorce from the Catholic princess Catherine of Aragon so that he could marry Anne Boleyn.

> The *protracted* delay in receiving an annulment was very *irritating* to the *impulsive* English king. . . . Gradually Henry's former *effusive* loyalty to Rome gave way to a settled conviction of the tyranny of the papal power, and there *rushed* to his mind the recollections of efforts of earlier English rulers to restrict that power. A few *salutary* enactments against the Church might *compel* a favorable decision from the Pope.

---

[5] "Women's Liberation: A Debate" (Penthouse International Ltd., 1970).

Henry seriously opened his campaign against the Roman Church in 1531, when he *frightened* the clergy into paying a fine of over half a million dollars for violating an *obsolete* statute . . . and in the same year he *forced* the clergy to recognize himself as supreme head of the Church. . . .

His *subservient* Parliament then empowered him to stop the payments of annates to the Pope and to appoint bishops in England without recourse to the papacy. *Without waiting longer* for the decision from Rome, he had Cranmer, *one of his own creatures*, whom he had just named Archbishop of Canterbury, declare his marriage null and void. . . .

Yet Henry VIII encountered considerable *opposition* from the *higher clergy*, from the monks, and from many *intellectual leaders*. . . . A *popular uprising* — the Pilgrimage of Grace — was *sternly* suppressed, and such men as the *brilliant* Sir Thomas More and John Fisher, the *aged* and *saintly* bishop of Rochester, were beheaded because they retained their former belief in papal supremacy. (Emphasis added)[6]

In the first paragraph the italicized words help make the following points: that Henry was rash, impulsive, and insincere and that he was intent on punishing the church (the word *salutary* means healthful or beneficial and is used sarcastically). In the second paragraph the choice of words stresses Henry's use of force and the cowardly submission of his followers. In the third paragraph the adjectives describing the opposition to Henry's campaign and those who were executed emphasize Henry's cruelty and despotism. Within the limits of this brief passage the author has offered some support for his strong indictment of Henry VIII's actions — defining the statute as obsolete, describing the popular opposition. In a longer exposition you would expect to find a more elaborate justification with facts and authoritative opinion from other sources.

The advocate of a position in an argument, unlike the reporter or the historian, must express a judgment, but the preceding examples demonstrate how the arguer should use language to avoid or minimize slanting and to persuade readers that he or she has come to a conclusion after careful analysis. The careful arguer must not conceal his or her judgments by presenting them as if they were statements of fact, must offer convincing support for his or her choice of words, and must respect the audience's feelings and attitudes by using temperate language.

## PICTURESQUE LANGUAGE

Picturesque language consists of words that produce images in the mind of the reader. Students sometimes assume that vivid picture-making language is the exclusive instrument of novelists and poets, but

---

[6] Carlton J. H. Hayes, *A Political and Cultural History of Modern Europe*, Vol. 1 (New York: Macmillan Company, 1933), pp. 172–73.

writers of arguments can also avail themselves of such devices to heighten the impact of their messages.

Picturesque language can do more than render a scene. It shares with other kinds of emotive language the power to express and arouse deep feelings. Like a fine painting or photograph, it can draw readers into the picture, where they partake of the writer's experience as if they were also present. Such power may be used to delight, to instruct, or to horrify. In 1741 the Puritan preacher Jonathan Edwards delivered his sermon ''Sinners in the Hands of an Angry God,'' in which people were likened to repulsive spiders hanging over the flames of Hell, to be dropped into the fire whenever a wrathful God was pleased to release them. The congregation's reaction to Edward's picture of the everlasting horrors to be suffered in the netherworld included panic, fainting, hysteria, and convulsions. Subsequently Edwards lost his pulpit in Northampton, in part as a consequence of his success at provoking such uncontrollable terror among his congregation.

Language as intense and vivid as Edwards's emerges under very strong emotion about a deeply felt cause. In an argument against abortion, a surgeon recounts a horrifying experience as if it were a scene in a movie.

> You walk toward the bus stop. . . . It is all so familiar. All at once you step on something soft. You feel it with your foot. Even through your shoe you may have the sense of something unusual, something marked by a special ''give.'' It is a foreignness upon the pavement. Instinct pulls your foot away in an awkward little movement. You look down, and you see . . . a tiny naked body, its arms and legs flung apart, its head thrown back, its mouth agape, its face serious. A bird, you think, fallen from the nest. But there is no nest here on 73rd Street, no bird so big. It is rubber, then. A model, a . . . a joke. And you bend to see. Because you must. And it is no joke. Such a gray softness can be but one thing. It is a baby, and dead. You cover your mouth, your eyes. You are fixed. Horror has found its chink and crawled in, and you will never be the same as you were. Years later you will step from a sidewalk to a lawn, and you will start at its softness and think of that upon which you have just trod.[7]

Here the use of the pronoun *you* serves to draw readers into the scene and intensify their experience.

The rules governing the use of picturesque language are the same as those governing other kinds of emotive language. Is the language appropriate? It is too strong, too colorful for the purpose of the message? Does it result in slanting or distortion? What will its impact be on a hostile or

---

[7] Richard Selzer, *Mortal Lessons: Notes on the Art of Surgery* (New York: Simon and Schuster, 1974), pp. 153–54.

indifferent audience? Will they be angered, repelled? Will they cease to read or listen if the imagery is too disturbing?

We expect strong language in arguments about life and death. For subjects about which your feelings are not so passionate, your choice of words will be more moderate. The excerpt below, from an article arguing against repeal of Sunday closing laws, creates a sympathetic picture of a market-free Sunday. Most readers, even those who oppose Sunday closing laws, would enjoy the picture and perhaps react more favorably to the argument.

> Think of waking in the city on Sunday. Although most people no longer worship in the morning, the city itself has a reverential air. It comes to life slowly, even reluctantly, as traffic lights blink their orders to empty streets. Next, joggers venture forth, people out to get the paper, families going to church or grandma's. Soon the city is its Sunday self: People cavort with their children, discuss, make repairs, go to museums, gambol. Few people go to work, and any shopping is incidental. The city on Sunday is a place outside the market. Play dominates, not the economy.[8]

## CONCRETE AND ABSTRACT LANGUAGE

Writers of argument need to be aware of another use of language — the distinction between concrete and abstract. Concrete words point to real objects and real experiences. Abstract words express qualities apart from particular things and events. *Beautiful roses* is concrete; we can see, touch, and smell them. *Beauty* in the eye of the beholder is abstract; we can speak of the quality of beauty without reference to a particular object or event. *Returning money found in the street to the owner, although no one has seen the discovery* is concrete. *Honesty* is abstract. In abstracting we separate a quality shared by a number of objects or events, however different from each other the individual objects or events may be.

Writing that describes or tells a story leans heavily on concrete language. Although arguments also rely on the vividness of concrete language, they use abstract terms far more extensively than other kinds of writing. Using abstractions effectively, especially in arguments of value and policy, is important for two reasons: (1) Abstractions represent the qualities, characteristics, and values that the writer is explaining, defending, or attacking; and (2) they enable the writer to make generalizations about his or her data. Equally important is knowing when to avoid abstractions that obscure the message.

---

[8]Robert K. Manoff, "New York City, It Is Argued, Faces 'Sunday Imperialism,' " *New York Times*, January 2, 1977, Sec. IV, p. 13.

In some textbook discussions of language, abstractions are treated as inferior to concrete and specific words, but such a distinction is misleading. Abstractions allow us to make sense of our experience, to come to conclusions about the meaning of the bewildering variety of emotions and events we confront throughout a lifetime. One writer summarized his early history as follows: "My elementary school had the effect of *destroying* any *intellectual motivation*, of *stifling* all *creativity*, of *inhibiting personal relationships* with either my teachers or my peers" (emphasis added). Writing in the humanities and in some social and physical sciences would be impossible without recourse to abstractions that express qualities, values, and conditions.

You should not, however, expect abstract terms alone to carry the emotional content of your message. The effect of even the most suggestive words can be enhanced by details, examples, and anecdotes. One mode of expression is not superior to the other; both abstractions and concrete detail work together to produce clear, persuasive argument. This is especially true when the meanings assigned to abstract terms vary from reader to reader.

In establishing claims based on support of values, for example, you may use such abstract terms as *religion, duty, freedom, peace, progress, justice, equality, democracy,* and *pursuit of happiness.* You can assume that some of these words are associated with the same ideas and emotions for almost all readers; others require further explanation. Suppose you write, "We have made great progress in the last fifty years." The dictionary defines *progress* as "a gradual betterment," another abstraction. How will you define "gradual betterment" for your readers? Can you be sure that they have in mind the same references for progress that you do? If not, misunderstandings are inevitable. You may offer examples: supersonic planes, computers, shopping malls, nuclear energy. Many of your readers will react favorably to the mention of these innovations, which to them represent progress; others, for whom these inventions represent change but not progress, will react unfavorably. You may not be able to persuade all of your readers that "we have made great progress," but all of them will now understand the meaning of the word. And intelligent disagreement is preferable to misunderstanding.

Abstractions tell us what conclusions we have arrived at; details tell us how we got there. But there are dangers in either too many details or too many abstractions. For example, a writer may present only concrete data without telling readers what conclusions are to be drawn from them. Suppose you read the following:

> To Chinese road-users, traffic police are part of the grass . . . and neither they nor the rules they're supposed to enforce are paid the least attention.

. . . Ignoring traffic-lights is only one peculiarity of Chinese traffic. It's normal for a pedestrian to walk straight out into a stream of cars without so much as lifting his head; and goodness knows how many Chinese cyclists I've almost killed as they have shot blindly in front of me across busy main roads.[9]

These details would constitute no more than interesting gossip until we read, "It's not so much a sign of ignorance or recklessness . . . but of fatalism." The details of specific behavior have now acquired a significance expressed in the abstraction *fatalism*.

A more common problem, however, in using abstractions is omission of details. Either the writer is not a skilled observer and cannot provide the details, or he feels that they are too small and quiet compared to the grand sounds made by abstract terms. These grand sounds, unfortunately, cannot compensate for the lack of clarity and liveliness. Lacking detailed support, abstract words may be misinterpreted. They may also represent ideas that are so vague as to be meaningless. Sometimes they function illegitimately as short cuts (discussed in the next section), arousing emotions but unaccompanied by good reasons for their use. The following paragraph exhibits some of these common faults. How would you translate it into clear English?

> We respectively petition, request and entreat that due and adequate provision be made, this day and the date hereinafter subscribed, for the satisfying of these petitioners' nutritional requirements and for the organizing of such methods of allocation and distribution as may be deemed necessary and proper to assure the reception by and for said petitioners of such quantities of baked cereal products as shall, in the judgment of the aforesaid petitioners, constitute a sufficient supply thereof.[10]

If you had trouble decoding this, it was because there were almost no concrete references — the homely words *baked* and *cereal* leap out of the paragraph like English signposts in a foreign country — and too many long words or words of Latin origin when simple words would do: *requirements* instead of *needs, petition* instead of *ask*. An absence of concrete references and an excess of long Latinate words can have a depressing effect on both writer and reader. The writer may be in danger of losing the thread of the argument, the reader at a loss to discover the message.

The paragraph above, according to James B. Minor, a lawyer who teaches courses in legal drafting, is "how a Federal regulation writer would probably write, 'Give us this day our daily bread.'" This brief

---

[9] Philip Short, "The Chinese and the Russians," *The Listener*, April 8, 1982, p. 6.
[10] *New York Times*, May 10, 1977, p. 35.

sentence with its short, familiar words and its origin in the Lord's Prayer has a deep emotional effect. The paragraph composed by Minor deadens any emotional impact because of its preponderance of abstract terms and its lack of connection with the world of our senses.

That passage was invented to educate writers in the government bureaucracy to avoid inflated prose. But writing of this kind is not uncommon among professional writers, including academics. If the subject matter is unfamiliar and the writer an acknowledged expert, you may have to expend a special effort in penetrating the language. But you may also rightly wonder if the writer is making unreasonable demands on you.

> The human race is now entering upon a new phase of evolutionary consciousness and progress, a phase in which, impelled by the forces of evolution itself, it must converge upon itself and convert itself into one single human organism infused by a reconciliation of knowing and being in their inner unity and destined to make a qualitative leap into a higher form of consciousness as we know it, or otherwise destroy itself. For the entire universe is one vast field, potential for incarnation, and achieving incandescence here and there of reason and spirit. And in the whole world of *quality* with which by the nature of our minds we necessarily make contact, we here and there apprehend pre-eminent value. This can be achieved only if we recognize that we are unable to focus our attention on the particulars of the whole, without diminishing our comprehension of the whole, and of course, conversely, we can focus on the whole only by diminishing our comprehension of the particulars which constitute the whole.[11]

You probably found this paragraph even more baffling than the previous example. Although there is some glimmer of meaning here, you should ask whether the extraordinary overload of abstract terms is justified. In fact, most readers would be disinclined to sit still for an argument with so little reference to the real world. One critic of social science prose maintains that if preeminent thinkers like Bertrand Russell can make themselves clear but social scientists are obscure, "then you can justifiably suspect that it might all be nonsense."

Finally, there are the moral implications of using abstractions that conceal a disagreeable reality. George Orwell pointed them out more than forty years ago in "Politics and the English Language." Another essayist, Joseph Wood Krutch, in criticizing the attitude that cheating "doesn't really hurt anybody," observed, " 'It really doesn't hurt anybody' means it doesn't do that abstraction called society any harm." The following news story reports a proposal with which Orwell and Krutch

---

[11]Ruth Nanda Anshen, "Credo Perspectives," introduction to *Two Modes of Thought* by James Bryant Conant (New York: Simon and Schuster, 1964), p. x.

might have agreed. His intention, says the author, is to "slow the hand of any President who might be tempted to unleash a nuclear attack."

> It has long been feared that a President could be making his fateful decision while at a "psychological distance" from the victims of a nuclear barrage; that he would be in a clean, air-conditioned room, surrounded by well-scrubbed aides, all talking in abstract terms about appropriate military reponses in an international crisis, and that he might well push to the back of his mind the realization that hundreds of millions of people would be exterminated.
>
> So Roger Fisher, professor of law at Harvard University, offers a simple suggestion to make the stakes more real. He would put the codes needed to fire nuclear weapons in a little capsule, and implant the capsule next to the heart of a volunteer, who would carry a big butcher knife as he accompanied the President everywhere. If the President ever wanted to fire nuclear weapons, he would first have to kill, with his own hands, that human being.
>
> He has to look at someone and realize what death is — what an innocent death is. "It's reality brought home," says Professor Fisher.[12]

The moral lesson is clear: It is much easier to do harm if we convince ourselves that the object of the injury is only an abstraction.

## SAMPLE ANALYSIS

# *Down, Down on America*

## JAN MORRIS

Crack! Something snapped in me, and I faced up to a conviction I    1
had been trying to stifle for years: the reluctant and terrible conviction that the greatest threat to the peace of humanity is the United States.

Thirty years ago, when I first came to America, it would have    2
seemed inconceivable. America, the Peacemaker, a threat to humanity! I had been brought to the States on a fellowship specifically intended to make a pro-American of me, and it worked like a charm. I loved the country from the start, and for 20 years or more I was able, with a clear conscience, to argue America's case in the world. I believed, generally speaking, in its policies. I admired its style. I welcomed its protection. I shared its purposes.

---

[12] *New York Times*, September 7, 1982, Sec. C, p. 1.

Jan Morris, who lives is Wales, is author of many books.

No longer. For one thing, I can no longer stomach America's insidi- 3
ous meddlings across the face of the world. I live a life of perpetual
travel, and wherever I go I find myself more and more repelled by the
apparently insatiable American urge to interfere in other people's business. Wriggling, probing, peering, intriguing, overt and covert, shady
and legitimate, patronizing, condescending and sometimes contemptuous, there is hardly a corner of the Earth where American officialdom is
not poking its nose and implanting its power.

Quite apart from the fact of it, too, I have become increasingly dis- 4
enchanted as the years have passed with the style of this neo-imperialism.
The G.I. of World War II was most people's idea of what a friendly soldier ought to be. The archetypal wandering Yank of the postwar period,
with his cigar and his jazzy hat, may have been laughed at but was by
common consent frank, straight and generous. But look at your arche-
types now! Look at the egregious ambassadors, the gung-ho admirals,
the creepy intelligence agents who are making the world's flesh creep in
your name this morning!

Like multitudes of my fellow citizens in Europe, Asia, Africa and 5
South America, nowadays I hardly believe a word official America says. I
didn't believe your spokesmen about the Korean airliner, I didn't believe them about Grenada and I certainly do not believe them about Soviet intentions upon the future of the world. And there's the real
crunch. Believe me I am not uttering some personal sour grapes: It is
hard I know for Americans to understand, but to millions and millions
of the rest of us, as liberty-loving as you are, the Soviets are less likely to
trigger World War III than you are yourselves.

Of course, you are both paranoiac — two ideologically stunted gi- 6
ants, neither of whom really wants to conquer the world by force but
whose preposterous dinosauran posturings menace the survival of everyone. But the Russians have cause to be paranoiac! Their history has been
one long misery, one long failure perhaps, distorted always from afar by
psychotic fear of the outside world — time and again, after all, the outside world has brutally attacked them. They are not as we are — of course
they aren't. They have different values — of course they do. But they are
a grand and tragic nation, struggling always, if often in ways we do not
like, to find some fulfillment of their own.

But you! The most powerful, the most enviable, the richest, the 7
most fortunate nation of the world. You have no excuse for paranoia,
and to people like me your incessant insulting goading of the Kremlin,
your habitual refusal even to consider the Soviet point of view on anything, has become unacceptable. Did anyone really believe, as your official spokesmen swore, that the Russians deliberately destroyed that Korean civil airliner knowing it to be harmless? Does anyone really suppose

**145**

that you went into Grenada to forestall the establishment of a Soviet military base? Baloney! Your crude abuse of everything more radical than the Democratic Party is not only vulgar and naïve, it is patently counterproductive: Many good people are Marxists, and many, many more of us, like Jefferson in his day, are proud to stand well on the left!

I had similar qualms in 1954, when McCarthyism was at its squalid   8
height, and Jefferson seemed equally out of favor. I declared them to Justice Felix Frankfurter, and he told me not to worry. The American pendulum was always swinging, he said, from the noble to the despicable, from the cheap to the tremendous, but it was weighted heavily toward the good. Give it time, he said, and I did, and that black period passed, and my faith was restored.

Will the pendulum swing again now, away from this unworthiness   9
of style and madness of purpose, back to the grand old presence? If an old friend feels as I do at this moment — more than an old friend; indeed, a passionate admirer, a grateful lover even — if even I feel as I feel, dear God, I hope for all our sakes it does!

## ANALYSIS

This fiercely angry denunciation of the United States probably says more about the feelings of the writer than about the object of her attack. Such an example of slanting and loaded words, however, is not often found among writers of Jan Morris's stature.

Slanting occurs first in the selection of data, reported in strong and partisan language. The United States is depicted as "the greatest threat to the peace of humanity." The country is condemned for its "insatiable American urge to interfere in other people's business." Notice the detailed indictment of American diplomacy in the seventh paragraph. The Soviet Union, however, is excused for its transgressions. In fact, none is mentioned. The choice of words to characterize Soviet actions is evasive, even slippery. "[The Soviets] are a grand and tragic nation, struggling always, if often in ways we do not like, to find some fulfillment of their own." She fails to mention that the "ways we do not like" include the murder of millions of Russians under Stalin or the suppression of revolts and dissension in Czechoslovakia, Hungary, and Poland, as well as the invasion of Afghanistan.

Eighty years ago Henry Adams, an American historian, wrote *Mont Saint Michel and Chartres*, contrasting the wonders of thirteenth-century Europe with the horrors of early-twentieth-century America. In his review of the book, one critic wrote:

> Adams arrived at his view of the Middle Ages by concentrating on a few
> great products of literature, thought, and architecture; ignoring everything

else, he asserted that these were the thirteenth century. He arrived at his view of the twentieth century by reversing the process. He thus deduced that the world was deteriorating, and so found a justification for his own state of mind.[13]

This is an apt description of the method used by Jan Morris to contrast the United States and the Soviet Union.

Throughout, words have been selected with a view to condemning only one side. The United States is guilty of "wriggling, probing, posturing, peering, intriguing," of being "overt and covert, shady and illegitimate, patronizing, condescending and sometimes contemptuous." Only Americans are characterized as "egregious [remarkably bad] ambassadors, the gung-ho admirals, the creepy intelligence agents who are making the world's flesh creep."

Such violent attacks may relieve an author's feelings. (Morris confesses that she has been trying to stifle her conviction about the United States for years.) But they are ineffective as arguments. Depending on the circumstances being described, exaggeration can be defined, in the words of one writer, as "a form of lying." An essay in *Time* magazine, "Watching Out for Loaded Words," points to the danger for the arguer in relying on exaggerated language as an essential part of the argument:

> The trouble with loaded words is that they tend to short-circuit thought. While they may describe something, they simultaneously try to seduce the mind into accepting a prefabricated opinion about the something described.[14]

## SHORT CUTS

Shorts cuts are arguments that depend on readers' response to words. Short cuts, like other devices we have discussed so far, are a common use of emotive language but are often mistaken for valid argument.

Although they have power to move us, these abbreviated substitutes for argument avoid the hard work necessary to provide facts, expert opinion, and the analysis of warrants. Even experts, however, can be guilty of using short cuts, and the writer who consults an authority should be alert to the authority's use of language. Two of the most common uses of short cuts are clichés and slogans.

---

[13] Yvor Winters, *The Anatomy of Nonsense* (Norfolk, CT: New Directions, 1943), p. 65.

[14] *Time*, May 24, 1982, p. 86.

## Clichés

"I'm against sloppy, emotional thinking. I'm against fashionable thinking. I'm against the whole cliché of the moment."[15] This statement by the late Herman Kahn, the founder of the Hudson Institute, a famous think tank, serves as the text for this section. A cliché is an expression or idea grown stale through overuse. Clichés of language are tired expressions that have faded like old photographs; readers no longer see anything when clichés are placed before them. Clichés include phrases like "cradle of civilization," "few and far between," "rude awakening," "follow in the footsteps of," "fly in the ointment."

But more important to recognize and avoid are clichés of thought. A cliché of thought may be likened to a formula, which one dictionary defines as "any conventional rule or method for doing something, especially when used, applied or repeated without thought." Clichés of thought represent ready-made answers to questions, stereotyped solutions to problems, "knee-jerk" reactions. Two writers who call these forms of expression "mass language" describe it this way: "Mass language is language which presents the reader with a response he is expected to make without giving him adequate reason for having this response."[16] These "clichés of the moment" are often expressed in single words or phrases.

Certain cultural attitudes encourage the use of clichés. The liberal American tradition has been governed by hopeful assumptions about our ability to solve problems. A professor of communications says that "we tell our students that for every problem there must be a solution."[17] But real solutions are hard to come by. In our haste to provide them, to prove that we can be decisive, we may be tempted to produce familiar responses that resemble solutions.

History teaches us that a solution to an old and serious problem is almost always accompanied by unexpected drawbacks. As the writer quoted in the previous paragraph warns us, "Life is not that simple. There is no one answer to a given problem. There are multiple solutions, all with advantages and disadvantages." By solving one problem, we often create another. Automobiles, advanced medical techniques, industrialization, and liberal divorce laws have all contributed to the solution of age-old problems: lack of mobility, disease, poverty, domestic unhap-

---

[15] *New York Times*, July 8, 1983, Sec. B, p. 1.

[16] Richard E. Hughes and P. Albert Duhamel, *Rhetoric: Principles and Usage* (Englewood Cliffs, NJ: Prentice-Hall, 1962), p. 161.

[17] Malcolm O. Sillars, "The New Conservatism and the Teacher of Speech," *Southern Speech Journal* 21 (1956), p. 240.

piness. We now see that these solutions bring with them new problems that we nevertheless elect to live with because the advantages seem greater than the disadvantages. A well-known economist puts it this way: "I don't look for solutions; I look for trade-offs. I think the person who asks, 'What is the solution to this problem?' has a fundamental misconception of the way the world works. We have trade-offs, and that's all we have."[18]

This means that we should be skeptical of solutions promising everything and ignoring limitations and criticism. Such solutions have probably gone round many times. Having heard them so often, we are inclined to believe that they have been tried and proven. Thus they escape serious analysis.

Some of these problems and their solutions represent the fashionable thinking to which Kahn objected. They confront us everywhere, like the public personalities who gaze at us week after week from the covers of magazines and tabloid newspapers at the checkout counter in the supermarket. Alarms about the failures of public education, about drug addiction or danger to the environment or teenage pregnancy are sounded throughout the media continuously. The same solutions are advocated again and again: "Back to basics"; "Impose harsher sentences"; "Offer sex education." Their popularity, however, should not prevent us from asking, Are the problems as urgent as their prominence in the media suggests? Are the solutions workable? Does sufficient evidence exist to justify their adoption?

Your arguments will not always propose solutions. They will sometimes provide interpretations of or reasons for social phenomena, especially for recurrent problems. Some explanations have acquired the status of folk wisdom, like proverbs, and careless arguers will offer them as if they needed no further support. One object of stereotyped responses is the problem of juvenile delinquency. Liberals attribute it to poverty, lack of community services, meaningless education, violence on TV. Conservatives blame parental permissivness, a decline in religious influence, lack of individual responsibility, lenient courts. Notice that the interpretations of the cause of juvenile delinquency are related to an ideology, to a particular view of the world that may prevent the arguer from recognizing any other way of examining the problem. Other stereotyped explanations for a range of social problems include inequality, competition, self-indulgence, alienation, discrimination, technology, lack of patriotism, excessive governmental regulation, lack of sufficient govern-

---

[18] Thomas Sowell, "Manhattan Report" (edited transcript of *Meet the Press*) (New York: International Center for Economic Policy Studies, 1981), p. 10.

mental regulation. All of these explanations are worthy of consideration, but they must be defined and supported if they are to be used in a thoughtful, well-constructed argument.

Although formulas change with the times, some are unexpectedly hardy and survive long after critics have revealed their weaknesses. Overpopulation is an often-cited cause of poverty, disease, and war. It can be found in the writing of the ancient Greeks 2500 years ago. "That perspective," says the editor of *Food Monitor*, a journal published by World Hunger Year, Inc., "is so pervasive that most Americans have simply stopped thinking about population and resort to inane clucking of tongues."[19] If the writer offering overpopulation as an explanation for poverty were to look further, he or she would discover that the explanation rested on shaky data. The Netherlands, the most densely populated country in the world (894 persons per square mile) is also one of the richest ($6700 per capita income per year). Chad, one of the most sparsely populated (9 persons per square mile) is also one of the poorest ($120 per capita income per year).[20] Strictly defined, overpopulation may serve to explain some instances of poverty; obviously it cannot serve as a blanket to cover all or even most instances. "By repeating stock phrases," one columnist reminds us, "we lose the ability, finally, to hear what we are saying."

Clichés sometimes appear in less familiar guise. In summer 1983 Nigeria elected a new government, an important, peaceful event that received less media attention than violent events of much more trivial significance. An editorial in the *Wall Street Journal* attributed this lack of interest to our inability to look beyond cherished clichés:

> Let's be frank about this: An awful lot of people in the industrialized West just can't take seriously the idea of these underdeveloped countries conducting their own affairs in any sensible or civilized way. The cliché on the right is that you're lucky if someone imposes stability on the country long enough to let a proper mix of economic policies take hold. And the left thinks that elections aren't as important as a government that will force a presumably more equal restructuring of the nation's wealth.[21]

## Slogans

The word *slogan* has a picturesque origin. A slogan was the war cry or rallying cry of a Scottish or Irish clan. From that early use it has come to mean a "catchword or rallying motto distinctly associated with a polit-

---

[19] Letter to the *New York Times*, October 4, 1982, Sec. A, p. 18.

[20] *Information Please Almanac 1980* (New York: Simon and Schuster, 1980), pp. 134–35.

[21] *Wall Street Journal*, August 15, 1983, p. 16.

ical party or other group" as well as a "catch phrase used to advertise a product."

Slogans, like clichés, are short, undeveloped arguments. They represent abbreviated responses to often complex questions. As a reader you need to be aware that slogans merely call attention to a problem; they cannot offer persuasive proof for a claim in a dozen words or less. As a writer you should avoid the use of slogans that evoke an emotional response "without giving [the reader] adequate reason for having this response."

Advertising slogans are the most familiar. Some of them are probably better known than nursery rhymes: "Reach out and touch someone," "It costs more, but I'm worth it," "Don't leave home without it." Advertisements may, of course, rely for their effectiveness on more than slogans. They may also give us interesting and valuable information about products, but most advertisements give us slogans that ignore proof — short cuts substituting for argument.

The persuasive appeal of advertising slogans is heavily dependent on the connotations associated with products. In Chapter 4 we discussed the way in which advertisements promise to satisfy our needs and protect our values. Wherever evidence is scarce or nonexistent, the advertiser must persuade us through skillful choice of words and phrases (as well as pictures), especially those that produce pleasurable feelings. "Coke — it's the real thing." "Real" — as opposed to artificial or unnatural — sounds like a desirable quality. But what is "real" about Coke? Probably even the advertiser would find it hard to define the "realness" of Coke. Another familiar slogan — "Noxzema, clean makeup" — also emphasizes a quality that we approve of, but what is "clean" makeup? Since the advertisers are silent, we are left with warm feelings about the word and not much more.

Advertising slogans are persuasive because their witty phrasing and punchy rhythms produce an automatic "yes" response. We react to them as we might react to the lyrics of popular songs, and we treat them far less critically than we treat more straightforward and elaborate arguments. Still, the consequences of failing to analyze the slogans of advertisers are usually not serious. You may be tempted to buy a product because you were fascinated by a brilliant slogan, but if the product doesn't satisfy, you can abandon it without much loss. However, ignoring ideological slogans, coined by political parties or special interest groups, may carry an enormous price, and the results are not so easily undone.

Ideological slogans, like advertising slogans, depend on the power of connotation, the emotional associations aroused by a word or phrase. In the 1960s and 1970s, a period of well-advertised social change, slogans flourished; they appeared by the hundreds of thousands on buttons, T-shirts, and bumper stickers. One of them read, "Student Power!" To some readers of the slogan, distrustful of young people and worried about student unrest on campuses and in the streets, the suggestion was frightening. To others, mostly students, the idea of power, however undefined, was intoxicating. Notice that "Student Power!" is not an argument; it is only a claim. (It might also represent a warrant.) Many people, whether they accepted or rejected the claim, supplied the rest of the argument without knowing exactly what the issues were and how a developed argument would proceed. They were accepting or rejecting the slogan largely on the basis of emotional reaction to words.

American political history is, in fact, a repository of slogans. Leaf through a history of the United States and you will come across "Tippecanoe and Tyler, too," "manifest destiny," "fifty-four forty or fight," "make the world safe for democracy," "the silent majority," "the domino theory," "the missile gap," "the window of vulnerability." Each administration tries to capture the attention and allegiance of the public by coining catchy phrases. Roosevelt's New Deal in 1932 was followed by the Square Deal and the New Frontier. Today, slogans must be carefully selected to avoid offending groups that are sensitive to the ways in which words affect their interests. In 1983 Senator John Glenn, announcing his candidacy for president, talked about bringing "old values and new horizons" to the White House. "New horizons" apparently carried positive connotations. His staff, however, worried that "old values" might suggest racism and sexism to minorities and women.

A professor of politics and international affairs at Princeton University explains why public officials use slogans, despite their obvious shortcomings:

> Officials long have tried to capture complicated events and to dominate public discussion of foreign policy by using simple phrases and slogans. They engage in phrase-making in order to reach wide audiences. . . .
>
> Slogans and metaphors often express the tendencies of officials and academics who have a common wish to be at once sweeping, unequivocal, easily understood and persuasive. The desire to capture complicated phenomena through slogans stems also from impatience with the particular and unwillingness or inability to master interrelationships.[22]

Over a period of time slogans, like clichés, can acquire a life of their own and, if they are repeated often enough, come to represent an unchanging truth we no longer need to examine. "Dangerously," says the writer quoted above, "policy makers become prisoners of the slogans they popularize."

---

[22] Henry Bienen, "Slogans Aren't the World," *New York Times*, January 16, 1983, Sec. IV, p. 19.

The arguments you write will not, of course, be one-sentence slogans. Unfortunately, many longer arguments amount to little more than
sloganeering or a series of suggestive phrases strung together to imitate
the process of argumentation. Following are two examples. The first is
taken from a full-page magazine advertisement in 1983, urging the formation of a new political party. The second is part of the second inaugural address of George C. Wallace, governor of Alabama, in 1971. These
extracts are typical of the full advertisement and the full speech.

> We can't dislodge big money from its domination over the two old
> parties, but we can offer the country something better: a new party that
> represents the people and responds to their needs. . . . How can we solve
> any problem without correcting the cause — the structure of the Dem/Rep
> machine and the power of the military-industrial establishment? . . .The
> power of the people could be a commanding force if only we could get to-
> gether — Labor, public-interest organizations, blacks, women, antinuclear
> groups, and all the others.[23]

> The people of the South and those who think like the South, repre-
> sent the majority viewpoint within our constitutional democracy, but they
> are not organized and do not speak with a loud voice. Until the day arrives
> when the voice of the people of the South and those who think like us is,
> within the law, thrust into the face of the bureaucrats, only then can the
> "people's power" express itself legally and ethically and get results. . . .
> Too long, oh, too long, has the voice of the people been silenced by their
> own disruptive government — by governmental bribery in quasi-govern-
> mental handouts such as H.E.W. and others that exist in America today!
> An aroused people can save this nation from those evil forces who seek our
> destruction. The choice is yours. The hour is growing late![24]

Whatever power these recommendations might have if their proposals were more clearly formulated, as they stand they are collections of
slogans and loaded words. (Even the language falters; can the voice of
the people be thrust into the face of the bureaucrats?) We can visualize
some of the slogans as brightly colored banners: "Dislodge Big Money!"
"Power of the People!" "Save This Nation from Evil Forces!" "The
Choice Is Yours!" Do all the groups mentioned share identical interests?
If so, what are they? Given the vagueness of the terms, it is not surprising
that arguers on opposite sides of the political spectrum — loosely characterized as liberal and conservative — sometimes resort to the same clichés
and slogans, the language of populism, or a belief in the virtues of the
"common people."

---

[23] *The Progressive*, September 1983, p. 38.
[24] Second Inaugural Address as Governor of Alabama, January 18, 1971.

Slogans have numerous shortcomings as substitutes for the development of an argument. First, their brevity presents serious disadvantages. Slogans necessarily ignore exceptions or negative instances that might qualify a claim. They usually speak in absolute terms without describing the circumstances in which a principle or idea might not work. Their claims therefore seem shrill and exaggerated. In addition, brevity prevents the sloganeer from revealing how he or she arrived at conclusions.

Second, slogans may conceal unexamined warrants. When Japanese cars were beginning to compete with American cars, the slogan "Made in America by Americans" appeared on the bumpers of thousands of American-made cars. A thoughtful reader would have discovered in this slogan several implied warrants: American cars are better than Japanese cars; the American economy will improve if we buy American; patriotism can be expressed by buying American goods. If the reader were to ask a few probing questions, he or she might find these warrants unconvincing.

Silent warrants that express values hide in other popular and influential slogans. "Pro-life," the slogan of those who oppose abortion, assumes that the fetus is a living being entitled to the same rights as individuals already born. "Pro-choice," the slogan of those who favor abortion, suggests that the freedom of the pregnant woman to choose is the foremost or only consideration. The words *life* and *choice* have been carefully selected to reflect desirable qualities, but the words are only the beginning of the argument.

Third, although slogans may express admirable sentiments, they often fail to tell us how to achieve their objectives. They address us in the imperative mode, ordering us to take an action or refrain from it. But the means of achieving the objectives may be nonexistent or very costly. If the sloganeer cannot offer workable means for implementing his goals, he or she risks alienating the audience.

Sloganeering is one of the recognizable attributes of propaganda. Propaganda for both good and bad purposes is a form of slanting, of selecting language and facts to persuade an audience to take a certain action. Even a good cause may be weakened by an unsatisfactory slogan. The slogans of some organizations devoted to fundraising for the physically handicapped have come under attack for depicting the handicapped as helpless. According to one critic, the popular slogan "Jerry's kids" promotes the idea that Jerry Lewis is the sole support of children afflicted with muscular dystrophy. Perhaps increased sensitivity to the needs of the handicapped will produce new words, new slogans. If you assume that your audience is sophisticated and alert, you will probably write your strongest arguments, devoid of clichés and slogans.

SAMPLE ANALYSIS

# *My Unprodigal Sons*

## CAROLYN LEWIS

My two sons live lives starkly different from my own. They make    1
their homes in small rural places, and theirs are lives of voluntary simplicity.

They have chosen work that gives service to others, requires no great    2
competitiveness and does no harm in the name of greater good. They
share a singular lack of interest in accruing possessions. Their clothes
would make Brooks Brothers shudder, and they drive automobiles that
are both ancient and uncomely.

They till the earth around their modest houses to grow vegetables,    3
trees and flowers. They are entertained by shared festivities with neighbors, wives and children. They have records for music, books for learning, and each lives close enough to the sea to enjoy the esthetic pleasures
of blue vistas and open sky.

This curious phenomenon — of ambitious, competitive, urban par-    4
ents spawning gentle, unambitious, country offspring — is not unique to
my own experience. I observe it all around me and listen with amusement to the puzzled comments of middle-aged parents faced with this
unexpected generational shift.

"We gave him everything, and he chooses to weave blankets in    5
Maine," they say accusingly. Or, "We invested in Andover and Harvard, and he cuts trees in Oregon." The refrain is sorrowful, even embarrassed, as though our children have somehow turned against us by choosing to live in ways different from our own.

But I confess that every time I return to the big city after visiting my    6
children, I am haunted by a psychic malaise. I go through my days comparing this with that, and more and more the *that* is looking better.

What my sons have is a world that is small enough to be readily un-    7
derstood, where those responsible wear a human face. When I talk about
the big city where I live, in the only terms that can grasp its enormity —
about groups and studies, trends and polls — my sons smile sweetly and

Carolyn Lewis is associate dean of the Columbia Graduate School of Journalism and
a former Washington reporter.

speak of people who live around the corner, have specific names and definitive problems. Theirs are flesh-and-blood realities instead of my pale, theoretical formulations. They remind me that the collective humanity I measure and label is far less interesting and vital than the individual who, mercifully, in the end will defy categorization.

When I ask him how he likes living in a town of 500 people three 8 hours away from the nearest large city, my son Peter says: "Just fine. You see, I know who I am here."

That statement resonates in my brain. It's true; he has definable 9 space to call his own. He has warming relationships with family and neighbors. He has what E. F. Schulmacher would call "good work."

On the other hand, he certainly cannot be labeled rich. His income 10 is hardly the kind that makes the GNP go into a tailspin. When the sophisticated instruments of measurement are applied to his life — husband, wife, two children (family of four earning so much) — they mark him low income.

I, by comparison, living in my overpriced city apartment, walking 11 to work past putrid sacks of street garbage, paying usurious taxes to local and state governments I generally abhor, I am rated middle class. This causes me to wonder, do the measurements make sense? Are we measuring only that which is easily measured — the numbers on the money chart — and ignoring values more central to the good life?

For my sons there is of course the rural bounty of fresh-grown vege- 12 tables, line-caught fish and the shared riches of neighbors' orchards and gardens. There is the unpaid baby-sitter for whose children my daughter-in-law baby-sits in return, and neighbors who barter their skills and labor. But more than that, how do you measure serenity? Sense of self? The feeling that, in order to get ahead, you don't have to trample on somebody else's skull?

I don't want to idealize life in small places. There are times when 13 the outside world intrudes brutally, as when the cost of gasoline goes up or developers cast their eyes on untouched farmland. There are cruelties, there is bigotry, there are all the many vices and meannesses in small places that exist in large cities. Furthermore, it is harder to ignore them when they cannot be banished psychologically to another part of town or excused as the vagaries of alien groups — when they have to be acknowledged as "part of us."

Nor do I want to belittle the opportunities for small decencies in cit- 14 ies — the eruptions of one-stranger-to-another caring that always surprise and delight. But these are, sadly, more exceptions than rules and are often overwhelmed by the awful corruptions and dangers that surround us.

In this society, where material riches and a certain notoriety are con- 15 sidered admirable achievements, it takes some courage to say, no thanks, not for me. The urban pleasures and delights — restaurants, museums, theater, crowds in the streets — continue to have an urgent seductiveness for many young people. For parents like myself, who strove to offer our children these opportunities and riches, it is hard to be reconciled to those same children spurning the offer and choosing otherwise.

Plainly, what my sons want and need is something different — something smaller, simpler and more manageable. They march to a different drummer, searching for an ethic that recognizes limits, that scorns overbearing competition and what it does to human relations, and that says simply and gently, enough is enough. 16

Is my sons' solution to the complexity and seeming intractability of modern problems the answer for everyone? Of course not. Some of us have to stay in the cities, do what we can, fight when it is necessary, compete in order to survive. Maybe if we are diligent, we can make things a little better where we are. 17

But to choose small places, modest ambitions and values that are tolerant and loving is surely an admirable alternative. It may in the end be the only alternative we have to an urban culture in which we have created so much ugliness, and where we deem to inflict so much pain on each other through neglect, selfishness and failure of will. 18

## ANALYSIS

Carolyn Lewis makes a by now familiar claim that can fairly be called a cliché: Country life is superior in almost every way to city life. The cliché is the dream of a golden age long ago when human beings lived peacefully in an innocent rural environment that satisfied all their needs. This pastoral dream has inspired writers and artists from the time of the ancient Greeks, despite historical evidence that such a world never existed. Today it remains alive among those who believe that one can escape from problems of the city to a rural paradise.

According to Lewis, not only is the country more physically satisfying, it is also inhabited by people who are emotionally and morally superior to those who live in the city. They have "modest ambitions and values that are tolerant and loving." The title is a revealing play on words. *Prodigal* means recklessly wasteful; Lewis's sons are the opposite. The title also brings to mind the biblical story of the wayward son who returned at last to his grieving father. Lewis apparently neither desires nor expects her sons to return to the city.

Lewis brings a fresh personal perspective to her argument, contrasting in some detail her own way of life in the city with that of her sons in the country. Her own way of life, she says, is characterized by "overpriced city apartments," "putrid sacks of street garbage," "usurious taxes.'' Her sons' way of life is represented by tilling of ''the earth around their modest homes,'' ''shared festivities with neighbors, wives, and children,'' ''shared riches of neighbors' orchards and gardens.''

But in elaborating this contrast, Lewis uses a questionable strategy. She offers in at least three paragraphs vivid details of the pleasures and benefits her sons derive from their simple country life; she disposes of the disadvantages in one brief paragraph without examples. On the other hand, the pleasures and benefits of living in cities are summed up in a parenthetical insertion — about restaurants, museums, theater, crowds in the streets — while the hateful aspects are clearly specified. In other words, she contrasts the worst characteristics of city life with the best characteristics of country life and incidentally omits any mention of the similarities, an acknowledgment that would undoubtedly weaken her claim. Such a practice is not uncommon, but it suggests that the author has been either careless or dishonest in the use of evidence.

In fact, it would not be hard to refute some of Lewis's generalizations. Getting ahead in the city doesn't always require that one ''trample on somebody else's skull.'' People in cities also do ''good work'' by providing needed services. Escape to rural areas is not always a sign of courage; it may be a sign of cowardice or an admission of failure.

Lewis's argument reflects the dangers in using evidence based entirely or even largely on personal expereince. No matter how vivid or moving, personal experience does not justify large generalizations about the whole society. Someone else may recall unpleasant experiences with country life. How, then, does a neutral reader decide between these rival expressions of opinion?

When Lewis concludes that a retreat to rural life may be the only alternative we have to ''an urban culture in which we have created so much ugliness,'' she reveals another weakness in accepting a time-worn belief without examining the consequences of acceptance. Since the world suggested by the formula seems so beautiful, she assumes that it also contains a solution to a problem. But it is unrealistic to think that all those who are disturbed by city life can escape to the country, however attractive that alternative may be.

READINGS FOR ANALYSIS

# The Speech
# the Graduates Didn't Hear

## JACOB NEUSNER

We the faculty take no pride in our educational achievements with   1
you. We have prepared you for a world that does not exist, indeed, that
cannot exist. You have spent four years supposing that failure leaves no
record. You have learned at Brown that when your work goes poorly, the
painless solution is to drop out. But starting now, in the world to which
you go, failure marks you. Confronting difficulty by quitting leaves you
changed. Outside Brown, quitters are no heroes.

With us you could argue about why your errors were not errors, why   2
mediocre work really was excellent, why you could take pride in routine
and slipshod presentation. Most of you, after all, can look back on honor
grades for most of what you have done. So, here grades can have meant
little in distinguishing the excellent from the ordinary. But tomorrow, in
the world to which you go, you had best not defend errors but learn from
them. You will be ill-advised to demand praise for what does not deserve
it, and abuse those who do not give it.

For four years we created an altogether forgiving world, in which   3
whatever slight effort you gave was all that was demanded. When you
did not keep appointments, we made new ones. When your work came
in beyond the deadline, we pretended not to care.

Worse still, when you were boring, we acted as if you were saying   4
something important. When you were garrulous and talked to hear yourself talk, we listened as if it mattered. When you tossed on our desks
writing upon which you had not labored, we read it and even responded,
as though you earned a response. When you were dull, we pretended
you were smart. When you were predictable, unimaginative and routine,
we listened as if to new and wonderful things. When you demanded free
lunch, we served it. And all this why?

Despite your fantasies, it was not even that we wanted to be liked by   5
you. It was that we did not want to be bothered, and the easy way out
was pretense: smiles and easy Bs.

It is conventional to quote in addresses such as these. Let me quote   6

---

Jacob Neusner is university professor and distinguished scholar of Judaic studies at
Brown University. He is currently translating the Palestinian Talmud.

someone you've never heard of: Prof. Carter A. Daniel, Rutgers University (*Chronicle of Higher Education*, May 7, 1979):

"College has spoiled you by reading papers that don't deserve to be  7
read, listening to comments that don't deserve a hearing, paying attention even to the lazy, ill-informed and rude. We had to do it, for the sake of education. But nobody will ever do it again. College has deprived you of adequate preparation for the last 50 years. It has failed you by being easy, free, forgiving, attentive, comfortable, interesting, unchallenging fun. Good luck tomorrow."

That is why, on this commencement day, we have nothing in which  8
to take much pride.

Oh, yes, there is one more thing. Try not to act toward your co-  9
workers and bosses as you have acted toward us. I mean, when they give you what you want but have not earned, don't abuse them, insult them, act out with them your parlous relationships with your parents. This too we have tolerated. It was, as I said, not to be liked. Few professors actually care whether or not they are liked by peer-paralyzed adolescents, fools so shallow as to imagine professors care not about education but about popularity. It was, again, to be rid of you. So go, unlearn the lies we taught you. To Life!

## Discussion Questions

1.  Pick out some of the words and phrases — especially adjectives and verbs — used by Neusner to characterize both students and teachers. Do you think these terms are loaded? Explain.
2.  Has Neusner chosen "facts" to slant his article? If so, point out where slanting occurs. If not, point out where the article seems to be truthful.
3.  As a student you will probably object to Neusner's accusations. How would you defend your behavior as a student in answer to his specific charges?

## Writing Suggestions

1.  Rewrite Neusner's article with the same "facts" — or others from your experience — using temperate language, in sadness rather than anger.
2.  Write a letter to Neusner responding to his attack. Support or attack his argument by providing evidence from your own experience.
3.  Write your own short commencement address. Do some things need to be said that commencement speakers seldom or never express?
4.  Write an essay using the same kind of strong language as Neusner uses about some aspect of your education of which you disapprove. Or write a letter to a teacher using the same form as "The Speech the Graduates Didn't Hear."

# A Hanging

## GEORGE ORWELL

We set out for the gallows. Two warders marched on either side of the prisoner, with their rifles at the slope; two others marched close against him, gripping him by arm and shoulder, as though at once pushing and supporting him. The rest of us, magistrates and the like, followed behind. Suddenly, when we had gone ten yards, the procession stopped short without any order or warning. A dreadful thing had happened — a dog, come goodness knows whence, had appeared in the yard. It came bounding among us with a loud volley of barks, and leapt round us wagging its whole body, wild with glee at finding so many human beings together. It was a large woolly dog, half Airedale, half pariah. For a moment it pranced round us, and then, before anyone could stop it, it had made a dash for the prisoner and, jumping up, tried to lick his face. Everyone stood aghast, too taken aback even to grab at the dog.

"Who let that bloody brute in here?" said the superintendent angrily. "Catch it, someone!"

A warder, detached from the escort, charged clumsily after the dog, but it danced and gamboled just out of his reach, taking everything as part of the game. A young Eurasian jailer picked up a handful of gravel and tried to stone the dog away, but it dodged the stones and came after us again. Its yaps echoed from the jail walls. The prisoner, in the grasp of the two warders, looked on incuriously, as though this was another formality of the hanging. It was several minutes before someone managed to catch the dog. Then we put my handkerchief through its collar and moved off once more, with the dog still straining and whimpering.

It was about forty yards to the gallows. I watched the bare brown back of the prisoner marching in front of me. He walked clumsily with his bound arms, but quite steadily, with that bobbing gait of the Indian who never straightens his knees. At each step his muscles slid neatly into place, the lock of hair on his scalp danced up and down, his feet printed themselves on the wet gravel. And once, in spite of the men who gripped him by each shoulder, he stepped slightly aside to avoid a puddle on the path.

It is curious, but till that moment I had never realized what it

George Orwell (1903–1950), whose real name was Eric Blair, was born in India, educated in England, and later served in the police force in Burma. In 1936 he fought with the Republicans in the Spanish Civil War. His best-known works are his political essays and novels, among them *Animal Farm* and *Nineteen Eighty-Four*.

means to destroy a healthy, conscious man. When I saw the prisoner step aside to avoid the puddle I saw the mystery, the unspeakable wrongness, of cutting a life short when it is in full tide. This man was not dying, he was alive just as we are alive. All the organs of his body were working — bowels digesting food, skin renewing itself, nails growing, tissues forming — all toiling away in solemn foolery. His nails would still be growing when he stood on the drop, when he was falling through the air with a tenth of a second to live. His eyes saw the yellow gravel and the gray walls, and his brain still remembered, foresaw, reasoned — reasoned even about puddles. He and we were a party of men walking together, seeing, hearing, feeling, understanding the same world; and in two minutes, with a sudden snap, one of us would be gone — one mind less, one world less.

The gallows stood in a small yard, separate from the main grounds  6
of the prison, and overgrown with tall prickly weeds. It was a brick erection like three sides of a shed, with planking on top, and above that two beams and a crossbar with the rope dangling. The hangman, a gray-haired convict in the white uniform of the prison, was waiting beside his machine. He greeted us with a servile crouch as we entered. At a word from Francis the two warders, gripping the prisoner more closely than ever, half led, half pushed him to the gallows and helped him clumsily up the ladder. Then the hangman climbed up and fixed the rope round the prisoner's neck.

We stood waiting, five yards away. The warders had formed in a  7
rough circle round the gallows. And then, when the noose was fixed, the prisoner began crying out to his god. It was a high, reiterated cry of "Ram! Ram! Ram! Ram!" not urgent and fearful like a prayer or cry for help, but steady, rhythmical, almost like the tolling of a bell. The dog answered the sound with a whine. The hangman, still standing on the gallows, produced a small cotton bag like a flour bag and drew it down over the prisoner's face. But the sound, muffled by the cloth, still persisted, over and over again: "Ram! Ram! Ram! Ram! Ram!"

The hangman climbed down and stood ready, holding the lever.  8
Minutes seemed to pass. The steady, muffled crying from the prisoner went on and on, "Ram! Ram! Ram!" never faltering for an instant. The superintendent, his head on his chest, was slowly poking the ground with his stick; perhaps he was counting the cries, allowing the prisoner a fixed number — fifty, perhaps, or a hundred. Everyone had changed color. The Indians had gone gray like bad coffee, and one or two of the bayonets were wavering. We looked at the lashed, hooded man on the drop, and listened to his cries — each cry another second of life; the same thought was in all our minds: oh, kill him quickly, get it over, stop that abominable noise!

Suddenly the suprintendent made up his mind. Throwing up his   9
head he made a swift motion with his stick. "Chalo!" he shouted almost
fiercely.

There was a clanking noise, and then dead silence. The prisoner had   10
vanished, and the rope was twisting on itself. I let go of the dog, and it
galloped immediately to the back of the gallows; but when it got there it
stopped short, barked, and then retreated into a corner of the yard,
where it stood among the weeds, looking timorously out at us. We went
round the gallows to inspect the prisoner's body. He was dangling with
his toes pointed straight downward, very slowly revolving, as dead as a
stone.

## Discussion Questions

1.  What is Orwell's thesis? Is it explicitly stated in the essay?
2.  Nowhere in the essay does Orwell mention the crime for which the man
    was executed. What is the significance of that omission?
3.  What purpose is served by the episode about the dog?
4.  Examine an article that argues against capital punishment without anec-
    dote or description. Which argument is more effective? Why?
5.  Would Orwell's argument be more persuasive with some audiences than
    with others? Explain.
6.  What other controversial subjects could be treated in the same way with
    vivid, picture-making language?
7.  What are the limitations, if any, of such linguistic strategies when they are
    used to support arguments?

## Writing Suggestions

1.  Compare "A Hanging" with "The Penalty of Death" by H. L. Mencken
    on page 394. Tell why you find one argument more convincing than the
    other.
2.  Choose another subject about which you feel strongly. Defend your point
    of view with picturesque language and narration.
3.  Find another article using picturesque language and analyze the effective-
    ness of the language as part of the argument.

# Say "I Love You" Today

## LEO BUSCAGLIA

As a professor, I'm constantly meeting people and working with 1
people — and I'm becoming so very concerned, because the people I
meet are afraid to show their wonder and to show their beauty. They are
in constant doubt about being beautiful and being wonderful. If there is
to be any hope for us as lovers, we've got to make sure to express our love
and caring, to bring it out into the open and not be afraid.

It's amazing — you may not realize it, but so much of what you are 2
*not* is because you are literally standing in your own way of becoming.
And what I'm pleading with you about is, fly — life and love are available to you; all you have to do is grasp them. So many people don't trust
themselves, don't believe in themselves, don't even *like* themselves. I
was in my office recently and I had a lovely girl, a student of mine, sitting across from me. I said, "Tell me about yourself. We're going to be
together for sixteen weeks in classes, and I don't want you to be a
stranger. You tell me about you and then I'll take over and tell you
about me."

She said, "I don't have anything to say." 3

I said, "What do you mean? Tell me about all your wonder." 4

She said, "Wonder?!" And then there was a long pause, and she 5
said, "Well, I'm too short."

You know, that had never occurred to me until she told me. I 6
thought, well, I'll counteract with something good. I said, "Yes, but
you're a darn good student. Do you know that you got an A in your mid-
term?"

And she said, "Sheer luck." 7

How do you like that? I said, "But you know that you're unique in 8
all the world — "

"Not me! I'm not unique." She said, "Stop the baloney! I know 9
I'm not very good-looking, and not a lot of people seek me out. And I'm
lonely a lot of the time."

It occurred to me that if she really believes she's short and ugly and 10
stupid and has nothing to contribute, why would anybody seek her out?

---

Leo Buscaglia (b. 1925) teaches education at the University of Southern California.
His message of the positive power of love has been disseminated through inspirational radio and television talks and several best-selling books.

Did I work on that one! When she walked out, she was four inches taller, and if I ever see her lean over again, there's going to be hell to pay.

Jack Parr says a wonderful thing. He says, "My life seems like one 11 long obstacle course, with me as the chief obstacle."

I love *Souls on Fire*, a book by Elie Weisel, in which there is a beau- 12 tiful statement. It says that when you die and go to meet your maker, you're not going to be asked why you didn't become a messiah or find a cure for cancer. All you're going to be asked is, why didn't you become you? Why didn't you become *all* that you are?

How often have you heard yourself say, "I'm nothing." Well, 13 you're nothing if you *think* you're nothing.

Mama would get me aside every night and say, "Some day you're 14 gonna be a *big* man." You know, I'd look at her and I'd say, "Am I?" She'd say, "Wait and see." She did that to *all* my brothers and sisters. Sometimes I get really sad, because in a supermarket I hear a mama with her little kid talking to her neighbor, saying, "This is the *dumb* one." She'll say, "Now, his sister — boy, she is the genius."

As if the little kid were deaf! It's a self-fulfilling prophecy. He 15 hears, and what is he hearing? That he's stupid. You become what you believe you are. I always heard at home, "What do you mean, you *can't* — go out and do it!"

I love the word *Yes*. Have you ever thought how beautiful that word 16 is? Sometimes I ask people, "What is the most beautiful word in the English language?" To me, it's *yes*. It's even a continuant. It goes on forever. Yessssssssss.

*No* is the end of the line. When you say *no*, that shuts the windows 17 and the doors. If you can't stand *yes*, if that scares you too much, try *maybe*. At least there's a chance, there's an opportunity! But "I won't?" That's sad. And then I hear, "That's the way it is, and there's nothing that can be done about it." You know, that *isn't* the way it is. And there's always something that *can* be done about it. Just get in there and try.

I really love this self-defeating idea: "It's a dog-eat-dog world." I 18 don't know about you, but I've never known a dog to eat another dog.

And then this one: "I've been hurt before, and I'm never going to 19 trust again." What's a little hurt? You can learn from pain. What a silly world we live in, where you believe that everything has to be on a high, joyous level all the time. It kills me. There's nothing wrong with a little pain. I've learned so many wonderful things over the years in painful situations. In fact, sometimes it takes death to teach us about life; it takes misery to teach us about joy. So embrace it when it comes. Say it's a part of life. Put your arms around it. Learn to feel it again. Don't deny it.

**165**

Maybe it does hurt. Say it's OK to hurt. Experience the pain. Cry. Bang on the table! Be angry! Let it come out. And then *forget* it. Otherwise you're going to store it up forever.

Where do we get these self-defeating ideas, these ideas that limit 20 us, that make us lonely? The ideas that keep us bored? The ideas that kill spontaneity and surprise?

Sometimes we learn them from the people we love the most. We 21 learn from our family. If you're going to learn personal growth and dignity, there is no better place to start than in your own home. Sometimes we show the least amount of loving to the people we love the most. We'll compliment people in the office, but we'll never compliment our own children, our own wives, our own husbands. Never let a day go by without seeing something good in the people who surround you. And tell them! Maybe it's going to be difficult that day. You've got to really search. But find *something* good and say, "That was really good." "That was well done."

I'm always telling teachers it's impossible for children to deal with a 22 concept that out of fifty, they got forty-nine wrong. Why not tell them, "Johnny, you got *one* right." Bravo! "Tomorrow we're going to make it *two!*" Remember that Grandma used to say, "You catch more flies with honey than you do with vinegar." So why do we concentrate on the vinegar all the time? What you *should* be. What you *should do*. And always under the guise, "I'm telling you this because I love you." This constant criticism is for your own good. So would compliments be! If you love me, say something nice. Isn't there *something* about me that's *nice*? Think about it. It's very dynamic and yet it's so real. Those people whom we should be reinforcing the most because we love them are often the people we tell the least. And that's a pity. So in your homes is where you begin to set this atmosphere of personal dignity. Recently I received a letter from a woman who was with me in elementary school. She had seen me on a TV show. That's the wonderful thing about being on television — all your old friends pop up. She wrote me saying, "There could only be one kook like you. Even as a kid you were crazy and now I can see it in you as an adult. And there's only one for sure who has a name like Felice Leonardo Buscaglia. You know that I remember about you, Felice?" And she conjured up something out of the past that I didn't remember anymore. She said "I remember once everybody surrounding you and making fun of you because you were in your sister's coat. It was winter and you were wearing your sister's coat."

Suddenly that memory came to me and I remembered how poor we 23 were. And I remembered that it was a very cold day, and Mama took my sister's coat. It had a little fur collar, and it buttoned on the wrong side. She put it on me. I said, "Mama, I don't want . . ." My mother was a wonderful nondirective counselor.

"Shut up!" she said. "You'll be grateful that you have something 24 to keep you warm. What about the people who don't even have a coat to keep them warm? Who cares if it's your sister's coat? If you wear it with pride, you will look good."

Well, it didn't work. But I'd forgotten. In retrospect, the thing 25 that's so wonderful is not the coat or the pain and the being made fun of — the thing that I remember is Mama, saying, "If you wear it with pride . . ." and "There are some people who don't have a coat to wear," That's learning something vital and positive for life, you see. I'm constantly telling this to people. They say, "Oh, loving is so difficult." I say, "Don't you know how easy it is? Loving is simple. It's we who are complex." Loving means sharing joy with people. When you see something beautiful, it means going over and telling them. When you see someone lovely, say, "You're lovely." And then back away! Because it's going to scare the hell out of them.

One of the funniest experiences I've ever had happened one day 26 when I saw this lovely girl on campus. She had golden hair and it was billowing in the sun. It looked so special. I passed her by and it flashed through my mind, what beautiful hair that girl has. As I walked by I thought, I should tell her. So I spun around and charged back toward her. And she could sort of feel me, you know how you can do. She turned around like "AAAACK!" And I said, "Don't be scared. All I want to do is tell you that you have the most beautiful hair with the sun on it, it's a real trip. I just *really* liked it. Thank you very much."

And then I moved slowly away, and as I got farther and farther 27 away, it began to dawn on her that someone had paid her a compliment. She started to smile. By the time I got to the university entrance, she even waved and said, "Thank you." It seemed to me that as she walked away, she stood even taller, bringing her closer to the sun.

What's so difficult about that? We have those opportunities every 28 single day of our lives, and we don't take them. We start with those people around us. We teach them self-respect and we make sure that everybody leaves with her beautiful compliment that day. People say, "Oh, but Buscaglia, that's artificial." It doesn't have to be artificial when you really see it. Don't tell me the people around you don't deserve an occasional compliment. What's artificial about that?

I remember that Mama loved to have her food praised. And we'd all 29 say, "Oh, Mama, this is wonderful!"

And she'd say, "I know, I know, you don't have to tell me." But 30
boy, if we didn't . . .

And it never hurts people to be told that they are loved, to say to 31
somebody, "I love you." People say — especially, this is true of men —
"Oh, she knows I love her. I don't have to tell her I love her." Oh, really? When she's gone, then maybe you'll wonder why. It's a simple
thing to say, "I love you." And if you can't say it, write it. If you can't
write it, dance it. But say it! And say it *many* times. One never tires of it.
One may say, "Oh, never mind telling me that. I know . . ." But it's so
nice to hear.

## Discussion Questions

1. What is the message of this article? Do you find it persuasive? Why or why
   not?
2. How does the first example of the author's encounter with the student establish the tone and purpose of the article?
3. What kinds of sayings and advice does Buscaglia favor? Why? Do they appeal to you?
4. Can the word *no* also be considered a "continuant"?
5. Is it always true that *yes* and *maybe* are better than *no*? Give examples to
   support your answer. What does the author mean by his celebration of *yes*?
   Do you agree?
6. What portion of this message might be characterized as cliché?
7. Have you heard this kind of advice before? How did you respond?
8. What does your experience tell you about how most people accept or respond to pain? Does Buscaglia's advice seem helpful?
9. Examine the language of this article. How would you characterize it? Do
   you find any relation between the language and the nature of the message?
10. Do you agree that loving is "simple"?

## Writing Suggestions

1. An Episcopalian priest writes: "Contrary to the facile exhortations of
   preachers, love — at least as it proceeds from our hearts and hands — is not
   a cure for the world's miseries but one of the prime causes of them." Defend or criticize this point of view.
2. Choose a proverb that offers advice, and analyze its value as a guide for behavior. Examples: If at first you don't succeed, try, try again. A bird in the
   hand is worth two in the bush. Early to bed, early to rise makes a man
   healthy, wealthy and wise.

# My Speech to the Graduates

## WOODY ALLEN

More than any other time in history, mankind faces a crossroads. 1
One path leads to despair and utter hopelessness. The other, to total ex-
tinction. Let us pray we have the wisdom to choose correctly. I speak, by
the way, not with any sense of futility, but with a panicky conviction of
the absolute meaninglessness of existence which could easily be misinterpreted as pessimism. It is not. It is merely a healthy concern for the predicament of modern man. (Modern man is here defined as any person
born after Nietzsche's edict that "God is dead," but before the hit recording "I Wanna Hold Your Hand.") This "predicament" can be
stated one of two ways, though certain linguistic philosophers prefer to
reduce it to a mathematical equation where it can be easily solved and
even carried around in the wallet.

Put in its simplest form, the problem is: How is it possible to find 2
meaning in a finite world given my waist and shirt size? This is a very difficult question when we realize that science has failed us. True, it has
conquered many diseases, broken the genetic code, and even placed human beings on the moon, and yet when a man of 80 is left in a room
with two 18-year-old cocktail waitresses nothing happens. Because the
real problems never change. After all, can the human soul be glimpsed
through a microscope? Maybe — but you'd definitely need one of those
very good ones with two eyepieces. We know that the most advanced
computer in the world does not have a brain as sophisticated as that of an
ant. True, we could say that of many of our relatives but we only have to
put up with them at weddings or special occasions. Science is something
we depend on all the time. If I develop a pain in the chest I must take an
X-ray. But what if the radiation from the X-ray causes me deeper problems? Before I know it, I'm going in for surgery. Naturally, while they're
giving me oxygen an intern decides to light up a cigarette. The next
thing you know I'm rocketing over the World Trade Center in bed
clothes. Is this science? True, science has taught us how to pasteurize
cheese. And true, this can be fun in mixed company — but what of the
H-bomb? Have you ever seen what happens when one of those things
falls off a desk accidentally? And where is science when one ponders the

Woody Allen (b. 1935) is an actor, writer, and award-winning film director for
*Annie Hall* and *Manhattan*. He has written humorous plays, stories, and essays, especially
for *The New Yorker*.

eternal riddles? How did the cosmos originate? How long has it been around? Did matter begin with an explosion or by the word of God? And if by the latter, could He not have begun it just two weeks earlier to take advantage of some of the warmer weather? Exactly what do we mean when we say, man is mortal? Obviously it's not a compliment.

Religion too has unfortunately let us down. Miguel de Unamuno 3 writes blithely of the "eternal persistence of consciousness," but this is no easy feat. Particularly when reading Thackeray. I often think how comforting life must have been for early man because he believed in a powerful, benevolent Creator who looked after all things. Imagine his disappointment when he saw his wife putting on weight. Contemporary man, of course, has no such peace of mind. He finds himself in the midst of a crisis of faith. He is what we fashionably call "alienated." He has seen the ravages of war, he has known natural catastrophes, he has been to singles bars. My good friend Jacques Monod spoke often of the randomness of the cosmos. He believed everything in existence occurred by pure chance with the possible exception of his breakfast, which he felt certain was made by his housekeeper. Naturally belief in a divine intelligence inspires tranquility. But this does not free us from our human responsibilities. Am I my brother's keeper? Yes. Interestingly, in my case I share that honor with the Prospect Park Zoo. Feeling godless then, what we have done is made technology God. And yet can technology really be the answer when a brand new Buick, driven by my close associate, Nat Persky, winds up in the window of Chicken Delight causing hundreds of customers to scatter? My toaster has never once worked properly in four years. I follow the instructions and push two slices of bread down in the slots and seconds later they rifle upward. Once they broke the nose of a woman I loved very dearly. Are we counting on nuts and bolts and electricity to solve our problems? Yes, the telephone is a good thing — and the refrigerator — and the air conditioner. But not every air conditioner. Not my sister Henny's, for instance. Hers makes a loud noise and still doesn't cool. When the man comes over to fix it, it gets worse. Either that or he tells her she needs a new one. When she complains, he says not to bother him. This man is truly alienated. Not only is he alienated but he can't stop smiling.

The trouble is, our leaders have not adequately prepared us for a 4 mechanized society. Unfortunately our politicians are either incompetent or corrupt. Sometimes both on the same day. The Government is unresponsive to the needs of the little man. Under five-seven, it is impossible to get your Congressman on the phone. I am not denying that democracy is still the finest form of government. In a democracy at least, civil liberties are upheld. No citizen can be wantonly tortured, imprisoned, or made to sit through certain Broadway shows. And yet this is a far cry from what goes on in the Soviet Union. Under their form of totalitarianism, a person merely caught whistling is sentenced to 30 years in a labor camp. If, after 15 years, he still will not stop whistling they shoot him. Along with this brutal fascism we find its handmaiden, terrorism. At no other time in history has man been so afraid to cut his veal chop for fear that it will explode. Violence breeds more violence and it is predicted that by 1990 kidnapping will be the dominant mode of social interaction. Overpopulation will exacerbate problems to the breaking point. Figures tell us there are already more people on earth than we need to move even the heaviest piano. If we do not call a halt to breeding, by the year 2000 there will be no room to serve dinner unless one is willing to set the table on the heads of strangers. Then they must not move for an hour while we eat. Of course energy will be in short supply and each car owner will be allowed only enough gasoline to back up a few inches.

Instead of facing these challenges we turn instead to distractions like ⁵ drugs and sex. We live in far too permissive a society. Never before has pornography been this rampant. And those films are lit so badly! We are a people who lack defined goals. We have never learned to love. We lack leaders and coherent programs. We have no spiritual center. We are adrift alone in the cosmos wreaking monstrous violence on one another out of frustration and pain. Fortunately, we have not lost our sense of proportion. Summing up, it is clear the future holds great opportunities. It also holds pitfalls. The trick will be to avoid the pitfalls, seize the opportunities, and get back home by six o'clock.

## Discussion Questions

1. Pick out as many of the clichés as you can in Allen's essay. Can you determine where they originated — that is, who uses them and what area of modern life they are associated with?
2. Do any of these clichés refer to real problems? If so, what are they?
3. Can you account for the persistence of some of these clichés?

## Writing Suggestions

1. Select one or two clichés from the speech and treat them seriously. Supply evidence to prove that they contain some truth.
2. Choose a subject you are familiar with — sports, theater, music, politics, health — and write a speech to some of its practitioners, using the clichés typical of the subject.

## Additional Writing Suggestions

1.  Select one or two related bumper stickers visible in your neighborhood. Examine the hidden warrants on which they are based and assess their validity.
2.  For a slogan found on a bumper sticker or elsewhere, supply the evidence to support the claim in the slogan. Or find evidence that disproves the claim.
3.  Examine a few periodicals from fifty or more years ago. Select either an advertising or a political slogan contained in them and relate it to beliefs or events of the period. Or tell why the slogan is no longer relevant.
4.  Discuss the origin of a cliché or slogan. Describe, as far as possible, the backgrounds and motives of its users.
5.  Make up your own slogan for a cause that you support. Explain and defend your slogan.
6.  Discuss the appeal to needs and values of some popular advertising or political slogan.
7.  Choose a cliché and find evidence to support or refute it. Examples: People were much happier in the past. Mother knows best. Life was much simpler in the past. Money can't buy happiness.
8.  Choose one of the statements in number 7 or another statement and write a paper telling why you think it has persisted as an explanation.
9.  Select a passage, perhaps from a textbook, written largely in abstractions and rewrite it, using simpler and more concrete language.

# 7 _Induction, Deduction, and Logical Fallacies_

Throughout the book we have pointed out the weaknesses that cause arguments to break down. In the vast majority of cases these weaknesses represent breakdowns in logic or the reasoning process. We call such weaknesses _fallacies_, a term derived from the Latin, meaning "false." Sometimes these false or erroneous arguments are deliberate; in fact, the Latin word _fallere_ means to deceive. But more often they are either careless or unknowing. Thoughtful readers learn to recognize them; thoughtful writers learn to avoid them.

The reasoning process was first given formal expression by Aristotle, the Greek philosopher, almost 2,500 years ago. In his famous treatises, he described the way we try to discover the truth — observing the world, selecting impressions, making inferences, generalizing. In this process Aristotle identified two forms of reasoning: _induction_ and _deduction_. Both forms, he realized, are subject to error. Our observations may be incorrect or insufficient, and our conclusions may be faulty because they have violated the rules governing the relationship between statements. The terms we've introduced may be unfamiliar, but the processes of reasoning, as well as the fallacies that violate these processes, are not. Induction and deduction are not reserved only for formal arguments about important problems; they represent our everyday thinking about the most ordinary matters. As for the fallacies, they, too, unfortunately, may crop up anywhere, whenever we are careless in our use of the reasoning process.

In this chapter we describe some of the most common fallacies. First, however, a closer look at induction and deduction will make clear what happens when fallacies occur.

# INDUCTION

Induction is the form of reasoning in which we come to conclusions about the whole on the basis of observations of particular instances. If you notice that prices on the four items you bought in the campus bookstore are higher than similar items in the bookstore in town, you may come to the conclusion that the campus store is a more expensive place to shop. If you also noticed that all three of the instructors you saw on the first day of school were wearing faded jeans and sandals, you might say that your teachers are generally informal in their dress. In both cases you have made an *inductive leap*, reasoning from what you have learned about a few examples to what you think is true of a whole class of things.

How safe are you in coming to these conclusions? As we've noticed in discussing data and generalization warrants, the reliability of your conclusion depends on the quantity and quality of your observations. Were four items out of the thousands available in the campus store a sufficiently large sample? Would you come to the same conclusion if you chose fifty items? Might another selection have produced a different conclusion? As for the casually dressed instructors, perhaps further investigation would disclose that the teachers wearing jeans were all teaching assistants and that associate and full professors usually wore business clothes. Or the difference might lie in the academic discipline; anthropology teachers might turn out to dress less formally than business school teachers.

In these two situations, you could come closer to verifying your conclusions by further observation and experience — that is, by buying more items at both stores over a longer period of time and by coming into contact with a greater number of professors during a whole semester. Even without pricing every item in both stores or encountering every instructor on campus, you would be more confident of your generalization as the quality and quantity of your samples increased.

In some cases you can observe all the instances in a particular situation. For example, by acquiring information about the religious beliefs of all the residents of the dormitory, you can arrive at an accurate assessment of the number of Buddhists. But since our ability to make definitive observations about everything is limited, we must also make an inductive leap about categories of things that we ourselves can never encounter in their entirety. For some generalizations, as we have learned about evidence, we rely on the testimony of reliable witnesses who report that they have experienced or observed many more instances of the phenomenon. A TV documentary may give us information about unwed teenage mothers in a city neighborhood; four girls are interviewed and followed for several days by the reporter. Are these girls typical of thousands of others? A sociologist on the program assures us that, in fact, they are. She herself has consulted with hundreds of other young mothers and can vouch for the fact that a conclusion about them, based on our observation of the four, will be sound. Obviously, though, our conclusion can only be probable, not certain. The sociologist's sample is large, but she can account only for hundreds, not thousands, and there may be unexamined cases that will seriously weaken our conclusions.

In other cases, we may rely on a principle known in science as "the uniformity of nature." We assume that certain conclusions about oak trees in the temperate zone of North America, for example, will also be true for oak trees growing elsewhere under similar climatic conditions. We also use this principle in attempting to explain the causes of behavior in human beings. If we discover that institutionalization of some children from infancy results in severe emotional retardation, we think it safe to conclude that under the same circumstances all children would suffer the same consequences. As in the previous example, we are aware that certainty about every case of institutionalization is impossible. With rare exceptions, the process of induction can offer only probability, not certain truth.

## DEDUCTION

While induction attempts to arrive at the truth, deduction guarantees sound relationships between statements. If each of a series of statements, called *premises*, is true, deductive logic tells us that the conclusion must also be true. Unlike the conclusions of induction, which are only probable, the conclusions of deduction are certain. The simplest deductive argument consists of two premises and a conclusion. In outline such an argument looks like this:

MAJOR PREMISE: All students with 3.5 averages and above for three years are invited to become members of Kappa Gamma Pi, the honor society.

MINOR PREMISE: George has had a 3.8 average for over three years.

CONCLUSION: Therefore, he will be invited to join Kappa Gamma Pi.

This deductive conclusion is *valid* or logically consistent because it follows necessarily from the premises. No other conclusion is possible. Validity, however, refers only to the form of the argument. The argument itself may not be satisfactory if the premises are not true — if Kappa Gamma Pi has imposed other conditions or if George has only a 3.4 average. The difference between truth and validity is important because it alerts us to the necessity for examining the truth of the premises before we decide that the conclusion is sound.

One way of discovering how the deductive process works is to look at the methods used by Sherlock Holmes, the most famous of literary detectives, in solving his mysteries. His reasoning process followed a familiar pattern. Through the inductive process, that is, observing the particulars of the world, he came to certain conclusions about those particulars. Then he applied deductive reasoning to come to a conclusion about a particular person or event.

On one occasion Holmes observed that a man sitting opposite him on a train had chalk dust on his fingers. From this observation Holmes deduced that the man was a schoolteacher. If his thinking were outlined, it would take the form of the syllogism, the classic form of deductive reasoning:

MAJOR PREMISE:   All men with chalk dust on their fingers are schoolteachers.

MINOR PREMISE:   This man has chalk dust on his fingers.

CONCLUSION:   Therefore, this man is a schoolteacher.

We see that the major premise, the first statement, is an inductive generalization, a statement arrived at after observation of a number of men with chalk dust on their fingers. The minor premise, the second statement, assigns a particular member to the general class of those who have chalk dust on their fingers. If these statements are true, then the conclusion must follow because it obeys the rules of logical consistency. The process of reasoning is valid.

But although the argument may be logical, it is faulty. The deductive argument is only as strong as its premises. As Lionel Ruby pointed out, Sherlock Holmes was often wrong.[1] Holmes once deduced from the size of a large hat found in the street that the owner was intelligent. He obviously believed that a large head meant a large brain and that a large brain indicated intelligence. Had he lived one hundred years later, new information would have enabled him to come to a different and better conclusion.

In this case, we might first object to the major premise, the general-

---

[1] *The Art of Making Sense* (Philadelphia, PA: Lippincott, 1954), chap. 17.

ization that all men with chalk dust on their fingers are schoolteachers. Is it true? Perhaps all the men with dusty fingers whom Holmes had so far observed had turned out to be schoolteachers, but was his sample sufficiently large to allow him to conclude that all dust-fingered men, even those with whom he might never have contact, were teachers? Were there no other vocations or situations that might require the use of chalk? All draftsmen or carpenters or tailors or artists might have fingers just as white as those of schoolteachers. In other words, Holmes may have ascertained that all schoolteachers have chalk dust on their fingers, but he had not determined that *only* schoolteachers can be thus identified. Sometimes it is helpful to draw circles representing the various groups in their relation to the whole.

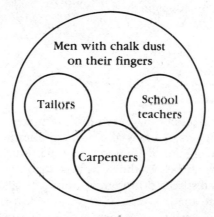

If the large circle represents all those who have chalk dust on their fingers, we see that several different groups may be contained in this universe. To be safe, Holmes should have deduced that the man on the train *might* have been a scoolteacher; he was not safe in deducing more than that. Obviously, if the inductive generalization or major premise is false, the conclusion of the particular argument is also false or invalid.

The deductive argument may also go wrong elsewhere. What if the minor premise is untrue? Could Holmes have mistaken the source of the white powder on the man's fingers? Suppose it was not chalk dust but flour or confectioner's sugar or talcum or heroin? Any of these possibilities would weaken or invalidate his conclusion.

Another example, closer to the kinds of arguments you will examine, reveals the same flaw.

MAJOR PREMISE:  All Communists oppose organized religion.

MINOR PREMISE:  Robert Roe opposes organized religion.

CONCLUSION:  Therefore, Robert Roe is a Communist.

The common name for this fallacy is "guilt by association." The fact that two things share an attribute does not mean that they are the same thing. As in the first example, the diagram makes clear that Robert Roe and Communists do not necessarily share all attributes.

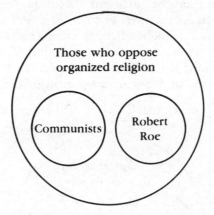

Remembering that Holmes may have misinterpreted the signs of chalk on the traveler's fingers, we may also want to question whether Robert Roe's opposition to organized religion has been misinterpreted.

An example from history shows us how such an argument may be used. In a campaign speech during the summer of 1952, Senator Joseph McCarthy, who had made a reputation as a tireless enemy of communism, said, "I do not tell you that Schlesinger, Stevenson's number one man, number one braintrust, I don't tell you he's a Communist. I have no information on that point. But I do know that if he were a Communist he would also ridicule religion as Schlesinger has done."[2] This is an argument based on a sign warrant. Clearly the sign referred to by Senator McCarthy, ridicule of religion, would not be sufficient to characterize someone as a Communist.

Some deductive arguments give trouble because one of the premises, usually the major premise, is omitted. As in the warrants we examined in Chapter 5, a failure to evaluate the truth of the unexpressed premise may lead to an invalid conclusion. When only two parts of the syllogism appear, we call the resulting form an *enthymeme*. Suppose we overhear the following snatch of conversation:

---

[2] Joseph R. McCarthy, "The Red-Tinted Washington Crowd," speech delivered to a Republican campaign meeting at Appleton, WI, November 3, 1952.

"Did you hear about my father? He had a heart attack last week."

"That's too bad. But I'm not surprised. I know he always refused to go for his annual physical checkups."

The second speaker has used an unexpressed major premise, the cause-effect warrant "If you have annual physical checkups, you can avoid heart attacks." He does not express it because he assumes that it is unnecessary to do so. The first speaker recognizes the unspoken warrant and may agree with it. Or the first speaker may produce evidence from reputable sources that such a generalization is by no means universally true, in which case the conclusion of the second speaker is suspect.

A knowledge of the deductive process can help guide you toward an evaluation of the soundness of your reasoning in an argument you are constructing. The syllogism is often clearer than an outline in establishing the relations between the different parts of an argument.

Suppose you wanted to argue that your previous high school should introduce a dress code. What would be the purpose of such a regulation? How could a dress code fulfill that purpose? What reasons could you provide to support your claim?

You might begin by setting down part of your argument this way:

Dressing in different styles makes students more aware of social differences among themselves.

The students in this school dress in many different styles.

Therefore, they are more aware of differences in social status among the student body.

As you diagram this first part of the argument, you should ask two sets of questions:

1. Is the major premise true? Do differences in dress cause awareness of differences in social status? Has my experience confirmed this?
2. Is the minor premise true? Has my observation confirmed this?

The conclusion, of course, represents something that you don't have to observe. You can deduce with certainty that it is true if both the major and minor premises are true.

So far the testing of your argument has been realtively easy because you have been concerned with the testing of observation and experience. Now you must examine something that does not appear in the syllogism. You have determined certain facts about perceptions of social status, but you have not arrived at the policy you want to recommend: that a dress code should be mandated. Notice that the dress code argument is based on acceptance of a moral value.

Reducing awareness of social differences is a desirable goal for the school.

A uniform dress code would help to achieve that goal.

Therefore, students should be required to dress uniformly.

The major premise in this syllogism is clearly different from the previous one. While the premise in the previous syllogism can be tested by examining sufficient examples to determine probability, this statement, about the desirability of the goal, is a value judgment and cannot be proved by counting examples. Whether equality of social status is a desirable goal depends on an appeal to other, more basic values.

Setting down your own or someone else's argument in this form will not necessarily give you the answers to questions about how to support your claim, but it should clearly indicate what your claims are and, above all, what logical connections exist between your statements.

## COMMON FALLACIES

In this necessarily brief review it would be impossible to discuss all the fallacies listed by logicians. But we can examine the ones most likely to be found in the arguments you will read and write. Inductive fallacies, as we know, result from the wrong use of evidence. Deductive fallacies, on the other hand, result from a failure to follow the logic of a series of statements.

### Hasty Generalization

In Chapter 4 we discussed the dangers in drawing conclusions on the basis of insufficient evidence. Many of our prejudices are a result of hasty generalization. A prejudice is literally a judgment made before the facts are in. On the basis of experience with two or three members of an ethnic group, for example, we may form the prejudice that all members of the group share the characteristics we have attributed to the two or three in our experience. (See Gordon Allport, "The Nature of Prejudice," on page 71.)

Superstitions are also based in part on hasty generalization. As a result of a very small number of experiences with black cats, broken mirrors, Friday the thirteenth, or spilled salt, some people will assume a cause-effect relation between these signs and misfortunes. Superstition has been defined as "a notion maintained despite evidence to the contrary." The evidence would certainly show that, contrary to the superstitious belief, in a lifetime hundreds of such "unlucky" signs are not followed by unfortunate events. To generalize about a connection is therefore unjustified.

## Faulty Use of Authority

The attempt to bolster claims by citing the opinions of experts was discussed in Chapter 4. Both writers and readers need to be especially aware of the testimony of authorities who may disagree with those cited. In circumstances where experts disagree, you were encouraged to undertake a careful evaluation and comparison of credentials.

## *Post Hoc* or Doubtful Cause

The whole Latin term for this fallacy is *post hoc, ergo propter hoc*, meaning "After this, therefore because of this." The arguer infers that because one event follows another event, the first event must be the cause of the second. But proximity of events or conditions does not guarantee a causal relation. The rooster crows every morning at 5:00 and, seeing the sun rise immediately after, decides that his crowing has caused the sun to rise. A month after A-bomb tests are concluded, tornadoes damage the area in which the tests were held, and residents decide that the tests caused the tornadoes. After the school principal suspends daily prayers in the classroom, acts of vandalism increase, and some parents are convinced that failure to conduct prayer is responsible for the rise in vandalism. In each of these cases, the fact that one event follows another does not prove a causal connection. The two events may be coincidental, or the first event may be only one, and an insignificant one, of many causes that have produced the second event. The reader or writer of causal arguments must determine whether another more plausible explanation exists and whether several causes have combined to produce the effect. Perhaps the suspension of prayer was only one of a number of related causes: a decline in disciplinary action, a relaxation of academic standards, a change in school administration, changes in family structure in the school community.

In the previous section we pointed out that superstitions are the result not only of hasty generalization but of the willingness to find a cause-effect connection in the juxtaposition of two events. A belief in astrological signs also derives from erroneous inferences about cause and effect. Not many of the millions of people who consult the astrology charts every day in newspapers and magazines have submitted the predictions to statistical analysis. A curious reader might try this strategy:

Save the columns, usually at the beginning or end of the year, in which astrologers and clairvoyants make predictions for events in the coming year allegedly based on their reading of the stars and other signs. At the end of the year evaluate the percentage of predictions that were fulfilled. The number will be very small. But even if some of the predictions prove true, there may be other, less fanciful explanations for their accuracy. Philosophers refer to a maxim called Occam's razor, the advice of a medieval philosopher and theologian, William of Occam, which says: "Entities are not to be multiplied without necessity." Bertrand Russell, the twentieth-century British philosopher, explained it this way:

> It is vain to do with more what can be done with fewer. That is to say, if everything in some science can be interpreted without assuming this or that hypothetical entity, there is no ground for assuming it. I have myself found this a most fruitful principle in logical analysis.[3]

In other words, choose the simpler, more credible explanation wherever possible.

We all share the belief that scientific experimentation and research can answer questions about a wide range of natural and social phenomena: evolutionary development, hurricanes, disease, crime, poverty. It is true that repeated experiments in controlled situations can establish what seem to be solid relations suggesting cause and effect. But even scientists prefer to talk not about cause but about an extremely high probability that under controlled conditions one event will follow another.

In the social sciences cause-effect relations are especially susceptible to challenge. Human experiences can seldom be subjected to laboratory conditions. In addition, the complexity of the social environment makes it difficult, even impossible, to extract one cause from among the many that influence human behavior.

## False Analogy

Problems in the use of analogy have been treated in Chapter 5. Many analogies are merely descriptive — like the analogy used by Malcolm X — and offer no proof of the connection between the two things being compared.

Historians are fond of using analogical arguments to demonstrate that particular circumstances prevailing in the past are being reproduced in the present. They therefore feel safe in predicting that the present

---

[3] *Dictionary of Mind, Matter and Morals* (New York: Philosophical Library, 1952), p. 166.

course of history will follow that of the past. British historian Arnold Toynbee argues by analogy that humans' tenure on earth may be limited.

> On the evidence of the past history of life on this planet, even the extinction of the human race is not entirely unlikely. After all, the reign of man on the Earth, if we are right in thinking that man established his present ascendancy in the middle paleolithic age, is so far only about 100,000 years old, and what is that compared to the 500 million or 900 million years during which life has been in existence on the surface of this planet? In the past, other forms of life have enjoyed reigns which have lasted for almost inconceivably longer periods — and which yet at last have come to an end.[4]

Toynbee finds similarities between the limited reigns of other animal species and the possible disappearance of the human race. For this analogy, however, we need to ask whether the conditions of the past, so far as we know them, at all resemble the conditions under which human existence on earth might be terminated. Is the fact that human beings are also members of the animal kingdom sufficient support for this comparison?

## Ad Hominem

The Latin term *ad hominem* translates as "against the man" and refers to an attack on the person rather than on the argument or the issue. The assumption in such a fallacy is that if the speaker proves to be unacceptable in some way, his or her statements must also be judged unacceptable. Attacking the author of the statement is a strategy of diversion that prevents the reader from giving attention where it is due — to the issue under discussion.

You might hear someone complain, "What can the priest tell us about marriage? He's never been married himself." This accusation ignores the validity of the advice the priest might offer. In the same way an overweight patient might reject the advice on diet by an overweight physician. In politics it is not uncommon for antagonists to attack each other for personal characteristics that may not be relevant to the tasks they will be elected to perform. They may be credited with infidelity to their partners, homosexuality, atheism, flamboyant social life. Even if certain accusations should be proved true, voters should not ignore the substance of what politicians do and say in their public offices.

---

[4] *Civilization on Trial* (New York: Oxford University Press, 1948), pp. 162–63.

This confusion of private life with professional record also exists in literature and the other arts. According to their biographers, the American writers Thomas Wolfe, Robert Frost, and William Saroyan — to name only a few — and numbers of film stars, including Charlie Chaplin, Joan Crawford, and Bing Crosby, made life miserable for those closest to them. Having read about their unpleasant personal characteristics, some people find it hard to separate the artist from his or her creation, although the personality and character of the artist are often irrelevant to the content of the work.

Accusations against the person do *not* constitute a fallacy if the characteristics under attack are relevant to the argument. If the politician is irresponsible and dishonest in the conduct of his or her personal life, we may be justified in thinking that the person will also behave irresponsibly and dishonestly in public office.

## False Dilemma

As the name tells us, the false dilemma, sometimes called the black-white fallacy, poses an either/or situation. The arguer suggests that only two alternatives exist, although there may be other explanations of or solutions to the problem under discussion. The false dilemma reflects the simplification of a complex problem. Sometimes it is offered out of ignorance or laziness, sometimes to divert attention from the real explanation or solution that the arguer rejects for doubtful reasons.

You can encounter the black-white situation in your personal life. "At the University of Georgia," says one writer, "the measure of a man was football. You either played it or worshiped those who did, and there was no middle ground."[5] Clearly this dilemma — "Love football or you're not a man" — ignores other measures of manhood.

Politics and government offer a wealth of examples. In an interview with the *New York Times* in 1975, the Shah of Iran was asked why he could not introduce into his authoritarian regime greater freedom for his subjects. His reply was, "What's wrong with authority? Is anarchy better?" Apparently he considered that only two paths were open to him — authoritarianism or anarchy. Of course, democracy was also an option, which, perhaps fatally, he declined to consider.

In this country some advocates of unilateral nuclear disarmament by the United States assume that only two alternatives exist as an end to the nuclear arms race — unilateral disarmament or nuclear war. Other possi-

---

[5] Phil Gailey, "A Nonsports Fan," *New York Times Magazine*, December 18, 1983, Sec. VI, p. 96.

bilities, however, may exist, at least one of which is the preservation of the status quo between the superpowers. In this argument the stakes are so high that the advocate needs to reassure the audience that he or she has examined the largest number of possible outcomes before proposing a solution.

## Slippery Slope

If an arguer predicts that taking a first step will lead inevitably to a second, usually undesirable step, he or she must provide evidence that this will happen. Otherwise, the arguer is guilty of a slippery slope fallacy.

Asked by an inquiring photographer on the street how he felt about censorship of a pornographic magazine, a man replied, "I don't think any publication should be banned. It's a slippery slope when you start making decision on what people should be permitted to read. . . . It's a dangerous precedent." Perhaps. But if questioned further, the man should offer evidence that a ban on some things leads inevitably to a ban on everything.

Predictions based on the danger inherent in taking the first step are commonplace:

Stationing military advisers in El Salvador will lead to another Vietnam.

Legalization of abortion will lead to murder of the old and the physically and mentally handicapped.

The Connecticut law allowing sixteen-year-olds and their parents to divorce each other will mean the death of the family.

If we ban handguns, we will end up banning rifles and other hunting weapons.

Distinguishing between probable and improbable predictions — that is, recognizing the slippery slope fallacy — poses special problems because only future developments can verify or refute predictions. For example, in 1941 the imposition of military conscription aroused some opponents to predict that the draft was a precursor of fascism in this country. Only after the war, when ten million draftees were demobilized, did it become clear that the draft had been an insufficient sign for a prediction of fascism. In this case the prediction of fascism might have been avoided if closer attention had been paid to other influences pointing to the strength of democracy.

Slippery slope predictions are simplistic. They ignore not only the dissimilarities between first and last steps but also the complexity of the developments in any long chain of events.

## Begging the Question

If the writer makes a statement that assumes that the very question being argued has already been proved, the writer is guilty of begging the question. In a letter to the editor of a college newspaper protesting the failure of the majority of students to meet the writing requirement because they had failed an exemption test, the writer said, "Not exempting all students who honestly qualify for exemption is an insult." But whether the students are honestly qualified is precisely the question that the exemption test was supposed to resolve. The writer has not proved that the students who failed the writing test were qualified for exemption. She has only made an assertion *as if* she had already proved it.

In an effort to raise standards of teaching, some politicians and educators have urged that "master teachers" be awarded higher salaries. Opponents have argued that such a proposal begs the question because it assumes that the term "master teachers" can be or has already been defined.

Circular reasoning is an extreme example of begging the question: "Women should not be permitted to join men's clubs because the clubs are for men only." The question to be resolved first, of course, is whether clubs for men only should continue to exist.

## Straw Man

This fallacy consists of an attack on a view similar to but not the same as the one your opponent holds. It is another familiar diversionary tactic.

One of the outstanding examples of the straw man fallacy occurred in the famous Checkers speech of then-Senator Richard Nixon. In 1952 during his vice-presidential campaign, Nixon was accused of having appropriated $18,000 in campaign funds for his personal use. At one point in the radio and television speech in which he defended his reputation, he said:

> One other thing I probably should tell you, because if I don't they will probably be saying this about me, too. We did get something, a gift, after the election.
>
> A man down in Texas heard Pat on the radio mention the fact that our two youngsters would like to have a dog, and, believe it or not, the day before we left on this campaign trip we got a message from Union Station in Baltimore saying they had a package for us. We went down to get it. You know what it was?
>
> It was a little cocker spaniel dog, in a crate that he had sent all the way

from Texas, black and white, spotted, and our little girl, Tricia, the six-year-old, named it Checkers.

And, you know, the kids, like all kids, loved the dog, and I just want to say this, right now, that regardless of what they say about it, we are going to keep it.[6]

Of course, Nixon knew that the issue was the alleged misappropriation of funds, not the ownership of the dog, which no one had asked him to return.

## Two Wrongs Make a Right

This is another example of the way in which attention may be diverted from the question at issue.

After a speech by President Jimmy Carter in March 1977 attacking the human rights record of the Soviet Union, Russian officials responded:

As for the present state of human rights in the United States, it is characterized by the following eloquent facts: millions of unemployed, racial discrimination, social inequality of women, infringement of citizens' personal freedom, the growth of crime and so on.[7]

The Russians made no attempt to deny the failure of *their* human rights record; instead they attacked by pointing out that the Americans are not blameless either.

## *Non Sequitur*

The Latin term *non sequitur*, which means "it does not follow," is another fallacy of irrelevance. An advertisement for a book, *Worlds in Collision*, whose theories about the origin of the earth and evolutionary development have been challenged by almost all reputable scientists, says:

Once rejected as "preposterous!" Critics called it an outrage! It aroused incredible antagonism in scientific and literary circles. Yet half a million copies were sold and for 27 years it remained an outstanding bestseller.

---

[6] Radio and television address of Senator Nixon from Los Angeles on September 23, 1952.

[7] *New York Times*, March 3, 1977, p. 1.

We know, of course, that the popularity of a book does not bestow scientific respectability. The number of sales, therefore, is irrelevant to proof of the book's theoretical soundness.

## Faulty Emotional Appeals

In some discussions of fallacies, appeals to the emotions of the audience are treated as illegitimate or "counterfeit proofs." All such appeals, however, are *not* illegitimate. As we saw in the chapter on support, appeals to the values and emotions of an audience are an appropriate form of persuasion. You can recognize fallacious appeals if (1) they are irrelevant to the argument or draw attention from the issues being argued and/or (2) they appear to conceal another purpose. Here we treat two of the most popular appeals — to pity and to fear.

Appeals to pity, compassion, and the natural willingness to help the unfortunate are particularly hard to resist. The requests for aid by most charitable organizations — for hungry children, victims of disaster, stray animals — offer examples of legitimate appeals. But these appeals to our sympathetic feelings should not divert us from considering other issues in a particular case. It would be wrong, for example, to allow a multiple murderer to escape punishment because he had experienced a wretched childhood. Likewise, if you are asked to contribute to a charitable cause, you should try to learn how many unfortunate people or animals are being helped and what percentage of the contribution will be allocated to maintaining the organization and its officers. In some cases the financial records are closed to public review, and only a small share of the contribution will reach the alleged beneficiaries.

Appeals to fear are likely to be even more effective. But they must be based on evidence that fear is an appropriate response to the issues and that it can move an audience toward a solution to the problem. (Fear can also have the adverse effect of preventing people from taking a necessary action.) Insurance companies, for example, make appeals to our fears of destitution for ourselves and our families as a result of injury, unemployment, sickness, and death. These appeals are justified if the possibilities of such destitution are real and if the insurance will provide for relief. It would also be legitimate to arouse fear of the consequences of drunk driving, provided, again, that the descriptions were accurate. On the other hand, it would be wrong to induce fear that fluoridation of public water supplies causes cancer without presenting sound evidence of the probability. It would also be wrong to instill a fear of school integration unless convincing proof were offered of undesirable social consequences.

An emotional response by itself is not always the soundest basis for making decisions. Your own experience has probably taught you that in the grip of a strong emotion like love or hate or anger you often overlook good reasons for making different and better choices. Like you, your readers want to be given the opportunity to consider all the available kinds of support for an argument.

## SAMPLE ANALYSIS

# ERA Could Swamp Courts: Women's Lib Amendment Not Simple Legal Formula

## JEFFREY ST. JOHN

"The legal position of woman," observed the late Supreme Court 1 Justice Felix Frankfurter, "cannot be stated in a simple formula, especially under a constitutional system, because her life cannot be expressed in a single simple relation." A procession of contemporary legal scholars made much of the same argument prior to congressional passage of the Women's Equal Rights Amendment now before various state legislatures for ratification.

Political pressures in this presidential year have given a militant mi- 2 nority of women powerful leverage for enactment. However, the respective state of the Union may come to regret ratification, if the two-thirds majority approves.

North Carolina Democratic Senator Sam Ervin has argued, along 3 with legal scholars from the University of Chicago, Yale, and Harvard, that while the amendment would have no effect upon discrimination, it would "nullify every existing federal and state law making any distinction whatever between men and women, no matter how reasonable the distinction may be, and rob Congress and the 50 states of the legislative power to enact any future laws making any distinction between men and women, no matter how reasonable the distinction may be."

In the wake of any ratification, moreover, a legal avalanche would 4 be unleashed that is likely to overwhelm the already overcrowded courts of the country.

---

Jeffrey St. John is a journalist and author of *Countdown to Chaos* (1968) about the violence that attended the Democratic National Convention in Chicago in 1968.

In reality, the aim of a minority of militant women's liberationists is 5 to bring about just such a state of legal and social anarchy. Like the disciples of Lenin in the early part of the century, Women's Lib seeks to use the law to destroy both existing law and social structure.

In abolishing a legal distinction between men and women, the way 6 is paved for sociological anarchy which militants can exploit for their own purposes of achieving political power.

The profound effect the Equal Rights Amendment would have on 7 marriage contracts, the home and children is precisely what Women's Lib wants: to sweep such established social units away as a prelude to pushing the country headlong into a life-style not unlike that now practiced in hippie communes.

Philosophically, at the root of the women's liberation movement is 8 an attempt to destroy the family structure as a means of bringing down the whole of society.

The form of "discrimination" upon which the Women's Lib movement bases much of its false, misleading, and dangerous campaign is less 9 in law than in custom and social attitudes, especially in the fields of career and employment.

Like the civil rights movement, Women's Lib is seeking, by using 10 the power of the state, to forbid individual discrimination as opposed to discrimination legally enforced.

This crucial distinction has not been made by most of Congress who 11 approved the Equal Rights Amendment for Women. Nor has it been made by the few state houses that have already ratified the amendment.

One can predict the same chaos will follow passage of this amend- 12 ment as that which followed the 1964 Civil Rights Act.

Legal scholars like the late dean of the Harvard Law School, Roscoe 13 Pound, have argued that the guarantee of "due process" in the Fifth Amendment and "equal protection" in the 14th Amendment provide the necessary legal instruments for reform now demanded by women's liberationists.

But like some elements of the civil rights movement, militant femi- 14 nists are not really interested in reform, but rather in revolution and destruction of the existing social fabric of society.

ANALYSIS

The article begins with a quotation from an impressive source and in the third and next to last paragraphs refers to other legal experts who support the author's negative view of the Equal Rights Amendment and the effect it will presumably have on legislation that would favor and protect women.

So far, so good. The rest of the article, however, falls into a number of logical traps that seriously weaken the argument. The obvious fallacies are *begging the question, slippery slope, false* or *questionable analogy,* and *ad hominem.* Other fallacies, less clearly defined, are also apparent.

*Begging the question.* The author often makes an allegation as if it had already been proved when the allegation is precisely the point of disagreement, or what remains to be proved. One form of *begging the question* is the use of loaded words. The author calls the campaign for the ERA "false, misleading, and dangerous," but the support for these emotionally charged terms is another unproved allegation — that advocates of the ERA want to overthrow the government. In other words, the question has been decided in advance of the argument.

*Slippery slope.* The author predicts that ratification of the ERA will lead to a "legal avalanche," "sociological anarchy," "a life-style not unlike that now practiced in hippie communes," and "chaos." But in none of these cases does he offer any proof that the first step — passage of the ERA — will lead to the consequences he foresees. Even his analogy with civil rights legislation, which led to an increase in law suits, is not persuasive; we have seen no evidence that such legislation led to "sociological anarchy" or "chaos."

*False or questionable analogy.* "Like the disciples of Lenin in the early part of the century, Women's Lib seeks to use the law to destroy both existing law and social structure." Again, there is no support for this comparison between the aims of the Bolsheviks who overthrew the Czarist regime in Russia in 1917 and those of the Women's Liberation movement of the 1970s. The advocates of the ERA are, in fact, working legally to change laws, a political activity in which every citizen has the right to engage.

*Ad hominem* (or in this case, *ad feminam*). Whenever we confront namecalling, we should ask whether the attacks are directed at the people who argue or at the issues themselves. In several places St. John uses the terms "a militant minority" and "militant women's liberationists" to suggest wrong-doing, but to a neutral reader, it's not clear that these terms can be used to condemn the motives of those who lobby for passage of the ERA. Rather they suggest an attack on the women for their militancy.

There are other contradictions and omissions. Notice how the author shifts ground — from attacking "a militant minority of women" to the whole women's liberation movement. Notice also that he condemns the civil rights movement because it attempted to change laws rather than the customs that supported discrimination. But the two things are not exclusive of each other; we can change laws *and* customs. And St. John ignores the obvious fact that laws can and do change customs. Most curious of all, although he quotes legal experts, the author provides not a single quotation from Women's Liberation literature to prove their subversive intentions.

## Exercise

Decide whether the reasoning in the following examples is faulty. Explain your answers.

1.  The presiding judge of a revolutionary tribunal, on being asked why people were being executed without trial: "Why should we put them on trial when we know that they're guilty?"
2.  Since good nutrition is essential to the health of its citizens, the government should punish people who eat junk food.
3.  A research study demonstrated that children who watch *M\*A\*S\*H* rather than *The Dukes of Hazzard* made higher grades in school. So *M\*A\*S\*H* must be more educational than *The Dukes of Hazzard*.
4.  The meteorologist was wrong in predicting the amount of rain for May. Obviously the meteorologist is unreliable.
5.  Women ought to be permitted to serve in combat. Why should men be the only ones to face death and danger?
6.  If Farrah Fawcett uses this shampoo, I'm confident that it will also make my hair look beautiful.
7.  People will gamble anyway, so why not legalize gambling in this state?
8.  Since so much money was spent on public education in the last decade while educational achievement declined, more money to improve education can't be the answer to reversing the decline.
9.  He's a columnist for the campus newspaper, so he must be a pretty good writer.
10. We tend to exaggerate the need for standard English. You don't need much standard English for most jobs in this country.
11. It's discriminatory to mandate that police officers must conform to a certain height and weight.
12. A doctor can consult books to make a diagnosis, so a medical student should be able to consult books when being tested.
13. Since this soft drink contains so many chemicals, it must be unsafe.
14. Core requirements should be eliminated. After all, students are paying for their education, so they should be able to earn a diploma by choosing the courses they want.
15. We should encourage a return to arranged marriages in this country since marriages based on romantic love haven't been very successful.
16. The popularity of the *Star Wars* trilogy proves that Americans have a mental age of ten years.
17. Supreme Court Justice Byron White was an All-American football player while at college, so how can you say that athletes are dumb?

18. Benjamin H. Sasway, a student at Humboldt State University in California, was indicted for failure to register for possible conscription. Barry Lynn, president of Draft Action, an antidraft group, said, "It is disgraceful that this Administration is embarking on an effort to fill the prisons with men of conscience and moral commitment."

19. You know that Jane Fonda's exercise salons must be a success. Look at the great shape she's in at age forty-five.

20. James A. Harris, former president of the National Education Association: "Twenty-three percent of schoolchildren are failing to graduate, and another large segment graduate as functional illiterates. If 23% of anything else failed — 23% of automobiles didn't run, 23% of the buildings fell down, 23% of stuffed ham spoiled — we'd look at the producer."

21. A professor at Rutgers University: "The arrest rate for women is rising three times as fast as that of men. Women, inflamed by the doctrines of feminism, are pursuing criminal careers with the same zeal as business and the professions."

22. Physical education should be required because physical activity is healthful.

23. George Meany, former president of the AFL-CIO, in 1968: "To these people who constantly say you have got to listen to these younger people, they have got something to say, I just don't buy that at all. They smoke more pot than we do and if the younger generation are the hundred thousand kids that lay around a field up in Woodstock, New York, I am not going to trust the destiny of the country to that group."

24. That candidate was poor as a child, so he will certainly be sympathetic to the poor if he's elected.

25. When the federal government sent troops into Little Rock, Arkansas, to enforce integration of the public school system, the governor of Arkansas attacked the action, saying that it was an act of brutal intervention as bad as Russia's sending troops into Hungary to squelch the Hungarians' rebellion. In both cases, the governor said, the rights of a freedom-loving, independent people were being violated.

26. Governor Jones was elected two years ago. Since that time constant examples of corruption and subversion have been unearthed. It is time to get rid of the man responsible for this kind of corrupt government.

27. Are we going to vote a pay increase for our teachers or are we going to allow our schools to deteriorate into substandard custodial institutions?

28. You see, the priests were right. After we threw those virgins into the volcano, it quit erupting.

29. The people of Rome lost their vitality and desire for freedom when their emperors decided that the way to keep them happy was to provide them with bread and circuses. What can we expect of our own country now that the government gives people free food and there is a constant round of entertainment provided by television?

30. From Mark Clifton, "The Dread Tomato Affliction" (proving that eating tomatoes is dangerous and even deadly): "Ninety-two point four percent of juvenile delinquents have eaten tomatoes. Fifty-seven point one percent

of the adult criminals in penitentiaries throughout the United States have eaten tomatoes. Eighty-four percent of all people killed in automobile accidents during the year have eaten tomatoes.''

31. A career criminal explaining his use of violence: ''So violence is wrong, on a fundamental level. I admit that. But on a day-to-day level it just happens that it's a tool of my trade and I use it — like an engineer uses a slide-rule, or a bus-driver the handbrake, or a dentist the drill.''

32. There's certainly some connection between the decline of public education and the fact that prayer has been banned in public schools.

PART TWO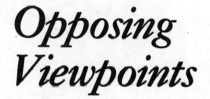

Opposing
Viewpoints

*T*HE FOLLOWING SECTION contains a variety of opposing viewpoints on six controversial questions. These questions generate conflict among experts and laypeople alike for two principal reasons. First, even when the facts are not in dispute, they may be interpreted differently by opposing sides. Example: Do the statistics prove that capital punishment is or is not a deterrent to crime? Second, and certainly more difficult to resolve, equally worthwhile values may be in conflict. Example: In dealing with harmful substances, should we decide in favor of the freedom of the individual to choose or the responsibility of the government to protect?

"Opposing Viewpoints" lends itself to classroom debates, both formal and informal, and to research papers that encourage you to investigate other sources and to argue for what you think are the most important issues.

In reading, analyzing, and preparing your own responses to the opposing viewpoints, you should ask the following questions about each controversy:

1. Are there two — or more — different points of view on the subject? Does each side make clear what it is trying to prove? Summarize their claims.

2. Do both sides share the same goals? If not, how are they different?

3. How important is definition of key terms? Do both sides agree on the definitions? If so, what are they? If not, how do they differ? Does definition become a significant issue in the controversy?

4. How important is factual and opinion evidence in support of the claims? Does the support fulfill the appropriate criteria? If not, what are its weaknesses? Is the support conflicting? Do the authorities — both the arguers and the experts they quote — have convincing credentials?

5. Do the arguers base any part of their arguments on needs and values that their readers are expected to share? What are they? Do the arguers provide examples of the ways these values function? Are these values implicit or explicit in the arguments? Is there a conflict of values? If so, which seem more important?

6. What warrants or assumptions underlie the claims? Are they implicit or explicit? Do the arguers examine them for the reader? Are the warrants acceptable? If not, point out their weaknesses.

7. What are the main issues? Is there a genuine debate — that is, does each side try to respond to arguments on the other side?

8. Do the arguers propose solutions to a problem? Are the advantages of their proposals clear? Are there obvious disadvantages to implementation of their solutions?

9. Does each argument follow a clear and orderly organization, one that lends itself to a good outline? If not, what are the weaknesses?

10. Does language play a part in the argument? Are there any examples of misuse of language — slanted or loaded words, clichés, slogans, euphemisms, or other short cuts?

12. Do the arguers show an awareness of audience? How would you describe the audience(s) for whom the various arguments are presented?

13. Do you think that one side won the argument? Explain your answer in detail.

# 1   *Affirmative Action*

The legal bases for affirmative action are the Civil Rights Act of 1964 and an executive order signed by President Johnson in 1965. Both of these measures prohibit discrimination by private employers and local governments that have contracts with the federal government, engage in interstate commerce, and employ more than fifteen persons. The law has since been extended to include affirmative action programs in colleges and universities for hiring of faculty and admission of students.

Affirmative action was designed to protect racial and ethnic minorities — and women — against discrimination in employment and schooling. In other words, business employers and schools were to base their selections on other criteria, such as merit or suitability for the job, rather than race, color, religion, sex, national origin, or handicap.

The law, however, has been carried out in ways that seem to suggest a change in its interpretation. Increasingly, quotas have been enforced, that is, employers and school officials are required to hire, or show that they have made an effort to hire, a specific percentage of blacks, Hispanics, native Americans, and women. Proponents argue that only the imposition of quotas can guarantee the fulfillment of affirmative action goals.

The controversy about affirmative action now revolves around this second interpretation. Almost everyone agrees — publicly, at least — that color and sex blindness should govern in hiring and school admissions. But sharp divisions arise over the implementation of quotas. Opponents charge that attention to the demands of the group rather than that of the individual violates an important democratic principle. And some white males have sued employers and universities, charging reverse discrimination.

# Views from Two Sides on How to Vault the Color Bar

**NEW YORK TIMES**

The election of a conservative President and the apparent disillu- 1
sionment of many voters with traditional modes of liberalism have recently brought unaccustomed attention to black conservatives. Academics and businessmen for the most part, they are dissenters from what
some call the "liberal orthodoxy" of established civil rights leaders. In
many respects, their views coincide with Ronald Reagan's and they are
likely to be heard from in coming months on issues such as tax credits for
private school tuition, a proposal that gained support last week from a
new study by Dr. James S. Coleman, the sociologist, who concluded that
private high schools provide a better education than public schools. To
explore the ideas of the black conservatives and how they contrast with
those of the traditional black leadership, Don Wycliff, an editor of The
Week in Review, interviewed separately Dr. Walter E. Williams, a professor of economics at George Mason University of Fairfax, Va., and a
leading exponent of black conservative views, and Benjamin L. Hooks,
the president of the National Association for the Advancement of Colored People. Excerpts from the interviews follow:

## WALTER WILLIAMS

Question. Black conservatives seem to focus on three issues in their 2
critique of the established black leadership: busing, affirmative action
and welfare. Wherein are these policies wrong or misguided?

Mr. Williams. Well, all of them aren't working. Take busing. As a 3
black person and an American, I'm for high-quality education. But it is
not clear to me that, to get high-quality education, black people have to
go out and capture a white kid for their children to sit beside. I'm not
suggesting I'm for segregated schools, but I'm saying there's considerable evidence that you can improve black education without busing.

The classic and most publicized example is Marva Collins in Chi- 4
cago. In the horrible slums of Chicago, her kids are reading one, two and
perhaps three years above grade level. They are doing math at or above
grade level. She didn't go out and capture white kids; there's no busing
involved. Perhaps more important, she does it for $60 a month (per

child). So it says two things: You can improve black education without busing and without huge financial resources.

Q. How about affirmative action and welfare?    5

A. Well, different people mean different things when they say af-   6 firmative action. Some mean equality of opportunity in jobs and some mean racial quotas. As a person who holds democratic principles, I find racial quotas offensive. I find that they don't deal with the issue and, furthermore, they cause race conflicts.

While doing a study, I came across a case of a black trucker in   7 Omaha, Neb., a fellow named Fred Ward, I believe. He made the lowest bid on an Air Force contract and he lost because he did not have I.C.C. authority to ship household effects across state lines. What is the classic civil rights leader's response to the fact that not many blacks have Federal contracts? Well, they push set-asides and quotas. Now a man like Fred Ward did not need a set-aside or quota; he needed the I.C.C. off his back. Set-asides and quotas do not deal with the monopoly problem caused by the Teamsters and the big trucking companies who maintain lawyers in Washington to keep other people out.

But in addition, there are many white guys like Fred Ward; they   8 can't get I.C.C. authority either. So you have a set-aside or a quota to insure that a guy like Fred Ward gets Federal contracts. Well, all these white guys are going to be pretty angry. So it enhances racial conflict where there otherwise would not be racial conflict. And the villain of the piece — the United States Government — goes unnoticed.

Q. Black conservatives seem to read the feelings and opinions of   9 black people differently than the established civil rights leadership. Assuming you are correct, why do you suppose they have misread?

A. Well, I don't know whether I have the correct reading or   10 whether they do. But there's been survey after survey that (shows) black people are against busing for the purpose of integration. A majority of black people are against racial quotas in employment and black people are strong on law and order. I think that, many times, these (black leaders) may be concerned with the white people's image of black people rather than what is necessary for black people.

Q. Do you believe that race has ceased to be a significant obstacle to   11 the advancement of black people?

A. It's less of an obstacle than it has been. Racial discrimination has   12 not come to an end in the United States, but if there is racial discrimination, many of the policies we have had make many, many black people worse off than they would be.

Q. What role do you see for the Reagan Administration in redirect-   13 ing Government action to help blacks or to cease hindering them?

A. One thing we have to recognize, in a time of people making   14 budget cuts, is that you're going to have to increase opportunities at the same time. Back in 1925, a poor, illiterate Italian in New York, if he had industry and ambition, would go out and buy a used car, write the word "taxi" on it and he was in business. For a poor person in New York now, if he's seeking a similar route to upward mobility, industry and ambition are not enough. He has to buy a $65,000 medallion, a license. Who does that discriminate against? It discriminates against people who don't have $65,000.

I would suggest that the Reagan Administration take a twofold ap- 15 proach. One that he has already suggested and I'd like to see him get a little bolder on, is deregulation. But when you're reducing the subsidies that people get, at the same time you need to make sure that there are opportunities for them to earn an honest living.

Q. Do you see any threat to the basic civil rights of blacks from the 16 Reagan Administration and its Congressional supporters?

A. If you're saying civil rights, referring to constitutional rights, I 17 don't see any near-term threat. What you do see is that, because of the relatively ineffective approaches taken to these problems, a lot of people are mad. The kind of strategy that traditional black leaders have developed is very dangerous. I think it's poor strategy to make the socio-economic welfare of so many black people depend on who happens to be President or on what happens to be the spending mood of the country. Because Presidents can change and spending moods can change.

Q. Is there any movement among black conservatives to bid actively 18 for support in the fashion of the N.A.A.C.P. or the Urban League?

A. No. There are some who have expressed interest in maybe setting 19 up groups or having meetings once a year or so to discuss some of these alternative solutions.

Q. Doesn't that then leave the field to people who you believe are 20 pursuing policies disadvantageous to blacks?

A. Well, I think people like Vernon Jordan and Benjamin Hooks 21 are well-intentioned, but they may misunderstand some things or they might not have explored some issues carefully enough. I in no way say that Vernon Jordan and Benjamin Hooks have to adopt my particular ideology. I just hope that they would not be like the dinosaur — I mean people who could not adapt to the changing environment and just pass away.


## BENJAMIN HOOKS

Question. Black conservatives focus on busing, affirmative action 22 and the welfare system in their critique of the current civil rights leadership. Are their criticisms valid and are those programs crucial?

Mr. Hooks. Black conservatives are basically a carbon copy of white 23
conservatives. They object to affirmative actions designed to overcome
preferences long accorded to white males; they object to busing, as one
effective remedy for rectifying a school system that has been deliberately
and historically segregated; they object, in some ways which are difficult
for me to understand, to Government spending to meet human needs
and to assist poor people.

They seem to favor a subminimum wage, which would have some 24
people working for a salary that would, upon receipt, put them below
the poverty level. They seem to favor disestablishment of the civil rights
enforcement machinery. The amazing thing is that they seem to say that
racial discrimination is a thing of the past. They do not understand or
appreciate or recognize the overwhelming evidence that racism continues.

Q. What of the charge that the welfare system, in particular, has 25
created a condition of permanent dependency on government?

A. The N.A.A.C.P. is not trying to perpetuate welfare or the wel- 26
fare state. Our emphasis is on trying to obtain jobs. But until the jobs are
obtained, no humane government should cut people off from some minimum standard of subsistence. If one talks about welfare dependency as
a way of life and says the present system has not worked — and I don't
concede that — then one would have to suppose that, had we not had
Social Security, unemployment insurance, old-age pensions, medical
care, we would be better off. Well, all one has to do is look at life expectancy today and look at the difference between a depression or recession
in 1980 and the one in 1930. It seems to me that, unless your philosophy
is the so-called cave man instinct, unless you go by the doctrine that right
is made by might and the weak ought not to survive, I don't understand
what they're talking about.

Q. How about the criticism that traditional civil rights leaders are 27
out of touch with the real views and feelings of black people?

A. I don't think it's any secret that most traditional black civil rights 28
leaders favored the re-election of Mr. Carter. That was the last public ref-
erendum in which black folk had a chance to express themselves. I think
the vote will show about 90 percent for Mr. Carter, perhaps a little more
or less than 5 percent for Mr. Reagan. And the black conservatives took
their position alongside Mr. Reagan. And if the people expressed themselves on Nov. 4, I don't know of anything that's happened since that
would make anybody believe that black people en masse have changed
their positions. It's an old ploy of the people who lead a small group to
claim that those who do represent some kind of establishment don't
have a consensus, don't have the people, don't have any following.

Q. Do you think it's reasonable to suggest that race is no longer an 29
obstacle to black advancement?

A. Well, I don't agree with that and I think all the evidence would 30 go the other way. I could take an hour citing the evidence: Only 2 percent of the doctors are black; 2 percent of the lawyers are black; less than 1 percent of the certified public accountants; the black median family income is only 57 percent of white family income; the unemployment rate is twice for the black community what it is for the white community; the percentages of blacks at or below the poverty level are much larger than for whites. I don't know of any evidence that does not point up that past pervasive racism has prevented blacks from achieving and being upwardly mobile.

Q. What do you hope for or fear from the Reagan Administration as 31 regards black people?

A. Well, I would hope Mr. Reagan could break the back of inflation 32 and create jobs. My worst fear is that the Administration's programs simply will not work. And if they don't, the country will be infinitely worse off at the end of a period of it not working than before. I think the Reagan Administration has, for some reason, chosen not to address the two major issues, inflation and joblessness, and has dealt with the third, balancing the budget, because of the sense, I guess, that it's something they feel they can do, while inflation is so pervasive, so widespread and there are so many systemic causes for it, that to deal with it demands a lot of ingenuity and imagination and it's not subject to simplistic answers.

Q. Do you see a danger of an erosion of basic civil rights, such as 33 with the Voting Rights Act, which comes up for renewal next year?

A. Well, yes, I think there is a serious danger. Senator (Orrin G.) 34 Hatch has introduced, I understand, a constitutional amendment to ban all forms of affirmative action. The fair housing law for which we fought so hard in the last Congress is sort of in limbo. There has been announced opposition to the Voting Rights Act by Senator (Strom) Thurmond and others. All of these are attacks on basic rights which we think this nation has to have. I'm not too sure where the black conservatives stand on those particular issues.

Q. Is it accidental or is it a reflection of the progress black people 35 have made that the two leading lights of black conservatism (Dr. Williams and Dr. Thomas Sowell of Stanford's Hoover Institution) are professional economists and that most black conservatives seem to be fairly affluent members of the middle class?

A. I don't know about that. All I do know is that, but for the very 36 programs they seem to be attacking, I doubt seriously if either of them would have positions in what we still call predominantly white institutions. The major question they raise, I guess, is that maybe we did need these programs, but we don't now. The only answer I could give is that I don't know of anything that has happened since we had these laws and opportunities and court suits and so forth, that would say to me that, if we were to dismantle all the laws that enabled us to come here, we could still maintain what we have and continue to move forward.

1981

# Why Blacks Need Affirmative Action

## JESSE JACKSON

Let me illustrate the point [this] way, using the familiar athletic example. "Runners to your mark, get set, go!" Two world-class distance runners begin the grueling human test of trying to run a sub-four-minute mile. Two minutes into the race, officials observe that one runner, falling far behind, still has running weights on his ankles. They stop the race, and hold both runners in their tracks. The weights are removed from the runner far behind, the officials re-fire the starting gun, and both runners continue from the points where they were when the race was stopped. Not surprisingly, the runner who ran the entire race without the ankle weights comes in with a sizable lead.

The fundamental moral question one could ask about that theoretical race must be, Would anyone call it fair? Again, not surprisingly, the answer would certainly be a simple and resounding No. If one could devise some means of compensating the second runner (for example, comparing the runners' times for the last two laps and projecting them over the entire race), a more accurate appraisal of each runner's ability and performance could be made. And if a reasonable means of compensation could be devised, no one would say that such compensation constituted "reverse discrimination" against the first runner or "preferential treatment" for the second. All would agree that compensation was fair and just.

Everyone can follow this example and see the "reasonableness" and morality of the solution because racial attitudes are not involved. Yet this is similar to the position in which blacks find themselves in the United States. We have been running the race with weights on our ankles — weights not of our own choosing. Weights of "no rights that a white must respect," weights of slavery, of past and present discrimination in jobs, in education, housing, and health care, and more.

---

Jesse Jackson is an ordained minister and founder of Operation Breadbasket and Operation PUSH. In 1984 he was also a candidate for president of the United States.

Some argue that there now are laws forbidding discrimination in 4 education, in public accommodations and employment, in politics, and in housing. But these laws only amount to removing the weights after years of disadvantage. Too often, when analyzing the race question, the analysts start at the end rather than at the beginning. To return to the track-meet example, if one saw only the last part of the race (without knowing about the first part), the compensation might seem unreasonable, immoral, discriminatory, or a form of preferential treatment. Affirmative action programs (in light of the history and experience of black people in the United States) are an extremely reasonable, even conservative, way of compensating us for past and present discrimination. According to a recent publication of the Equal Employment Opportunity Commission (*Black Experience and Black Expectations*, Melvin Humphrey), at the present rate of "progress" it will take forty-three years to end job discrimination — hardly a reasonable timetable.

If our goal is educational and economic equity and parity — and it 5 is — then we need affirmative action to catch up. We are behind as a result of discrimination and denial of opportunity. There is one white attorney for every 680 whites, but only one black attorney for every 4,000 blacks; one white physician for every 649 whites, but only one black physician for every 5,000 blacks; and one white dentist for every 1,900 whites, but only one black dentist for every 8,400 blacks. Less than 1 percent of all engineers — or of all practicing chemists — is black. Cruel and uncompassionate injustice created gaps like these. We need creative justice and compassion to help us close them.

Actually, in the U.S. context, "reverse discrimination" is illogical 6 and a contradiction in terms. Never in the history of mankind has a majority, with power, engaged in programs and written laws that discriminate against itself. The only thing whites are giving up because of affirmative action is unfair advantage — something that was unnecessary in the first place.

Blacks are not making progress at the expense of whites, as news ac- 7 counts make it seem. There are 49 percent more whites in medical school today and 64 percent more whites in law school than there were when affirmative action programs began some eight years ago.

In a recent column, William Raspberry raised an interesting ques- 8 tion. Commentating on the *Bakke* case, he asked, "What if, instead of setting aside 16 of 100 slots, we added 16 slots to the 100?" That, he suggested, would allow blacks to make progress and would not interfere with what whites already have. He then went on to point out that this, in fact, is exactly what has happened in law and medical schools. In 1968, the year before affirmative action programs began to get under way, 9,571 whites and 282 members of minority groups entered U.S. medical schools. In 1976, the figures were 14,213 and 1,400 respectively. Thus, under affirmative action, the number of "white places" actually rose by 49 percent: white access to medical training was not diminished, but substantially increased. The trend was even more marked in law schools. In 1969, the first year for which reliable figures are available, 2,933 minority-group members were enrolled; in 1976, the number was up to 8,484. But during the same period, law school enrollment for whites rose from 65,453 to 107,064 — an increase of 64 percent. In short, it is a myth that blacks are making progress at white expense.

# Dissenting from Liberal Orthodoxy

## THOMAS SOWELL

The grand assumption that body count proves discrimination proceeds as if people would be evenly distributed in the absence of deliberate barriers. There isn't a speck of evidence for this assumption, and there is a mountain of evidence against it. Even in activities wholly within each individual's control, people are not evenly distributed: The choices made as to what television programs to watch, what games to play, what songs to listen to, what candidates to vote for, all show the enormous impact of social, cultural, religious and other factors. One-fourth of the professional hockey players in the United States come from one state;[1] more than a quarter of all American Nobel prize winners are Jewish; more than half of all professional basketball stars are black. Can one state discriminate against the other forty-nine? Can Jews stop Gentiles from getting Nobel prizes, or blacks keep whites out of basketball? Obviously there are reasons of climate, tradition and interest that cause some groups' attention to be drawn strongly toward some activities, and that of other groups toward other activities. It need not even involve "ability." Some groups that have been tremendously successful in some activities have been utter failures in other activities requiring no more talent. Even such an economically successful urban group as American Jews had an unbroken string of financial disasters in farming, while immigrants from a peasant background succeeded, even though peasant

Thomas Sowell, an economist, is a senior fellow at the Hoover Institution and the author of several books on economics and race.

[1] Minnesota.

immigrants could not begin to match the Jews' performance in an urban setting. As a noted historian once said, "We do not live in the past, but the past in us."

It takes no imagination at all to see the heavy weight of the past  2
among both minorities and women. Even those minority and female individuals who are able to take advantage of higher educational opportunities do not specialize in the same fields as others, but disproportionately choose such fields as education and the humanities — where most people are poorly paid, regardless of sex or race. There are good historical explanations for such choices, but these are not necessarily good economic reasons. However, unless we are prepared to deny free choice to the supposed beneficiaries of "affirmative action," it is arbitrary social dogma to expect an even distribution of results.

Should we do nothing? That is the bogeyman of unbridled discrim-  3
ination that "affirmative action" spokesmen try to scare us with. But we were not doing "nothing" before quotas came in. The decade of the 1960s saw some of the strongest antidiscrimination laws passed anywhere, backed up by changing public opinion and by a new awareness and militancy among minorities and women. The dramatic improvement in the economic position of blacks was just one fruit of these developments. Despite the tendency of "affirmative action" proponents to conjure up images of discrimination in decades past, the question is, what existed just before the quotas, and what has happened since? That is the relevant question, and the answer shows a mountain laboring to bring forth a mouse — and often not succeeding. . . . The ratio of black income to white income has never been as high since mandatory quotas as it was just before such "goals and timetables."

Why is "affirmative action" so ineffective, despite all the furor it  4
stirs up? Simply because its shotgun statistical approach hits the just and the unjust alike. Just as the crime does not consist of demonstrable discrimination against someone, but of a failure to meet governmental preconceptions, so the punishment does not usually consist of penalties imposed at the end of some adjudicatory process but of having to go through the process itself. For example, the University of Michigan had to spend $350,000 just to collect statistics for "affirmative action." For all practical purposes, that is the same as being assessed a $350,000 fine without either a charge or proof of anything. Most "affirmative action" proceedings do not end up in proof of guilt or innocence, or in any penalty, though many end up settled by "peace with honor" in the form of elaborate plans with good intentions spelled out in statistical detail: 1.3 more black accountants per year, 2.7 more female chemists, etc. If King Solomon had operated under "affirmative action," he would have *promised* each woman 0.5 children, and gone back to business as usual.

# *Quotas Are Tough If All Are Minorities*

## WILCOMB E. WASHBURN

Minority preferences/quotas/affirmative action are emerging as 1 critical issues dividing Republicans and Democrats in this presidential election year. While the ambiguity surrounding such concepts allows for vague and evasive responses to questions concerning candidate commitment to "minority rights," there seems to be a clear division on the issue.

In the fight over minority rights, whether in the form of rigid quo- 2 tas or more flexible affirmative-action measures to enlarge the opportunities for minorities, one of the strongest arguments against minority preferences has been overlooked: There is no "majority" in the U.S. against which "minority" rights can be measured. All elements of the American population constitute minorities, the largest being the English at 14%, followed by the German at 13%, the black at 12%, the Irish at 8% and the Hispanic at 7%. Only the term "white" keeps the concept of a majority alive. By combining the wide variety of groups traditionally designated white, one masks the enormous inequalities among such minorities in the proportions represented in the professions, school admissions and the like.

By breaking down the stereotypical opposition of minority/major- 3 ity, opponents of quotas could more easily note the logical necessity — but moral absurdity — of reducing the numbers of higher-achieving minorities in order to bring up those of the lower-achieving minorities. If Jews, who are usually lumped into the category of whites, have a disproportionate achievement in many areas (which they do) not only against blacks, but against all other whites, then the implications of such inequality of results should be argued either in terms of its essential justice in a society in which all have equal opportunity but no guarantee of equal results, or in terms of the need to bring Jews (and Orientals) down so that more Poles and Italians, as well as blacks and Hispanics, can achieve equivalent rates of success.

It is now time for the candidates, as well as for those who question 4 them, to confront the basic definitional as well as philosophical implications of minority preferences.

---

Wilcomb E. Washburn is director of the Office of American Studies of the Smithsonian Institution.

# Affirmative Action:
# The Answer to Discrimination?

## AMERICAN ENTERPRISE INSTITUTE

PAUL SEABURY: . . . I would like to sharpen a couple of points be- 1
cause it takes an awfully long time, given the nature of the language that
is employed in these debates about affirmative action, before some of
the basic issues and principles become clear. As was previously brought
out, the phrase "affirmative action" itself well shows this confusion: it is
a form — kind of an Orwellian expression — and can mean many things
to many people. But you know to certain people affirmative action does
mean discrimination, and reverse discrimination. It seems to me that the
issue that the federal government, the universities, and perhaps the business and professional worlds have been struggling with as well, has been
what kind of equality we are talking about in American life.

Are we talking about equality of opportunity or about equality of 2
results? This is a very important issue, because the idea of equality of opportunity has always meant, as Mr. Posner stressed, a concept of merit,
by which an individual is judged according to his or her qualifications —
the skills, the inner qualities; and these don't always have to be those of
intelligence alone, as some simpleminded people believe. But equality
of results is a very different thing and here we begin to get into the numbers game. What is it that we are aiming toward? How do we want the
race to come out? These questions, of course, take us well into the depths
of the metaphysical view of the notion of equality.

We have an affirmative action program oriented toward equality of 3
results, and we can be sure that the victim is going to be equal opportunity because these things are very difficult to square. For example, when
a contract is made with HEW, as was done a couple of weeks ago at
Berkeley, the university commits itself to so-called goals, hiring goals.
Nobody, incidentally, was happy when they heard the outcome of this
agreement: the women were mad; the minorities were mad; the bureaucrats and university administrators were frustrated; and the faculty
thought that the university had capitulated to a satanic system of federal
public-utility regulation. In any event, the principle that was adopted
here is one based upon the notion of equality of results. Under that principle, one sets a timetable for certain things to come to pass.

---

The American Enterprise Institute is an organization for research and education on
public policy located in Washington, D.C.

And it has never been clear to me how anyone — especially a bu- 4
reaucrat — can accurately prophesy the outcome, if the processes are followed fairly. How can you tell how this particular ethnic or sexual category is going to come out if you are treating people fairly on an
individual basis?

Now, it isn't really the case that a goal is not a quota. I once looked 5
it up in the dictionary, and the word "quota" means a part of a whole.
And if one plays around the goals that are in the contracts, such as we
have at Berkeley, those goals are numerical and they are part of a whole;
therefore, they are quotas. I have invented two animals to illustrate this
point: one is called a "go-ta," which is a fast-moving form of discrimination, and the other is called a "qu-oal," which is a very slow form of
moving towards a goal.

I think we have got to face this issue because it is fundamental for 6
the future patterns not only of our university life but of the whole quality of our culture. Does the value of individual merit have any intrinsic
meaning in a culture which is dominated by collective group rights, and
group rights expressed in these fashions? . . .

PROFESSOR WINTER: Now let us . . . talk more specifically about 7
the constitutionality of preferential treatment. How does one determine
which groups may be given preferential treatment on the basis of ethnic
background, race, or sex, and how would we identify people as members of those particular groups — the constitutionally permissible ways,
that is?

PROFESSOR FISS: Well, I think the question that you pose is a diffi- 8
cult one. I would think that preferential treatment would be permissible
by a state university, for example, if the group occupies a certain social
position which could, just for shorthand purposes, be described as perpetual subordination. If you had a group that, in many respects, had occupied the lowest social rung for an extraordinarily long time, as the
blacks have, it would be permissible to afford them preferential treatment on the theory that it is permissible for a state agency or state university to try to elevate the position of that group. The pure case would
be blacks — a group that has occupied a position of subordination for
two centuries or more. Other groups could find themselves in roughly
analogous positions, and I would say they are also entitled to the same
kind of preferential treatment.

My point is this: Given the function of the equal protection clause, 9
which I view to be one of protecting subordinated classes from hostile
state action, it would be ironical to use that legal instrument to prevent a
state from taking action that is corrective and tries to elevate such a class.

PROFESSOR WINTER: What other groups would you include? 10

PROFESSOR FISS: I would include Chicanos, certainly the American 11

Indian — the list can go on; but I would certainly include the racial minorities. I think the most difficult issue would be posed by the women. I say "difficult" not because one couldn't make comparisons in terms of their social position in America. But part of the rationale for, say, a state university or a state agency giving preferential treatment to blacks, and for the court tolerating it, would be, I think, their political position. And I suspect that women, constituting something greater than a minority — indeed, having a much stronger political position — might not be regarded in the same light as, say, blacks or Chicanos or some other racial minority. They are a harder category for me. But as to racial minorities, the groups concerned in the *DeFunis* case, I would certainly say the state is entitled to give them preferential treatment.[1] . . .

PROFESSOR POSNER: . . . I have reservations about Professor Fiss's theory regarding racial minorities. As I read the background of the equal protection clause, it was designed to deal with racial discrimination and closely similar practices. Although the primary focus in the deliberations on the amendment was on the situation of the blacks, a question did arise about another unpopular group at the time: "What about the Chinese on the West Coast? Do we have to accord equal protection to them?" And the grudging agreement of the congressmen debating the proposed amendment was that you couldn't limit the equal protection clause to one racial group. So it seems to me that the clause protects anybody against racial discrimination. I don't think it's possible to limit the principle, as Professor Fiss suggests, to groups that have been historically oppressed or that we somehow view as oppressed minorities. I think that's too slippery, too amorphous. There's too much judgment involved in deciding, "What about Armenians? Are they an oppressed minority? If they're not an oppressed minority, does it mean that the state university of Washington can decide not to accept any Armenians because it wants to promote some other group?" And if, in a particular area, some racial minority has an electoral majority, does that mean that it is free to discriminate against people who are members of a majority group in the larger society but in the minority in that area? . . .

MR. RASPBERRY: . . . One of the advantages of the affirmative action program is that it says to despised minorities and discriminated-against minorities that, yes, it's worthwhile doing the hard work of training, beginning in grade school; that there is some payoff at the end. I think that, in itself, sends a message back down the line.

---

[1] The *DeFunis* case (1974) was predecessor to the *Bakke* case in which the Supreme Court refused to decide whether professional schools can constitutionally give preference to minorities in their admissions processes.

PROFESSOR SEABURY: . . . If one shifts the issues here from the uni- 14
versities to, say, a baseball team, it seems to me that the team manager
has a very high incentive to hire the best baseball players he can get. The
test here is winning, and it is very easy to see who wins, because at the
end, somebody wins in the World Series. You know, that's harder to do
when you are choosing between people from Harvard and people from
Berkeley, but still, one of the basic things that we are concerned about is
excellent education, and that means really hunting for the best people
for the best jobs.

One may say that that principle ought not to apply in the universi- 15
ties and colleges of lesser stature, although I think that's a very patronizing view to take of the matter. The question of excellence should apply
in all sectors and it should be answered on the basis of the innate qualifications of the people being considered in exactly the same way that a
baseball team operates.

MR. RASPBERRY: The difficulty with that is that it presupposes that 16
it's possible to rate a dozen applicants for a single job as one rates the
batting averages from .347 down to .314. As a matter of fact, it is simply
not possible in every instance to rate applicants for most jobs in that
manner.

# *Discrimination in Higher Education*

## HOWARD GLICKSTEIN

It would be nice if we could make up for the disadvantages that 1
some groups have suffered without any inconveniences to the advantaged group. I doubt whether this is possible, however. Undoubtedly,
there are many individuals who feel that they have been disadvantaged
because of the preferences we give to our veterans. But the sacrifices
made by veterans, as a group, justify according them preferences, as a
group. Similarly, our laws contain numerous examples of preferences for
Indians, including preferences in employment, but because of the cruelty this group has suffered such preferences have been allowed.

When a society has committed past injustices or when historically 2
disadvantaged groups exist side by side with more advantaged groups, it
simply is not possible to achieve equality and fairness by applying neu-

Howard Glickstein is director of the Center for Civil Rights at the University of No-
tre Dame. Earlier he was director of the U.S. Commission on Civil Rights.

tral principles. This has been recognized by India, whose laws accord many preferences to "scheduled castes." This has been recognized by Israel, where so-called "colored Jews" receive preferred treatment. It is not pure fantasy, therefore, to believe that it is possible to "create color blindness out of color consciousness, and nondiscrimination out of preferential treatment."

Just a few months ago, the Court of Appeals for the Fifth Circuit 3 upheld a lower-court order which required the Alabama Department of Public Safety to hire one qualified black trooper or support person for each white so hired until approximately 25 percent of both the state troopers and support-personnel force was comprised of blacks. Judge Coleman's reasoning is equally applicable to the situation we are discussing.

> . . . the affirmative hiring relief instituted . . . [here] fails to transgress either the letter or the spirit of the Fourteenth Amendment. . . . No one is denied any right conferred by the Constitution. It is the collective interest, governmental as well as social, in effectively ending unconstitutional racial discrimination, that justifies temporary carefully circumscribed resort to racial criteria, whenever the chancellor determines that it represents the only rational, nonarbitrary means of eradicating past evils.
>
> By mandating the hiring of those who have been the object of discrimination, quota relief promptly operates to change the outward and visible signs of yesterday's racial distinctions and thus, to provide an impetus to the process of dismantling the barriers, psychological or otherwise, erected by past practices. It is a temporary remedy that seeks to spend itself as promptly as it can by creating a climate in which objective, neutral employment criteria can successfully operate to select public employees solely on the basis of job-related merit. For once an environment where merit can prevail exists, equality of access satisfies the demand of the Constitution. (*NAACP v. Allen*.)

In addition to our differences over what must be done to overcome 4 the effects of past discrimination, I imagine we differ on what constitutes "merit" and "competence." Many of those who oppose affirmative-action efforts argue that such efforts will upset systems that have been run strictly on the basis of merit and competence. They suggest that in the past the rule has been "may the best man (and I use the word intentionally) win" and that advocates of affirmative action are intent on destroying this principle.

Aside from the fact that in so many instances the only ones allowed 5 to demonstrate their "merit" were white males, I do not believe that even within that limited category merit and competence were generally the decisive factors. We paid lip-service to merit and competence, but so many hiring decisions are made on the basis of extraneous factors. If there were some foolproof litmus test for determining merit, perhaps I would be fearful of tampering with the system. But the rules have been so rubbery in the past that I become a bit suspicious when a new rigidity is demanded as women and minorities appear at the gates.

Nor, I suspect, do we agree on who is "competent" to be a teacher. 6 I have known all too many persons, as I am sure you have, with a string of degrees who did not have the vaguest idea of what he or she was doing in the classroom. The conventional badges of accomplishment in terms of certificates, diplomas, and degrees are not necessarily what we should be looking for to provide the best teachers for young Americans. Perhaps our efforts to insure that women and minorities have greater access to academic positions will force us to reevaluate our standards for determining competence.

# Discrimination, Color Blindness, and the Quota System

## SIDNEY HOOK

It is not hard to demonstrate the utter absurdity of the directives issued by the Office of Civil Rights of the Department of Health, Education, and Welfare. I shall use two simple instances. A few years ago, it was established that more than 80 percent of the captains of tugboats in the New York Harbor were Swedish. None were black. None were Jewish. And this in a community in which blacks and Jews outnumbered Swedes by more than a hundred to one. If one were to construe these figures along the lines laid down by the Office of Civil Rights of HEW, this would be presumptive proof of crass discrimination against Negroes and Jews. But it is nothing of the sort. Negroes and Jews, for complex reasons we need not here explore, have never been interested in navigating tugboats. They have not applied for the positions. They have therefore never been rejected.

The faculties of many Negro colleges are overwhelmingly black out 2 of all proportion to their numbers in the country, state, or even local community. It would be a grim jest therefore to tax them with discriminatory practices. Until recently, they have been pathetically eager to employ qualified white teachers, but they have been unable to attract them.

Sidney Hook, who is considered America's leading philosopher of pragmatism, is a prolific author and a senior research fellow at the Hoover Institution.

The fact that HEW makes a distinction between women and minor- 3
ities, judging sexual discrimination not by simple proportion of women
teachers and researchers in universities to their proportion in the general
population, but only to their proportion among *applicants*, shows that it
has a dim understanding of the relevant issue. There are obviously various occupational fields — military, mining, aeronautical, and so forth,
for which women have, until now, shown little inclination. Neither the
school nor the department can be faulted by the scarcity of female appli-
cations. But the main point is this: no matter how many applicants there
are for a post, whether they are male or female, the only relevant criterion is whether or not they are qualified. Only when there is antecedent
determination that the applicants, with respect to the job or post specifi-
cations are equally or even roughly equally qualified, and there is a
marked and continued disparity in the relative numbers employed, is
there legitimate ground for suspicion and inquiry.

The effect of the ultimata to universities to hire blacks and women 4
under threat of losing crucial financial support is to compel them to hire
*unqualified* Negroes and women, and to discriminate *against* qualified
nonblacks and men. This is just as much a manifestation of racism, even
if originally unintended, as the racism the original presidential directive
was designed to correct. Intelligent, self-respecting Negroes and women
would scorn such preferential treatment. The consequences of imposing
any criterion other than that of qualified talent on our educational establishments are sure to be disastrous on the quest for new knowledge and
truth as well as subversive of the democratic ethos. Its logic points to the
introduction of a quota system, of the notorious *numerus clausus* of repressive regimes of the past. If blacks are to be hired merely on the basis
of their color and women merely on the basis of their sex, because they
are *under*represented in the faculties of our universities, before long the
demand will be made that Jews or men should be fired or dismissed or
not hired as Jews or men, no matter how well qualified, because they are
*over*represented in our faculties.

## Discussion Questions

1. Some writers contend that those who are hired as a result of affirmative
   action programs can never be sure that they have been chosen for merit
   rather than race or sex. Does this seem like a valid criticism of affirmative
   action programs and policies? Why or why not?
2. If quotas or goals are established, how should schools and employers decide
   which disadvantaged groups to favor? Jews and Asiatics, for example, have
   been the victims of severe discrimination in the past. Should they be ac-

corded the same preferential treatment as women, blacks, and Hispanics? Consider what Professors Winter, Fiss, and Posner (in the AEI Roundtable) have to say about this. With whom do you agree? Why?

3. Affirmative action has been interpreted by many people as a means of guaranteeing equal opportunity, by others as a means of guaranteeing equal results. Define these two positions and examine the arguments for them presented by Walter Williams, Benjamin Hooks, Jesse Jackson, Thomas Sowell and Professor Seabury in the American Enterprise Institute Roundtable. What are the principal issues? What are the social implications of these differing interpretations? Which one do you support? Why?

4. If an affirmative action program exists on your campus, do some research to find out how it works and what kinds of results it has achieved. Evaluate the results. Explain why you think the program is or is not justified.

5. Choose one of the "debates" in this section — between Walter Williams and Benjamin Hooks or between Howard Glickstein and Sidney Hook — and decide whether one side is more convincing than the other. Consider the issues raised, whether each side is responsive to the other, the amount and quality of the support, the appeal to values, the validity of the warrants. Consider also any weaknesses in the reasoning. Rather than treat them all, consider two or three of these elements in depth.

# 2  *Animal Rights*

Advocates for the rights of animals object to several different kinds of human exploitation of animals — for food, clothing, research, and recreation (as in hunting and bullfighting). In this section we confine our discussion to the uses of animals for food and research.

Although organized concern for the rights of animals is at least 200 years old in the West, the movement has acquired new momentum, perhaps as a result of human rights movements, which have succeeded in raising people's consciousness about the rights of women, minorities, homosexuals, the handicapped, and others whose interests have often been ignored by those who are more powerful.

Ethical vegetarianism, based on the belief that the lives of animals are as sacred as those of human beings, is very old. Strict Hindus have practiced vegetarianism for 2,000 years. But it is relatively new in the West. Especially in the last quarter of a century the growth of factory farming of animals has induced numbers of people to stop eating meat.

Experimentation with animals for medical and other scientific research has proliferated dramatically with immeasurable benefits for human beings, above all in medicine — in the conquest of rabies, bacterial infection, sterile surgical techniques, syphilis, and organ transplants.

Less defensible experimentation has been performed by cosmetic companies.

The question is to what extent the welfare of human beings should take precedence over the rights of animals. The answer will rest on religious and philosophical grounds that define the relationship between human beings and their fellow creatures.

# Animal Liberation

## PETER SINGER

We are familiar with Black Liberation, Gay Liberation, and a variety 1 of other movements. With Women's Liberation some thought we had come to the end of the road. Discrimination on the basis of sex, it has been said, is the last form of discrimination that is universally accepted and practiced without pretense, even in those liberal circles which have long prided themselves on their freedom from racial discrimination. But one should always be wary of talking of "the last remaining form of discrimination." If we have learned anything from the liberation movements, we should have learned how difficult it is to be aware of the ways in which we discriminate until they are forcefully pointed out to us. A liberation movement demands an expansion of our moral horizons, so that practices that were previously regarded as natural and inevitable are now seen as intolerable.

*Animals, Men and Morals* is a manifesto for an Animal Liberation 2 movement. The contributors to the book may not all see the issue this way. They are a varied group. Philosophers, ranging from professors to graduate students, make up the largest contingent. There are five of them, including the three editors, and there is also an extract from the unjustly neglected German philosopher with an English name, Leonard Nelson, who died in 1927. There are essays by two novelist/critics, Brigid Brophy and Maureen Duffy, and another by Muriel the Lady Dowding, widow of Dowding of Battle of Britain fame and the founder of "Beauty Without Cruelty," a movement that campaigns against the use of animals for furs and cosmetics. The other pieces are by a psychologist, a botanist, a sociologist, and Ruth Harrison, who is probably best described as a professional campaigner for animal welfare.

Whether or not these people, as individuals, would all agree that 3

---

Peter Singer teaches philosophy at Monash University in Melbourne, Australia. This essay is a review of a book, *Animals, Men, and Morals*, edited by Stanley and Roslind Godlovitch and John Harris.

they are launching a liberation movement for animals, the book as a whole amounts to no less. It is a demand for a complete change in our attitudes to nonhumans. It is a demand that we cease to regard the exploitation of other species as natural and inevitable, and that, instead, we see it as a continuing moral outrage. Patrick Corbett, Professor of Philosophy at Sussex University, captures the spirit of the book in his closing words:

> . . . We require now to extend the great principles of liberty, equality and fraternity over the lives of animals. Let animal slavery join human slavery in the graveyard of the past.

The reader is likely to be skeptical. "Animal Liberation" sounds   4 more like a parody of liberation movements than a serious objective. The reader may think: We support the claims of blacks and women for equality because blacks and women really are equal to whites and males — equal in intelligence and in abilities, capacity for leadership, rationality, and so on. Humans and nonhumans obviously are not equal in these respects. Since justice demands only that we treat equals equally, unequal treatment of humans and nonhumans cannot be an injustice.

This is a tempting reply, but a dangerous one. It commits the non-   5 racist and non-sexist to a dogmatic belief that blacks and women really are just as intelligent, able, etc., as whites and males — and no more. Quite possibly this happens to be the case. Certainly attempts to prove that racial or sexual differences in these respects have a genetic origin have not been conclusive. But do we really want to stake our demand for equality on the assumption that there are no genetic differences of this kind between the different races or sexes? Surely the appropriate response to those who claim to have found evidence for such genetic differences is not to stick to the belief that there are no differences, whatever the evidence to the contrary; rather one should be clear that the claim to equality does not depend on IQ. Moral equality is distinct from factual equality. Otherwise it would be nonsense to talk of the equality of human beings, since humans, as individuals, obviously differ in intelligence and almost any ability one cares to name. If possessing greater intelligence does not entitle one human to exploit another, why should it entitle humans to exploit nonhumans?

Jeremy Bentham expressed the essential basis of equality in his fa-   6 mous formula: "Each to count for one and none for more than one." In other words, the interests of every being that has interests are to be taken into account and treated equally with the like interests of any other being. Other moral philosophers, before and after Bentham, have made the same point in different ways. Our concern for others must not depend on whether they possess certain characteristics, though just what concern involves may, of course, vary according to such characteristics.

Bentham, incidentally, was well aware that the logic of the demand 7
for racial equality did not stop at the equality of humans. He wrote:

> The day *may* come when the rest of the animal creation may acquire those
> rights which never could have been withholden from them but by the hand
> of tyranny. The French have already discovered that the blackness of the
> skin is no reason why a human being should be abandoned without redress
> to the caprice of a tormentor. It may one day come to be recognized that
> the number of the legs, the villosity of the skin, or the termination of the
> *os sacrum*, are reasons equally insufficient for abandoning a sensitive being
> to the same fate. What else is it that should trace the insuperable line? Is it
> the faculty of reason, or perhaps the faculty of discourse? But a full-grown
> horse or dog is beyond comparison a more rational, as well as a more con-
> versable animal, than an infant of a day, or a week, or even a month, old.
> But suppose they were otherwise, what would it avail? The question is not,
> Can they *reason*? nor Can they *talk*? but, Can they *suffer*?[1]

Surely Bentham was right. If a being suffers, there can be no moral justification for refusing to take that suffering into consideration, and, indeed, to count it equally with the like suffering (if rough comparisons
can be made) of any other being.

So the only question is: Do animals other than man suffer? Most 8
people agree unhesitatingly that animals like cats and dogs can and do
suffer, and this seems also to be assumed by those laws that prohibit
wanton cruelty to such animals. Personally, I have no doubt at all about
this and find it hard to take seriously the doubts that a few people apparently do have. The editors and contributors of *Animals, Men and Morals*
seem to feel the same way, for although the question is raised more than
once, doubts are quickly dismissed each time. Nevertheless, because this
is such a fundamental point, it is worth asking what grounds we have for
attributing suffering to other animals.

It is best to begin by asking what grounds any individual human has 9
for supposing that other humans feel pain. Since pain is a state of consciousness, a "mental event," it can never be directly observed. No observations, whether behavioral signs such as writhing or screaming or
physiological or neurological recordings, are observations of pain itself.
Pain is something one feels, and one can only infer that others are feeling
it from various external indications. The fact that only philosophers are
ever skeptical about whether other humans feel pain shows that we regard such inference as justifiable in the case of humans.

Is there any reason why the same inference should be unjustifiable 10
for other animals? Nearly all the external signs which lead us to infer
pain in other humans can be seen in other species, especially "higher"

---

[1] *The Principles of Morals and Legislation*, ch. XVII, sec. 1, footnote to paragraph 4.

animals such as mammals and birds. Behavioral signs — writhing, yelping, or other forms of calling, attempts to avoid the source of pain, and many others — are present. We know, too, that these animals are biologically similar in the relevant respects, having nervous systems like ours which can be observed to function as ours do.

So the grounds for inferring that these animals can feel pain are 11 nearly as good as the grounds for inferring other humans do. Only nearly, for there is one behavioral sign that humans have but nonhumans, with the exception of one or two specially raised chimpanzees, do not have. This, of course, is a developed language. As the quotation from Bentham indicates, this has long been regarded as an important distinction between man and other animals. Other animals may communicate with each other, but not in the way we do. Following Chomsky, many people now mark this distinction by saying that only humans communicate in a form that is governed by rules of syntax. (For the purposes of this argument, linguists allow those chimpanzees who have learned a syntactic sign language to rank as honorary humans.) Nevertheless, as Bentham pointed out, this distinction is not relevant to the question of how animals ought to be treated, unless it can be linked to the issue of whether animals suffer.

This link may be attempted in two ways. First, there is a hazy line of 12 philosophical thought, stemming perhaps from some doctrines associated with Wittgenstein, which maintains that we cannot meaningfully attribute states of consciousness to beings without language. I have not seen this argument made explicit in print, though I have come across it in conversation. The position seems to me very implausible, and I doubt that it would be held at all if it were not thought to be a consequence of a broader view of the significance of language. It may be that the use of a public, rule-governed language is a precondition of conceptual thought. It may even be, although personally I doubt it, that we cannot meaningfully speak of a creature having an intention unless that creature can use a language. But states like pain, surely, are more primitive than either of these, and seem to have nothing to do with language.

Indeed, as Jane Goodall points out in her study of chimpanzees, 13 when it comes to the expression of feelings and emotions, humans tend to fall back on non-linguistic modes of communication which are often found among apes, such as a cheering pat on the back, an exuberant embrace, a clasp of hands, and so on.[2] Michael Peters makes a similar point in his contribution to *Animals, Men and Morals* when he notes that the basic signals we use to convey pain, fear, sexual arousal, and so on are not

---

[2] Jane van Lawick-Goodall, *In the Shadow of Man* (Boston: Houghton Mifflin, 1971), p. 225.

specific to our species. So there seems to be no reason at all to believe that a creature without language cannot suffer.

The second, and more easily appreciated way of linking language 14 and the existence of pain is to say that the best evidence that we can have that another creature is in pain is when he tells us that he is. This is a distinct line of argument, for it is not being denied that a non-language-user conceivably could suffer, but only that we could know that he is suffering. Still, this line of argument seems to me to fail, and for reasons similar to those just given. "I am in pain" is not the best possible evidence that the speaker is in pain (he might be lying) and it is certainly not the only possible evidence. Behavioral signs and knowledge of the animal's biological similarity to ourselves together provide adequate evidence that animals do suffer. After all, we would not accept linguistic evidence if it contradicted the rest of the evidence. If a man was severely burned, and behaved as if he were in pain, writing, groaning, being very careful not to let his burned skin touch anything, and so on, but later said he had not been in pain at all, we would be more likely to conclude that he was lying or suffering from amnesia than that he had not been in pain.

Even if there were stronger grounds for refusing to attribute pain to 15 those who do not have a language, the consequences of this refusal might lead us to examine these grounds unusually critically. Human infants, as well as some adults, are unable to use language. Are we to deny that a year-old infant can suffer? If not, how can language be crucial? Of course, most parents can understand the responses of even very young infants better than they understand the responses of other animals, and sometimes infant responses can be understood in the light of later development.

This, however, is just a fact about the relative knowledge we have of 16 our own species and other species, and most of this knowledge is simply derived from closer contact. Those who have studied the behavior of other animals soon learn to understand their responses at least as well as we understand those of an infant. (I am not referring to Jane Goodall's and other well-known studies of apes. Consider, for example, the degree of understanding achieved by Tinbergen from watching herring gulls.)[3] Just as we can understand infant human behavior in the light of adult human behavior, so we can understand the behavior of other species in the light of our own behavior (and sometimes we can understand our own behavior better in the light of the behavior of other species).

The grounds we have for believing that other mammals and birds 17

---

[3] N. Tinbergen, *The Herring Gull's World* (New York: Basic Books, 1961).

suffer are, then, closely analogous to the grounds we have for believing that other humans suffer. It remains to consider how far down the evolutionary scale this analogy holds. Obviously it becomes poorer when we get further away from man. To be more precise would require a detailed examination of all that we know about other forms of life. With fish, reptiles, and other vertebrates the analogy still seems strong, with molluscs like oysters it is much weaker. Insects are more difficult, and it may be that in our present state of knowledge we must be agnostic about whether they are capable of suffering.

If there is no moral justification for ignoring suffering when it occurs, and it does occur in other species, what are we to say of our attitudes toward these other species? Richard Ryder, one of the contributors to *Animals, Men and Morals*, uses the term "speciesism" to describe the belief that we are entitled to treat members of other species in a way in which it would be wrong to treat members of our own species. The term is not euphonious, but it neatly makes the analogy with racism. The non-racist would do well to bear the analogy in mind when he is inclined to defend human behavior toward nonhumans. "Shouldn't we worry about improving the lot of our own species before we concern ourselves with other species?" he may ask. If we substitute "race" for "species" we shall see that the question is better not asked. "Is a vegetarian diet nutritionally adequate?" resembles the slave-owner's claim that he and the whole economy of the South would be ruined without slave labor. There is even a parallel with skeptical doubts about whether animals suffer, for some defenders of slavery professed to doubt whether blacks really suffer in the way whites do.

I do not want to give the impression, however, that the case for Animal Liberation is based on the analogy with racism and no more. On the contrary, *Animals, Men and Morals* describes the various ways in which humans exploit nonhumans, and several contributors consider the defenses that have been offered, including the defense of meat-eating mentioned in the last paragraph. Sometimes the rebuttals are scornfully dismissive, rather than carefully designed to convince the detached critic. This may be a fault, but it is a fault that is inevitable, given the kind of book this is. The issue is not one on which one can remain detached. As the editors state in their Introduction:

> Once the full force of moral assessment has been made explicit there can be no rational excuse left for killing animals, be they killed for food, science, or sheer personal indulgence. We have not assembled this book to provide the reader with yet another manual on how to make brutalities less brutal. Compromise, in the traditional sense of the term, is simple unthinking weakness when one considers the actual reasons for our crude relationships with the other animals.

18

19

The point is that on this issue there are few critics who are genuinely 20
detached. People who eat pieces of slaughtered nonhumans every day
find it hard to believe that they are doing wrong; and they also find it
hard to imagine what else they could eat. So for those who do not place
nonhumans beyond the pale of morality, there comes a stage when
further argument seems pointless, a stage at which one can only accuse
one's opponent of hypocrisy and reach for the sort of sociological account
of our practices and the way we defend them that is attempted by David
Wood in his contribution to this book. On the other hand, to those unconvinced by the arguments, and unable to accept that they are merely
rationalizing their dietary preferences and their fear of being thought peculiar, such sociological explanations can only seem insultingly arrogant.

The logic of speciesism is most apparent in the practice of experi- 21
menting on nonhumans in order to benefit humans. This is because the
issue is rarely obscured by allegations that nonhumans are so different
from humans that we cannot know anything about whether they suffer.
The defender of vivisection cannot use this argument because he needs
to stress the similarities between man and other animals in order to justify the usefulness to the former of experiments on the latter. The researcher who makes rats choose between starvation and electric shocks to
see if they develop ulcers (they do) does so because he knows that the rat
has a nervous system very similar to man's, and presumably feels an electric shock in a similar way.

Richard Ryder's restrained account of experiments on animals made 22
me angrier with my fellow men than anything else in this book. Ryder, a
clinical psychologist by profession, himself experimented on animals before he came to hold the view he puts forward in his essay. Experimenting on animals is now a large industry, both academic and commercial.
In 1969, more than 5 million experiments were performed in Britain, the
vast majority without anesthetic (though how many of these involved
pain is not known). There are no accurate U.S. figures, since there is no
federal law on the subject, and in many cases no state law either. Estimates vary from 20 million to 200 million. Ryder suggests that 80 million
may be the best guess. We tend to think that this is all for vital medical
research, but of course it is not. Huge numbers of animals are used in
university departments from Forestry to Psychology, and even more are
used for commercial purposes, to test whether cosmetics can cause skin
damage, or shampoos eye damage, or to test food additives or laxatives
or sleeping pills or anything else.

A standard test for foodstuffs is the "LD50." The object of this test 23
is to find the dosage level at which 50 percent of the test animals will die.
This means that nearly all of them will become very sick before finally

succumbing or surviving. When the substance is a harmless one, it may be necessary to force huge doses down the animals, until in some cases sheer volume or concentration causes death.

Ryder gives a selection of experiments, taken from recent scientific 24 journals. I will quote two, not for the sake of indulging in gory details, but in order to give an idea of what normal researchers think they may legitimately do to other species. The point is not that the individual researchers are cruel men, but that they are behaving in a way that is allowed by our speciesist attitudes. As Ryder points out, even if only 1 percent of the experiments involve severe pain, that is 50,000 experiments in Britain each year, or nearly 150 every day (and about fifteen times as many in the United States, if Ryder's guess is right). Here then are two experiments:

O. S. Ray and R. J. Barrett of Pittsburg gave electric shocks to the feet of 1,042 mice. They then caused convulsions by giving more intense shocks through cup-shaped electrodes applied to the animals' eyes or through pressure spring clips attached to their ears. Unfortunately some of the mice who "successfully completed Day One training were found sick or dead prior to testing on Day Two." [*Journal of Comparative and Physiological Psychology*, vol. 67, 1969, pp. 110–116]

At the National Institute for Medical Research, Mill Hill, London, W. Feldberg and S. L. Sherwood injected chemicals into the brains of cats — "with a number of widely different substances, recurrent patterns of reaction were obtained. Retching, vomiting, defaecation, increased salivation and greatly accelerated respiration leading to panting were common features." . . .

The injection into the brain of a large dose of Tubocuraine caused the cat to jump "from the table to the floor and then straight into its cage, where it started calling more and more noisily whilst moving about restlessly and jerkily . . . finally the cat fell with legs and neck flexed, jerking in rapid clonic movements, the condition being that of a major [epileptic] convulsion . . . within a few seconds the cat got up, ran for a few yards at high speed and fell in another fit. The whole process was repeated several times within the next ten minutes, during which the cat lost faeces and foamed at the mouth."

The animal finally died thirty-five minutes after the brain injection. [*Journal of Physiology*, vol. 123, 1954, pp. 148–167]

There is nothing secret about these experiments. One has only to 25 open any recent volume of a learned journal, such as the *Journal of Comparative and Physiological Psychology*, to find full descriptions of experiments of this sort, together with the results obtained — results that are frequently trivial and obvious. The experiments are often supported by public funds.

It is a significant indication of the level of acceptability of these 26
practices that, although these experiments are taking place at this moment on university campuses throughout the country, there has so far as
I know, not been the slightest protest from the student movement. Students have been rightly concerned that their universities should not discriminate on grounds of race or sex, and that they should not serve the
purposes of the military or big business. Speciesism continues undisturbed, and many students participate in it. There may be a few qualms
at first, but since everyone regards it as normal, and it may even be a required part of a course, the student soon becomes hardened and, dis-
missing his earlier feelings as "mere sentiment," comes to regard animals as statistics rather than sentient beings with interests that warrant
consideration.

Argument about vivisection has often missed the point because it 27
has been put in absolutist terms: Would the abolitionist be prepared to
let thousands die if they could be saved by experimenting on a single animal? The way to reply to this purely hypothetical question is to pose another: Would the experimenter be prepared to experiment on a human
orphan under six months old, if it were the only way to save many lives?
(I say "orphan" to avoid the complication of parental feelings, although
in doing so I am being overfair to the experimenter, since the nonhuman
subjects of experiments are not orphans.) A negative answer to this question indicates that the experimenter's readiness to use nonhumans is
simple discrimination, for adult apes, cats, mice, and other mammals are
more conscious of what is happening to them, more self-directing, and,
so far as we can tell, just as sensitive to pain as a human infant. There is
no characteristic that human infants possess that adult mammals do not
have to the same or a higher degree.

(It might be possible to hold that what makes it wrong to experi- 28
ment on a human infant is that the infant will in time develop into more
than the nonhuman, but one would then, to be consistent, have to oppose abortion, and perhaps contraception, too, for the fetus and the egg
and sperm have the same potential as the infant. Moreover, one would
still have no reason for experimenting on a nonhuman rather than a human with brain damage severe enough to make it impossible for him to
rise above infant level.)

The experimenter, then, shows a bias for his own species whenever 29
he carries out an experiment on a nonhuman for a purpose that he would
not think justified him in using a human being at an equal or lower level
of sentience, awareness, ability to be self-directing, etc. No one familiar
with the kind of results yielded by these experiments can have the slightest doubt that if this bias were eliminated the number of experiments
performed would be zero or very close to it.

* * *

If it is vivisection that shows the logic of speciesism most clearly, it is 30
the use of other species for food that is at the heart of our attitudes
toward them. Most of *Animals, Men and Morals* is an attack on meat-
eating — an attack which is based solely on concern for nonhumans,
without reference to arguments derived from considerations of ecology,
macrobiotics, health, or religion.

The idea that nonhumans are utilities, means to our ends, pervades 31
our thought. Even conservationists who are concerned about the slaughter of wild fowl but not about the vastly greater slaughter of chickens for
our tables are thinking in this way — they are worried about what we
would lose if there were less wildlife. Stanley Godlovitch, pursuing the
Marxist idea that our thinking is formed by the activities we undertake in
satisfying our needs, suggests that man's first classification of his environment was into Edibles and Inedibles. Most animals came into the first
category, and there they have remained.

Man may always have killed other species for food, but he has never 32
exploited them so ruthlessly as he does today. Farming has succumbed to
business methods, the objective being to get the highest possible ratio of
output (meat, eggs, milk) to input (fodder, labor costs, etc.). Ruth
Harrison's essay "On Factory Farming" gives an account of some aspects
of modern methods, and of the unsuccessful British campaign for effective controls, a campaign which was sparked off by her *Animal Machines*
(London: Stuart, 1964).

Her article is in no way a substitute for her earlier book. This is a 33
pity since, as she says, "Farm produce is still associated with mental pictures of animals browsing in the fields . . . of hens having a last forage
before going to roost. . . ." Yet neither in her article nor elsewhere in
*Animals, Men and Morals* is this false image replaced by a clear idea of
the nature and extent of factory farming. We learn of this only indirectly, when we hear of the code of reform proposed by an advisory committee set up by the British government.

Among the proposals, which the government refused to implement 34
on the grounds that they were too idealistic, were *"Any animal should at
least have room to turn around freely."*

Factory farm animals need liberation in the most literal sense. Veal 35
calves are kept in stalls five feet by two feet. They are usually slaughtered
when about four months old, and have been too big to turn in their stalls
for at least a month. Intensive beef herds, kept in stalls only proportionately larger for much longer periods, account for a growing percentage of
beef production. Sows are often similarly confined when pregnant,
which, because of artificial methods of increasing fertility, can be most of

the time. Animals confined in this way do not waste food by exercising, nor do they develop unpalatable muscle.

*"A dry bedded area should be provided for all stock."* Intensively 36 kept animals usually have to stand and sleep on slatted floors without straw, because this makes cleaning easier.

*"Palatable roughage must be readily available to all calves after one* 37 *week of age."* In order to produce the pale veal housewives are said to prefer, calves are fed on an all-liquid diet until slaughter, even though they are long past the age at which they would normally eat grass. They develop a craving for roughage, evidenced by attempts to gnaw wood from their stalls. (For the same reason, their diet is deficient in iron.)

*"Battery cages for poultry should be large enough for a bird to be* 38 *able to stretch one wing at a time."* Under current British practice, a cage for four or five laying hens has a floor area of twenty inches by eighteen inches, scarcely larger than a double page of the *New York Review of Books.* In this space, on a sloping wire floor (sloping so the eggs roll down, wire so the dung drops through) the birds live for a year or eighteen months while artificial lighting and temperature conditions combine with drugs in their food to squeeze the maximum number of eggs out of them. Table birds are also sometimes kept in cages. More often they are reared in sheds, no less crowded. Under these conditions all the birds' natural activities are frustrated, and they develop "vices" such as pecking each other to death. To prevent this, beaks are often cut off, and the sheds kept dark.

How many of those who support factory farming by buying its pro- 39 duce know anything about the way it is produced? How many have heard something about it, but are reluctant to check up for fear that it will make them uncomfortable? To non-speciesists, the typical consumer's mixture of ignorance, reluctance to find out the truth, and vague belief that nothing really bad could be allowed seems analogous to the attitudes of "decent Germans" to the death camps.

There are, of course, some defenders of factory farming. Their argu- 40 ments are considered, though again rather sketchily, by John Harris. Among the most common: "Since they have never known anything else, they don't suffer." This argument will not be put by anyone who knows anything about animal behavior, since he will know that not all behavior has to be learned. Chickens attempt to stretch wings, walk around, scratch, and even dustbathe or build a nest, even though they have never lived under conditions that allowed these activities. Calves can suffer from maternal deprivation no matter at what age they were taken from their mothers. "We need these intensive methods to provide protein for a growing population." As ecologists and famine relief organizations know, we can produce far more protein per acre if we grow the right vegetable crop, soy beans for instance, than if we use the land to grow crops to be converted into protein by animals who use nearly 90 percent of the protein themselves, even when unable to exericse.

There will be many readers of this book who will agree that factory farming involves an unjustifiable degree of exploitation of sentient creatures, and yet will want to say that there is nothing wrong with rearing animals for food, provided it is done "humanely." These people are saying, in effect, that although we should not cause animals to suffer, there is nothing wrong with killing them.

There are two possible replies to this view. One is to attempt to show that this combination of attitudes is absurd. Roslind Godlovitch takes this course in her essay, which is an examination of some common attitudes to animals. She argues that from the combination of "animal suffering is to be avoided" and "there is nothing wrong with killing animals" it follows that all animal life ought to be exterminated (since all sentient creatures will suffer to some degree at some point in their lives). Euthanasia is a contentious issue only because we place some value on living. If we did not, the least amount of suffering would justify it. Accordingly, if we deny that we have a duty to exterminate all animal life, we must concede that we are placing some value on animal life.

This argument seems to me valid, although one could still reply that the value of animal life is to be derived from the pleasures that life can have for them, so that, provided their lives have a balance of pleasure over pain, we are justified in rearing them. But this would imply that we ought to produce animals and let them live as pleasantly as possible, without suffering.

At this point, one can make the second of the two possible replies to the view that rearing and killing animals for food is all right so long as it is done humanely. This second reply is that so long as we think that a nonhuman may be killed simply so that a human can satisfy his taste for meat, we are still thinking of nonhumans as means rather than as ends in themselves. The factory farm is nothing more than the application of technology to this concept. Even traditional methods involve castration, the separation of mothers and their young, the breaking up of herds, branding or ear-punching, and of course transportation to the abattoirs and the final moments of terror when the animal smells blood and senses danger. If we were to try rearing animals so that they lived and died without suffering, we should find that to do so on anything like the scale of today's meat industry would be a sheer impossibility. Meat would become the prerogative of the rich.

I have been able to discuss only some of the contributions to this book, saying nothing about, for instance, the essays on killing for furs and for sport. Nor have I considered all the detailed questions that need to be asked once we start thinking about other species in the radically different way presented by this book. What, for instance, are we to do

41

42

43

44

45

about genuine conflicts of interest like rats biting slum children? I am not sure of the answer, but the essential point is just that we *do* see this as a conflict of interest, that we recognize that rats have interests too. Then we may begin to think about other ways of resolving the conflict — perhaps by leaving out rat baits that sterilize the rats instead of killing them.

I have not discussed such problems because they are side issues com- 46 pared with the exploitation of other species for food and for experimental purposes. On these central matters, I hope that I have said enough to show that this book, despite its flaws, is a challenge to every human to recognize his attitudes to nonhumans as a form of prejudice no less objectionable than racism or sexism. It is a challenge that demands not just a change of attitudes, but a change in our way of life, for it requires us to become vegetarians.

Can a purely moral demand of this kind succeed? The odds are cer- 47 tainly against it. The book holds out no inducements. It does not tell us that we will become healthier, or enjoy life more, if we cease exploiting animals. Animal Liberation will require greater altruism on the part of mankind than any other liberation movement, since animals are incapable of demanding it for themselves, or of protesting against their exploitation by votes, demonstrations, or bombs. Is man capable of such genuine altruism? Who knows? If this book does have a significant effect, however, it will be a vindication of all those who have believed that man has within himself the potential for more than cruelty and selfishness.

## *Animal Rights Versus Human Health*

### ALBERT ROSENFELD

Stray dogs and cats by the hundreds of thousands roam the streets of 1 our cities. Usually they wind up in animal shelters, where hard-pressed staffs must find ways to dispose of them. One legitimate disposal route has been the research laboratory. But in southern California — with its impressive collection of research centers — antivivisectionists and animal rights groups recently have been leaning hard on animal shelters, effectively cutting off much of the supply.

About 30 years ago Los Angeles voters soundly defeated a proposal 2 to prohibit the release of animals for laboratory use. But today, with new

Albert Rosenfeld is a professor of biology at the University of Texas, Galveston, and a journalist and author of books on scientific and biomedical topics.

proposals being submitted to city councils and county boards, the results could well be different. And the new proposals are much more sweeping. They would, for instance, create review boards for all animal experimentation, requiring researchers to justify in advance any experiment they were planning and to submit a detailed research protocol before even applying for a grant. Alarmed, a group of southern California investigators have organized a committee for animal research in medicine.

"Most scientists don't realize the danger." says Caltech neurobiologist John M. Allman, who uses monkeys to study the organization of the brain. "Such movements in the past — in this country, at least — have largely been the efforts of small, fragmented, and relatively ineffective groups. But this new movement is carefully orchestrated, well organized, and well financed. Moreover, this is not just a local issue. It is going on intensively at the national and even at the international level. We'd be foolish to underestimate these people. They have clout. And if they attain their goals, it will effectively kill a lot of important research."

To doubly ensure the protection of human experimental subjects, a number of restrictions and regulations that admittedly are burdensome have been adopted over recent years. They take a great deal of time and energy. They generate a considerable amount of extra paper work. They often slow research (indeed, make some projects impossible) and render it much more difficult and costly at a time when budgets are shrinking and inflation is making further inroads. While these procedures are accepted as the price of seeing that human subjects volunteer freely and with fully informed consent, are we willing to pay a similar price on behalf of animal subjects who can in no way either give or withhold consent?

It is easy to look at the history of animal experimentation and compile a catalog of horrors. Or, for that matter, to look around today and find research projects that might be hard to justify. But the day is long past when a researcher can take any animal and do anything he pleases to it with a total disregard for its welfare and comfort. "People don't realize," says Allman, "that we are already extensively reviewed. In my work I must follow the ethical codes laid down by the National Institutes of Health and the American Physiological Society, among others. And we might have a surprise visit at any time from the U.S. Department of Agriculture's inspectors. It's the USDA field veterinarians who do the enforcing. Believe me, these inspections are anything but routine, and these fellows have a great deal of power. Because their reports can adversely affect federal funding, their recommendations are, in reality, orders.

"More than that, we are all required to keep detailed reports on all our animal experiments. And if pain or surgery is involved, we must tell them what anesthetics we used and in what dosages, what postoperative pain relievers and care were given, and so on. These reports are filed annually with the USDA, and they keep tabs on what goes on all over the country."

For all these precautions, however, it is fair to say that millions of 7 animals — probably more rats and mice than any other species — are subjected to experiments that cause them pain, discomfort, and distress, sometimes lots of it over long periods of time. If you want to study the course of a disease with a view to figuring out its causes and possible therapies, there is no way that the animal to whom you give the disease is going to be happy about it. All new forms of medication or surgery are tried out on animals first. Every new substance that is released into the environment, or put on the market, is tested on animals.

In fact, some of the tests most objected to by animal advocates are 8 those required by the government. For instance, there is a figure called the LD-50 (short for "lethal dose for 50 percent") that manufacturers are required to determine for any new substance. In each such case, a great many animals are given a lot of the stuff to find out how much it takes to kill half of them — and the survivors aren't exactly in the pink.

The animal rights advocates, except for the more extreme and un- 9 compromising types, are not kooks or crackpots. They tend to be intelligent, compassionate individuals raising valid ethical questions, and they probably serve well as consciousness raisers. It is certainly their prerogative — or anyone's — to ask of a specific project: Is this research really necessary? (What's "really necessary" is of course not always obvious.)

But it's important that they not impose their solutions on society. It 10 would be tragic indeed — when medical science is on the verge of learning so much more that is essential to our health and welfare — if already regulation-burdened and budget-crunched researchers were further hampered.

In 1975, Australian philosopher Peter Singer wrote his influential 11 book called *Animal Liberation*, in which he accuses us all of "speciesism" — as reprehensible, to him, as racism or sexism. He freely describes the "pain and suffering" inflicted in the "tyranny of human over nonhuman animals" and sharply challenges our biblical license to exercise "dominion over the fish of the sea, and over the fowl of the air, and over every living thing that moveth upon the Earth."

Well, certainly we are guilty of speciesism. We do act as if we had 12 dominion over other living cratures. But domination also entails some custodial responsbility. And the questions continue to be raised: Do we have the right to abuse animals? To eat them? To hunt them for sport? To keep them imprisoned in zoos — or, for that matter, in our households? Especially to do experiments on these creatures who can't fight back? To send them into orbit, spin them on centrifuges, run them through mazes, give them cancer, perform experimental surgery?

Hardly any advance in either human or veterinary medicine — cure, 13
vaccine, operation, drug, therapy — has come about without experiments on animals. And it may be impossible to get the data we need to
determine the hazards of, say, radiation exposure or environmental pollutants without animal testing. I certainly sympathize with the demand
that we look for ways to get the information we want without using animals. Most investigators are delighted when they can get their data by
means of tissue cultures or computer simulations. But as we look for alternative ways to get information, do we meanwhile just do without?

I wonder about those purists who seek to halt all animal experimen- 14
tation on moral grounds: Do they also refuse, for themselves and others,
to accept any remedy — or information — that was gained through animal experimentation? And do they ask themselves if they have the right
to make such moral decisions on behalf of all the patients in cancer wards
and intensive care units and on behalf of all the victims of the maladies
that afflict our species? And what of the future generations that will be
so afflicted — but who might not have been — had the animal rightists
not intervened?

# *The Rights of Animals*

## BRIGID BROPHY

Were it announced tomorrow that anyone who fancied it might, 1
without risk of reprisals or recriminations, stand at a fourth-storey window, dangle out of it a length of string with a meal (labelled ''Free'') on
the end, wait till a chance passer-by took a bite and then, having entan-
gled his cheek or gullet on a hook hidden in the food, haul him up to the
fourth floor and there batter him to death with a knobkerry, I do not
think there would be many takers.

Most sane adults would, I imagine, sicken at the mere thought. Yet 2
sane adults do the equivalent to fish every day: not in panic, sexual jealousy, ideological frenzy or even greed — many of our freshwater fish are
virtually inedible, and not one of them constitutes a threat to the life,
love or ideology of a human on the bank — but for amusement. Civilisa-
tion is not outraged at their behaviour. On the contrary: that a person's
hobby is fishing is often read as a guarantee of his sterling and innocent
character.

The relationship of *homo sapiens* to the other animals is one of un- 3

---

Brigid Brophy is a British novelist, literary critic, and essayist on moral and political
topics.

remitting exploitation. We employ their work; we eat and wear them. We exploit them to serve our superstitions: whereas we used to sacrifice them to our gods and tear out their entrails in order to foresee the future, we now sacrifice them to Science and experiment on their entrails in the hope — or on the mere off chance — that we might thereby see a little more clearly into the present. When we can think of no pretext for causing their death and no profit to turn it to, we often cause it nonetheless, wantonly, the only gain being a brief pleasure for ourselves, which is usually only marginally bigger than the pleasure we could have had without killing anything; we could quite well enjoy our marksmanship or crosscountry galloping without requiring a real dead wild animal to shew for it at the end.

It is rare for us to leave wild animals alive; when we do, we often do     4
not leave them wild. Some we put on display in a prison just large enough for them to survive, but not in any full sense to live, in. Others we trundle about the country in their prisons, pausing every now and then to put them on public exhibition performing, like clockwork, "tricks" we have "trained" into them. However, animals are not clockwork but instinctual beings. Circus "tricks" are spectacular or risible as the case may be precisely *because* they violate the animals' instinctual nature — which is precisely why they ought to violate both our moral and our aesthetic sense.

But where animals are concerned humanity seems to have switched     5
off its morals and aesthetics — indeed, its very imagination. Goodness knows those faculties function erratically enough in our dealings with one another. But at least we recognise their faultiness. We spend an increasing number of our cooler moments trying to forestall the moral and aesthetic breakdowns which are liable, in a crisis, to precipitate us into atrocities against each other. We have bitter demarcation disputes about where the rights of one man end and those of the next man begin, but most men now acknowledge that there are such things as the rights of the next man. Only in relation to the next animal can civilised humans persuade themselves that they have absolute and arbitrary rights — that they may do anything whatever that they can get away with.

The reader will have guessed in some detail by now what sort of person     6
he confronts in me: a sentimentalist; probably a killjoy; a person with no grasp on economic realities; a twee anthropomorphist, who attributes human feelings (and no doubt human names and clothes as well) to animals, and yet actually prefers animals to humans and would sooner succour a stray cat than an orphan child; a latter-day version of those folklore English spinsters who in the nineteenth century excited the ridicule of the natives by walking round Florence requesting them not to ill-treat their donkeys; and *par excellence*, of course, a crank.

Well. To take the last item first: if by "crank" you mean "abnormal," yes. My views are shared by only a smallish (but probably not so small as you think) part of the citizenry — as yet. Still, that proves nothing either way about the validity of our views. It is abnormal to be a lunatic convinced you are Napoleon, but equally (indeed, numerically considered, probably even more) abnormal to be a genius. The test of a view is its rationality, not the number of people who endorse it. It would have been cranky indeed in the ancient world to raise the question of the rights of slaves — so cranky that scarcely a voice went on record as doing so. To us it seems incredible that the Greek philosophers should have scanned so deep into right and wrong and yet never *noticed* the immorality of slavery. Perhaps three thousand years from now it will seem equally incredible that we do not notice the immorality of our oppression of animals. 7

Slavery was the ancient world's patch of moral and aesthetic insensitivity. Indeed, it was not until the eighteenth and nineteenth centuries of our own era that the human conscience was effectively and universally switched on in that respect. Even then, we went on with economic and social exploitations which stopped short of slavery only in constitutional status, and people were found to justify them. But by then the exploiters had at least been forced onto the defensive and felt obliged to produce the feeble arguments that had never even been called for in the ancient world. Perhaps it is a sign that our conscience is about to be switched on in relation to animals that some animal-exploiters are now seeking to justify themselves. When factory farmers tell us that animals kept in "intensive" (i.e. concentration) camps are being kindly spared the inclemency of a winter outdoors, and that calves do not mind being tethered for life on slats because they have never known anything else, an echo should start in our historical consciousness: do you remember how the childlike blackamoors were kindly spared the harsh responsibilities of freedom, how the skivvy didn't feel the hardship of scrubbing all day because she was used to it, how the poor didn't mind their slums because they had never known anything else? 8

The first of the factory farmers' arguments is, of course, an argument for ordinary farms to make better provision for animals in winter, not for ordinary farms to be replaced by torture chambers. As for the one about the animals' never having known anything else, I still shan't believe it valid but I shall accept that the factory farmers genuinely believe it themselves when they follow out its logic by using their profits to finance the repatriation of every circus and zoo animals that was caught in the wild, on the grounds that those *have* known something else. 9

Undismayed by being a crank, I will make you free gift of another stick to beat me with, by informing you that I am a vegetarian. Now, 10

237

surely, you have me. Not only am I a more extreme crank, a member of an even smaller minority, than you had realised; surely I *must*, now, be a killjoy. Yet which, in fact, kills more joy: the killjoy who would deprive you of your joy in eating steak, which is just one of the joys open to you, or the kill-animal who puts an end to all the animals' joys along with its life?

Beware, however (if we may now take up the first item in your Identikit portrait of me), how you call me a sentimentalist in this matter. I 11 may be less of one than you are. I won't kill an animal in order to eat it, but I am no respecter of dead bodies as such. If our chemists discovered (as I'm sure they quickly would were there a demand) how to give tenderness and hygiene to the body of an animal which had died of old age, I would willingly eat it; and in principle that goes for human animals, too. In practice I suspect I should choke on a rissole which I knew might contain bits of Great-Aunt Emily (whether through love for or repulsion from her I am not quite sure), and I admit I might have to leave rational cannibalism to future generations brought up without my irrational prejudice (which is equally irrational whether prompted by love or by repulsion for the old lady). But you were accusing me, weren't you, of sentimentality and ignorance of economic realities. Have you thought how much of the world's potential food supply *you* unrealistically let go waste because of your sentimental compunction about eating your fellow citizens after they have lived out their natural lives?

If we are going to rear and kill animals for our food, I think we have 12 a moral obligation to spare them pain and terror in both processes, simply because they are sentient. I can't *prove* they are sentient; but then I have no proof *you* are. Even though you are articulate, whereas an animal can only scream or struggle, I have no assurance that your "It hurts" expresses anything like the intolerable sensations I experience in pain. I know, however, that when I visit my dentist and say "It hurts," I am grateful that he gives me the benefit of the doubt.

I don't myself believe that, even when we fulfill our minimum obli- 13 gation not to cause pain, we have the right to kill animals. I know I would have no right to kill you, however painlessly, just because I liked your flavour, and I am not in a position to judge that your life is worth more to you than the animal's to it. If anything, you probably value yours less; unlike the animal, you are capable of acting on an impulse to suicide. Christian tradition would permit me to kill the animal but not you, on the grounds that you have, and it hasn't, an immortal soul. I am not a Christian and do not avail myself of this licence; but if I were, I should in elementary justice see the soul theory as all the more reason to let the animal live out the one mortal life it has.

The only genuine moral problem is where there is a direct clash be- 14 tween an animal's life and a human one. Our diet proposes no such clash, meat not being essential to a human life; I have sustained a very healthy one for ten years without. And in fact such clashes are much rarer in reality than in exam papers, where we are always being asked to rescue either our grandmother or a Rubens from a blazing house. . . .

The most genuine and painful clash is, of course, on the subject of 15 vivisection. To hold vivisection never justified is a hard belief. But so is its opposite. I believe it is never justified because I can see nothing (except our being able to get away with it) which lets us pick on animals that would not equally let us pick on idiot humans (who would be more useful) or, for the matter of that, on a few humans of any sort whom we might sacrifice for the good of the many. If we do permit vivisection, here if anywhere we are under the most stringent minimum obligations. The very least we must make sure of is that no experiment is ever duplicated, or careless, or done for mere teaching's sake or as a substitute for thinking. Knowing how often, in every other sphere, pseudowork proliferates in order to fill time and jobs, and how often activity substitutes for thought, and then reading the official statistics about vivisection, do you truly believe we *do* make sure? . . .

Our whole relation to animals is tinted by a fantasy — and a fal- 16 lacy — about our toughness. We feel obliged to demonstrate we can take it; in fact, it is the animals who take it. So shy are we of seeming sentimental that we often disguise our humane impulses under "realistic" arguments: foxhunting is snobbish: factory-farmed food doesn't taste so nice. But foxhunting would still be an atrocity if it were done by authenticated, pedigreed proletarians, and so would factory-farming even if a way were found of making its corpses tasty. So, incidentally, would slavery, even if it were proved a hundred times more economically realistic than freedom.

The saddest and silliest of the superstitions to which we sacrifice 17 animals is our belief that by killing them we ourselves somehow live more fully. We might live more fully by entering imaginatively into their lives. But shedding their blood makes us no more full-blooded. It is a mere myth, often connected with our myth about the *savoir vivre* and sexiness of the sunny south (which is how you managed to transform me into a frustrated British virgin in Florence). There is no law of nature which makes *savoir vivre* incompatible with "live and let live." The bullfighter who torments a bull to death and then castrates it of an ear has neither proved nor increased his own virility; he has merely demonstrated that he is a butcher with balletic tendencies.

Superstition and dread of sentimentality weight all our questions 18 against the animals. We *don't* scrutinise vivisection rigorously — we somehow think it would be soft of us to do so, which we apparently think a worse thing to be than cruel. When, in February of this year, the House of Lords voted against a Bill banning animal acts from circuses, it was pointed out that animal-trainers would lose their jobs. (Come to think of it, many human-trainers must have lost theirs when it was decided to ban gladiator acts from circuses.) No one pointed out how many unemployed acrobats and jugglers would *get* jobs to replace the animals. (I'm not, you see by the way, the sort of killjoy who wants to abolish the circus as such.) Similarly with the anthropomorphism argument, which works in both directions but is always wielded in one only. In the same House of Lords debate, Lady Summerskill, who had taken the humane side, was mocked by a noble lord on the grounds that were *she* shut up in a cage she would indeed suffer from mortification and the loss of her freedom, but an animal, not being human, wouldn't. Why did no one point out that a human, in such circumstances, dreadful as they are, would have every consolation of the human intellect and imagination, from reading books to analysing his circumstances and writing to the Home Secretary about them, whereas the animal suffers the raw terror of not comprehending what is being done to it?

In point of fact, I am the very opposite of an anthropomorphist. I 19 don't hold animals superior or even equal to humans. The whole case for behaving decently to animals rests on the fact that we are the superior species. We are the species uniquely capable of imagination, rationality and moral choice — and that is precisely why we are under the obligation to recognise and respect the rights of animals.

# Lab Animals' Use

## LYNN MORRISON AND GERALD S. LEVEY

While all of us have benefited from the ability of modern medicine 1 to prevent and treat many devastating diseases, there are critics who fail to realize that the improvement of medical care depends upon research involving animals and who insist that the use of animals in research is inhumane and unnecessary. They are mistaken.

Animals are of course used as substitutes for humans in research re- 2 garding the diagnosis, treatment and prevention of disease. Virtually

---

Lynn Morrison is staff associate of the Association of Professors of Medicine. Gerald S. Levey, M.D., chairman of the department of medicine of the University of Pittsburgh School of Medicine, is an association member.

every major advance in medical science has been based on knowledge gained through such research. A good case in point is the development of insulin for the treatment of diabetes. There are in America alone some 11 million diabetics, most of whom live normal lives with the aid of insulin injections. Previous treatment for diabetes consisted of a starvation diet to delay, however briefly, inevitable death. Equally good examples are the development of polio vaccine, improved treatment for heart attacks and high blood pressure, the development of transplant procedures, kidney dialysis and vaccines against numerous diseases.

Nonetheless, important medical questions remain unanswered. 3 Biomedical researchers are seeking methods to prevent, or improve the treatments for, a wide range of diseases including cancer, multiple sclerosis and heart disease. Animals are essential to this research. While such knowledge is often supplemented by information obtained through alternative methods, and while scientists avoid using animals whenever possible (there has been a 50 percent decline in their use in research since 1968), the functions of human organs such as the heart and brain cannot be simulated in a test tube or through use of a computer. Improvements in medical care will continue to depend — at least in part — on the use of animals.

Considerable publicity and misinformation has surrounded isolated 4 incidents of mistreatment of laboratory animals. Along with the general public, research scientists are appalled by such abuse whether in a scientific, industrial or sports environment.

Researchers themselves make sure that laboratory animals receive 5 proper care for humanitarian reasons as well as in the interest of scientific quality. Universities and medical schools have committees that inspect animal care facilities and actively oversee the use of animals in research. As for external controls, the Government has established standards for the care of laboratory animals. They must be housed in sufficiently large cages that are kept clean and adequately ventilated. Anesthesia must be used for potentially painful procedures. Animal care facilities are also inspected by the Animal and Plant Health Inspection Service of the Agriculture Department. Despite these assurances, public confusion regarding this issue persists and, unfortunately, has been exacerbated by the misguided efforts of certain well-intentioned animal rights groups.

However, there is an important distinction between these groups 6 and organizations that seek to limit — or totally eliminate — the use of animals in research. Such organizations act in a variety of ways. Many have raised large sums of money to lobby for legislation that would inhibit or ban research involving animals. Some have successfully advocated the repeal of local laws that permit laboratories to obtain unwanted animals from shelters — facilities that last year alone had to destroy about 13 million homeless dogs and cats. Some of the more radical organizations have orchestrated demonstrations or break-ins at research facilities to "liberate" animals. Others go so far as to suggest that the use of prisoners or elderly patients as research subjects would be preferable to the use of animals.

For obvious reasons, there is sharp disagreement between these organizations and research scientists. The biomedical community finds it hard to understand why there is opposition to using animals — even rats and mice — when such research might lead to vaccines or cures for diseases such as muscular dystrophy and leukemia, which strike thousands of children each year. Clearly, the scientific community shares the public's interest in assuring that laboratory animals are treated humanely. But it is important to recognize that the use of animals will remain essential in the search for medical knowledge that will save lives and relieve human suffering.

7

# Monkey Business
## TIMOTHY NOAH

"This is vivisection," proclaimed scores of posters that appeared overnight all over Washington to designate April 24 an International Day for Laboratory Animals. "Don't let anyone tell you differently." The posters were illustrated with a lurid photograph of a monkey trapped in an elaborate scaffold, its neck wedged in a narrow aperture and its arms extended, Christ-like, to the outer bars, where they were tightly bandaged. The photograph was a little deceptive. The scaffold was really a restraining chair whose "seat" was obscured by the head-on angle, and though the monkey appeared to be choking, more likely it was simply trying to jerk its head free, and was only seconds short of surrendering. This unmistakable image of suffering, however, was strong enough to lure two hundred demonstrators on the appointed day to a solemn funeral procession, led by a real hearse, that circled the Capitol, drove past the White House, and ended in Bethesda, Maryland, where an empty coffin was unloaded before the National Institute of Health [NIH].

1

In a world of malnutrition, yellow rain, and prison rape, it seems more than a little dilettantish to invoke "animal welfare," "animal rights," or, at the most self-parodistic level, "animal liberation." Despite such silly slogans, however, animals lovers can at least make a dimly

2

plausible case for some of their doctrine. Vegetarianism, for instance, may not rank up there with vaccinating ghetto schoolchildren, but it's a good many ethical notches up from, say, practicing tax law. Even when militancy on behalf of animals leads to socially embarrassing situations, such as the denunciation of an impoverished Eskimo whale hunter by a Scarsdale housewife, one might argue that shining through the wealthy woman's arrogance is the faint glimmering of an ethical principle. After all, didn't the justly admired Albert Schweitzer admonish us to consider a man ethical "only when life as such is sacred to him, that of plants and animals as that of his fellow man"? (Let's ignore for the moment less admirable exemplars like Caligula, who loved his horse so much that he made him a senator, and Hermann Goering, who kept a sign in his Berlin office which read, "He who tortures animals wounds the feelings of the German people.")

It's different with anti-vivisectionists. Overtly or implicitly, they re- 3 ject *in principle* the use of animals in experimentation. (Many will add the caveat, "experimentation that causes pain," but in practice that means just about everything except rats in mazes.) The issue is not human appetites; their concern is not for cattle at the slaughterhouse. Nor is it human vanity. Sealskin coats may be distasteful (though more from an economic point of view than a humanitarian one), but anti-vivisection has nothing to do with the skinning of seals. To be sure, most anti-vivisectionists object to these other forms of cruelty to animals. But by strict definition, anti-vivisection is opposition to animal suffering that may ease human suffering. As philosopher Peter Singer writes in *Animal Liberation*, a very silly 1975 tract that grew out of an article in the *New York Review of Books* and became the bible of the anti-vivisection movement, "An experiment cannot be justifiable unless the experiment is so important that the use of a retarded human being would also be justifiable." In other words, the ethical rules governing animal experimentation are the same thorny rules that govern human experimentation.

The three major anti-vivisection societies in America — the Na- 4 tional, American, and New England "AVs" — are seeking to prevent scientists from harming animals to help human beings. With a combined and partly overlapping membership of under 100,000, their numbers are small. But add to that perhaps as many as ten million members and supporters of various Humane Societies, SPCAs, and other animal welfare groups, which are showing an inclination to join the crusade against animal experimentation, and you have what a prudent futurologist might call an incipient national movement. The Humane Society of America, for instance, is currently seeking to prevent "pound seizure," or the use for medical experiments of animals turned over to local pounds. It recently had a victory in the city of Los Angeles, and is now seeking a statewide ban in California. A spokeswoman for the group argues that these animals are pets — though only a fraction of all pound animals are ever reclaimed by their owners — and denies that the Human Society is anti-vivisectionist. It may not be in theory, but clamping down on the supply of laboratory animals is an effective way to put anti-vivisection into practice. Another factor that may help anti-vivisection blossom into a nationwide movement is the odd tendency many of us have to care more deeply about cruelty to animals than about cruelty to human beings. This was illustrated vividly in 1973, when Representative Les Aspin, Democrat of Wisconsin, discovered that the Defense Department intended to use two hundred beagle puppies to test poisonous gases. To be sure, this was not an experiment whose benefit to mankind was immediately apparent. But when the volume of mail surpassed the number of letters Defense had received over the bombings of North Vietnam and Cambodia, true humanitarians had cause to wonder. Anti-vivisectionists, on the other hand, ought to have broken out the champagne. (They were much too surly to do that, of course; Singer gripes that the beagle protest demonstrated "a remarkable ignorance of the nature of quite standard experiments performed by the armed services, research establishments, universities, and commercial firms of many different kinds.") Anti-vivisection has broad appeal insofar as all of us hate the idea of cruelty to animals. But it is, on three levels, a deeply misanthropic movement.

The first level is the most familiar: good, old-fashioned hatred of a ⁵ particular individual. In this case, the individual is a biologist in Silver Spring, Maryland, named Edward Taub. Taub has become a national scapegoat for the anti-vivisection movement because of his alleged (and wholly unproven) mistreatment of seventeen monkeys that were seized from the Institute for Behavioral Research by Montgomery County police last September at the instigation of one of Taub's lab assistants, an undercover animal welfare advocate from People for the Ethical Treatment of Animals. (It was PETA that sponsored the "funeral procession" in April, and one of Taub's monkeys that illustrated the poster. The photograph also appeared in the *Washington Post* the day after the raid.) Taub has received surprisingly unkind treatment from a movement that calls itself humanitarian. "The man was guilty of cruelty on every single count he was charged with." seethes Cleveland Amory, the former *TV Guide* critic and columnist for *Saturday Review*, whose Fund for Animals contributed $20,000 to Taub's legal harassment. Not a very merciful point of view, especially considering that the state of Maryland found Taub *innocent* of all but six of the one hundred and thirteen counts brought against him. And those six counts really amount to one count brought six times, in an odd legal arrangement whereby six wronged monkeys were treated rather more like plaintiffs than like collective property. The charge each of the monkeys brought against their keeper was "unnecessarily failing to provide veterinary care" by an outside vet. For this heinous crime. Taub was fined $3,000.

Mild punishment, perhaps, if it had ended there. But with all the awkward publicity, the NIH was compelled to review Taub's $200,000 grant. Two months previous to the September raid, a routine site inspection by the Department of Agriculture had approved Taub's laboratory. Now, however, NIH's eyes were opened to Taub's negligence, and it suspended his grant. Most significant among the reasons, again, was Taub's failure to keep a veterinarian around the lab. The result was that a lot of sores on the monkey's limbs went unbandaged. Some explanation is required here. Taub's experiments involved severing the sensory nerves of monkeys (we'll get to the reason later). Once a limb was numbed, or "deafferented," the monkey had a habit of biting and scratching it. Since the monkey could feel no pain — a point anti-vivisectionists like to overlook — it tended to bite and scratch so much that bad sores appeared on its deafferented limb. Veterinarians questioned at Taub's trial voiced outrage over his failure to bandage the monkeys. But Taub argued — along with five other scientists, two of them also veterinarians who had had experience with deafferented monkeys — that bandaging only made things worse, because the monkeys tended then to bite and scratch at the *unbandaged* part. The court and NIH rejected Taub's argument. Then NIH, to whom the court assigned custody of the monkeys, proceeded to follow Taub's advice: in its own treatment of the deafferented limbs, it didn't bandage them either.

Two other reasons NIH cited for suspension of Taub's grant were poor ventilation and dirty animal cages. Dr. William Raub, Associate Director for Extramural Research and Training, says these were the "major issues." Taub dismisses the criticism of his ventilation system as a technical violation of NIH guidelines that even labs at NIH's research campus in Bethesda routinely violate. NIH guidelines say nothing about cages. Let's assume, however, that ventilation was poor and the cages were dirty. Would Taub routinely expose *himself* to an environment that was unclean enough to threaten health? For if the monkeys were in danger, surely anyone who handled them as much as Taub did might also be in danger. Remember also that a lab that was dirty enough to be unhygienic was not likely to go unnoticed by the inspector from the Department of Agriculture who had dropped by, unannounced, in July. Likelier than not, NIH was troubled by appearances, not by ethics. The best way to keep up appearances was to agree with the anti-vivisectionists that

Taub shouldn't be allowed to experiment on monkeys. So NIH suspended Taub's grant.

Consequently, Edward Taub can't at the moment experiment with 8 monkeys, as he has for the past twenty-five years. (He claims he has spent more time studying deafferented monkeys than anyone else alive.) Is the world any worse off? The answer is yes, and the reason brings us to the second level of misanthropy in anti-vivisection: to rule out animal suffering is to condone human suffering. Taub's experiments were directed at a phenomenon known as "learned nonuse." It is common among stroke victims, and also occurs sometimes to sufferers of spinal injuries. Learned nonuse is exactly what it sounds like: when life doesn't depend on using a limb deadened to sensation, a person (or monkey) may never make the effort to use it. Although muscles may function normally, the loss of sensation results in a kind of voluntary paralysis. Victims thus must relearn how to use the limbs. Taub says his research may be applicable to roughly one-sixth of all stroke victims, and has already been adapted into clinical technique at two hospitals in the United States. This is "inhumane" research that anti-vivisectionists have curtailed. They would also like to end the practice of poisoning laboratory animals to determine the lethality of potential drugs and cosmetics. They argue that lethality varies wildly from species to species, particularly in the oral LD 50 test, in which sixty to a hundred animals are fed enough of a substance to kill 50 percent of them. That's true. But the alternatives they suggest — tests on tissue cultures and computer models — are even more unreliable. Such methods are fine for use in preliminary tests, to weed out obviously toxic substances. But those substances not weeded out inevitably must be tested on whole systems. And, as Dr. Raub testified before the House Subcommittee on Science, Research, and Technology, in the study of "the integrated functions of an intact higher organism or the interaction of organ systems, animal experimentation is inevitable." The only alternative — releasing a drug without such testing — amounts to *human* experimentation.

In response to the anti-vivisectionist cry against animal experimentation, Representative Douglas Walgren, Democrat of Pennsylvania and chairman of the Science, Research, and Technology Subcommittee, has submitted the Humane Care and Development of Substitutes for Animals in Research Act. The main features of the bill are the addition of red tape in the processing of animal research grants, including the creation of an "animal care committee" on which one place is reserved for an animal welfare advocate, and the appropriation of $75 million over the next three years for development of alternative research methods and "improving animal care facilities." The first provision — red tape — is at best needless (the NIH and Department of Agriculture are already responsible for review and inspection of animal treatment) and at worst a blow to biological (and consequently medical) science. Anti-vivisection-ists like to bring up the example of Britain when they try to seem reasonable; licensing for animal experimentation is severely restricted there. British fondness for animals is one of that culture's most endearing qualities. Who among us wasn't touched when the Duke of Edinburgh recently complained that the Falklands conflict might lead to the death of many whales, who emit echoes that sound like Argentine submarines? Deference to the animal kingdom is also, some scientists say, the reason animal research in Britain lags behind in an otherwise impressive tradition of biological research. And as psychiatrist Jeri A. Sechzer has written in the British journal, *Social Science and Medicine,* whatever limits are placed on scientists in Britain would have much worse effect in the U.S., "where there are thousands of research centers and scientists" as compared to the relatively small scientific community in Britain. "Should the use of animals for research and teaching be curtailed as a result of hastily conceived legislation," Sechzer writes, "progress in gaining knowledge crucial to human and animal well being would be disrupted."

The problems inherent in this sort of regulation are illustrated in 10 the troubling issue of anesthesia. Everyone agrees that animals should not be exposed to unnecessary pain. But neither should scientists be hamstrung by the requirement to use anesthesia in every animal experiment that might cause pain. There are too many experiments — particularly those testing the effects of drugs — that would be impossible to conduct in any scientifically reliable way if this additional chemical variable were made mandatory. The Walgren bill requires "in any case involving surgery or other invasive procedures on animals, appropriate assurances of the proper use of tranquilizers." A subcommittee staffer says the word "proper" allows researchers to fudge when anesthesia might threaten results. But would an "animal care committee" interpret its mandate the same way?

The appropriation of $75 million for upgrading facilities and 11 searching for alternatives to animal experimentation is also a blow to the progress of human well-being. No one is anxious to guess where the money will come from, but in the current economic climate it isn't likely this nonsense would be paid for with a new addition to the budget. Rather, the Department of Health and Human Services, which is placed in charge of this program, would have to raid the people kitty. Thus we would witness the absurdity of cutting appropriations for Medicaid, Aid to Families with Dependent Children, and food stamps to pay for welfare for animals. And taking a large view, what benefits would such research provide? Given the likelihood that in 2025 none of us will feel any better about taking pills that haven't been tested on living animals, not much.

\* \* \*

The third and most ethereal level of misanthropy in the anti-vivisec-  12
tion movement is so intuitive that to launch on an extended attack of it
would be sophomoric. It's that, fundamentally, animal welfare makes
no distinction between the value of human life and that of animal life.
The ease with which anti-vivisectionists pass from one to the other in ethical arguments is downright scary. Peter Singer's equation between the
lot of a retarded person and that of a laboratory animal crystallizes the
point. "I ask you to recognize that your attitudes to members of other
species are a form of prejudice no less objectionable than prejudice about
a person's race or sex," writes Singer in introducing the bogeyman of
"speciesism," the animal kingdom's equivalent to ethnocentricity. Either this sort of talk makes you angry or it doesn't. An example helps.
Alex Pacheco, the undercover animal liberationist who freed Edward
Taub's monkeys, argues that the same premise upon which speciesism is
based "was used by the slave owners and by white males against blacks
and women. And it was used by the Nazis and by Hitler to justify the
murder of millions of Jews." Pacheco should ask a ghetto black or an
Auschwitz survivor how he likes the analogy. And he shouldn't be surprised when he gets an uncivil answer.

Anti-vivisection may never amount to much, although it has al-  13
ready caused Edward Taub some distress. But this is a case where a little
paranoia among liberals would be justified. The right has creationism,
the know-nothing doctrine that we aren't related to the apes; the left
should avoid creationism's mirror image of anti-vivisection, the know-
nothing doctrine that apes are members of the immediate family. Both
are anti-scientific ways of thinking that do more harm than good to the
prospect that the human race may someday cure its various, far more
worrisome ills.

## Discussion Questions

1. Choose one of the arguments — or part of an argument — in this section
   and evaluate its validity. Consider the soundness of the different kinds of
   support and the warrants. For example, is Brigid Brophy's analogy between
   slavery and the exploitation of animals or between eating animals and eating human beings effective? Does Timothy Noah answer all the objections
   that he raises against antivivisection?
2. If you disagree with Brigid Brophy, tell in what way her argument for ethical vegetarianism fails to convince you. Minimize attention to questions of
   taste and preference. Emphasize instead the principles that underlie your
   own claim.

3.  Some people believe that experimentation on animals unrelated to us, such as rats and rabbits, is acceptable but that experimentation on primates — rhesus monkeys and chimpanzees — is not. Or to put it in more extreme terms, is there a difference between experimentation on a chimpanzee and on a human being with very low intelligence? Is there some point on the evolutionary scale when it becomes immoral to continue experimentation? Explain your position as fully as possible.
4.  If you have ever seen animals slaughtered for food, either on a farm or in a stockyard, describe your reactions and tell whether the experience influenced your attitude toward meat eating.
5.  What values do the antivivisectionists, especially Peter Singer and Brigid Brophy appeal to? Might these same values be held by those on the other side? If so, which side seems to you to have the better right to make such appeals?

# 3   *Euthanasia*

Euthanasia means "good death" or "mercy killing," that is, causing the death of one who is so ill or disabled that continued existence will produce intolerable suffering. Euthanasia may be active or passive; in the first case, death is deliberately inflicted, sometimes by a relative; in the second case, life-support systems are withdrawn and the patient dies naturally.

Controversy surrounding the morality of euthanasia has been heightened enormously in recent years because of advances in medical technology that make it possible for human beings, both newborn and old, to be kept alive almost indefinitely, although severely impaired. As the life span lengthens, more and more people will reach an age when illness and disability create the possibility of euthanasia.

In those cases where the patient cannot make a rational choice, decisions to prolong or terminate life must be left to families, doctors, and, not infrequently, the courts. Even the definition of "life" is at issue. A person may be declared "brain dead" while vital functions persist.

On one side are those who regard the problems posed by euthanasia as essentially religious: life is sacred, no matter how severely disabled the patient may be, and no human being can arrogate to him- or herself a decision reserved for God. On the other side are those who insist that it is the quality of life that should influence the decision and that death may be preferable to a severely impaired life. Euthanasia thus becomes an act of charity.

One more problem has emerged: Will the widespread acceptance of euthanasia lead to a more careless attitude toward taking life in general and especially taking the lives of those in need of constant and lifelong attention?

# Death by Choice:
# Who Should Decide?

## DANIEL C. MAGUIRE

Who would dare arrogate to himself the decision to impose death 1
on a child or unconscious person who is not in a position to assent or dissent to the action? What right does any person have to make decisions
about life and death in any way that assumes absolute and ultimate authority over another human being? Could a doctor make such a decision?
It would seem that he could not. His medical skills are one thing, the
moral decision to end a life is another. How would a family feel who
learned that a doctor had reached an independent decision to terminate
their father's life?

Could the family make such a decision? It would seem not, for sev- 2
eral good reasons. There might be a conflict of interest arising from ava-
rice, spite, or impatience with the illness of the patient. And even if
these things were not present, the family might be emotionally trau-
matized when their pain of loss is complicated by the recollection of their
decision. Also, the family might constitute a split and therefore a hung
jury. Then what?

Could a court-appointed committee of impartial persons make the 3
decision? No, it would seem not. They would not only be impartial but
also uninformed about the personal realities of the patient. The decision
to terminate life requires a full and intimate knowledge of all the reality-
constituting circumstances of the case. Strangers would not have this.

The conclusion, therefore, would seem inescapable that there is no 4
moral way in which death could be imposed on a person who is incapable
of consent because of youth or irreversible loss of consciousness.

This objection contains so much truth that my reply to it will con- 5
tain much agreement as well as disagreement. To begin with, it should
be noted that we are discussing not the legality but the morality of terminating life without the consent of the patient. Terminating life by a deliberate act of commission in the kinds of cases here discussed is illegal in
this country. By an ongoing fiction of American law it would be classified as murder in the first degree. Terminating by calculated omission is
murky at best and perilous at worst under current law. Therefore, it can

---

Daniel Maguire is a professor of ethics at Marquette University and a former Roman
Catholic priest.

be presumed that any conclusion we reach here will probably be illegal. This is a morally relevant fact; it is not to be presumed morally decisive, however, since there may be good moral gounds to assume the risk of illegality. As we have stated, morality and legality are not identical.

With this said, then, let us face up to the objection. There are two parts to my response. First, holding the question of *who should decide* in abeyance for the moment, I would suggest that there are cases where, if that difficult question could be satisfactorily answered, it would seem to be a morally good option (among other morally good options) to terminate a life. In other words, there are cases where the termination of a life could be defended as a moral good if the proper authority for making the decision could be located. Of course, if the objections raised against all those who could decide are decisive, then this otherwise morally desirable act would be immoral by reason of improper agency. **6**

There are cases where it would appear to be arguably moral to take the necessary action (or to make the necessary omission) to end a life. Dr. Ruth Russell tells this story: **7**

> I used to annually take a class of senior students in abnormal psychology to visit the hospital ward in a training school for medical defectives. There was a little boy about 4 years old the first time we visited him in the hospital. He was a hydrocephalic with a head so immensely large that he had never been able to raise it off the pillow and he never would. He had a tiny little body with this huge head and is very difficult to keep him from developing sores. The students asked, "Why do we keep a child like that alive?"
>
> The next year we went back with another class. This year the child's hands had been padded to keep him from hitting his head. Again the students asked, "Why do we do this?" The third year we went back and visited the same child. Now the nurses explained that he had been hitting his head so hard that in spite of the padding he was injuring it severely and they had tied his arms down to the sides of his crib.[1]

What are the defensible moral options in this kind of case? One might be to keep the child alive in the way that was being done. This might show a great reverence for life and re-enforce society's commitment to weak and defective human life. It may indeed be the hallmark of advancing civilization that continuing care would be taken of this child. Termination of this child's life by omission or commission might set us on the slippery slope that has led other societies to the mass murder of physically and mentally defective persons. **8**

---

[1] See *Dilemmas of Euthanasia*, a pamphlet containing excerpts, papers, and discussions from the Fourth Euthanasia Conference, held in New York on December 4, 1971; this is a publication of the Euthanasia Educational Council, Inc., New York, p. 35.

All of this is possibly true but it is by no means self-evidently true to  9
the point that other alternatives are apodictically excluded. This case is a
singularly drastic one. Given its special qualities, action to end life here
is not necessarily going to precipitate the killing of persons in distin-
guishably different circumstances.

Furthermore, keeping this child alive might exemplify the material-  10
istic error of interpreting the sanctity of life in merely physical terms.
This interpretation, of course, is a stark oversimplification. It is just as
wrong as the other side of the simplistic coin, which would say that life
has no value until it attains a capacity for distinctively personal acts such
as intellectual knowledge, love, and imagination. A fetus, while not yet
capable of intellectual and other distinctively personal activity, is on a
trajectory towards personhood and already shares in the sanctity of human life. (This does not mean that it may never be terminated when
other sacred values outweigh its claim to life in a conflict situation.)

The sanctity of life is a generic notion that does not yield a precisely  11
spelled-out code of ethics. Deciding what the sanctity of life requires in
conflict situations such as the case of the hydrocephalic child described
by Dr. Russell, may lead persons to contradictory judgments. To say that
the sanctity of life requires keeping that child alive regardless of his condition and that all other alternatives impeach the perception of life as sacred, is both arrogant and epistemologically unsound. In this case, maintaining this child in this condition might be incompatible with its sacred
human dignity. It might not meet the minimal needs of human physical
existence. In different terms, the sanctity of death might here take precedence over a physicalist interpretation of the sanctity of life. There is a
time when human death befits human life, when nothing is more ger-
mane to the person's current needs. This conclusion appears defensible
in the case of the hydrocephalic boy.

Also, to keep this child alive to manifest and maintain society's re-  12
spect for life appears to be an unacceptable reduction of this child to the
status of means. Society should be able to admit the value of death in
this case and still maintain its respect for life. Our reverence for life
should not be dependent on this sort of martyrdom.

The decision, therefore, that it is morally desirable to bring on this  13
boy's death is a defensible conclusion from the facts and prognosis of this
case. (We are still holding in abeyance the question of who should make
that decision.) There are two courses of action that could flow from that
decision. The decision could be made to stop all special medication and
treatment and limit care to nourishment, or the decision could be made
in the light of all circumstances to take more direct action to induce
death.

There is another case, a famous one . . ., where the life of a radi-  14

254

cally deformed child was ended. This is the tragic case of Corinne van de Put, who was a victim of thalidomide, a drug that interfered with the limb buds between the sixth and eighth weeks of pregnancy. Corinne was born on May 22, 1962, with no arms or shoulder structure and with deformed feet. It would not even be possible to fit the child with artificial limbs since there was no shoulder structure, but only cartilage. Some experts said the chances for survival were one in ten and a Dr. Hoet, a professor of pathological embryology at the Catholic University of Louvain, was of the opinion that the child had only a year or two to live. Eight days after the baby was born, the mother, Madame Suzanne van de Put, mixed barbiturates with water and honey in the baby's bottle and thus killed her daughter.

During the trial, Madame van de Put was asked why she had not 15 followed the gynecologist's advice to put the child in a home. "I did not want it," she replied. "Absolutely not. For me, as an egoist, I could have been rid of her. But it wouldn't have given her back her arms." The president of the court pointed out that the child appeared to be mentally normal. "That was only worse," said Madame van de Put. "If she had grown up to realize the state she was in, she would never have forgiven me for letting her live."[2]

Is Madame van de Put's decision to be seen as one of the several 16 morally defensible options available in this case? I think that it is. Again, this does not say that other solutions have no moral probability. As Norman St. John-Stevas points out in his discussion of this case, there are individuals who, though terribly disadvantaged, live fruitful and apparently happy lives. He speaks of Arthur Kavanagh, who was born in 1831 without limbs. No mechanical mechanism could be devised to help him. According to St. John-Stevas, however, Kavanagh managed to achieve some mystifying successes.

> Yet throughout his life he rode and drove, traveled widely, shot and fished. From 1868 until 1880 he sat as Member for Carlow and spoke in the Commons. In addition, he was a magistrate, a grand juror, a poor-law guardian, and he organized a body to defend the rights of landlords.[3]

St. John-Stevas, however, does admit that "Not everyone can be an 17 Arthur Kavanagh. . . ." Neither could everyone be a Helen Keller. The problem is that no one knows this when these decisions are made. The option to let the person live and find out is not necessarily safe. The per-

---

[2] For an account of this case and a negative judgment on Madame van de Put's action, see Norman St. John-Stevas, *The Right to Life* (New York, Chicago, San Francisco: Holt, Rinehart & Winston, 1964), pp. 3–24.

[3] Ibid., p. 16.

son may not have the resources of a Kavanagh or a Keller and may rue both the day of birth and the decision to let him live. As Madame van de Put said, Corinne may "never have forgiven me for letting her live." The decision to let live is not inherently safe. It may be a decision for a personal disaster. There are persons living who have found their lives a horror, who do not think they have the moral freedom to end their lives, and who ardently wish someone had ended life for them before they reached consciousness. It is little consolation to these people to be told that they were let live on the chance that they might have been a Beethoven. The presumption that the decision to let live will have a happy moral ending is gratuitous and is not a pat solution to the moral quandary presented by such cases.

Interestingly, in the van de Put case, the defense counsel told the 18 jury that he did not think Madame van de Put's solution was the only one, but that it was not possible to condemn her for having chosen it.[4] It could have been moral also to muster all possible resources of imagination and affection and give Corinne the ability to transcend her considerable impairments and achieve fullness of life. In this very unclear situation, this could have been a defensible option. It was not, however, one without risks. It could have proved itself wrong.

The decision to end Corinne's life was also arguably moral, though, 19 again, not without risks. It could not be called immoral on the grounds that it is better to live than not to live regardless of the meaning of that life. This is again a physicalist interpretation of the sanctity of life. It also could not be called immoral on the grounds that this kind of killing is likely to spill over and be used against unwanted children, etc., since this case has its own distinguishing characteristics which make it quite exceptional. It could not be called immoral because it is direct killing since . . . the issue is not directness or indirectness, but whether there is proportionate reason.

In this case, then, as in the case of the hydrocephalic boy, we have a 20 situation where the imposition of death could seem a moral good, prescinding still from the question of who should decide. There could be other cases, too, where death could be seen as a good. Suppose someone suffers severe cerebral damage in an accident but due to continuing brainstem activity can be kept alive almost indefinitely through tubal nourishing and other supportive measures. Would it not seem a clear good if a decision could be made to withdraw support and allow death to have its final say? The spectacle of living with the breathing but deper-

---

[4] Ibid., pp. 7–8.

sonalized remains of a loved one, could make death seem a needed blessing. In conclusion, then, there are cases where the imposition of death would seem a good. It was logically indicated to state that conclusion before going to the main thrust of the objection, the question of who could decide when the person in question can give no consent.

# That Right Belongs Only to the State

## MORTIMER OSTOW

To the Editor:

Nine members of the Kennedy Institute for the Study of Human Reproduction and Bioethics commented on May 18 on your May 2 editorial "Who Shall Make the Ultimate Decision?" Their assertion that it is important to establish precise criteria to guide the judgment of reasonable people cannot be faulted. 1

I believe comment is called for, however, on your argument that vital decisions respecting life and death belong to the patient or, when he is incompetent to make them, to those who are presumed to have his best interests at heart. The members of the Kennedy Institute concur. 2

It is a basic assumption of our society that individual members possess no right to determine matters of life and death respecting other individuals, or even themselves. That right belongs only to the state. The prohibition of murder, suicide and, until recently, abortion, has rested on this assumption. The right to determine whether life-preserving efforts are to be continued or discontinued therefore belongs neither to the physician nor to the patient or his guardian, but to the state. 3

In practical terms, when such a decision is called for, the decision is to be made only by some agency or agent of the state, and it is to be made only by due process. To cede the right to the individuals involved is to license murder. 4

Aside from the philosophic argument, which not everyone will find cogent, there are two practical reasons for requiring due process in such instances. In discussion of matters of continuing or withholding life-support systems and euthanasia, the arguments usually offered relate to the best interests of the patient or to the economic cost to society. Abortion, too, is discussed in these terms. A far more important consider- 5 ation, it seems to me, is what making life-and-death decisions does to the individuals who decide.

While most of us will doubt that having made a decision to termi- 6 nate life support to a suffering relative will then incline one to commit murder, still, making such a decision does condition the unconditional respect for life, and does weaken the concept of the distinction between what is permitted and what is forbidden.

One can see a tendency to pass from withdrawing life support from 7 the moribund to facilitating the death of the suffering, and from there to the neglect or even abandonment of the profoundly defective, and from there to the degradation or liquidation of any whom society might consider undesirable. The undisciplined making of life-and-death decisions tends to corrupt the individual who makes them, and corrupted individuals tend to corrupt society.

Second, it is not necessarily true that the individual himself has his 8 own interests at heart. Afflicted with a painful and long-drawn-out illness, many individuals will wish for death, even when objectively there is a reasonable possibility of recovery. Permitting the patient to make the decision to die may amount to encouraging his suicide. Anyone familiar with the ambivalence which prevails in family relationships will not take it for granted that family members will necessarily represent the patient's best interests.

It is important for the morale and morality of our society that "the 9 ultimate decision" be made only by a disinterested agent or agency of our society, and only by due process.

MORTIMER OSTOW, M.D.
Bronx, May 25, 1977

# *The Right to Die*

## NORMAN COUSINS

The world of religion and philosophy was shocked recently when 1 Henry P. Van Dusen and his wife ended their lives by their own hands. Dr. Van Dusen had been president of Union Theological Seminary; for more than a quarter-century he had been one of the luminous names in Protestant theology. He enjoyed world status as a spiritual leader. News of the self-inflicted death of the Van Dusens, therefore, was profoundly

---

Norman Cousins, longtime editor of *Saturday Review*, now teaches at the University of California, Los Angeles, School of Medicine.

disturbing to all those who attach a moral stigma to suicide and regard it as a violation of God's laws.

Dr. Van Dusen had anticipated this reaction. He and his wife left 2 behind a letter that may have historic significance. It was very brief, but the essential point it made is now being widely discussed by theologians and could represent the beginning of a reconsideration of traditional religious attitudes toward self-inflicted death. The letter raised a moral issue: does an individual have the obligation to go on living even when the beauty and meaning and power of life are gone?

Henry and Elizabeth Van Dusen had lived full lives. In recent years, 3 they had become increasingly ill, requiring almost continual medical care. Their infirmities were worsening, and they realized they would soon become completely dependent for even the most elementary needs and functions. Under these circumstances, little dignity would have been left in life. They didn't like the idea of taking up space in a world with too many mouths and too little food. They believed it was a misuse of medical science to keep them technically alive.

They therefore believed they had the right to decide when to die. In 4 making that decision, they weren't turning against life as the highest value; what they were turning against was the notion that there were no circumstances under which life should be discontinued.

An important aspect of human uniqueness is the power of free will. 5 In his books and lectures, Dr. Van Dusen frequently spoke about the exercise of this uniqueness. The fact that he used his free will to prevent life from becoming a caricature of itself was completely in character. In their letter, the Van Dusens sought to convince family and friends that they were not acting solely out of despair or pain.

The use of free will to put an end to one's life finds no sanction in 6 the theology to which Pitney Van Dusen was committed. Suicide symbolizes discontinuity; religion symbolizes continuity, represented at its quintessence by the concept of the immortal soul. Human logic finds it almost impossible to come to terms with the concept of nonexistence. In religion, the human mind finds a larger dimension and is relieved for the ordeal of a confrontation with nonexistence.

Even without respect to religion, the idea of suicide has been abhor- 7 rent throughout history. Some societies have imposed severe penalties on the families of suicides in the hope that the individual who sees no reason to continue his existence may be deterred by the stigma his self-destruction would inflict on loved ones. Other societies have enacted laws prohibiting suicide on the grounds that it is murder. The enforcement of such laws, of course, has been an exercise in futility.

Customs and attitudes, like individuals themselves, are largely 8 shaped by the surrounding environment. In today's world, life can be prolonged by science far beyond meaning or sensibility. Under these circumstances, individuals who feel they have nothing more to give to life, or to receive from it, need not be applauded, but they can be spared our condemnation.

The general reaction to suicide is bound to change as people come 9 to understand that it may be a denial, not an assertion, of moral or religious ethics to allow life to be extended without regard to decency or pride. What moral or religious purpose is celebrated by the annihiliation of the human spirit in the triumphant act of keeping the body alive? Why are so many people more readily appalled by an unnatural form of dying than by an unnatural form of living?

"Nowadays," the Van Dusens wrote in their last letter, "it is diffi- 10 cult to die. We feel that this way we are taking will become more usual and acceptable as the years pass.

"Of course, the thought of our children and our grandchildren 11 makes us sad, but we still feel that this is the best way and the right way to go. We are both increasingly weak and unwell and who would want to die in a nursing home?

"We are not afraid to die. . . ." 12

Pitney Van Dusen was admired and respected in life. He can be ad- 13 mired and respected in death. "Suicide," said Goethe, "is an incident in human life which, however much disputed and discussed, demands the sympathy of every man, and in every age must be dealt with anew."

Death is not the greatest loss in life. The greatest loss is what dies 14 inside us while we live. The unbearable tragedy is to live without dignity or sensitivity.

## Active and Passive Euthanasia

### JAMES RACHELS

The distinction between active and passive euthanasia is thought to 1 be crucial for medical ethics. The idea is that it is permissible, at least in some cases, to withhold treatment and allow a patient to die, but it is never permissible to take any direct action designed to kill the patient. This doctrine seems to be accepted by most doctors, and it is endorsed in a statement adopted by the House of Delegates of the American Medical Association on December 4, 1973:

James Rachels, a professor at the University of Miami, Coral Gables, is editor of *Moral Problems*, a reader on the ethical aspects of contemporary social issues.

The intentional termination of the life of one human being by an-other — mercy killing — is contrary to that for which the medical profession stands and is contrary to the policy of the American Medical Association.

The cessation of the employment of extraordinary means to prolong the life of the body when there is irrefutable evidence that biological death is imminent is the decision of the patient and/or his immediate family. The advice and judgment of the physician should be freely available to the patient and/or his immediate family.

However, a strong case can be made against this doctrine. In what follows I will set out some of the relevant arguments, and urge doctors to reconsider their views on this matter.

To begin with a familiar type of situation, a patient who is dying of incurable cancer of the throat is in terrible pain, which can no longer be satisfactorily alleviated. He is certain to die within a few days, even if present treatment is continued, but he does not want to go on living for those days since the pain is unbearable. So he asks the doctor for an end to it, and his family joins in the request. 2

Suppose the doctor agrees to withhold treatment, as the conventional doctrine says he may. The justification for his doing so is that the patient is in terrible agony, and since he is going to die anyway, it would be wrong to prolong his suffering needlessly. But now notice this. If one simply withholds treatment, it may take the patient longer to die, and so he may suffer more than he would if more direct action were taken and a lethal injection given. This fact provides strong reason for thinking that, once the initial decision not to prolong his agony has been made, active euthanasia is actually preferable to passive euthanasia, rather than the reverse. To say otherwise is to endorse the option that leads to more suffering rather than less, and is contrary to the humanitarian impulse that prompts the decision not to prolong his life in the first place. 3

Part of my point is that the process of being "allowed to die" can be relatively slow and painful, whereas being given a lethal injection is relatively quick and painless. Let me give a different sort of example. In the United States about one in 600 babies is born with Down's syndrome. Most of these babies are otherwise healthy — that is, with only the usual pediatric care, they will proceed to an otherwise normal infancy. Some, however, are born with congenital defects such as intestinal obstructions that require operations if they are to live. Sometimes, the parents and the doctor will decide not to operate, and let the infant die. Anthony Shaw describes what happens then: 4

> . . . When surgery is denied [the doctor] must try to keep the infant from suffering while natural forces sap the baby's life away. As a surgeon whose natural inclination is to use the scalpel to fight off death, standing by and watching a salvageable baby die is the most emotionally exhausting

experience I know. It is easy at a conference, in a theoretical discussion, to decide that such infants should be allowed to die. It is altogether different to stand by in the nursery and watch as dehydration and infection wither a tiny being over hours and days. This is terrible ordeal for me and the hosptial staff — much more so than for the parents who never set foot in the nursery.[1]

I can understand why some people are opposed to all euthanasia, and insist that such infants must be allowed to live. I think I can also understand why other people favor destroying these babies quickly and painlessly. But why should anyone favor letting "dehydration and infection wither a tiny being over hours and days"? The doctrine that says that a baby may be allowed to dehydrate and wither, but may not be given an injection that would end its life without suffering, seems so patently cruel as to require no further refutation. The strong language is not intended to offend, but only to put the point in the clearest possible way.

My second argument is that the conventional doctrine leads to decisions concerning life and death made on irrelevant grounds.    5

Consider again the case of the infants with Down's syndrome who    6
need operations for congenital defects unrelated to the syndrome to live. Sometimes, there is no operation, and the baby dies, but when there is no such defect, the baby lives on. Now, an operation such as that to remove an intestinal obstruction is not prohibitively difficult. The reason why such operations are not performed in these cases is, clearly, that the child has Down's syndrome and the parents and doctor judge that because of that fact it is better for the child to die.

But notice that this situation is absurd, no matter what view one    7
takes of the lives and potential of such babies. If the life of such an infant is worth preserving, what does it matter if it needs a simple operation? Or, if one thinks it better that such a baby should not live on, what difference does it make that it happens to have an unobstructed intestinal tract? In either case, the matter of life and death is being decided on irrelevant grounds. It is the Down's syndrome, and not the intestines, that is the issue. The matter should be decided, if at all, on that basis, and not be allowed to depend on the essentially irrelevant question of whether the intestinal tract is blocked.

What makes this situation possible, of course, is the idea that when    8
there is an intestinal blockage, one can "let the baby die," but when there is no such defect there is nothing that can be done, for one must not "kill" it. The fact that this idea leads to such results as deciding life or death on irrelevant grounds is another good reason why the doctrine should be rejected.

---

[1] A. Shaw, "Doctor, Do We Have a Choice?" *New York Times Magazine*, January 30, 1972, p. 54.

One reason why so many people think that there is an important 9
moral difference between active and passive euthanasia is that they think
killing someone is morally worse than letting someone die. But is it? Is
killing, in itself, worse than letting die? To investigate this issue, two
cases may be considered that are exactly alike except that one involves
killing whereas the other involves letting someone die. Then, it can be
asked whether this difference makes any difference to the moral assessments. It is important that the cases be exactly alike, except for this one
difference, since otherwise one cannot be confident that it is this difference and not some other that accounts for any variation in the assessments of the two cases. So, let us consider this pair of cases:

In the first, Smith stands to gain a large inheritance if anything 10
should happen to his six-year-old cousin. One evening while the child is
taking his bath, Smith sneaks into the bathroom and drowns the child,
and then arranges things so that it will look like an accident.

In the second, Jones also stands to gain if anything should happen 11
to his six-year-old cousin. Like Smith, Jones sneaks in planning to drown
the child in his bath. However, just as he enters the bathroom Jones sees
the child slip and hit his head, and fall face down in the water. Jones is
delighted; he stands by, ready to push the child's head back under if it is
necessary, but it is not necessary. With only a little thrashing about, the
child drowns all by himself, "accidentally," as Jones watches and does
nothing.

Now Smith killed the child, whereas Jones "merely" let the child 12
die. That is the only difference between them. Did either man behave
better, from a moral point of view? If the difference between killing and
letting die were in itself a morally important matter, one should say that
Jones's behavior was less reprehensible than Smith's. But does one really
want to say that? I think not. In the first place, both men acted from the
same motive, personal gain, and both had exactly the same end in view
when they acted. It may be inferred from Smith's conduct that he is a
bad man, although that judgment may be withdrawn or modified if certain further facts are learned about him — for example, that he is mentally deranged. But would not the very same thing be inferred about
Jones from his conduct? And would not the same further considerations
also be relevant to any modification of this judgment? Moreover, suppose Jones pleaded, in his own defense, "After all, I didn't do anything
except just stand there and watch the child drown. I didn't kill him; I
only let him die." Again, if letting die were in itself less bad than killing, this defense should have at least some weight. But it does not. Such
a "defense" can only be regarded as a grotesque perversion of moral reasoning. Morally speaking, it is no defense at all.

Now, it may be pointed out, quite properly, that the cases of eutha- 13
nasia with which doctors are concerned are not like this at all. They do

not involve personal gain or the destruction of normal healthy children. Doctors are concerned only with cases in which the patient's life is of no further use to him, or in which the patient's life has become or will soon become a terrible burden. However, the point is the same in these cases: the bare difference between killing and letting die does not, in itself, make a moral difference. If a doctor lets a patient die, for humane reasons, he is in the same moral position as if he had given the patient a lethal injection for humane reasons. If his decision was wrong — if, for example, the patient's illness was in fact curable — the decision would be equally regrettable no matter which method was used to carry it out. And if the doctor's decision was the right one, the method used is not in itself important.

The AMA policy statement isolates the crucial issue very well; the 14 crucial issue is "the intentional termination of the life of one human being by another." But after identifying this issue, and forbidding "mercy killing," the statement goes on to deny that the cessation of treatment is the intentional termination of a life. This is where the mistake comes in, for what is the cessation of treatment, in these circumstances, if it is not "the intentional termination of the life of one human being by another"? Of course it is exactly that, and if it were not, there would be no point to it.

Many people will find this judgment hard to accept. One reason, I 15 think, is that it is very easy to conflate the question of whether killing is, in itself, worse than letting die, with the very different question of whether most actual cases of killing are more reprehensible than most actual cases of letting die. Most actual cases of killing are clearly terrible (think, for example, of all the murders reported in the newspapers), and one hears of such cases every day. On the other hand, one hardly ever hears of a case of letting die, except for the actions of doctors who are motivated by humanitarian reasons. So one learns to think of killing in a much worse light than of letting die, for it is not the bare difference between killing and letting die that makes the difference in these cases. Rather, the other factors — the murderer's motive of personal gain, for example, contrasted with the doctor's humanitarian motivation — account for different reactions to the different cases.

I have argued that killing is not in itself any worse than letting die; 16 if my contention is right, it follows that active euthanasia is not any worse than passive euthanasia. What arguments can be given on the other side? The most common, I believe, is the following:

"The important difference between active and passive euthanasia is 17 that, in passive euthanasia, the doctor does not do anything to bring about the patient's death. The doctor does nothing, and the patient dies of whatever ills already afflict him. In active euthanasia, however, the doctor does something to bring about the patient's death: he kills him. The doctor who gives the patient with cancer a lethal injection has himself caused his patient's death; whereas if he merely ceases treatment, the cancer is the cause of the death.''

A number of points need to be made here. The first is that it is not exactly correct to say that in passive euthanasia the doctor does nothing, for he does do one thing that is very important: he lets the patient die. ''Letting someone die'' is certainly different in some respects, from other types of action — mainly in that it is a kind of action that one may perform by way of not performing certain other actions. For example, one may let a patient die by way of not giving medication, just as one may insult someone by way of not shaking his hand. But for any purpose of moral assessment, it is a type of action nonetheless. The decision to let a patient die is subject to moral appraisal in the same way that a decision to kill him would be subject to moral appraisal: it may be assessed as wise or unwise, compassionate or sadistic, right or wrong. If a doctor deliberately let a patient die who was suffering from a routinely curable illness, the doctor would certainly be to blame for what he had done, just as he would be to blame if he had needlessly killed the patient. Charges against him would then be appropriate. If so, it would be no defense at all for him to insist that he didn't ''do anything.'' He would have done something very serious indeed, for he let his patient die. [18]

Fixing the cause of death may be very important from a legal point of view, for it may determine whether criminal charges are brought against the doctor. But I do not think that this notion can be used to show a moral difference between active and passive euthanasia. The reason why it is considered bad to be the cause of someone's death is that death is regarded as a great evil — and so it is. However, if it had been decided that euthanasia — even passive euthanasia — is desirable in a given case, it has also been decided that in this instance death is no greater an evil than the patient's continued existence. And if this is true, the usual reason for not wanting to be the cause of someone's death simply does not apply. [19]

Finally, doctors may think that all of this is only of academic interest — the sort of thing that philosophers may worry about but that has no practical bearing on their own work. After all, doctors must be concerned about the legal consequences of what they do, and active euthanasia is clearly forbidden by the law. But even so, doctors should also be concerned with the fact that the law is forcing upon them a moral doctrine that may well be indefensible, and has a considerable effect on their practices. Of course, most doctors are not now in the position of being coerced in this matter, for they do not regard themselves as merely going along with what the law requires. Rather, in statements such as the AMA [20] policy statement that I have quoted, they are endorsing this doctrine as a central point of medical ethics. In that statement, active euthanasia is condemned not merely as illegal but as "contrary to that for which the medical profession stands," whereas passive euthanasia is approved. However, the preceding considerations suggest that there is really no moral difference between the two, considered in themselves (there may be important moral differences in some cases in their *consequences*, but, as I pointed out, these differences may make active euthanasia, and not passive euthanasia, the morally preferable option). So, whereas doctors may have to discriminate between active and passive euthanasia to satisfy the law, they should not do any more than that. In particular, they should not give the distinction any added authority and weight by writing it into official statements of medical ethics.


# *Still, a Person Owns Himself*

## WILLARD GAYLIN

Every competent adult is considered to be the master of his own  1
body. He may treat it wisely or foolishly. He may even refuse life-saving treatment, and it's nobody else's business. Certainly not the state's. That is the law of the land.

Cold comfort for Peter Cinque of Lynbrook, L.I., who, locked in  2
like an uncharged prisoner, was kept joined to a life-sustaining device — from which he had begged to be released — until reduced to a comatose, vegetative state. His last few days were shorn of dignity, his family was humiliated and his death became a media event.

Mr. Cinque was in the terminal phases of diabetes, which had al-  3
ready ravaged him beyond reasonable repair. He had lost both legs, was blind, wracked with pain and was barely kept alive by continuous maintenance on a kidney dialysis machine. He asked on Oct. 8 that treatment be discontinued. For reasons that strain credulity, the administrators of Lydia E. Hall Hospital in Freeport, L.I., arrogating powers not clearly placed in their hands by anyone, delayed a decision until Mr. Cinque could be subjected to interviews with two psychiatrists to verify his mental competence.

---

Willard Gaylin, M.D., is president of The Hastings Center, an institute that focuses on ethics and the life sciences, and coeditor, with Ruth Macklin, of *Who Speaks for the Child: The Problems of Proxy Consent*.

Why this should have been questioned at all is not part of the public record. After the psychiatrists found him competent, Mr. Cinque signed the forms that should have released him from the agony of an artificially extended life. Instead, the hospital, in its litigious zeal, that very night went to state Supreme Court in Mineola, L.I., and obtained an order requiring Mr. Cinque to continue the dialysis. The hospital's skill in the courtroom did not seem to extend to its intensive-care unit, for on that Sunday, Oct. 17, Mr. Cinque, unnoticed, stopped breathing for an unspecified period of time, suffering severe and irreversible brain damage.

Five days later, after two court hearings at bedside, what remained of Mr. Cinque received permission to do that which the same court had previously denied the autonomous and conscious man: the right to exercise his constitutional right of self-determination. Treatment was discontinued with an inexplicable urgency that denied his family the time to be present at the bedside. Peter Cinque died alone.

How did we get into this Alice-in-Wonderland world, where a man must beg for his legal rights, prove his sanity, endure court hearings and finally be reduced to a living cadaver to do that which has been generally accepted as his privilege?

The case of Karen Ann Quinlan, the young New Jersey woman who was disconnected from a respirator in 1976 and who remains in a coma, certainly gave impetus to all of this. Her parents asked the court: Who should be authorized to speak for the unconscious girl? (This is the problem of proxy consent.) Before this, it had been assumed to be the right of the family — and the family only — to act as surrogate. The Quinlan decision upheld that right. But the publicity surrounding the case encouraged a rush to litigation. Every termination of treatment in a case of proxy consent would now be viewed as a candidate for court intervention. This was a complication that no one anticipated.

Further, these cases touched the hearts of Nervous Nellies across the country who seemed to find difficulty distinguishing between the proxy consent necessary for a comatose patient and the free choice of a competent, conscious patient. Nowhere was such an abridgment of autonomy anticipated, nor was it ever condoned by law. Autonomy has been at the heart of our concept of dignity at least since Immanuel Kant fused the two ideas.

We live under laws that demand informed consent. It does not matter what authority may think you need treatment; it cannot be forced upon you — not in this country. The threat to do so and the laying on of hands could constitute assault and battery. We have statutes that protect even the criminal from illegal detention and false imprisonment. Why wasn't the justice system protecting Peter Cinque rather than meddling in personal decisions that are reserved to self and family?

267

In an age of increasing technological capacities in medicine, ethical  10
questions involving the quality of life and the cessation of treatment will
be increasingly troublesome. We must stop the rush to litigation — and
legislation — in moral areas where they are least useful. Such action de-
means the court as it diminishes the patient.

Our most precious right is not the right to something but the right  11
to be free of something. Justice Louis D. Brandeis said it best: "The
makers of the Constitution sought to protect Americans in their beliefs,
their emotions, and their sensations. They conferred, as against the government, the right to be let alone. . . . the most comprehensive of
rights, and the right most valued by civilized man."

## Discussion Questions

1. Look up the case of Baby Doe, a severely deformed infant born in 1982.
   Her case aroused national attention after her parents and doctors decided
   that she should be allowed to die. The federal government intervened to
   block the action until they had reviewed her medical records. After carefully examining the case, argue either for or against the decision of the parents and the doctors. Analyze the assumptions on which they based their
   claim that the baby should be allowed to die. What principles should govern our decisions about the right to live of severely handicapped infants?
   Refer to James Rachels's discussion of infants with Down's syndrome.
2. Look up the case of Elizabeth Bouvia, a thirty-four-year-old cerebral palsy
   victim who asked hospital personnel to allow her to starve herself to death.
   Argue for or against her right to commit suicide.
3. A society in Great Britain has issued a pamphlet describing different ways
   to commit suicide. The publication of the pamphlet raised protests from
   groups who thought it was both dangerous and immoral. Do you agree?
   What issues should be considered in arguing either for or against the right
   of the society to publish such a pamphlet?
4. A number of states have legalized the "living will," which enables a terminally ill patient to authorize suspension of life-support systems and medication that prolongs life. Read one of these wills and argue either for or
   against its legalization. What are the advantages and/or disadvantages of
   such a document?
5. If you are opposed to euthanasia, what alternatives can you propose for al-
   leviating the suffering of terminally ill patients? Find out about the hospice
   system in Great Britain and elsewhere.

# 4 _Immigration Policy_

The United States is a nation of immigrants. Between 1820 and 1920 more than 33 million immigrants, fleeing poverty and oppression, arrived in this country from parts of Europe, China, and Japan. Today millions of additional immigrants, escaping similar conditions, are entering the United States, both legally and illegally, from Latin America and the Far East.

Problems develop when immigrants arrive unschooled and unskilled and bring with them different ways of thinking and living. We have always found it easier to accept those who assimilate more readily into mainstream culture, such as white northern Europeans. In addition, unskilled workers may have greater difficulty in finding employment today than they did at the turn of the century, a time of booming factories and unmechanized farms.

Immigration affects a variety of groups in this country — farmers, businesses, labor unions, ethnic and religious organizations — who lobby either for or against the admission of aliens based on the way immigration will improve or weaken their own interests. On one side of the controversy are the advocates of a liberal immigration policy; they argue not only that our humanity should encourage us to open our doors to refu-

gees but that immigrants contribute to the social and economic enrich-
ment of the country. On the other side are advocates of a tighter immigration policy, who argue that new waves of immigrants are straining our
resources and changing the cultural character of our country.

Various bills have been introduced into Congress that may or may
not satisfy the opposing constituencies: bills that punish employers who
hire illegal aliens, that grant amnesty to illegal aliens arriving before
1982, that tighten immigration controls, and that change quota systems
presently in force.

# U.S. Immigration Policy

## JIM BATES

There are areas in the United States, for both reasons of geography 1
and climate, that have borne the brunt of immigration into this country.
These areas in many ways constitute a test-tube experiment in the forced
mixing of cultures, life-styles, economic systems, and government policy.

San Diego County, nestled along the populous Mexican border, is a 2
popular transit point for undocumented immigrants heading northward.
The flow of these illegal immigrants has become a river of uncertain proportions and economic effects.

The climate and the culture of Southern California have also drawn 3
the legal immigrants from Southeast Asia — the boat people, the refugees, and those dispossessed by the war in Vietnam. The ballooning population of Cambodians, Hmong, Vietnamese, Laotians, and other ethnic
and national groups has been drawn here by the weather — similar in
many respects to that of their native land — and by "seed" populations
of previous immigrants.

Federal, state, and local governments have sought to alleviate some 4
of the suffering of these immigrants. The result has become a jungle of
aid programs, quotas, and illegal immigration. One cannot speak of the
problems of illegal Mexican immigration without considering the federally funded programs for Pan-Asians. Bilingual education has become a
cruel joke as the number of common dialects spoken in a single elementary school reaches a dozen or more, and interpreters and aides must be
employed for each.

Without a goal on which we can agree at both the national and local 5
level, no effective means to deal with the problem can be devised. The
goal for the local government has become mere survival in this web of
conflicting laws and objectives.

## OBLIGATIONS

There seems to be a sound basis for the recognition of our responsi- 6
bility for the less fortunate of other countries. In the past, we have encouraged immigration into the United States as a national policy. But
that was when the nation was young and labor was scarce. Newly arrived

---

Jim Bates, San Diego County Supervisor for the Fourth District, is a long-time resident of San Diego who has worked actively in local politics for many years.

residents could pass through the ports and find work almost immediately.

The situation has changed, but the change is far more societal than 7 related to employment. Mexicans illegally cross the border to find jobs; there are obviously still jobs available. The impact of Pan-Asians on the job market has been, so far as can be determined, negligible. Yet the resistance to these new immigrants is increasing.

The mainstream of America still seems willing to extend a helping 8 hand to individual refugees and immigrants; yet, as a class or group, the immigrants are spurned.

There are countless theories about the growing resistance to immi- 9 gration, and I'll offer what seems to be a growing consensus: dwindling resources of our society are making it more and more difficult to be generous. Perhaps the test of a nation's character lies in its willingness to extend a hand when times are bad, since it's easy to be generous when there is plenty. If that is an accurate test of our nation's character, then perhaps we are failing the test.

Yet this begs the question: What are the obligations of a nation to 10 the citizens of another nation? We obviously cannot be expected to extend our social services to everyone in need the world over. There are two compelling reasons to limit the sharing of our resources. In the first place, the physical ability of our nation to supply even a minimum of aid to the world's needy is very limited. Latest estimates indicate some two billion in such need around the world. To provide even two months' aid to these people would require, in purely economic terms, almost $400 billion. The resources of this country would soon be stretched to the point where not only would we be unable to care for the world's poor but even to provide for our own citizens.

The other side of the coin is the effect upon the social and political 11 order of those countries to which we provide aid. Strings attached to the aid become "economic imperialism," and the no-strings approach often results in the purchase of tanks and jets rather than rice and flour.

If our aid outside the United States must be limited, so must the aid 12 within. For similar reasons, we cannot accept unlimited immigration into the nation; our resources would soon be inadequate to provide basic needs. Also, the effects upon the social fabric of a greatly expanded immigration would probably cause considerable dislocations, both in the United States and in the country "donating" the immigrants.

There is undeniably a "which came first" question about Mexico. 13 For instance, many social problems are responsible for the flood of immigrants. But it is also true that, if we skim off the vigorous portion of a developing nation's population, we can expect a serious rending of the social fabric in that country.

Our obligations are, in sum, to provide all that we can to the 14
world's poor, but to recognize that our resources are very limited and the
problem, at least in numbers, is growing every day. We can point to a
general responsibility to provide "aid" to needy populations — not necessarily countries. We can also identify an obligation on our part to provide a home for a certain number of immigrants.

## WHO AND HOW

There are two separate groups of immigrants for which reasonable 15
policies must be designed: those arriving in the United States and those
already here. In the realm of social services, those already in the United
States pose the most serious problems.

There are between three million and seven million illegal residents 16
in the United States, and the practical obstacles to deporting this vast
number are the strongest arguments for a limited amnesty program that
gives citizenship to those who have been here a specified length of time.
These immigrants now contribute to the economy, the tax system, and to
the necessary labor force. Beyond any sense of equity, we need to keep
these residents.

There is also the argument that, without legalizing the status for 17
current illegal residents, future limitations would be meaningless. Thus,
the limitation on immigration is necessary to protect the institutions and
the social structure of the nation. The nation cannot continue to bear the
burden of overpopulation, social injustice, labor unrest, and unemployment in other countries without damaging our country as well.

The National Association of Counties has proposed a three-year res- 18
idence limit for citizen status: if an illegal immigrant has stayed continuously in the United States for three years without running afoul of the
law, he or she should be granted citizen status. The Association has also
proposed a humane policy of allowing close relatives of those who gain
citizenship through amnesty to come to the United States and apply for
residency.

Once the status of our current immigrant population is resolved, it 19
will be time to devise a process that allows for new residents. We need a
system that grants legal immigration and penalizes illegal immigration,
both by deportation of illegal immigrants as well as by imposing stiff
penalties on those who employ them. The proposed guest worker program is severely lacking in this sense, as it would require a large and cum-
bersome (and probably ineffective) bureaucracy as well as encourage illegal immigration.

## SOCIAL SERVICES

It is evident that a number of groups within our immigrant popula- 20 tion need extensive social and health services. Beyond even the moral sense of obligation to these, many of whom are unwilling refugees from oppression, the practical needs of a society to provide for those on the lowest rungs of the social ladder are compelling.

We dare not create an "underclass" of underprivileged, under- 21 served, and uninvolved citizens. For public health reasons we must provide basic health services. For the health of the society, we must provide the social programs that ameliorate the poverty and distress. It is shortsighted in the extreme to think that we can ignore with impunity the social and physical needs of immigrants.

If they are ever to become fully assimilated and productive members 22 of our society, they need our help now.

The investment in social services to immigrants, legal or otherwise, 23 will be repaid time and time again. The relatively small costs associated with health and social care are easy to justify when compared with the costs of not preventing the social and physical disease at the outset.

It is unfortunate that the greatest problems and pressures of immi- 24 gration have come upon this nation in a time of rapidly dwindling government and natural resources. It is an almost automatic reaction to think in terms of services to those who have been here the longest, but that is a reaction that will harm us in the long run.

By allocating a substantial portion of our social services budget for 25 the immigrants, the refugees in our society will pay dividends in better management of resources, a greatly reduced drain on the system in the near future, and a wealth of new, vital blood into our society.

# *When the Door Is Closed to Illegal Aliens, Who Pays?*

## WAYNE A. CORNELIUS

A very predictable thing happens in this country whenever the 1 economy takes a sharp turn for the worst: The illegal alien is rediscovered. Politicians, journalists, organized labor, and other interest groups rush to blame him for every imaginable problem afflicting American so-

---

Wayne A. Cornelius is associate professor of political science at the Massachusetts Institute of Technology and director of a study of Mexican migration to the United States.

ciety, from high unemployment to rising crime rates, escalating social-service costs, overpopulation, and balance-of-payments deficits.

Immigration authorities crank out ever-more-frightening "guess- 2 timates" of the numbers of illegal aliens "simply invading" the country. The public is warned in urgent and ominous tones that illegal aliens are out to take their jobs away and add billions of dollars to their tax bills.

We are now witnessing yet another "rediscovery" of the illegal 3 alien. Pressures for new restrictive measures — particularly legislation that would impose civil or criminal penalties and fines on United States employers who "knowingly" hire illegal aliens — have mounted steadily. Such restrictive measures form the core of the policy package reportedly recommended to President Carter by his cabinet-level task force on illegal aliens, and they have been proposed repeatedly by various members of Congress.

The case for a more restrictive immigration policy is based on three 4 principal assumptions: that illegal aliens compete effectively with, and replace, large numbers of American workers; that the benefits to American society resulting from the aliens' contribution of low-cost labor are exceeded by the "social costs" resulting from their presence here; and that most illegal aliens entering the United States eventually settle here permanently, thus imposing an increasingly heavy, long-term burden upon the society.

There is as yet no direct evidence to support any of these assump- 5 tions, at least with respect to illegal aliens from Mexico, who still constitute at least 60 to 65 percent of the total flow and more than 90 percent of the illegal aliens apprehended each year.

Where careful independent studies of the impact of illegal immi- 6 gration on local labor markets have been made, they have found no evidence of large-scale displacement of legal resident workers by illegal aliens. Studies have also shown that Mexican illegals make amazingly little use of tax-supported social services while they are in the United States, and that the cost of the services they do use is far out-weighed by their contributions to Social Security and income tax revenues.

There is also abundant evidence indicating that the vast majority of 7 illegal aliens from Mexico continue to maintain a pattern of "shuttle" migration, most of them returning to Mexico after six months or less of employment in the United States. In fact, studies have shown that only a small minority of Mexican illegals even aspire to settle permanently in the United States.

While illegal aliens from countries other than Mexico do seem to 8 stay longer and make more use of social services, there is still no reliable evidence that they compete effectively with American workers for desirable jobs. The typical job held by the illegal alien, regardless of nationality, would not provide the average American family with more than a subsistence standard of living. In most states, it would provide less income than welfare payments.

Certainly in some geographic areas, types of enterprises, and job 9 categories, illegal aliens may depress wage levels or "take jobs away" from American workers. But there is simply no hard evidence that these effects are as widespread or as serious as most policy-makers and the general public seem to believe.

The notion that curtailing illegal immigration will significantly re- 10 duce unemployment among the young, the unskilled, members of minority groups, and other sectors of the United States population allegedly being displaced by illegal aliens may prove to be a cruel illusion.

Many of the jobs "liberated" in this way are likely to be eliminated 11 through mechanization or through bankruptcy of the enterprises involved, and many others cannot be "upgraded" sufficiently — even with higher wages and shorter hours — to make them attractive to native workers.

While the benefits of a more restrictive immigration policy to the 12 American worker have been grossly exaggerated, the costs of such a policy to both the United States and the illegal aliens' countries of origin have been consistently underestimated.

The impact of "closing the door" to illegal aliens will be felt by the 13 American consumer, in the form of higher prices for food and many other products currently produced with alien labor. Failures among small businesses — those with 25 or fewer employees, which hire more than half of the illegal aliens from Mexico — will also increase, eliminating jobs not only for illegals but for native Americans.

But the adverse impact of restrictive measures will be felt most in- 14 tensely in Mexico, which is currently struggling to recover from its most serious economic crisis since the 1930's. At least 20 percent of the population — and a much higher proportion of the rural poor — depend upon wages earned in the United States for a large share of their cash income.

An employer-sanction law that is even partly effective in denying 15 jobs to illegal aliens is likely to produce economic dislocations and human suffering on a massive scale within Mexico. This will not be simply a problem for Mexico; the implications for United States economic and foreign policy interests are obvious.

All available evidence indicates that employer sanctions and other 16 restrictive measures — short of erecting a Berlin-type wall — will fail to deter economically desperate Mexicans from seeking employment in the United States.

In the long run, every dollar that is spent trying to enforce new re- 17 strictive policies would be much better spent on programs to reduce the "push" factors within Mexico and other sending countries that are primarily responsible for illegal immigration: rural unemployment and underemployment, low incomes, and rapid population growth.

For example, studies indicate that resources invested in labor-inten- 18 sive, small-scale rural industries could significantly reduce the flow of illegal aliens within five to eight years.

In the short run, the best approach would be an expanded program 19 of temporary worker visas permitting up to six months of employment in the United States each year. A temporary-worker program that did not require a prearranged contract between the alien worker and a particular United States employer (in contrast to the former *bracero* program of contract labor) would minimize exploitation of alien workers while reducing illegal immigration and keeping open a critically important safety valve for Mexico. It would also benefit United States workers, since the use of legal alien labor is likely to have a less depressing effect on wages and working conditions than the use of illegal alien labor.

It is ironic that a more restrictive immigration policy is being advo- 20 cated by many at a point in our history when declining birth rates, the end of unlimited legal immigration, and an American labor force with more education and higher job expectations than ever before all foreshadow a shortage of workers to fill low-skill, low-wage, low-status jobs in the United States economy. When this occurs, in the not-too-distant future, the aliens who are now viewed as a burden on United States society may be seen as a highly valuable asset.

# *America Needs Fewer Immigrants*

## RICHARD D. LAMM

One of the major problems in making public policy is that politi- 1 cians, like von Clausewitz's generals, always tend to fight the last war. It is deceptively simple to define the future in terms of our past. Abraham Lincoln said it so well: "As our case is new, so we must think and act anew. We must disenthrall ourselves."

Few issues facing the United States are as important as the question 2 of immigration and in no other issue are we so blinded by our past myths.

---

Richard D. Lamm, a Democrat, is governor of Colorado.

As children and grandchildren of immigrants, we have made immi- 3
gration such a part of our mythology and folklore that it is immensely
difficult to come to grips with the new realities that face us.

But history plays strange tricks on civilizations. Yesterday's solu- 4
tions becomes today's problems. The historian Arnold Toynbee said that
the same elements that build up an institution eventually lead to its
downfall. When the United States was an empty frontier, it needed immigrants to people an empty continent. Those days are gone, never to return, yet the myth lingers.

Frontier America is gone, replaced by an America of 7.6 percent un- 5
employment, with dramatically higher unemployment in many industries and appallingly high unemployment among youth who are minority-group members. Our increasingly scarce resources, our own severe
economic problems, and our own social fabric demand a rational immigration policy.

Immigration is already at the highest level in our history: 808,000 6
legal immigrants in 1980 — including the special status given to the Cu-
bans and Haitians. That is *twice* the number of immigrants accepted by
*all* the rest of the world combined.

In addition to these legal immigrants, illegal immigration is at a 7
high, though not a quantifiable, level. We do know that we had more
than one million apprehensions of illegal immigrants in the last few
years — 10 times the level of apprehensions in the early 1960's with the
same level of enforcement.

It is usually not recognized but the nation's largest number of im- 8
migrants came not in 1911 or 1893 but in 1980. Legal and illegal immigration accounts for half the United States' population-growth rate and a
rising percentage of its crime and welfare statistics.

When Jimmy Carter ordered the Immigration and Naturalization 9
Service to deport Iranians who had entered this country to study and
then dropped out of school, the agency had to admit it had no idea how
many Iranian students were in the United States, or who or where they
were.

Whatever the pressures are now, they will soon grow dramatically 10
worse. The demographers tell us we will add one billion people to the
world's population in the next 11 years.

The population of Mexico has nearly tripled since 1945 and is ex- 11
pected to double within the next 20 years. Mexico has a labor force of 19
million people — of whom 50 percent are unemployed or seriously un-
deremployed. And by the year 2000, it will be 45 million. Considering
the great discrepancy between per-capita income in Mexico and in this
country, the pull is tremendous.

We have to get our hearts in line with our heads and our myths in 12
line with reality. We know we cannot accept all the people who want to

come to the United States. We know our immigration policy has to be designed in the interest of the United States.

We hate to say "no" to that worthy individual from the poverty-stricken country who just wants to do a little better. It seems selfish to us to set limits. The Lady in the Harbor would not understand. However, I believe dramatic reform is necessary and inevitable, and that the sooner we recognize this, the better off we will be. 13

As others have observed, every year the United States is importing a new poverty class. 14

This year, with the bipartisan cooperation of Senator Alan K. Simpson, Republican of Wyoming, and Representative Romano L. Mazzoli, Democrat of Kentucky, who are chairmen of subcommittees studying immigration reform, it is possible to amend our immigration laws to achieve realistic limits on legal immigration and realistic powers to curtail illegal entry. 15

America owes its first duty to our own disadvantaged, unemployed, and poor to maintain the strength of the United States. 16

We can only meet our commitments by placing realistic limits on immigration. The Lady in the Harbor symbolizes *Liberty*, not *immigration*. We must, like Abraham Lincoln, "disenthrall ourselves" from our past myths and deal with the realities of the "stormy present" — which means not overwhelming the Lady in the Harbor with more immigrants than she can absorb. 17

# *Across the River to the Farm*

## GINA ALLEN

I met my first wetback thirty years ago in the middle of a cold February night on a farm near the Rio Grande in New Mexico. The farm was, at that moment, 3.2 miles from the river which designated the international border between Mexico and the United States. The Rio Grande is an unpredictable river, sometimes tearing a new course through the earth as it rages, swollen and swirling, uprooting trees, rolling boulders downstream, destroying homes, threatening and taking lives. At other times the river is lazy and sluggish. Sometimes the farm was a few miles from the river, sometimes ten miles, sometimes flooded during the spring runoff. At one time the river had wandered right 1

Gina Allen was, for many years, a cowhand on the Rio Grande in southern New Mexico. A writer, she now lives in San Francisco and is vice-president of the American Humanist Association.

through the farm, stranding the farmhouse on the Mexican side of the water. Whatever its course, this capricious border river strikes through the heart of the southwestern Hispanic community, arbitrarily dividing it.

My husband, Ted, and I had recently moved to the Southwest and the farm with our infant daughter, Ginita. But we knew about wetbacks — or thought we did. They were dirty and shiftless, often dishonest, quick to wield a knife if crossed. They were frequently syphilitic and carried other dread diseases, even leprosy. They were a drain on U.S. social services and took jobs from law-abiding U.S. citizens who needed the work. They would try to sleep in our hay barn and might burn it down. For all these reasons we hired only U.S. citizens. We were always short-handed.

Our two white German shepherds alerted us to the wetback. They barked and growled menacingly into the night. The man cried out. Backed against the corral fence by the dogs, the man didn't look dangerous or diseased, rather cold and scared. He was a man in his thirties, slight, wiry, muscled. He spoke only Spanish. his name was Andres. He was looking for work.

We explained that we had no work, that if he tried to sleep in the hay barn we would let the dogs at him, but that he was welcome to spend the night in the adobe barn before he set out in the morning to look for work. He slept in the adobe barn. In the morning he found work — right outside the barn door.

By the time we got up, he had fed and watered the animals and had hitched the horse to the plow. We watched amazed as he plowed the field that had been left half finished when the light faded the night before. Not that plowing a field is any big deal, even when it's done with a horse in this age of the tractor. (Our lone tractor was on a rush leveling job at the other end of the farm.) What was amazing was the way Andres handled that particular horse who, bred and trained to the saddle, objected strenuously to working in the fields. But he worked obediently for Andres.

Andres stayed. He continued to live in the barn, which seemed safer than giving him quarters in the tenant houses where the "legal" help lived. The tenant houses faced a road at one edge of the farm, and a wet there might be seen and reported to La Migra, the Border Patrol.

Andres missed his family and spent spare moments with Ginita. When I worked on the farm, I always parked her near, in a buggy, and when I worked with Andres he frequently got to her faster than I when she cried. He was adept at feeding her from a bottle, changing her diaper, or propping her up so she could see around after a nap. When Ted and I played with her on the lawn on Sunday afternoons, he frequently joined us. Sometimes we used him as a babysitter.

Ginita, a radio, his pipe, and a picture of his family were the only 8
diversions Andres had. He didn't read or write. He was afraid to go into
town; he might be picked up by La Migra. On Saturdays, paydays, I did
his shopping for him and sent a money order to his wife in Mexico. The
money he sent each week was enough to feed and clothe her and the children, he explained to me, and to pay two men to farm the few acres that
were his in Mexico. The money order was always for fifty dollars.

The radio that provided Andres's entertainment also taught him 9
English, as did the men with whom he worked. He learned eagerly and
used his newly acquired language with pride. It was a strange mixture of
textbook formality and field-hand coarseness.

"I beg your pardon, please," he would say to me. "You want out 10
the corral I shovel the sheet?" *Manure* was apparently not part of the vocabulary he learned daily from his radio teacher.

One duty Andres and I performed each evening at the height of the 11
wetback season was a trip through the hay barn with the dogs on leashes
and Andres calling out the message that it was forbidden to sleep in the
hay. Soon the dogs would be unleashed to enforce the prohibition.
There was no work on this farm, but they were welcome to stay the
night. There were cots and food in the adobe barn.

The men heard the message and moved. Andres kept chili and 12
beans on the back of the stove and baked tortillas on its flat surface for
his guests. Spanish music poured from the radio. Sometimes the men
sang. Sometimes they talked and laughed together. At times there were
eight to a dozen men, or there might be one or two or four. Andres occasionally spent the evening alone. No longer did we have to run out in the
night to investigate when the dogs barked or growled. Andres took care
of the wets who arrived through the night and sent them off again in the
morning.

Though we knew we had a jewel in Andres, we thought he was the 13
exception among wetbacks. We continued to send away those who came
from the river and to depend on the employment office for our workers.
But the "legal" Anglos, blacks, and Spanish Americans who came to
live in our tenant houses usually stayed only long enough to make the
money it took to carry them on to Arizona or California, where, it was
rumored, jobs were more plentiful and easier, the pay higher, the hours
shorter.

The jobs we had to offer weren't easy and the hours were long. We 14
were practicing intensive farming — trying to pay off the mortgage,
while increasing and improving our herd of Guernseys as quickly as possible. The cows needed consistent, careful management by caretakers
who knew them and whom they knew. Our crops were top-paying mel-
ons, vegetables, onion seed, and long-staple cotton, some of which had

**281**

to be planted by hand, all of which had to be harvested by hand. During round-the-clock irrigation, water had to be managed carefully so that all corners of the fields being watered were reached and no spot flooded nor any water allowed to leak onto crops that were being harvested.

With so much at stake, careless transient labor was about to be our 15 undoing. Andres timidly suggested a solution. "Let me pick some good workers from the wets who cross the river," he suggested. So that's what he did when we needed more help. The men were good, as Andres was good — bright, hard working, quick to learn, cooperative, interested in what they were doing.

They stayed on as Andres had stayed on. We moved old barracks 16 into the tenant house area, because there were utilities there, but these new quarters were off the road, backed against the irrigation ditch, and, at one point, bordering a neighbor's acreage.

The neighbor, Mr. Garcia, complained. "You've brought mojados 17 to my back door."

"They're good men," I told him. 18

"Scum, that's what they are," he countered. "Mexicans! We are 19 Spanish Americans," he said proudly. Then he warned, "If one of them so much as speaks to my Juanita, I'll report them to La Migra."

I thought it unlikely that any of them would speak to Juanita, or 20 even see her. A young woman in her late teens or early twenties, she was carefully protected, mostly sequestered. She hadn't even gone to school. The excuse was her crossed eyes. Because of this disability, school had given her violent headaches.

Still, Mr. Garcia's threat disturbed me, even though at that time 21 the Immigration and Naturalization Service had a policy of comparative lenience toward illegal workers from Mexico. Such policies are always subject to change, and we now had several illegals to worry about.

The one who gave us the most concern was the Indian. He spoke a 22 dialect that no one could understand and came from a village so remote that there was no way to send money to his family. The Indian took it back himself every few months, braving the Border Patrol, the rednecks who shot wetbacks for sport on this side of the border, and bandits in Mexico who would waylay and rob them. We worried while he was gone and constantly checked the federal prison at La Tuna.

Several times we found him there. If he had been caught coming 23 back from Mexico, he bore detention well; but if he had been caught before he had delivered money to his family, he stalked his cell like a crazed man. Then we argued, begged, and pleaded with the warden to let him go on his way before his family starved.

One summer day, when the Indian was safely on the farm and all 24 seemed well, the Border Patrol arrived. Two officers got out of the patrol car. "We have come for your man, Andres," they explained. "We know he's a good man and we hate to pick him up, but he's been reported so we must." (Mr. Garcia swore later that he had not done the reporting.)

The officers went back to the corrals, guns drawn. Andres was the 25 only wet around. The others had disappeared. Andres was leaning against a corral fence, a horse nibbling at his elbow. The officers frisked him, handcuffed him, and led him away. I followed, crying. The horse whinnied. The officers put their prisoner in the car. Andres smiled up at me. "Don't cry, please," he said. "I come back."

He did. Then they took him away again, and he came back again. It 26 happened repeatedly as the years passed. Ginita grew to be a toddler and toddled every morning to the barn where Andres still lived. She preferred his tortillas to anything we had to offer at home. She missed them, and him, during his absences, which became more frequent.

The immigration service policy had changed. Operation Wetback 27 was in full swing: a crackdown on illegals. But there were hundreds of contract Mexican workers about, brought here through the Bracero Program. With work permits, they were free to go to town on Saturday nights. Little restaurants and bars catered to them. There were Saturday night dances. With so much social activity beckoning our illegal workers, even Andres became less cautious, despite the new vigilance of La Migra.

The men didn't always return from their Saturday night revels. 28 Sometimes some of them got picked up. Looking for them in the jails, including La Tuna, became a regular Sunday morning expedition. Weekend tragedies became commonplace. One Saturday night, two of our men got into a car with a drunken driver and were killed in a highway accident.

Lupe, who had moved his family to Juarez and went to see them on 29 Saturday nights, repeatedly got caught trying to get back again. In Juarez, a crowded border city, Lupe and his family lived in one room with three other families. Lupe became ill and despondent and stopped trying to make it back across the border.

Andres had found a lady friend, Ofelia, who had seven children. 30 She was a U.S. citizen. Andres sent her and her children into Juarez each week, dressed in layers and layers of clothing for Lupe's family and carrying money to keep them alive. Lupe and his family eventually disappeared and Ofelia couldn't find them again. Our hope was that they had gone back to their village and found a way to make a living there.

Nice things happened, too, and Andres's lady friend was the nicest. 31 She came with her family to live on the farm and work in our house. She was a big, kindly woman who mothered everybody. Ginita adored her. We all did. We hoped that with Ofelia on the farm Andres would take fewer chances of being picked up in town. Still, he envied the freedom of the braceros. Who could blame him? And he had an idea: he would become a bracero.

Ted objected. As a bracero, Andres would not have a choice as to where he worked. His time in the States would be limited and when it was up he could not legally stay. Moreoever, the pickup points in Mexico for braceros were crowded with tens of thousands of hopefuls, of which only a few would be admitted to the program. Andres's chances of being one of those were slim. 32

But Andres had been talking to braceros. Ted knew the way the program was supposed to work. Andres knew the way it really worked. With *mordida*. Literally, "the bite." In our terms, "the bribe." You had only to bribe the right men at a pickup point in Mexico and you got transported to the United States as a bracero. Another bribe or two got you assigned to the farm of your choice. All Ted had to do was ask and pay for a bracero under the program. He would eventually get Andres. 33

When Andres's term as a bracero was up, he would be sent back to Mexico. There he would buy the papers of someone who had died. Papers are never destroyed in Mexico, he explained. They are too valuable. They are recycled. Then, with a new identity, he would bribe his way into the program again and return to the farm. 34

It worked. Time and again it worked. When Andres's term as a bracero was over, he went back to Mexico and I sent him fifteen dollars for the mordida. Then he returned as somebody else. But one year, just before he was due to leave, Mexican officials announced a government reform. No more mordida. "Mexico has been cleaned up," I warned Andres. "Your scheme may not work this time." I still sent the fifteen dollars and, shortly thereafter, got a collect call from Mexico. 35

"You were right, Gina," Andres said at the other end of the line. "Mexico cleaned up now. It will take fifty dollars for mordida." Fifty dollars did it. Andres returned. 36

# Smokescreens and Evasions

## GARRETT HARDIN

Though insisting on their commitment to democracy, most Americans conveniently close their eyes to two facts. First, ours is not a democracy in the original Greek sense but a representative government in which the many vote for a few and then the few make the laws that gov- 1

Garrett Hardin is a professor of human ecology of the University of California, Riverside.

ern all. The consequences of this arrangement have never been fully worked out in political theory. Particularly — and this brings us to the second aspect of our willful blindness — it should be noted that very frequently the will of the majority can be thwarted for a long time by the normal working of the machinery of representation. This fact deserves the closest study by those who want the will of the majority to prevail.

A clear instance of the frustration of the majority's will is found in the management (more exactly, the *non*management) of immigration. In the summer of 1977 the Roper organization took a reading of public opinion in this area. Ninety-one percent of the sample agreed that we should make an all-out effort to stop the illegal entry of approximately 1.5 million foreigners each year. In commenting on this finding, Burns Roper remarked, "It is rare on any poll question to find such a lopsided result." 2

Two years later the Roper poll repeated the question and got exactly the same result — 91 percent. Probably, 91 percent is as close to unanimity as national opinion can reach. 3

It cannot be successfully maintained that this near-unanimity is the result of media indoctrination. Until the summer of 1976 the media had little to say about immigration, though the Immigration and Naturalization Service repeatedly called attention to the rapid increase in illegal entries. Residents of cities near the Mexican border had enough personal experience to be willing to bet that the situation was getting worse. Even many people in manufacturing centers in the Midwest and Northeast began to suspect what was happening. Hard data are hard to come by, but the INS, under the direction of General Leonard F. Chapman, raised its esimtate of illegal immigration to 1.7 million during the last year of the Ford administration. 4

Of course the figures for any illegal activity are necessarily imprecise, a fact that can be used to thwart any attempt to institute corrective action. It seems so scientific to say, "Let's find out the *exact* facts before we act," but in the real world, action often cannot wait for precision (which may never come). Since time has no stop, not to act is to act. As Robert Allen said, "If you jump out of an airplane you are better off with a parachute than an altimeter." Obstructionists insist that we should take an altimeter reading before we buy a parachute — and then they throw sand in the altimeter. When Jimmy Carter became President, he replaced General Chapman with Leonel J. Castillo, a politician from the Mexican-American community. One of Commissioner Castillo's first acts was to clamp a secrecy lid on all estimates of illegal immigration. 5

The label "liberal" has been much overused, but I think most people feel that allowing immigrants in is a liberal sort of thing to do, and that keeping them out is illiberal. Some might argue that the Roper polls merely revealed how bigoted Americans are. This is the sort of arrogance 6 that periodically leads "intellectuals" to say "Everybody's out of step but me." Unfortunately, "intellectuals" are the ones who run most of the media; the 91 percent is a rather silent majority — or has been silent until quite recently.

No responsible agency has asserted that the right to migrate *into* a country is a fundamental human right, though the opposite right is proclaimed in Article 13, Section 2 of the United Nations Universal Declaration of Human Rights: "Everyone has the right *to leave* any country, including his own, and *to return to his country*" (italics added). To assert a person's right to enter a country not his own would be tantamount to claiming the right of invasion. That the invasion might be gradual and peaceful is only secondarily relevant to the moral question.   7

Let us begin by sweeping several red herrings off the path. First, I do not assert that immigrants are inferior to citizens. The problem of innate quality is so complicated (and perhaps insoluble) that it is operationally wise to assume an innate equality between immigrants and long-time occupants of the land. The issue discussed here will be concerned with quantity only, not quality.   8

Second, I know of no thoughtful person who would (if he could) stop *all* immigration. The benefits of variety, of periodic fresh infusions of new peoples and new ideas are real. No adventurous, lively nation wants to forego them. But how many immigrants are needed to secure these benefits? A thousand per year? Ten thousand? Surely no more, Moreover, *if* the seasoning of variety is what we desire to secure by immigration, we should discriminate among immigrants, preferentially admitting those who personally embody more of the culture of their homeland rather than those who carry a lesser load; bluntly, we should discriminate in favor of the talented and highly trained against the untrained and incompetent. (This would, of course, raise another difficult moral issue, that of the "brain drain," which harms the country of origin.)   9

Adding legal immigrants to the illegals, it appears that the United States is now being invaded by approximately 2 million immigrants per year. Of all the other sovereign countries in the United Nations, not one is subject to anything like such an invasion. In fact, the annual immigration into the United States exceeds the immigration into all other 150-odd nations combined. To reduce the U.S. immigration rate to a fraction of its present value (as desired by more than three-quarters of our citizens) would merely be to bring our country in line with international norms. Entry is rigidly and narrowly rationed by almost all other countries.   10

We need to take the word "development" seriously. The development of every organism includes a juvenile period when growth is very   11 rapid, followed by an adult period (often quite prolonged in time) during which *no* growth takes place. (Normally, that is: a cancerous tissue may continue the juvenile rate of growth indefinitely in the adult years, in the absence of surgical intervention.) The development of nations also has its juvenile and mature phases. The United States is surely in the mature phase now. There is no rational excuse for encouraging an immigration rate that was appropriate to, and beneficial in, our juvenile phase. Large numbers of immigrants, particularly if unskilled and ill-trained, cannot be acculturated rapidly. They undermine the shared culture. They erode national unity.

Vietnam and Watergate had a destabilizing effect on our national 12 psyche. Perhaps it is a national identity crisis that explains our reluctance to take the steps needed to conserve our national culture, but this is a poor excuse. Our psychological uncertainty makes it all the more necessary that we closely control the inflow of immigrants while we work through our problems.

There is no clearer indication of our psychological insecurity than 13 the 1975 extension of the U.S. Voting Rights Act which decreed that ballots must be provided in the language of any foreign-language group that exceeds 5 percent of the voters in a district. The expense of voting — a necessary expense in a democracy — is escalating in area after area. In San Francisco, instructional material and ballots are now being printed in English, Spanish, Chinese, Korean, and Tagalog. (Tagalog, in case you don't know, is one of the many languages spoken in the Philippines.)

The good intentions underlying this law are obvious and praisewor- 14 thy: they are to make minorities feel more welcome, to help them preserve their familiar and comforting subcultures. But of this well-intentioned act, as of all good intentions, we must ask the ecologist's question, "And then what?" As we continue to pursue this policy, what will the ultimate consequences be? Plainly Babel, against which the Bible warns us. How can we achieve anything like national unity if we lack the courage to insist that the language of the majority — the vast majority, be it noted — must be the only language for exercising the franchise of citizenship? We have become a passel of poltroons who quail at the word "minority." We have lost our common sense.

The desire to encourage widespread knowledge of other cultures is, 15 of course, a worthy one, but it can be better served by other means. We must distinguish between two meanings of the word "culture." As the anthropologist uses the word, every people, no matter how poor or uneducated, has a culture — call it the A-culture. The humanist, however, uses the word in a more value-laden sense to include knowledge and love of the arts, the literature, and the history of a particular people. Call this the H-culture. It is a degree of pluralism in H-cultures that we want to encourage. Immigrants who come here to escape grinding poverty bring (by definition) a standard load of A-culture, but most of them (in fact) bring precious little H-culture. Such immigrants should not be blamed: their deficiency is just one of the consequences of poverty. But how much will the immigrants' retention of their H-culture, or their acquisition of a new H-culture, be furthered by excusing them from learning English? Certainly the native majority receives little benefit from the expense of the Voting Rights Act.

If we are serious about diminishing the provincialism of the native 16 majority, let us make a working knowledge of at least one foreign language a requirement of citizenship for all. Immigrants should be able to fulfill this requirement more easily than natives. For both groups, language education should be continued until the associated H-culture can be comprehended. Without doubt, such a proposal would be dismissed as utopian.

"The road to Hell is paved with good intentions." No more telling 17 example of this truth can be found than the Voting Rights Act of 1975 and the subsequent legal compulsion to institute "bilingual" education in the public schools. The taxpayers of California, perhaps the most affected of all the states, were paying for instructors in 79 different languages as of 1981. Of the state's four million students about one million were Hispanic, with a similar number divided among the other 78 language groups. One can hardly be called an alarmist if he worries about the eventual consequences of the Voting Rights Act and "bilingual" education. To encourage the retention of multiple languages, as (in practice) "bilingual" education does, is to encourage the growth of tribalism in a nation. In the not too distant future we may face the task of welding together a multitude of feuding tribes to form, once more, a single nation. The second time may not be as easy as the first — which was something of a miracle.

Immigration can be understood only in the framework of popula- 18 tion theory. The most basic fact for population policy is that ours is a finite world. The rapid growth of world population during the past two decades — nearly 2 percent per year — has befuddled our minds. For the past million years (including the past two decades) the *average* rate of growth of the human population has been but two-thousandths of 1 percent per year — scarcely more than zero. Realistically, the most optimistic accomplishment of the near future (i.e., during the next century) will be a reestablishment of zero population growth. At least as realistic, and far more pessimistic, is the possibility of a harrowing negative population growth rate.

Deliberate population control is the greatest need facing every na- 19
tion today, and it cannot be solved by emigration. When we make it possible for another nation to get rid of its excess population by shipping it
to us, we merely encourage the leaders of that nation to evade the hard
problem of population control. Through emigration an overpopulated
country can export its problems to any country that is foolish enough to
permit uncontrolled immigration.

Massive immigration damages the receiving nation even in the near 20
term. Every new baby or new immigrant imposes acculturation costs —
both monetary and other — on the nurturant nation. Unless the utter
disruption of the native H-culture is regarded as a matter of no moment,
the public costs of acculturating immigrants and the children of immigrants are much greater than the public costs of acculturating the children of longtime residents. The present U.S. population of 235 million,
with a fertility rate of fifteen per thousand, produces 3.5 million children in a year. If the year's inflow of immigrants (legal and illegal) is 2
million, this means that the load of immigrants to be acculturated is 57
percent as great as the acculturation load of new babies. This underesti-
mates the load because many of the new babies are born into immigrant
homes. Next year there will be a new wave of fertile immigrants.

The total cost of acculturation imposed by immigrants is difficult to 21
determine, but with rising immigration and falling native fertility these
costs must be increasing. To survive as a people, every nation must produce and acculturate the next generation, but accomplishing this largely
by immigration is not the most economic way, whether one undertstand
economics in a broad sense or a narrow. Who would propose, as a matter
of policy, that immigration be the preferred way for producing the next
generation?

From the point of view of welfare economics, illuminated by human 22
ecological insights, the case against unrestricted immigration in a
crowded world is overwhelming. The common folk who live outside
idealistic and bemused Academia understand this perfectly well, and always have. Unfortunately, those who dominate the American media are
more influenced by Academia than by the common folk. "Intellectuals" — more accurately described as "verbals" — are reluctant to reexamine old cliches. "A nation of immigrants," "the open door policy,"
"my brother's keeper," "fortress America," "isolationism," "bigotry," "for whom the bell tolls" — these are only a few of the verbal
blockages to independent thought.

No discussion of immigration is complete if we neglect to deal with 23
this argument: "Immigrants will do the work Americans are unwilling to
do. Therefore they do not displace Americans, and they are good for the

economy.'' It is undoubtedly true that the newest immigrants will work harder for less money at unpleasant jobs than will Americans. To the employer who pays only for the daily work, immigrants may be a bargain. Service jobs in restaurants and hotels have long been held by the latest wave of immigrants; employers maintain they could not stay in business if they had to depend on native labor. In the short run they may be right.

If we were honest with ourselves we would see that our attitude  24 toward immigration reveals the hypocrisy in our praise of the economic dogma of "the market." In a true market economy the price of a product should reflect all the costs, including labor, that go into it. If the price is high, economic demand will be less. The true cost may be greater than anyone is willing to pay, in which case the product "prices itself out of the market." (How long has it been since you bought a jar of pheasants' tongues in the supermarket?)

Growers of California lettuce long maintained they could stay in  25 business only if they had available low-priced "stoop labor" — illegal immigrants or "green card" holders (temporary guest workers). But there are other possibilities: the price of the product could be raised to reflect higher labor costs; in that case New Yorkers would either eat higher-priced lettuce or do without. In the latter event, lettuce farms could be devoted to growing something else.

Cheap labor, like cheap manufacturing processes, fails to internal-  26 ize all the costs. The owner of a smoky factory produces a cheap product because he imposes external costs on the community at large, which must pay the bills for cleaning clothes and buildings. Air pollution can increase medical costs also: lung diseases don't come cheap: *The public interest dictates that all costs be internalized*. In a total accounting a clean factory is generally more economical than a smoky one — but it often takes public action to internalize all the costs.

What is the true cost of labor? It is not only the cost of food to fuel a  27 laborer's muscles; it is also the cost of clothing, housing, and a modicum of luxuries — automobiles, TV sets, public parks, etc. More important, since labor will not settle for an unalterable second-class citizenship, the true cost of labor includes whatever it takes to bring the laborer and his children ultimately into a condition of full membership in the community. Many of these costs are mostly externalized as far as the employer is concerned: schools, health services, welfare payments.

It takes a tremendous community investment — during one or more  28 generations — to bring the immigrant and his family fully into the community. Employers pay few of these external costs. Most are paid by the citizens at large. It takes a lot of money to turn new immigrants into fully acculturated citizens. The nominal low cost of immigrant labor is an illusion; but without community action — the passage and enforcement of laws — individual business enterprisers will continue to benefit from a dishonest accounting system.

At first glance one might expect strong opposition to immigration 29 from individual laborers, if not from their leaders. But times have changed. In the days before the welfare state, if a laborer had no job he and his family were in danger of starving. No longer is this true. The welfare state has created a domestic commons into which unemployed laborers can dip. Life on unemployment and welfare payments is not as plush as it is on a weekly paycheck — reality does not yet quite live up to the Marxian ideal of "to each according to his need" — but the living is good enough to weaken the springs of action of any worker who might perceive a causal connection between immigration and unemployment. Conviction and vigor are needed to fight against the ever-recurring threat of making our territory a part of a global commons. The creation of the domestic commons of the welfare state has debilitated the forces that otherwise might be fighting for survival.

The interests of the whole community, though great, are diffuse. I 30 know that I lose every time one more immigrant comes across the border. To acculturate fully one more immigrant and his family may cost my nation $80,000. But that cost (whatever its true magnitude) is divided among some 80 million taxpayers: my proportionate share is a tenth of a cent. The cost of a million immigrants is, of course, much more — a thousand dollars per taxpayer. But this cost is invisibly spread over several decades. Only insightful intellectual analysis enables us to see that immigrants do not come cheap. Our direct, "intuitive" appreciation of this reality is almost nil.

*It takes imagination to see the truth.* 31

At the present time no constituency in the United States is suffi- 32 ciently informed and powerful to secure the end desired by the vast majority, namely a sharp curtailment of immigration. We suspect that democracy may be in jeopardy because of its apparent inability to meet the first test of any system — survival. The constituency opposed to community control of population growth has a pretty tight control of the media.

As the proportion of recent immigrants increases, their political 33 power will increase proportionately. We already see signs of this in the growing intransigence of "Chicano" leaders, the younger generation of Mexican-Americans. At some level of population — five percent of the total population? ten percent? — the recent immigrants may well reach a "critical mass" (to borrow a concept from nuclear physics) whose power the more comfortable and passive multitude of longtime residents will find irresistible. As militant immigrants fight to keep the borders open, they will be aided by native political activists, left over from the 1960s, who seek new worlds to conquer. When the political power of this coalition becomes irresistible, the United States will have lost control of its destiny. Hoping to diminish world poverty by neglecting to control movements across our borders, the nation will merely have become sucked into a global commons that universalizes poverty.

## Discussion Questions

1.  If immigrants are enrolled in your school or living in your community, argue that they have (or have not) made a contribution to the cultural or material richness of life there.

2.  To what extent should immigrants be expected to assimilate into the majority culture — by learning English, attending public schools, adopting the cultural practices of those around them? Be specific in pointing out the degree of acculturation that you think desirable, and explain why. Use examples from your own experience with immigrants, if possible.

3.  Garrett Hardin cites the use of language — ''bigotry,'' ''a nation of immigrants,'' ''the open door policy,'' ''my brother's keeper,'' ''isolationism,'' ''fortress America,'' ''for whom the bell tolls'' — as an obstacle to clear thinking about immigration policy. Choose some of these terms and explain how they are used by ''intellectuals'' to support a liberal immigration policy. (It would be interesting and helpful to examine the origins of these terms and tell how they have been appropriated for use in arguments about immigration.) Do you agree with Hardin's attack on the use of these terms?

4.  The writers in this section make appeals to our heads and to our hearts. Summarize briefly the two kinds of appeals (although there is overlap) and explain why you do or do not find one more effective than the other in supporting your own view of immigration policy. Make specific references to the readings.

5.  Look up the pending legislation on immigration into this country. Pick out one section (for example, granting amnesty to illegal aliens who arrived before 1982) and argue for or against it. What problem was it intended to solve? Why will it be successful or unsuccessful in solving the problem? Is it based on moral principles? You may need to do some research before coming to a conclusion.

# 5   *Pornography*

The debate over pornography opposes two views of the rights of citizens. On the one hand, advocates of legal access to pornography argue that adults should be free to read or see whatever they wish. On the other hand, those who are opposed argue that widespread distribution of pornographic material degrades society and especially women, who are often seen as its victims.

In any debate about pornography the first problem to emerge is that of definition. One dictionary defines *pornography* as "the depiction of erotic behavior (as in pictures or writing) intended to cause sexual excitement." But, as numerous court cases have demonstrated, this definition does not make a clear distinction between pornography and art. In 1973 the Supreme Court held that material was *obscene* (the legal term for pornographic) if "the material is offensive because it offends community standards." But this definition did no more than previous ones to settle the controversy. For example, can the conservative majority in a community impose its standards without violating the rights of a more liberal minority in that community?

Nevertheless, despite these difficulties of interpretation, any definition of pornography must rest on the values of the community. As these values change, so do our attitudes toward offensive material. The Puritan and Victorian standards of sexual morality that prevailed earlier in our history dictated restraint in the portrayal of sexual behavior. The novel *Ulysses* by James Joyce, now considered one of the masterpieces of twentieth-century literature, was banned in Britain and America in 1922. The United States Post Office Department charged the novel with obscenity and banned it from this country. Not until 1933 was the ban lifted. Censorship also affected the reception of *Lady Chatterley's Lover* (1928) by D. H. Lawrence, which was available for many years only in expurgated form.

Today our tolerance for "obscenity" makes the descriptions in these books seem tame, even commonplace. Laws based on the First Amendment that protect freedom of speech for the most flagrant depictions of sexual activity reflect our more permissive attitudes.

In recent years, however, the demands for censorship have been strongly revived. At least two social phenomena are propelling them. One is the growth of evangelical religion, whose practitioners adopt a conservative position on explicit displays of erotic behavior. The other is the growth of the women's liberation movement, which regards pornography not only as degrading to women but as threatening to their physical safety. In a novel interpretation, feminists in Minneapolis tried — unsuccessfully — to make purveyors of pornographic materials subject to civil rights laws because, they argued, pornography violates women's civil rights.

# What Is a Civil Libertarian to Do When Pornography Becomes So Bold?

## WALTER GOODMAN

As pornography has proliferated across the land, from centers of 1
sexual technology such as New York and Los Angeles to less advanced
communities, a suspicion that something may be awry has begun to nag
at even that enlightened vanguard which once strove to save Lady Chatterley from the philistines. Having opened the door to sex for art's sake,
they have found that it is no longer possible to close it against sex for
profit's sake.

Where does duty lie today for the dutiful civil libertarian con- 2
fronted by efforts around the country to prosecute the purveyors of porn?
One may wish that Al Goldstein, an avant-garde publisher of the stuff,
would go away, but no civil libertarian can cheer the efforts by lawmen
in Wichita, Kansas, to have him put away. One might doubt that Harry
Reems, who has filled many X-rated screens, is contributing much to the
art of the cinema, yet no civil libertarian wants the assistant U.S. Attorney in Memphis, Tennessee, to clap him in irons. What to do?

To grapple with this matter, I brought together two figures known 3
to have provocative — and sharply conflicting — views on the subject: author Gay Talese, whose ongoing research for a book about sex in America
includes the management of two New York City massage parlors, and
psychoanalyst Ernest van den Haag, adjunct professor of social philosophy at New York University and a favorite "expert witness" of pornography prosecutors everywhere.

Our conversation began with an effort by Professor van den Haag to 4
identify the animal which he believes ought to be locked up:

VAN DEN HAAG: I would call pornographic whatever is blatantly of- 5
fensive to the standards of the community.

TALESE: But does the public have the right to ban *Ulysses* because 6
some people find it offensive?

VAN DEN HAAG: I think anyone who reads *Ulysses* for the sake of 7
pornographic interests ought to get a medal! The characteristic focus of
pornography is precisely that it leaves out all human context and reduces
the action to interaction between organs and orifices — and that I find
obscene, degrading to sex and dehumanizing to its audiences.

TALESE: So if you have a picture of a girl, including the genitals, 8
then that is pornographic.

VAN DEN HAAG: Not necessarily.  9

TALESE: But if she's making love it would be?  10

VAN DEN HAAG: I'm not even opposed to that altogether. But, if  11
the love-making picture focuses on the operation of the genitals . . .

TALESE: You mean if it shows the genitals while the love-making is  12
going on?

VAN DEN HAAG: If the genitals are shown incidentally, that does  13
not greatly disturb me. But if it is clearly focused on the operation of the
genitals and the persons are only shown incidentally, then I think the
stuff is pornographic.

TALESE: There's no agreement on a definition at all, even by the  14
people who want to ban it. Obscenity is the *one* crime that cannot be defined. Unlike murder, burglary, forgery, the word means different
things to different people — to judges, to newspaper editors, to pornographic film-makers.

VAN DEN HAAG: That's why we have courts of law and laywers.  15

TALESE: And it means different things to different lawyers — it's the  16
most imprecise of crimes.

VAN DEN HAAG: Gay, if you were to see a man walking down the  17
street, fully clothed except that his genitals were exposed, would you regard that as obscene?

TALESE: On the issue of whether the cop on the beat has the right to  18
stop public behavior that is unseemly and offensive we have no quarrel.
But no policeman ought to have the right to stop two homosexuals in a
Holiday Inn in Teaneck, New Jersey, from doing whatever they want together. They have that right, and I have the right to see a film or a play
even if it is considered offensive by Sidney Baumgarten of the Mayor's
Midtown Enforcement Project. I don't want policemen to tell me what is
moral or immoral in my private life. I think we have too much government and where sex is concerned, I want next to no government.

VAN DEN HAAG: I certainly agree, Gay, that you or I should be al-  19
lowed to indulge in sexual acts in our homes. That's our business. I am
not in the least disturbed about that. But when anyone can see the spectacle we are no longer dealing with a private matter, but with a public
matter.

TALESE: If I want to pay five dollars to go into a theater to go see  20
"Deep Throat," that's a private matter.

VAN DEN HAAG: Then you regard a public spectacle as a private act.  21

TALESE: How about buying a book?  22

VAN DEN HAAG: If it is publicly available to anyone who pays the  23
price, it's a public matter.

TALESE: So, according to you, I have the right to read *Ulysses* or *The*  24
*Story of O* or *The Sex Life of a Cop* in my home — only I shouldn't be
allowed to get it into my home in the first place.

VAN DEN HAAG: The police should not come into your home and 25 check what you're reading — but the police can accuse a seller of selling something pornographic. The matter can then be brought up before a jury and if the jury feels that what the seller sold publicly is pornography, then the seller can be convicted.

TALESE: So you'd ban such magazines as *Playboy* or *Oui* or *Screw*? 26

VAN DEN HAAG: I have testified against *Screw* and I am in favor of 27 banning it. As for *Playboy* and so on, I would leave those to juries in particular communities. If I'm invited as an expert to testify about the effects they will have on a particular community, I will testify that these effects are deleterious, but it is not for me to decide whether they should be prohibited or not.

GOODMAN: Ernest, why should it be any more the business of a jury 28 what Gay likes to read or watch than it is what he likes to do in bed?

VAN DEN HAAG: Gay's view — one that is widespread — is that soci- 29 ety consists of individuals, each independent of each other, and that the task of the government is merely to protect one individual from interference by others. That is not my view. My view is that no society can survive unless there are bonds among its members, unless its members identify with each other, recognize each other as humans and do not think of each other simply as sources of pleasure or unpleasure. For once they do, then they may come to think of people as kinds of insects. If one disturbs you, you kill it. Once you no longer recognize that a person is fully human, like yourself, you can do what the Germans did to the Jews — use the gold in their teeth. Human solidarity is based on our ability to think of each other not purely as means, but as ends in ourselves. Now the point of all pornography, in my opinion, is that it invites us to regard the other person purely as a subject of exploitation for sexual pleasure.

GOODMAN: Gay, am I right in assuming that you don't agree that 30 pornography has such dire consequences?

TALESE: Government interference in these areas is usually justified 31 on the grounds that obscenity is harmful to the morals of society, harmful to family life, harmful to juveniles. But in fact there is no proof that exposure to pornography leads to anti-social behavior. There is no proof that watching a pornographic movie leads anybody to go out and commit rape.

VAN DEN HAAG: You're not getting my point. I do not maintain 32 that reading pornorgraphy leads to an increase in crime. It may, but I don't think there's conclusive evidence either way. I feel that the main damage pornography does is not to the individual but to the social climate.

TALESE: Tell me how. 33

VAN DEN HAAG: You and I both write books, and our books are 34 somehow meant to influence what people feel and think. Sexual mores,

297

you certainly will agree, have changed over the past century. Why have they changed? Basically because of the ideas of people who write books, make movies, produce things. The biology of sex hasn't changed. What has changes is our perception of it and our reaction to it. So I don't think it can be denied that books do have an influence. If that is so, we come to the question of whether the government has the right or duty to limit it. Here my point is a very simple one. Every community has a right to protect what it regards as its important shared values. In India, I would vote for the prohibition against the raising of pigs for slaughter. In the United States, where a certain amount of sexual reticence has been a central value of traditional culture, I would vote for the rights of communities to protect their sexual reticence.

TALESE: And I'm saying that the government should not have the 35 right to deal with this "crime" that it cannot define. The Supreme Court has never been able to define what is obscene to the satisfaction of most Americans. If you are going to give government the power to tell us what is obscene and to restrict our freedom to read books, see films or look at pictures, if you give government that kind of power over the individual, you are not going to maintain a democracy.

VAN DEN HAAG: I am for freedom, too, but you ignore the fact that 36 freedom can be used for good or bad. For instance, if the Weimar Republic had banned its political pornographers such as Hitler, then perhaps six million Jews would not have been killed. The dogmatic insistence on freedom as the only value to be protected by the government disregards such things as survival and community traditions which are essential to survival.

TALESE: But you seem to forget that Hitler himself opposed pornog- 37 raphy. Almost the first thing he did on taking power was to ban *Ideal Marriage*, a classic work on sex and marriage.

GOODMAN: Would you put any limits at all on individual liberties 38 in this area, Gay?

TALESE: I believe there should be censorship — in the home. I have 39 two daughters, and in my home I do exercise censorship. I subscribe to magazines and newspapers that I do not leave on the coffee table. But I do not want government to tell me what I can have in my house or what I can have my daughters read.

VAN DEN HAAG: I congratulate you on having this family that you 40 describe. Let me point out that many American families are not so structured. Not all parents are able to exercise such parental discipline.

GOODMAN: But isn't Gay's response to government intrusions into 41 family life in accord with your own principles as a conservative?

VAN DEN HAAG: In an ideal society, things that we now regulate by 42 law, would be regulated by custom and by the authority of parents. We don't live in this ideal society. The authority of parents has been under-mined by all kinds of things, starting with progressive education. If we could strengthen the hand of parents and integrate families more, that would be much better. I have found no way of doing so for the time being.

TALESE: So you're willing to give this power to a policeman. 43

VAN DEN HAAG: I am not proposing that we trust the government 44 with the power of censorship. I'm opposed to censorship, opposed to prior restraint which is unconstitutional. I am in favor of traditional American legislation. Whereby each state, and more recently each com-munity, may determine for itself what it wishes and what it does not wish to be publicly sold. In each case, Ralph Ginzburg or Al Goldstein or you or anyone can publish whatever he wishes. Until the bounds have been exceeded . . .

TALESE: What bounds? It's all so hypocritical. One night these peo- 45 ple have been at an American Legion smoker enjoying hard-core porn and the next day they are deciding to put a pornographer in jail. What a member of the jury is likely to say in public has nothing to do with the way he behaves in private. That seems to me socially unhealthy. Many of the people who would go on record to have Times Square closed down because it has too many massage parlors patronize the places. We're dealing here with something very private — sexual desires. Very private.

GOODMAN: But is the expression of these desires around an area 46 such as Times Square really all that private? It seems pretty public to me.

TALESE: Sure, Times Square has always been a center of public en- 47 tertainment. What some people can't stand is that it is today a center of entertainment for the working class instead of for the elite. There are two kinds of pornography. You have the pornography for the working man, like the 42d Street peep shows, and you have the "legitimate theater," where the elite can see "Let My People Come," "Oh, Calcutta!" or the works of Edward Albee or Arthur Miller or Tennessee Williams. The gov-ernment does not as readily interfere with the pornography of the elite as it does with the pornography of the man who buys his magazine at the corner newsstand, which is the museum of the man in the street, or the man who pays 25 cents to see copulating couples in a coin-operated ma-chine. Pornography is primarily denied to the blue collar classes. That has always been the case. Strong government tries always to control the masses — just as much in China and Cuba as in Times Square. The peo-ple who get their pleasure from going to an art gallery to look at Goya's "The Naked Maja" aren't bothered by government.

GOODMAN: Ernest, under your definition of pornography, is there 48 any difference between a picture of a copulating couple on a musuem wall and in the centerfold of a girly magazine?

VAN DEN HAAG: Yes, effect and intent are different, and I think  49
the courts are correct in taking the context into consideration. That is, if
Hugh Hefner had put "The Naked Maja" in Playboy a few years ago, it
might have become pornographic in that context though Goya had not
intended it that way.

TALESE: So pornography is all right for the elite, but not for the  50
working man.

VAN DEN HAAG: It may appear that way, but the reason, as you  51
yourself pointed out, is that the working man gets his pornography in a
more public way. A theater at which you've made a reservation and paid
$10 is much less public than the 25-cent arcade; therefore, there is more
justification, if you are against pornography, to intervene against one
than against the other.

GOODMAN: You don't deny, Gay, that Times Square has in fact be-  52
come a place of public pornography.

TALESE: Yes, our sensibilities are assaulted. I wish the 42nd Street  53
pornographer would be more subtle. But people have as much right to
put a quarter in a machine as to pay $5 for "Deep Throat" or $10 for
"Let My People Come." I do not want to give to law enforcement officials the right to clean up Times Square, to deny pornography to those
who want it. If crimes are being committed, people being mugged, that
should be prevented. But nobody is forced to go into a peep show or a
massage parlor or to pay for sex with a prostitute.

GOODMAN: I take it you're opposed to laws against prostitution.  54

TALESE: I would really like to see prostitution legalized, but I know  55
that would be the worst thing for prostitution, because it would mean
that women would have to be fingerprinted.

VAN DEN HAAG: You would simply decriminalize it.  56

TALESE: I would like to see that happen.  57

GOODMAN: And you, Ernest?  58

VAN DEN HAAG: For call girls yes; for street prostitution no.  59

GOODMAN: Isn't that a trifle elitist, as Gay terms it?  60

VAN DEN HAAG: No. A call girl is an entirely private proposition.  61
You call her. In the case of the street prostitute, the initiative must come
from the soliciting girl, and that makes a difference.

TALESE: Have you ever been assaulted by a prostitute on the street?  62
All the girls do is ask a question.

VAN DEN HAAG: There's more to it than that. In the United States,  63
for some reason, prostitution has always been connected with crime. The
sort of thing that exists around Times Square attracts not only prostitutes
and their customers, but people who prey on prostitutes and customers
and make the whole area unsafe. I believe that crime must not only be
prosecuted; it must also be prevented.

TALESE: What offends the white New Yorker, the customer on his  64 way to the bus terminal, about Times Square is that he walks through the neighborhood and sees the great number of blacks there — the black prostitutes and black pimps. That's what makes people fearful. There is more crime all over the country today, but it has nothing to do with prostitutes working Eighth Avenue. You see, I don't think it's a crime to have sex with a person. The prostitutes are there, on the street in great numbers, because men — not the children Ernest is legitimately concerned about but middle class married white men — want them. For some reason, they find prostitutes necessary. That's their private affair. I don't want to have Times Square become acceptable to Franco Spain. I don't want government to clean it up.

VAN DEN HAAG: You're saying that people should be allowed to 65 have what they want. But should people be forced to have what they don't want? Suppose that a town in Ohio votes that it doesn't want prostitutes on its streets or pornographic movies? You are in favor of pornography in principle, regardless of what the majority wants.

TALESE: I am in favor of freedom of expression. 66

VAN DEN HAAG: The men who wrote Article I of the Bill of Rights 67 intended to make sure that the government would not suppress opposition. They did not intend to include such things as pornography.

TALESE: They wrote that Congress shall make no law abridging free- 68 dom of speech or the press; they didn't add, "except when it comes to sexual expression."

GOODMAN: Gentlemen, I am not sure how much light we have 69 shed on pornography but your respective positions are clear as day. And I thank you.

# The Pornography Debate Goes On

## NEW YORK TIMES MAILBAG

To the Editor:

Here in my prosperous area the government can tell me whether or 1 not I can open a fruit stand on my own property. I cannot. It is assumed that the community can enforce such standards. Saying that the poor folk trapped on West 46th Street can expect no such defense against the invasion of far more objectionable business ventures is sheer elitism.

AL HORMEL
Weston, Conn.

To the Editor:

I do not think it would violate the First Amendment to prohibit the   2
public display and advertising of sexually explicit pictures. Indeed, I feel
instead that *my* right to privacy is being invaded by my being forced to
see this sort of thing in public places whether I want to or not.

LESLIE S. GENSBURG
East Burke, Vt.

To the Editor:

The discussion concerning pornography apparently regarded the   3
subject as an abstruse point concerning individual ''rights'' without regard to urban consequences. However we must never forget that pornographic establishments can poison a neighborhood overnight, and I
think it more than dubious that Gay Talese — and his two daughters —
would welcome a marquee proclaiming ''Live Sex Acts on Stage'' next to
their apartment house. Urban degradation is the price of pornography,
and this, I think, transcends the specious arguments of the prurient few.

G. E. KIDDER SMITH
New York City

To the Editor:

Perhaps the zoning concept would provide an answer to the ques-   4
tion raised by Gay Talese in his debate with Ernest van den Haag. If Mr.
Talese proposed to operate a pig farm at Times Square, he would be told
that the area was not zoned for farming. He could have his pig farm,
they would point out, but he couldn't have it *there*.

Applying this principle to the porn business, the city could desig-   5
nate areas where the sex merchants could legally operate, and other areas, such as Times Square and Fifth Avenue, where they could not. In
this way the merchants and their patrons could interact, civil liberties un-
impaired, in the zones prescribed by ordinance. And by the same token,
citizens who wished to walk up Broadway with their families could do so
without embarrassment.

JAMES C. MOISE
Franklin Park, N.J.

To the Editor:

My reactions on my way from Times Square to the New York Public   6
Library are quite different from those of Gay Talese's ''customer on *his*
way to the bus terminal.'' As a woman, I feel profoundly offended by

the grotesque display of female nudity, and no amount of sophistry can persuade me that such displays are comparable to selected passages of *Ulysses* and that my freedom of speech is dependent upon the continued existence of such exhibitions.

The fact is that women are the victims of pornography in every way. 7 It is the naked female body that is flaunted on billboards. It is female flesh that is exploited in prostitution as both call girls and streetwalkers, and the female genitals that are used to arouse prurient interest in films and peep shows. And it is women like myself who are assaulted daily in public places by youths hawking the wares of massage parlors and live sex shows.

Until the day when male genitalia are displayed in this fashion, por- 8 nography cannot be regarded as anything but blatant exploitation of women. Of course, on that day and not a moment before, the male powers that control society will see to it that pornography is abolished.

LYNN GARAFOLA
New York City

To the Editor:

Gay Talese is right in maintaining that legal restriction of pornogra- 9 phy, which many would like to see extended to the portrayal of crime and violence, is inconsistent with the democratic principal of freedom of expression. We do not want to see "art tongue-tied by authority." But he errs in not combining that freedom with responsibility. Ernest van den Haag is right in expressing concern over community traditions, but censorship is not the way of instilling values and standards.

I would therefore like to present a third view, not as a compromise 10 but rather as a reasonable approach to the problem — namely, self-discipline and social responsibility. Publishers and producers, as informal but strong educational agencies, should give as much thought to responsibilities as to rights. And their commonly advanced claim that they give the public what it wants is utterly fallacious. Pandering to people's unbridled animal instincts merely intensifies and lowers them still more, a condition which then leads to more elaborate portrayals of criminal violence and pornography — in short, a vicious cycle.

To be sure, the media are business enterprises and are entitled to a 11 fair margin of profit. But they could still be successful by encouraging creativity based on a meaningful and absorbing interpretation of the human experience.

BENJAMIN BRICKMAN
New York City

# Deep Throat

## NORA EPHRON

The sign on the door says "Film Productions," and it all couldn't   1
seem blander. The receptionist is a plump, pleasant woman named
Frances, who looks like any receptionist in any office. But this is not,
Frances assures me, any office. "No way," she says. "I used to work at
the *Catholic News*. That was interesting. Then I worked at an ad agency.
We had the Rheingold account and Nat 'King' Cole used to come in all
the time. That was interesting. But *this* is *really* interesting." This, as it
happens, is the office which produced the most successful pornographic
film in the short, recent history of mass-market pornographic films.
*Deep Throat*, as I write, is currently in its twenty-second record-breaking
week at "the mature World Theatre" on Times Square, and is thirty-
seventh on the list of *Variety*'s top grossers, having so far taken in some
$1,500,000. The film cost $40,000 to make, and its profits are such that
Frank Yablans of Paramount Pictures, who speaks in sentences that
sound suspiciously like *Variety* headlines, calls it "The *Godfather* of the
sex pix."

I am here at the offices of Film Productions because one week ago,   2
on one of those evenings when it was almost impossible to find a movie
someone in the group had not seen, we ended in a packed theatre watching the 7:30 show of *Deep Throat*, ended up there having read in Suzy
Knickerbocker's column that Mike Nichols had seen it three times and
having heard, from friends, that it was not only the best film of its kind
but actually funny. *Screw* magazine had given it 100 points on the Peter
Meter. There was an interview with the star of the film, one Miss Linda
Lovelace, in *Women's Wear Daily* — "I'm just a simple girl who likes to
go to swinging parties and nudist colonies," she said — and a column by
Pete Hamill in *New York* magazine. In short, there was an overwhelming amount of conversation and column space concerning the film; not
to have seen it seemed somehow . . . derelict.

The plot of *Deep Throat* — that it has one at all is considered a   3
breakthrough of a sort — concerns a young woman, Linda Lovelace playing herself, who cannot find sexual satisfaction through intercourse. "I
want to hear bells ringing, dams bursting, rockets exploding," she says.
She goes to a doctor and he discovers that her problem is simply that her

---

Nora Ephron is a journalist and novelist known for her diversity of styles and approaches and her frequent focus on popular culture.

clitoris is in her throat. (Ah, yes, the famous clitoris-in-the-throat syndrome.) Once diagnosed, she embarks on an earnest program of compensatory behavior — I should say here that her abilities have mainly to do with the fact that, like circus sword-swallowers, she has learned to control her throat muscles to the point where she seems to have no gag reflex whatsoever — and before long, dams burst and rockets explode.

"I do not know what their reasonings were or why," Lou Perry is    4
saying, "but every top motion-picture company in the United States has called us and asked to borrow a print for the weekend." Perry is the producer of *Deep Throat*. He is thirty-five years old, dark-haired, a bit paunchy, and until all this began to happen he was Lou Perino. He is sitting in his office at Film Productions in the midst of what passes for a crisis in the sex-pix business: Hugh Hefner's aide has just called to request a print of *Deep Throat* for Hefner's personal film collection, and all the available prints are in use. "Look," Perry is saying to a tattooed person named Vinny, who works for him, "call Fort Lee. Call Atlanta. This is a very important thing. *Playboy* is giving us a three-page spread in the February issue. We gotta find a print." There are other things on Perry's mind — one is an impending trial on the obscenity of the *Deep Throat* advertising; another is the forthcoming sequel, *Deep Throat II*, which is about to go into production with a $100,000 budget; and a third is the Los Angeles premiere of *Deep Throat*, to be held at the Hollywood Cat in two weeks, complete with searchlights and Linda Lovelace herself. "She's going to do some radio interviews out there," says Perry, "and we think maybe Johnny Carson."

Exactly what Perry was doing prior to entering the pornographic    5
film business he prefers not to say, but he is perfectly willing to tell the story of his big break. "How I got into this," he says, "is I lent — I mean, I invested money in a company that went bankrupt that was into this. We then made two pictures. One was *Sex U.S.A.* The other was called *This Film Is All About* . . . That's right. Blank. The original title was going to be a four-letter word, but we realized no newspaper would take the ad. New York papers won't even take the word 'Sex' on movies like this. To give you a for instance, *Sex U.S.A.* in the *Daily News* was printed *Xex U.S.A.* Both these films were documentaries, about events that were happening, sex shows, interviews with people about what did they think about sex shows. *Sex* cost about twelve to fifteen thousand dollars. So far, it's grossed six hundred thousand. The way *Deep Throat* came about was we decided to do another film. We didn't want to do a documentary. There was this film, *Mona*, that we had seen. It was different. It had a story. It was done with what you would call improvisational.

We thought of doing possibly the same exact thing, so we decided, let's pick out a subject.

"To be honest about it, we couldn't come up with anything too good. We were just going to do another *Mona*. Then, somehow, Jerry Damiano, the writer and director, he seen this girl at a party. I assume he got fixed up with her. And he came in the next day and he said as he was driving over the Fifty-ninth Street Bridge he was thinking of her. What she had done was fantastic. He's never seen anybody do like she did. So he thought, let's make a picture about this girl. 6

"We started out with a fifteen-thousand-dollar picture, and then it went up to twenty-two thousand and then thirty thousand and then we said, oh the hell with it, let's go all the way. By the time we finished, we spent forty thousand. I was very worried. How would it be accepted? Before we released it, we had a screening. Personal friends, exhibitors, sub-distributors. I tell you, I was on pins and needles as to what their reaction would be. Well, I've been to many X-rated movie screenings, but this picture — in the screening, when she first gives throat, four or five of the men in the audience said, 'Hurray,' and by the end of the sequence there were fifteen guys standing and they went into a very big applause. At that point, we knew we had a hit on our hands. *Screw* reviewed it a week before it opened and said it was the best porn film ever made. That had a lot to do with what happened. We opened up against *Cabaret* and the sequel to *Shaft*, and we outgrossed both of them." 7

It may be a terrible mistake to take *Deep Throat* and its success seriously. These things may just happen. Their success may not mean a thing. The publicity machine marches on, and all that. But I can't help thinking that pornography that has this sort of impact must have some significance. I have seen a lot of stag films in my life — well, that's not true; I've seen about five or six — and although most of them were raunchy, a few were also sweet and innocent and actually erotic. *Deep Throat*, on the other hand, is one of the most unpleasant, disturbing films I have ever seen — it is not just anti-female but anti-sexual as well. I walked into the World Theatre feeling thoroughly unshockable — after all, I can toss off phrases like "split beaver" with almost devil-may-care abandon — and I came out of the theatre a quivering fanatic. Give me the goriest Peckinpah any day. There is a scene in *Deep Throat*, for example, where a man inserts a hollow glass dildo inside Miss Lovelace, fills it with Coca-Cola, and drinks it with a surgical straw — the audience was bursting with nervous laughter, while I sat through it literally faint. All I could think about was what would happen if the glass broke. I always cringe when I read reviews of this sort — crazy feminists carrying on, criticizing nonpolitical films in political terms — but as I sat through the film 8

I was swept away in a bromidic wave of movement rhetoric. "Demeaning to women," I wailed as we walked away from the theatre. "Degrading to women." I began muttering about the clitoris backlash. The men I was with pretended they did not know me, and then, when I persisted in addressing my mutterings to them, they assured me that I was overreacting, that it was just a movie and that they hadn't even been turned on by it. But I refused to calm down. "Look, Nora," said one of them, playing what I suppose he thought was his trump card by appealing to my sense of humor, "there's one thing you have to admit. The scene with the Coca-Cola was hilarious."

Exactly what Linda Lovelace did for a living before becoming the 9 first superstar of her kind is something she prefers not to be explicit about. She will say, though, that she is twenty-one years old, from Bryan, Texas, and that she decided to come to New York almost two years ago. She had met a man she calls J.R., a former Marine, who is now her manager and who taught her the trick of relaxing her throat muscles, and the two of them set off for the big city together. "I was just going to get a job as a topless dancer or something," said Miss Lovelace. "I really didn't think what happened would happen." A few months after arriving in New York, Linda and J.R. went to a party. "J.R. met Jerry Damiano and they got to talking about what I could do," said Miss Lovelace. "And when he saw me, he liked me and the way I looked and he got carried away. The next day he was riding to work across the Brooklyn Bridge and he decided on the whole script for the movie."

Everything that has happened to Linda Lovelace since then is kind 10 of a goof. Making the film was kind of a goof. Its success is kind of a goof. Being recognized in public is kind of a goof. "I totally enjoyed myself making the movie and all of a sudden I'm what they call a superstar," she says. "It's kind of a goof." I am talking to Miss Lovelace long distance — she is living in Texas with J.R. — and we are having a conversation that leaves something to be desired. For instance, Linda Lovelace's idea of candor is to insist that her name really is Linda Lovelace, and her idea of a clever response to the question of whether she has any idiosyncrasies is to say, "I swallow well." As if all this were not enough, it turns out that Linda Lovelace thinks the scene with the Coca-Cola and glass dildo was even funnier than my friend thinks it is. "Actually," she says, "I think the funniest thing that happened when we were shooting was when we did that scene. They were going to shoot a little bit more, but someone said something and I started laughing and the glass dildo went flying into the air and cracked into a million pieces." I am not sure what I expected from this interview — I honestly did not expect Linda Lovelace to be Jane Fonda in *Klute*, not did I think that she would, as a result of our conversation, see the light and leave the pornographic film business forever. On the other hand, I did not expect what is happening, which is that we seem to be spending as much time talking about me and what Miss Lovelace clearly thinks of as my problems as we are about her and what I clearly think of as her problems. As in this exchange:

"How do you feel about being recognized on the street?" I ask. 11

"It's kind of a goof," she says. 12

"But," I say, "Lou Perry told me that it made you a little ner- 13
vous."

"Why should it make me nervous?" 14

"I don't know," I say. "I might be nervous if someone recognized 15
me as the star of a pornographic film. Especially in the Times Square
area."

"Would you be nervous," she asks, "if you walked around nude 16
and strangers saw you?"

"Yes." 17

"See? I wouldn't." 18

Or in this exchange: 19

"Why do you shave off your pubic hair in the film?" I ask. 20

"I always do," Linda Lovelace replies. "I like it." 21

"But why do you do it?" 22

"Well," she says, "it's kinda hot in Texas." 23

That stops me for a second. "Well," I say, "I think it's weird." 24

"Weird? Why?" 25

"Well, I don't know anyone who does that." 26

"Now you do," says Linda Lovelace. 27

"I don't have any inhibitions about sex," she says. "I just hope 28
that everybody who goes to see the film enjoys it and maybe learns something from it." Like what? "I don't know. Enjoys their sex life better.
Maybe loses some of their inhibitions." In the meantime, Linda Lovelace
is about to make the sequel. She is under exclusive contract to Film Productions and receives $250 a week when she isn't working and $10,000
plus a piece of the profits for the next film. Does she want to make regular films as well as pornographic films? "Look," she says, "you make a
separation between movies and this kind of movie. To me, it's just a
movie, like all other movies. Only it has some much better things in it."
Like what? "Like me," says Linda Lovelace.

And there we are. Linda Lovelace, "just a simple girl who likes to go 29
to swinging parties and nudist colonies." And me, a hung-up, uptight,
middle-class, inhibited, possibly puritanical feminist who lost her sense
of humor at a skin flick. It's not exactly the self-image I had in mind, but
I can handle it.

# The Real Linda Lovelace

## GLORIA STEINEM

Remember *Deep Throat*? It was the porn movie that made porn    1
movies chic; the first stag film to reach beyond the bounds of X-rated
theaters and into much bigger audiences. Though it was created in 1972
as a cheap feature that took only forty thousand dollars and a few days to
make, it ended the decade with an estimated gross income of six hundred million dollars from paying customers for the film itself plus its sub-
industry of sequels, cassettes, T-shirts, bumper stickers, and sexual aids.
In fact, so much of the media rewarded it with amusement or approval
that *Deep Throat* entered our language and our consciousness, whether
we ever saw the film or not. From the serious Watergate journalists of the
Washington *Post* who immortalized "Deep Throat" by bestowing that
title on their top-secret news source, to the sleazy pornocrats of *Screw*
magazine — a range that may be, on a scale of male supremacy, the distance from *A* to *B* — strange media bedfellows turned this cheap feature
into a universal dirty joke and an international profit center.

At the heart of this dirty joke was Linda Lovelace (née Linda Bore-    2
man) whose innocent face and unjaded manner was credited with much
of the film's success. She offered moviegoers the titillating thought that
even the girl next door might love to be the object of porn-style sex.

Using Linda had been the idea of Gerry Damiano, the director-    3
writer of *Deep Throat*. "The most amazing thing about Linda, the truly
amazing thing," she remembers him saying enthusiastically to Lou Peraino, who bankrolled the movie, "is that she still looks sweet and innocent." Nonetheless, Peraino (who was later arrested by the FBI as a figure in alleged organized-crime activities in the illicit-film industry)
complained that Linda wasn't the "blond with big boobs" that he had
in mind for his first porn flick. He continued to complain, even after she
had been ordered to service him sexually.

In fact, watching Linda perform in public as a prostitute had given    4
Damiano the idea for *Deep Throat* in the first place. He had been at a
party where men lined up to be the beneficiaries of the sexual sword-
swallower trick Linda had been taught by her husband and keeper,
Chuck Traynor. By relaxing her throat muscles, she learned to receive the
full-length plunge of a penis without choking; a desperate survival technique for her, but a constant source of amusement and novelty for cli-

---

Gloria Steinem was a founder and editor of *New York* and *Ms.* magazines and a
founding member of the National Women's Political Caucus.

ents. Thus creatively inspired, Damiano had thought up a movie gimmick, one that was second only to Freud's complete elimination of the clitoris as a proper source of female pleasure and invention of the vaginal orgasm. Damiano decided to tell the story of a woman whose clitoris was in her throat and who was constantly eager for oral sex with men.

Though his physiological fiction about *one* woman was far less ambitious than Freud's fiction about *all* women, his porn movie had a whammo audiovisual impact; a teaching device that Freudian theory had lacked.

Literally millions of women seem to have been taken to *Deep Throat* by their boyfriends or husbands (not to mention prostitutes who were taken by their pimps) so that each one might learn what a woman could do to please a man *if she really wanted to*. This instructive value seems to have been a major reason for the movie's popularity and its reach beyond the usual male-only viewers.

Of course, if the female viewer were really a spoilsport, she might identify with the woman on screen and sense her humiliation, danger, and pain — but the smiling, happy face of Linda Lovelace could serve to cut off empathy, too. *She's there because she wants to be. Who's forcing her? See how she's smiling? See how a real woman enjoys this?*

Eight years later, Linda told us the humiliating and painful answer in *Ordeal*, her autobiography. She described years as a sexual prisoner during which she was tortured and restricted from all normal human contact.

Nonetheless, it's important to understand how difficult it would have been at the time (and probably still is, in the case of other victims) to know the truth.

At the height of *Deep Throat*'s popularity, for instance, Nora Ephron wrote an essay about going to see it. She was determined not to react like those "crazy feminists carrying on, criticizing nonpolitical films in political terms." Nonetheless, she sat terrified through a scene in which a hollow glass dildo is inserted in Linda Lovelace's vagina and then filled with Coca-Cola, which is drunk through a surgical straw. ("All I could think about," she confessed, "was what would happen if the glass broke.") Feeling humiliated and angry, but told by her male friends that she was "overreacting," that the Coca-Cola scene was "hilarious," she used her license as a writer to get a telephone interview with Linda Lovelace. "I totally enjoyed myself making the movie," she was told by Linda. "I don't have any inhibitions about sex. I just hope that everybody who goes to see the film . . . loses some of their inhibitions."

So Nora wrote an article that assumed Linda to be a happy and willing porn queen who was enjoying ". . . $250 a week . . . plus a piece of the profits.'' And she wrote off her own reaction as that of a ''puritanical feminist who lost her sense of humor at a skin flick.''

What she did not know (how could any interviewer know?) was that 12 Linda would later list these and other answers as being dictated by Chuck Traynor for just such journalistic occasions; that he punished her for showing any unacceptable emotion (when, for instance, she cried while being gang-banged by five men in a motel room, thus causing one customer to refuse to pay); in fact, that she had been beaten and raped so severely and regularly that she suffered rectal damage plus permanent injury to the blood vessels in her legs.

What Nora did not know was that Linda would also write of her 13 three escape attempts and three forcible returns to this life of sexual servitude: first by the betrayal of another prostitute; then by her own mother who was charmed by Chuck Traynor's protestations of remorse and innocence into telling him where her daughter was hiding; and finally by Linda's fear for the lives of two friends who had sheltered her after hearing that she had been made to do a sex film with a dog, and outside whose home Traynor had parked a van that contained, Linda believed, his collection of hand grenades and a machine gun.

Even now, these and other facts about Traynor must be read with 14 the word ''alleged'' in front of them. Because of Linda's long period of fear and hiding after she escaped, the time limitations of the law, and the fact that Traynor forced her to marry him, legal charges are difficult to bring. Linda's book documents her account of more than two years of fear, sadism, and forced prostitution. Traynor had been quoted as calling these charges ''so ridiculous I can't take them seriously.'' He has also been quoted as saying: ''when I first dated her she was so shy, it shocked her to be seen nude by a man. . . . *I created Linda Lovelace.*''

Linda's account of being ''created'' includes guns put to her head, 15 turning tricks while being watched through a peephole to make sure she couldn't escape, and having water forced up her rectum with a garden hose if she refused to offer such amusements as exposing herself in restaurants or to passing drivers on the highway.

*Ordeal* is a very difficult book to read. It must have been far more 16 difficult to write. But Linda says she wanted to purge forever the idea that she had become ''Linda Lovelace'' of her own free will.

Was profit a motive for this book? Certainly she badly needs money 17 for herself, her three-year-old son, her imminently expected second baby, and her husband, a childhood friend named Larry Marchiano, whose work as a TV cable installer has been jeopardized by his co-workers' discovery of Linda's past. For a while, they were living partially on welfare. But Linda points out that she has refused offers of more than three million dollars to do another porn movie like *Deep Throat*. (For that filming, Linda was paid twelve hundred dollars; a sum that, like her fees for turning tricks as a prostitute, she says she never saw.)[1] "I wouldn't do any of that again," she says, "even if I could get fifty million dollars."

A different motive for writing *Ordeal* is clear from Linda's response 18 to a postcard written by a young woman who had been coerced into prostitution, a woman who said she got the courage to escape after seeing Linda on television. "Women have to be given the courage to try to escape, and to know that you *can* get your self-respect back," she says. "It meant the whole world to me to get that postcard."

Ironically, her own hope of escape came with the surprising success 19 of *Deep Throat*. She had become a valuable property. She had to be brought into contact with outsiders occasionally, with a world that she says had been denied to her, even in the form of radio or newspapers. Now, she says soberly, "I thank God today that they weren't making snuff movies back then. . . ."

She says she escaped by feigning trustworthiness for ten minutes, 20 then a little longer each time, until, six months later, she was left unguarded during rehearsals for a stage version of *Linda Lovelace*. Even then, she spent weeks hiding out in hotels alone, convinced she might be beaten or killed for this fourth try at escape, but feeling stronger this time for having only her own life to worry about. It took a long period of hiding, with help and disguises supplied by a sympathetic secretary from Traynor's newly successful Linda Lovelace Enterprises (but no help from police, who said they could do nothing to protect her "until the man with the gun is in the room with you"), before the terror finally dwindled into a nagging fear. Traynor continued to issue calls and entreaties for her return. He filed a lawsuit against her for breach of contract. But he had also found another woman to star in his porn films — Marilyn Chambers, the model who appeared in a comparatively nonviolent porn movie called *Behind the Green Door*.

And then suddenly, she got word through a lawyer that Traynor was 21 willing to sign divorce papers. The threats and entreaties to return just stopped.

Free of hiding and disguises at last, she tried to turn her created 22 identity into real acting by filming *Linda Lovelace for President*, a comedy that was supposed to have no explicit sex, but she discovered that

---

[1]Since this writing, a judgment has been brought against Linda for "contract failure" during what she says was her period of imprisonment, and her payments for *Ordeal* have been attached. The book may end by financially benefiting Traynor's former lawyer. The punishment goes on.

producers who offered her roles always expected nudity in return. She went to a Cannes Film Festival but was depressed by her very acceptance among celebrities she respected. "I had been in a disgusting film with disgusting people. . . . What were they doing watching a movie like that in the first place?"

Once she started giving her own answers to questions and trying to 23 explain her years of coercion, she discovered that reporters were reluctant to rush into print. Her story was depressing, not glamorous or titillating at all. Because she had been passed around like a sexual trading coin, sometimes to men who were famous, there was also fear of lawsuits.

Only in 1978, when she was interviewed by Mike McGrady, a re- 24 spected newspaper reporter on Long Island where she had moved with her new husband, did her story begin the long process of reaching the public. McGrady believed her. In order to convince publishers, he also put her through an eleven-hour lie-detector test with the former chief polygraphist of the New York district attorney's office, a test that included great detail and brutal cross-questioning. But even with those results and with McGrady himself as a collaborator, several major book publishers turned down the manuscript. It was finally believed and accepted by Lyle Stuart, a maverick in the world of publishing who often takes on sensational or controversial subjects.

One wonders: Would a male political prisoner or hostage telling a 25 similar story have been so disbelieved? *Ordeal* attacks the myth of female masochism that insists women enjoy sexual domination and even pain, but prostitution and pornography are big businesses built on that myth. When challenged about her inability to escape earlier, Linda wrote: "I can understand why some people have such trouble accepting the truth. When I was younger, when I heard about a woman being raped, my secret feeling was *that could never happen to me.* I would never *permit* it to happen. Now I realize that can be about as meaningful as saying I won't permit an avalanche."

There are other, nameless victims of sexual servitude: the young 26 blonds from the Minnesota Pipeline, runaways from the Scandinavian farming towns of Minnesota, who are given drugs and "seasoned" by pimps and set up in Times Square; the welfare mothers who are pressured to get off welfare and into prostitution; the "exotic" dancers imported from poorer countries for porn films and topless bars; the torture victims whose murders were filmed in Latin America for snuff movies popular here, or others who bodies were found buried around a California filmmaker's shack; the body of a prostitute found headless and handless in a Times Square hotel, a lesson to her sisters. Perhaps some of their number will be the next voiceless, much-blamed women to speak out and begin placing the blame where it belongs. Perhaps Linda's example will give them hope that, if they return, some of society will accept them. Right now, however, they are just as disbelieved as rape victims and battered women were a few years ago.

To publicize her book, Linda is sitting quiet and soft-spoken on 27 TV's "Phil Donahue Show." Under her slacks she wears surgical stockings to shield the veins that were damaged by the beatings in which she curled up, fetuslike, to protect her stomach and breasts from kicks and blows: this she explains under Donahue's questioning. Probably, she will need surgery after her baby is born. The silicone injected in her breasts by a doctor (who, like many other professionals to whom she was taken, was paid by Linda's sexual services) has shifted painfully, and surgery may be necessary there, too.

Yet Donahue, usually a sensitive interviewer, is asking her psycho- 28 logical questions about her background: How did she get along with her parents? What did they tell her about sex? Didn't her fate have something to do with the fact that she had been pregnant when she was nineteen and had given birth to a baby that Linda's mother put up for adoption?

Some of the women in the audience take up this line of question- 29 ing, too. *They* had been poor. *They* had strict and authoritarian parents; yet *they* didn't end up as part of the pornographic underground. The air is thick with self-congratulation. Donahue talks on about the tragedy of teenage pregnancy, and what parents can do to keep their children from a Linda-like fate.

Because Traynor did have a marriage ceremony performed some- 30 where along the way (Linda says this was to make sure she couldn't testify against him on drug charges), she has to nod when he is referred to as "your husband." On her own, however, she refers to him as "Mr. Traynor."

Linda listens patiently to doubts and objections, but she never gives 31 up trying to make the audience understand. If another woman had met a man of violence and sadism who "got off on pain," as Linda has described in her book, *she might have ended up exactly the same way*. No, she never loved him: he was the object of her hatred and terror. Yes, he was very nice, very gentlemanly when they first met. They had no sexual relationship at all. He had just offered an apartment as a refuge from her strict childlike regime at home. *And then he did a 180-degree turn*. She became, she says quietly, a prisoner. A prisoner of immediate violence and the fear of much more.

She describes being so isolated and controlled that she was not al- 32 lowed to speak in public or to go to the bathroom without Traynor's permission. *There was no choice. It could happen to anyone.* She says this simply, over and over again, and to many women in the audience the point finally comes through. But to some, it never does. Donahue continues to ask questions about her childhood, her background. What attracted her to this fate? How can we raise our daughters to avoid it? If you accept the truth of Linda's story, the questions are enraging, like saying, "What in your background led you to a concentration camp?"

No one asks how we can stop raising men who fit Linda's terrified 33 description of Chuck Traynor. Or what attracted the millions of people who went to *Deep Throat*. Or what to do about the millions of "normal" men who assume that some violence and aggression in sex are quite okay.

A woman in the audience asks if this isn't an issue for feminism. 34 Linda says that yes, she has heard there are anti-pornography groups, she is getting in touch with Susan Brownmiller who wrote *Against Our Will*. That definitive book on rape has led Brownmiller to attack other pornographic violence against women.

But it's clear that, for Linda, this is a new hope and new connection. 35

For women who want to support Linda now and to save others being 36 used sexually against their will, this may be the greatest sadness. At no time during those months of suffering and dreams of escape, not even during the years of silence that followed, was Linda aware of any signal from the world around her that strong women as a group or feminists or something called the women's movement might be there to help her.

Surely, a victim of anti-Semitism would know the Jewish commu- 37 nity was there to help, or a victim of racism would look to the civil rights movement. But feminist groups are not yet strong enough to be a public presence in the world of pornography, prostitution, and gynocide; or in the world of welfare and the working poor that Linda then joined. Even now, most of her help and support come from sympathetic men: from McGrady who believed her life story, from her husband who loses jobs in defense of her honor, from the male God of her obedient Catholic girlhood to whom she prayed as a sexual prisoner and prays now in her daily life as homemaker and mother.

Even her feelings of betrayal are attached to her father, not her 38 mother. During her long lie-detector test, the only time she cried and completely broke down was over an innocuous mention of his name. "I was watching that movie *Hardcore*," she explained, "where George C. Scott searches and searches for his daughter. Why didn't my father come looking for me? He saw *Deep Throat*. He should've known. . . . He should've done something. Anything!"

After all, who among us had mothers with the power to rescue us, 39 to *do something*? We don't even expect it. In mythology, Demeter rescued her daughter who had been abducted and raped by the King of the Underworld. She was a strong and raging mother who turned the earth to winter in anger at her daughter's fate. Could a powerful mother now rescue her daughter from the underworld of pornography? Not even Hollywood can fantasize that plot.

But Linda has begun to uncover her own rage, if only when talking   40 about her fears for other women as pornography becomes more violent. "Next," she says quietly, as if to herself, "they're going to be selling women's skins by the side of the road."

And women have at least begun to bond together to rescue each   41 other as sisters. There are centers for battered women, with publicized phone numbers for the victims but private shelters where they cannot be followed. It's a system that might work for victims of prostitution and pornography as well, if it existed, and if women knew it was there.

In the meantime, Linda takes time out from cleaning her tiny house   42 on Long Island ("I clean it twice a day," she says proudly) to do interviews, to send out her message of hope and strength to other women who may be living in sexual servitude right now, and to lecture against pornography with other women, who are now her friends. She keeps answering questions, most of them from interviewers who are far less sympathetic than Donahue.

How could she write such a book when her son will someday read it?   43 "I've already explained to him," she says firmly, "that some people hurt Mommy — a long time ago." How can her husband stand to have a wife with such a sexual past? ("It wasn't sexual. I never experienced any sexual pleasure, not one orgasm, nothing. I learned how to fake pleasure so I wouldn't get punished for doing a bad job.") And the most popular doubt of all: *If she really wanted to, couldn't she have escaped sooner?*

Linda explains as best she can. As I watch her, I come to believe the   44 question should be different: *Where did she find the courage to escape at all?*

Inside the patience with which she answers these questions — the   45 result of childhood training to be a "good girl" that may make victims of us all — there is some core of strength and stubbornness that is itself the answer. She *will* make people understand. She will *not* give up.

In the microcosm of this one woman, there is a familiar miracle: the   46 way in which women survive — and fight back.

And a fight there must be.   47

*Deep Throat* plays continuously in a New York theater and proba-   48 bly in many other cities of the world. Bruises are visible on Linda's legs in the film itself, supporting her testimony that she was a prisoner while she made it. Do viewers see the bruises or only her smile?

So far, no invasion of privacy or legal means has been found to stop   49 this film. Money continues to be made.

*Deep Throat* has popularized a whole new genre of pornography. 50
Added to all the familiar varieties of rape, there is now an ambition to
rape the throat. Porn novels treat this theme endlessly. Some emergency-
room doctors belive that victims of suffocation are on the increase.

As for Chuck Traynor himself, he is still the husband and manager 51
of Marilyn Chambers.

Larry Fields, a columnist for the Philadelphia *Daily News*, remem- 52
bers interviewing them both for his column a few years ago when Marilyn
was performing a song-and-dance act in a local nightclub. Traynor
bragged that he had taught Linda Lovelace everything she knew, but
that "Marilyn's got what Linda never had — talent."

While Traynor was answering questions on Marilyn's behalf, she 53
asked him for permission to go to the bathroom. Permission was refused. "Not right now," Fields remembers him saying to her. And when
she objected that she was about to appear onstage: "Just sit there and
shut up."

When Fields also objected, Raynor was adamant. "I don't tell you 54
how to write your column," he said angrily. "Don't tell me how to treat
my broads."

# Pornography and Censorship

## IRVING KRISTOL

Being frustrated is disagreeable, but the real disasters in life begin 1
when you get what you want. For almost a century now, a great many intelligent, well-meaning and articulate people — of a kind generally
called liberal or intellectual, or both — have argued eloquently against
any kind of censorship of art and / or entertainment.

And within the past 10 years, the courts and the legislatures of most 2
Western nations have found these arguments persuasive — so persuasive
that hardly a man is now alive who clearly remembers what the answers
to these arguments were. Today, in the United States and other democracies, censorship has to all intents and purposes ceased to exist.

Is there a sense of triumphant exhilaration in the land? Hardly. 3
There is, on the contrary, a rapidly growing unease and disquiet. Somehow, things have not worked out as they were supposed to, and many
notable civil libertarians have gone on record as saying this was not what
they meant at all.

---

Irving Kristol teaches urban values at New York University and is founder and editor of the journal *Public Interest*.

They wanted a world in which "Desire Under the Elms" could be  4
produced, or *Ulysses* published, without interference by philistine busy-
bodies holding public office. They have got that, of course; but they
have also got a world in which homosexual rape takes place on the stage,
in which the public flocks during lunch hours to witness varieties of professional fornication.

But disagreeable as this may be, does it really matter? Might not our  5
unease and disquiet be merely a cultural hangover — a "hangup," as
they say? What reason is there to think that anyone was ever corrupted
by a book?

This last question, oddly enough, is asked by the very same people  6
who seem convinced that advertisements in magazines or displays of violence on television do indeed have the power to corrupt. It is also asked,
incredibly enough and in all sincerity, by people — e.g., university professors and school teachers — whose very lives provide all the answers one
could want.

After all, if you believe that no one was ever corrupted by a book,  7
you have also to believe that no one was ever improved by a book (or a
play or a movie). You have to believe, in other words, that all art is morally trivial and that, consequently, all education is morally irrelevant. No
one, not even a university professor, really believes that.

To be sure, it is extremely difficult, as social scientists tell us, to  8
trace the effects of any single book (or play or movie) on an individual
reader or any class of readers. But we all know, and social scientists know
it too, that the ways in which we use our minds and imaginations shape
our characters and help define us as persons. That those who certainly
know this are nevertheless moved to deny it merely indicates how a dogmatic resistance to the idea of censorship can — like most dogmatism —
result in a mindless insistence on the absurd.

I have used these harsh terms — "dogmatism" and "mindless" —  9
advisedly. I might also have added "hypocritical." For the plain fact is
that none of us is a complete civil libertarian. We all believe that there is
some point at which the public authorities ought to step in to limit the
"self-expression" of an individual or a group, even where this might be
seriously intended as a form of artistic expression, and even where the artistic transaction is between consenting adults.

A playwright or theatrical director might, in this crazy world of  10
ours, find someone willing to commit suicide on the stage, as called for
by the script. We would not allow that — any more than we would permit scenes of real physical torture on the stage, even if the victim were a
willing masochist.

The basic point that emerges is one that Walter Berns has power-  11 fully argued in his superb essay, "Pornography vs. Democracy": No society can be utterly indifferent to the ways its citizens publicly entertain themselves.

Bearbaiting and cockfighting are prohibited only in part out of 12 compassion for the suffering animals; the main reason they were abolished was that it was felt they debased and brutalized the citizenry who flocked to witness such spectacles. And the question we face with regard to pornography and obscenity is whether, now that they have such strong legal protection from the Supreme Court, they can or will brutalize and debase our citizenry.

We are, after all, not dealing with one passing incident — one 13 book, or one play, or one movie. We are dealing with a general tendency that is suffusing our entire culture.

I say pornography and obscenity because, though they have differ- 14 ent dictionary definitions and are frequently distinguishable as "artistic" genres, they are nevertheless in the end identical in effect. Pornography is not objectionable simply because it arouses sexual desire or lust or prurience in the mind of the reader or spectator; this is a silly Victorian notion.

A great many nonpornographic works — including some parts of 15 the Bible — excite sexual desire very successfully. What is distinctive about pornography is that, in the words of D. H. Lawrence, it attempts "to do dirt on (sex) . . . (It is an) insult to a vital human relationship."

In other words, pornography differs from erotic art in that its whole 16 purpose is to treat human beings obscenely, to deprive human beings of their specifically human dimension. That is what obscenity is all about. It is light years removed from any kind of carefree sensuality — there is no continuum between Fielding's *Tom Jones* and the Marquis de Sade's *Justine.*

It may well be that Western society, in the latter half of the 20th 17 century, is experiencing a drastic change in sexual mores and sexual relationships. We have had many such "sexual revolutions" in the past — and the bourgeois family and bourgeois ideas of sexual propriety were themselves established in the course of a revolution against 18th century "licentiousness" — and we shall doubtless have others in the future.

It is, however, highly improbable (to put it mildly) that what we are 18 witnessing is the final revolution which will make sexual relations utterly unproblematic, permit us to dispense with any kind of ordered relationships between the sexes, and allow us freely to redefine the human condition. And so long as humanity has not reached that utopia, obscenity will remain a problem.

Sex — like death — is an activity that is both animal and human. 19

There are human sentiments and human ideals involved in this animal activity. But when sex is public, the viewer does not see — cannot see — the sentiments and the ideals. He can only see the animal coupling.

And that is why, when men and women make love, as we say, they 20 prefer to be alone — because it is only when you are alone that you can make love, as distinct from merely copulating in an animal and casual way. And that, too, is why those who are voyeurs, if they are not irredeemably sick, also feel ashamed at what they are witnessing. When sex is a public spectacle, a human relationship has been debased into a mere animal connection.

The basic psychological fact about pornography and obscenity is 21 that it appeals to and provokes a kind of sexual regression. The sexual pleasure one gets from pornography and obscenity is autoerotic and infantile; to put it bluntly, it is a masturbatory exercise of the imagination, when it is not masturbation pure and simple. Now, people who masturbate do not get bored with masturbation, just as sadists don't get bored with sadism, and voyeurs don't get bored with voyeurism.

In other words, infantile sexuality is not only a permanent temptation for the adolescent or even the adult — it can quite easily become a permanent, self-reinforcing neurosis. 22

What is at stake is civilization and humanity, nothing less. The idea 23 that "everything is permitted," as Nietzsche put it, rests on the premise of nihilism and his nihilistic implications. I will not pretend that the case against nihilism and for civilization is an easy one to make. We are here confronting the most fundamental of philosophical questions, on the deepest levels.

But that is precisely my point — that the matter of pornography and 24 obscenity is not a trivial one, and that only superficial minds can take a bland and untroubled view of it.

In this connection, I might also point out that those who are pri- 25 marily against censorship on liberal grounds tell us not to take pornography or obscenity seriously, while those who are for pornography and obscenity on radical grounds, take it very seriously indeed.

I believe the radicals — writers like Susan Sontag, Herbert Marcuse, 26 Norman O. Brown, and even Jerry Rubin — are right, and the liberals are wrong. I also believe that those young radicals at Berkeley, some five years ago, who provoked a major confrontation over the public use of obscene words, showed a brilliant political instinct.

Once the faculty and administration had capitulated on this issue 27 saying: "Oh, for God's sake, let's be adult: What difference does it make anyway?" — once they said that, they were bound to lose on every other issue. And once Mark Rudd could publicly ascribe to the president of Columbia a notoriously obscene relationship to his mother, without provoking any kind of reaction, the SDS had already won the day. The occupation of Columbia's buildings merely ratified their victory.

Men who show themselves unwilling to defend civilization against 28 nihilism are not going to be either resolute or effective in defending the university against anything.

I am already touching upon a political aspect of pornography when 29 I suggest that it is inherently and purposefully subversive of civilization and its institutions. But there is another and more specifically political aspect, which has to do with the relationship of pornography and/or obscenity to democracy, and especially to the quality of public life on which democratic government ultimately rests.

Though the phrase, ''the quality of life,'' trips easily from so many 30 lips these days it tends to be one of these clichés with many trivial meanings and no large, serious one. Rarely does it have anything to do with the way the citizen in a democracy views himself—his obligations, his intentions, his ultimate self-definition.

There is an old idea of democracy—one which was fairly common 31 until about the beginning of this century—for which the conception of the quality of public life is absolutely crucial. This idea starts from the proposition that democracy is a form of self-government, and that if you want it to be a meritorious polity, you have to care about what kind of people govern it. Indeed, it puts the matter more strongly and declares that, if you want self-government, you are only entitled to it if that ''self'' is worthy of governing.

And because the desirability of self-government depends on the 32 character of the people who govern, the older idea of democracy was very solicitous of the condition of this character. It was solicitous of that collective self which we call public opinion and which, in a democracy, governs us collectively.

And because it cared, this older idea of democracy had no problem 33 in principle with pornography and/or obscenity. It censored them—and it did so with a perfect clarity of mind and a perfectly clear conscience. It was not about to permit people capriciously to corrupt themselves.

I have, it may be noticed, uttered that dreadful word, ''censor- 34 ship.'' And I am not about to back away from it. If you think pornography and/or obscenity is a serious problem, you have to be for censorship. I'll go even further and say that if you want to prevent pornography and/or obscenity from becoming a problem, you have to be for censorship. And lest there be any misunderstanding as to what I am saying, I'll put it as bluntly as possible: If you care for the quality of life in our American democracy, then you have to be for censorship.

But can a liberal be for censorship? Unless one assumes that being a 35 liberal must mean being indifferent to the quality of American life, then the answer has to be: yes, a liberal can be for censorship — but he ought to favor a liberal form of censorship.

Is that a contradiction in terms? I don't think so. We have no prob- 36 lem in contrasting repressive laws governing alcohol and drugs and to-bacco with laws regulating (i.e., discouraging the sale of) alcohol and drugs and tobacco. Laws encouraging temperance are not the same thing as laws that have as their goal prohibition or abolition.

We have not made the smoking of cigarets a criminal offense. We 37 have, however, and with good liberal conscience, prohibited cigaret ad-vertising on television, and may yet, again with good liberal conscience, prohibit it in newspapers and magazines. The idea of restricting individual freedom, in a liberal way, is not at all unfamiliar to us.

I therefore see no reason why we should not be able to distinguish 38 repressive censorship from liberal censorship of the written and spoken word.

This possibility, of course, occasions much distress among artists 39 and academics. It is a fact, one that cannot and should not be denied, that any system of censorship is bound, upon occasion, to treat unjustly a particular work of art — to find pornography where there is only gentle eroticism, to find obscenity where none really exists, or to find both where its existence ought to be tolerated because it serves a larger moral purpose.

It is such works of art that are likely to suffer at the hands of the cen- 40 sor. That is the price one has to be prepared to pay for censorship — even liberal censorship.

But just how high is this price? If you believe, as so many artists 41 seem to believe today, that art is the only sacrosanct activity in our pro-fane and vulgar world — that any man who designates himself an artist thereby acquires a sacred office — then obviously censorship is an intoler-able form of sacrilege. But for those of us who do not subscribe to this religion of art, the costs of censorship do not seem so high at all.

But I must repeat and emphasize: What kind of laws we pass gov- 42 erning pornography and obscenity, what kind of censorship or — since we are still a federal nation — what kinds of censorship we institute in our various localities may indeed be difficult matters to cope with; never-theless the real issue is one of principle.

I myself subscribe to a liberal view of the enforcement problem: I 43 think that pornography should be illegal and available to anyone who wants it so badly as to make a pretty strenuous effort to get it. We have lived with under-the-counter pornography for centuries now in a fairly comfortable way. But the issue of principle, of whether it should be over or under the counter, has to be settled before we can reflect on the advantages of alternative modes of censorship.

I think the settlement we are living under now, in which obscenity 44 and democracy are regarded as equals, is wrong; I believe it is inherently unstable: I think it will, in the long run, be incompatible with any authentic concern for the quality of life in our democracy.

# Hers

## SUSAN JACOBY

It is no news that many women are defecting from the ranks of civil 1 libertarians on the issue of obscenity. The conviction of Larry Flynt, publisher of *Hustler* magazine — before his metamorphosis into a born-again Christian — was greeted with unabashed feminist approval. Harry Reems, the unknown actor who was convicted by a Memphis jury for conspiring to distribute the movie *Deep Throat*, has carried on his legal battles with almost no support from women who ordinarily regard themselves as supporters of the First Amendment. Feminist writers and scholars have even discussed the possibility of making common cause against pornography with adversaries of the women's movement — including opponents of the equal rights amendment and "right to life" forces.

All of this is deeply disturbing to a woman writer who believes, as I 2 always have and still do, in an absolute interpretation of the First Amendment. Nothing in Larry Flynt's garbage convinces me that the late Justice Hugo L. Black was wrong in this opinion that "the Federal Government is without any power whatsoever under the Constitution to put any type of burden on free speech and expression of ideas of any kind (as distinguished from conduct)." Many women I like and respect tell me I am wrong; I cannot remember having become involved in so many heated discussions of a public issue since the end of the Vietnam War. A feminist writer described my views as those of a "First Amendment junkie."

Many feminist arguments for controls on pornography carry the im- 3 . plicit conviction that porn books, magazines and movies pose a greater threat to women than similarly repulsive exercises of free speech pose to

---

Susan Jacoby is a journalist and essayist who writes frequently on feminist concerns.

other offended groups. This conviction has, of course, been shared by everyone — regardless of race, creed or sex — who has ever argued in favor of abridging the First Amendment. It is the argument used by some Jews who have withdrawn their support from the American Civil Liberties Union because it has defended the right of American Nazis to march through a community inhabited by survivors of Hitler's concentration camps.

If feminists want to argue that the protection of the Constitution 4 should not be extended to *any* particularly odious or threatening form of speech, they have a reasonable argument (although I don't agree with it). But it is ridiculous to suggest that the porn shops on 42d Street are more disgusting to women than a march of neo-Nazis is to survivors of the extermination camps.

The arguments over pornography also blur the vital distinction be- 5 tween expression of ideas and conduct. When I say I believe unreservedly in the First Amendment, someone always comes back at me with the issue of "kiddie porn." But kiddie porn is not a First Amendment issue. It is an issue of the abuse of power — the power adults have over children — and not of obscenity. Parents and promoters have no more right to use their children to make porn movies than they do to send them to work in coal mines. The responsible adults should be prosecuted, just as adults who use children for back-breaking farm labor should be prosecuted.

Susan Brownmiller, in *Against Our Will: Men, Women and Rape*, 6 has described pornography as "the undiluted essence of anti-female propaganda." I think this is a fair description of some types of pornography, especially of the brutish subspecies that equates sex with death and portrays women primarily as objects of violence.

The equation of sex and violence, personified by some glossy rock 7 record album covers as well as by *Hustler*, has fed the illusion that censorship of pornography can be conducted on a more rational basis than other types of censorship. Are all pictures of naked women obscene? Clearly not, says a friend. A Renoir nude is art, she says, and *Hustler* is a trash. "Any reasonable person" knows that.

But what about something between art and trash — something, say, 8 along the lines of *Playboy* or *Penthouse* magazines? I asked five women for their reactions to one picture in *Penthouse* and got responses that ranged from "lovely" and "sensuous" to "revolting" and "demeaning." Feminists, like everyone else, seldom have rational reasons for their preferences in erotica. Like members of juries, they tend to disagree when confronted with something that falls short of 100 percent vulgarity.

In any case, feminists will not be the arbiters of good taste if it be-  9
comes easier to harass, prosecute and convict people on obscenity
charges. Most of the people who want to censor girlie magazines are
equally opposed to open discussion of issues that are of vital concern to
women: rape, abortion, menstruation, contraception, lesbianism — in
fact, the entire range of sexual experience from a women's viewpoint.

Feminist writers and editors and film makers have limited financial  10
resources: Confronted by a determined prosecutor, Hugh Hefner will
fare better than Susan Brownmiller. Would the Memphis jurors who
convicted Harry Reems for his role in *Deep Throat* be inclined to take a
more positive view of paintings of the female genitalia done by sensitive
feminist artists? *Ms.* magazine has printed color reproductions of some of
those art works; *Ms.* is already banned from a number of high school libraries because someone considers it threatening and/or obscene.

Feminists who want to censor what they regard as harmful pornog-  11
raphy have essentially the same motivation as other would-be censors:
They want to use the power of the state to accomplish what they have
been unable to achieve in the marketplace of ideas and images. The impulse to censor places no faith in the possibilities of democratic persuasion.

It isn't easy to persuade certain men that they have better uses for  12
$1.95 each month than to spend it on a copy of *Hustler*? Well, then,
give the men no choice in the matter.

I believe there is also a connection between the impulse toward cen-  13
sorship on the part of people who used to consider themselves civil libertarians and a more general desire to shift responsibility from individuals
to institutions. When I saw the movie "Looking for Mr. Goodbar," I
was stunned by its series of visual images equating sex and violence,
coupled with what seems to me the mindless message (a distortion of the
fine Judith Rossner novel) that casual sex equals death. When I came out
of the movie, I was even more shocked to see parents standing in line
with children between the ages of 10 and 14.

I simply don't know why a parent would take a child to see such a  14
movie, any more than I understand why people feel they can't turn off a
television set their child is watching. Whenever I say that, my friends tell
me I don't know how it is because I don't have children. True, but I do
have parents. When I was a child, they did turn off the TV. They didn't
expect the Federal Communications Commission to do their job for
them.

I am a First Amendment junkie. You can't OD on the First Amend-  15
ment, because free speech is its own best antidote.

# Pornography Is
# a Social Disease

## JANE RULE

I think one of the basic failures in recent debates about pornogra- 1
phy and censorship is some women's inability to see that censorship
won't work, and some men's inability to see that pornography is an issue
as important as, and separate from, freedom of expression.

If we are not talking about writing laws, defining pornography 2
doesn't pose as serious a problem. We do have different tastes. Maybe
some of mine come from my middle-class background (my mother
wouldn't think so!). I don't like bodies presented without heads, particularly female bodies. The motive may sometimes be the protection of
the individual, but the impression is decapitation, and I also happen to
be someone who is attracted to people's faces. This is a matter of taste.

What I object to is the representation of acts of violence against 3
bodies in the name of sexual freedom. Live rats, guns and hot hair-curl-
ing irons placed in women's vaginas are not sexual acts, any more than
dismemberment and murder are sexual acts. If these were images only to
be found in the archives of criminal pathology, women might not be as
concerned as they are, but these are, in fact, images found in widely distributed films. There are apparently a great many people willing to pay
money to look at images of that sort.

I don't find evidence, as some radical feminists do, for the claim 4
that all men are rapists and murderers. If all men are, potentially, rapists
and murders, then they are so only as women, too, have a potential for
destructive behavior. Women, however, have been traditionally trained
away from such behaviour (how else would the two-year-olds of the
world survive?), except as we can turn it on ourselves in madness and
self-destruction. Why else would Sylvia Plath's suicide inspire myths
rather than simple pity? Men are trained to kill in circumstances of war.
Because for most men such behaviour is abhorrent, it must continually
be glorified to persuade them against their own moral sense to destroy
rather than protect other members of their own species.

We have come to a point in the history of our species where individ- 5
ual and even national survival don't have any meaning apart from the
survival of the entire planet. The destructive impulse, therefore, hasn't

---

Jane Rule has published five novels, two collections of short stories, and a book of
criticism and social comment called *Lesbian Images*.

any claim to social usefulness (if it ever did). Only a very small percentage of the population actually commits suicide or rapes or kills without specific training to do so; that education in self-destruction or murder must be reversed, so that no woman can ever again romanticize suicide, so that the chorus, "Hell no, we won't go" becomes universal.

I find the preoccupation with violence in the daily fare on television 6 just as frightening as violent pornography. Men are presented to us hourly as heroes who beat up, torture, maim and kill other men. Their victims are "bad guys" who deserve what they get, much as the women in violent pornographic films are presented as beneath contempt. That these are the most common images given to men for their power and self-worth should be as energetically protested by men as by women.

It is not only women but men who must stand up and say. "No, 7 that is not who we are." Women, in stating our own case against our misrepresentation in the fantasy-life of the world, and therefore our lack of representation in the real world, sometimes don't want to hear that men are as victimized, if differently. The generation of women currently involved in the feminist movement are mostly too young to remember world wars. I remember, with horror, the old stars in windows marking proudly a house which had lost a son, brother or father. I remember, with horror, a mother proudly receiving her country's honour for having "given" five sons to victory. Whole generations of young men were killed in both these wars. Any woman who proudly sees men off to war has very little moral claim to insistence on the sanctity of her own life, exempt from the violence she condones.

Men's indifference to pornography as a basic threat to our humane 8 survival is akin to the indifference of men and women alike to the daily glorification of male violence when it is directed against other men, not only in thrillers but on the nightly news, where we are supposed to go on applying the brutish morality of "good guys" and "bad guys."

It is not a matter of wanting to turn away from "things unpleas- 9 ant," from "reality." Both the glory and the terrible vulnerability of human creatures grows from our ability to learn. But we do also have some capacity to resist our educations, to influence the world we live in, to change our perceptions of ourselves and other people. If this were not so, those in authority would have no fear of dissenters.

Not so very long ago, children worked in the mines from the age of 10 six, women died young of yearly breeding, and men died exhausted working for their betters. In the world today, there is not even that minimal ritual of life in huge refugee populations, in many indigenous populations. But we do know, because as a culture we have experienced it, that a more humane way to be children and to be women and men is possible.

If we refuse to help create a climate which glorifies mutilation and 11
death, if we protest against it, we can begin to change it. What makes all
human atrocities on a large scale possible is the passive acceptance of
them by the majority of people, who have been conditioned either to
feel helpless or to be indifferent to the suffering of others.

The wide gap between trying to suppress violent pornography, ei- 12
ther by calling in the police or destroying private property, and helping
to sell the stuff offers plenty of comfortable moral and political space to
live in. In this consumer society, not helping to sell and not buying are
very strong weapons in the hands of the people.

Men and women can be together on this issue. Women don't have 13
to play into the traps of the moral majority by demanding censorship
which will be politically abused. Men don't have to condone pornography degrading to women in the name of sexual freedom and freedom of
expression. We won't sell it. We won't buy it. We will instead do everything we can to change the image of man as a defiler of the earth, proving his superiority to nature by destroying it.

The terrifying message of gay liberation is that men are capable of 14
loving their brothers. It should be sweet news to every woman in the
world, for if the capacity of men to love those whom they've been taught
to treat as competitors and enemies can transcend their education, the
world can begin to heal. The message of women's liberation is that
women can love each other and ourselves against degrading education. It
is not necessary for men to protect and despise women, nor for women to
nurture and fear men. It is time for us to share subversive truths about
the courage of men and women to live in diversity and peace.

## Discussion Questions

1. A few years ago a purveyor of pornographic films requested permission to
   show some of his films on a large northeastern campus. One of the objections raised against permitting him to do so was that educational institutions should observe standards different from the community outside. Defend or attack this argument.
2. Irving Kristol says that "none of us is a complete civil libertarian." That is,
   we all draw the line at some point where we think "public authorities
   ought to step in to limit the 'self-expression' of an individual or a group."
   Do you draw the line somewhere? For example, would you deny the right
   of American Nazis to march among the survivors of concentration camps?
3. Discuss the persuasive effect of Gloria Steinem's article on Linda Lovelace.
   Does it offer a legitimate argument against pornographic movies? Or is it
   merely grotesquely sensational? Or perhaps both? If you find the article
   persuasive, tell in what way the story of Linda Lovelace supports Steinem's
   principal complaint against pornography.

4. Do you agree with Jane Rule that violence by men against men in war and fiction represents essentially the same behavior as violence by men against women in pornography? Why or why not?

5. Susan Jacoby quotes a friend who said, "A Renoir nude is art, . . . and *Hustler* is trash." Define the differences, using more examples to make your point. Or disagree, making the case that art and pornography are really indistinguishable.

6. Do some research to discover what experts say about the influence of pornography on violent conduct, especially by men against women. If the experts differ, evaluate the relative merits of their evidence in order to come to a conclusion, if possible, that one set of data is more reliable than another.

PART THREE  *Anthology*

# The Ignored Lesson of Anne Frank

## Bruno Bettelheim

Anne Frank, the fourteen-year-old Dutch Jewish author of *The Diary of a Young Girl*, is probably the best-known victim of the Nazi extermination program that killed 6 million Jews before and during World War II. In this essay Bruno Bettelheim, a writer and psychologist and himself a survivor of a Nazi concentration camp, argues with some bitterness against the universal admiration for the way the Franks continued to live their beloved family life while the world around them was being destroyed. Our admiration for what Bettelheim calls a senseless fate is based, he says, on our desire to repress the horror of the Holocaust.

When the world first learned about the Nazi concentration and death camps, most civilized people felt the horrors committed in them to be so uncanny as to be unbelievable. It came as a severe shock that supposedly civilized nations could stoop to such inhuman acts. The implication that modern man has such inadequate control over his cruel and destructive proclivities was felt as a threat to our views of ourselves and our humanity. Three different psychological mechanisms were most frequently used for dealing with the appalling revelation of what had gone on in the camps:

1. its applicability to man in general was denied by asserting — contrary to evidence — that the acts of torture and mass murder were committed by a small group of insane or perverted persons;
2. the truth of the reports was denied by declaring them vastly exaggerated and ascribing them to propaganda (this originated with the German government, which called all reports on terror in the camps "horror propaganda" — *Greuelpropaganda*);
3. the reports were believed, but the knowledge of the horror repressed as soon as possible.

All three mechanisms could be seen at work after liberation of those prisoners remaining. At first, after the discovery of the camps and their death-dealing, a wave of extreme outrage swept the Allied nations. It was soon followed by a general repression of the discovery in people's minds. Possibly this reaction was due to something more than the blow dealt to modern man's narcissism by the realization that cruelty is still

rampant among men. Also present may have been the dim but extremely threatening realization that the modern state now has available
the means for changing personality, and for destroying millions it deems
undesirable. The ideas that in our day a people's personalities might be
changed against their will by the state, and that other populations might
be wholly or partially exterminated, are so fearful that one tries to free
oneself of them and their impact by defensive denial, or by repression.

The extraordinary world-wide success of the book, play, and movie 3
*The Diary of Anne Frank* suggests the power of the desire to counteract
the realization of the personality-destroying and murderous nature of
the camps by concentraing all attention on what is experienced as a demonstration that private and intimate life can continue to flourish even
under the direct persecution by the most ruthless totalitarian system.
And this although Anne Frank's fate demonstrates how efforts at disre-
garding in private life what goes on around one in society can hasten
one's own destruction.

What concerns me here is not what actually happened to the Frank 4
family, how they tried — and failed — to survive their terrible ordeal. It
would be very wrong to take apart so humane and moving a story, which
aroused so much well-merited compassion for gentle Anne Frank and her
tragic fate. What is at issue is the universal and uncritical response to her
diary and to the play and movie based on it, and what this reaction tells
about our attempts to cope with the feelings her fate — used by us to
serve as a symbol of a most human reaction to Nazi terror — arouses in
us. I believe that the world-wide acclaim given her story cannot be explained unless we recognize in it our wish to forget the gas chambers,
and our effort to do so by glorifying the ability to retreat into an extremely private, gentle, sensitive world, and there to cling as much as
possible to what have been one's usual daily attitudes and activities, although surrounded by a maelstrom apt to engulf one at any moment.

The Frank family's attitude that life could be carried on as before 5
may well have been what led to their destruction. By eulogizing how
they lived in their hiding place while neglecting to examine first whether
it was a reasonable or an effective choice, we are able to ignore the crucial
lesson of their story — that such an attitude can be fatal in extreme circumstances.

While the Franks were making their preparations for going passively 6
into hiding, thousands of other Jews in Holland (as elsewhere in Europe)
were trying to escape to the free world, in order to survive and/or fight.
Others who could not escape went underground — into hiding — each
family member with, for example, a different gentile family. We gather
from the diary, however, that the chief desire of the Frank family was to
continue living as nearly as possible in the same fashion to which they
had been accustomed in happier times.

Little Anne, too, wanted only to go on with life as usual, and what 7
else could she have done but fall in with the pattern her parents created
for her existence? But hers was not a necessary fate, much less a heroic
one; it was a terrible but also a senseless fate. Anne had a good chance to
survive, as did many Jewish children in Holland. But she would have had
to leave her parents and go to live with a gentile Dutch family, posing as
their own child, something her parents would have had to arrange for
her.

Everyone who recognized the obvious knew that the hardest way to 8
go underground was to do it as a family; to hide out together made detection by the SS most likely; and when detected, everybody was
doomed. By hiding singly, even when one got caught, the others had a
chance to survive. The Franks, with their excellent connections among
gentile Dutch families, might well have been able to hide out singly,
each with a different family. But instead, the main principle of their
planning was continuing their beloved family life — an understandable
desire, but highly unrealistic in those times. Choosing any other course
would have meant not merely giving up living together, but also realizing the full measure of the danger to their lives.

The Franks were unable to accept that going on living as a family as 9
they had done before the Nazi invasion of Holland was no longer a desirable way of life, much as they loved each other; in fact, for them and
others like them, it was most dangerous behavior. But even given their
wish not to separate, they failed to make appropriate preparations for
what was likely to happen.

There is little doubt that the Franks, who were able to provide 10
themselves with so much while arranging for going into hiding, and even
while hiding, could have provided themselves with some weapons had
they wished. Had they had a gun, Mr. Frank could have shot down at
least one or two of the "green police" who came for them. There was no
surplus of such police, and the loss of an SS with every Jew arrested
would have noticeably hindered the functioning of the police state. Even
a butcher knife, which they certainly could have taken with them into
hiding, could have been used by them in self-defense. The fate of the
Franks wouldn't have been very different, because they all died anyway
except for Anne's father. But they could have sold their lives for a high
price, instead of walking to their death. Still, although one must assume
that Mr. Frank would have fought courageously, as we know he did when
a soldier in the first World War, it is not everybody who can plan to kill
those who are bent on killing him, although many who would not be
ready to contemplate doing so would be willing to kill those who are
bent on murdering not only them but also their wives and little daughters.

An entirely different matter would have been planning for escape in 11 case of discovery. The Franks' hiding place had only one entrance; it did not have any other exit. Despite this fact, during their many months of hiding, they did not try to devise one. Nor did they make other plans for escape, such as that one of the family members — as likely as not Mr. Frank — would try to detain the police in the narrow entrance way — maybe even fight them, as suggested above — thus giving other members of the family a chance to escape, either by reaching the roofs of adjacent houses, or down a ladder into the alley behind the house in which they were living.

Any of this would have required recognizing and accepting the desperate straits in which they found themselves, and concentrating on how best to cope with them. This was quite possible to do, even under the terrible conditions in which the Jews found themselves after the Nazi occupation of Holland. It can be seen from many other accounts, for example from the story of Marga Minco, a girl of about Anne Frank's age who lived to tell about it. Her parents had planned that when the police should come for them, the father would try to detain them by arguing and fighting with them, to give the wife and daughter a chance to escape through a rear door. Unfortunately it did not quite work out this way, and both parents got killed. But their short-lived resistance permitted their daughter to make her escape as planned and to reach a Dutch family who saved her.[1]    12

This is not mentioned as a criticism that the Frank family did not    13
plan or behave along similar lines. A family has every right to arrange their life as they wish or think best, and to take the risks they want to take. My point is not to criticize what the Franks did, but only the universal admiration of their way of coping, or rather of not coping. The story of little Marga who survived, every bit as touching, remains totally neglected by comparison.

Many Jews — unlike the Franks, who through listening to British ra-    14
dio news were better informed than most — had no detailed knowledge of the extermination camps. Thus it was easier for them to make themselves believe that complete compliance with even the most outrageously debilitating and degrading Nazi orders might offer a chance for survival. But neither tremendous anxiety that inhibits clear thinking and with it well-planned and determined action, nor ignorance about what happened to those who responded with passive waiting for being rounded up for their extermination, can explain the reaction of audiences to the play and movie retelling Anne's story, which are all about such waiting that results finally in destruction.

I think it is the fictitious ending that explains the enormous success    15

---

[1]Marga Minco, *Bitter Herbs* (New York: Oxford University Press, 1960).

of this play and movie. At the conclusion we hear Anne's voice from the beyond, saying, "In spite of everything, I still believe that people are really good at heart." This improbable sentiment is supposedly from a girl who had been starved to death, had watched her sister meet the same fate before she did, knew that her mother had been murdered, and had watched untold thousands of adults and children being killed. This statement is not justified by anything Anne actually told her diary.

Going on with intimate family living, no matter how dangerous it 16 might be to survival, was fatal to all too many during the Nazi regime. And if all men are good, then indeed we can all go on with living our lives as we have been accustomed to in times of undisturbed safety and can afford to forget about Auschwitz. But Anne, her sister, her mother, may well have died because her parents could not get themselves to believe in Auschwitz.

While play and movie are ostensibly about Nazi persecution and 17 destruction, in actuality what we watch is the way that, despite this terror, lovable people manage to continue living their satisfying intimate lives with each other. The heroine grows from a child into a young adult as normally as any other girl would, despite the most abnormal conditions of all other aspects of her existence, and that of her family. Thus the play reassures us that despite the destructiveness of Nazi racism and tyranny in general, it is possible to disregard it in one's private life much of the time, even if one is Jewish.

True, the ending happens just as the Franks and their friends had 18 feared all along: their hiding place is discovered, and they are carried away to their doom. But the fictitious declaration of faith in the goodness of all men which concludes the play falsely reassures us since it impresses on us that in the combat between Nazi terror and continuance of intimate family living the latter wins out, since Anne has the last word. This is simply contrary to fact, because it was she who got killed. Her seeming survival through her moving statement about the goodness of men releases us effectively of the need to cope with the problems Auschwitz presents. That is why we are so relieved by her statement. It explains why millions loved play and movie, because while it confronts us with the fact that Auschwitz existed it encourages us at the same time to ignore any of its implications. If all men are good at heart, there never really was an Auschwitz; nor is there any possibility that it may recur.

The desire of Anne Frank's parents not to interrupt their intimate 19 family living, and their inability to plan more effectively for their survival, reflect the failure of all too many others faced with the threat of Nazi terror. It is a failure that deserves close examination because of the inherent warnings it contains for us, the living.

Submission to the threatening power of the Nazi state often led 20 both to the disintegration of what had once seemed well-integrated personalities and to a return to an immature disregard for the dangers of reality. Those Jews who submitted passively to Nazi persecution came to depend on primitive and infantile thought processes: wishful thinking and disregard for the possibility of death. Many persuaded themselves that they, out of all the others, would be spared. Many more simply disbelieved in the possibility of their own death. Not believing in it, they did not take what seemed to them desperate precautions, such as giving up everything to hide out singly; or trying to escape even if it meant risking their lives in doing so; or preparing to fight for their lives when no escape was possible and death had become an immediate possibility. It is true that defending their lives in active combat before they were rounded up to be transported into the camps might have hastened their deaths, and so, up to a point, they were protecting themselves by "rolling with the punches" of the enemy.

But the longer one rolls with the punches dealt not by the normal 21 vagaries of life, but by one's eventual executioner, the more likely it becomes that one will no longer have the strength to resist when death becomes imminent. This is particularly true if yielding to the enemy is accompanied not by a commensurate strengthening of the personality, but by an inner disintegration. We can observe such a process among the Franks, who bickered with each other over trifles, instead of supporting each other's ability to resist the demoralizing impact of their living conditions.

Those who faced up to the announced intentions of the Nazis pre- 22 pared for the worst as a real and imminent possibility. It meant risking one's life for a self-chosen purpose, but in doing so, creating at least a small chance for saving one's own life or those of others, or both. When Jews in Germany were restricted to their homes, those who did not succumb to inertia took the new restrictions as a warning that it was high time to go underground, join the resistance movement, provide themselves with forged papers, and so on, if they had not done so long ago. Many of them survived.

Some distant relatives of mine may furnish an example. Early in the 23 war, a young man living in a small Hungarian town banded together with a number of other Jews to prepare against a German invasion. As soon as the Nazis imposed curfews on the Jews, his group left for Budapest — because the bigger capital city with its greater anonymity offered chances for escaping detection. Similar groups from other towns converged in Budapest and joined forces. From among themselves they selected typically "Aryan" looking men who equipped themselves with false papers and immediately joined the Hungarian SS. These spies were then able to warn of impending persecution and raids.

Many of these groups survived intact. Furthermore, they had also 24
equipped themselves with small arms, so that if they were detected, they
could put up enough of a fight for the majority to escape while a few
would die fighting to make the escape possible. A few of the Jews who
had joined the SS were discovered and immediately shot, probably a
death preferable to one in the gas chambers. But most of even these Jews
survived, hiding within the SS until liberation.

Compare these arrangements not just to the Franks' selection of a 25
hiding place that was basically a trap without an outlet but with Mr.
Frank's teaching typically academic high-school subjects to his children
rather than how to make a getaway: a token of his inability to face the
seriousness of the threat of death. Teaching high-school subjects had, of
course, its constructive aspects. It relieved the ever-present anxiety about
their fate to some degree by concentrating on different matters, and by
implication it encouraged hope for a future in which such knowledge
would be useful. In this sense such teaching was purposeful, but it was
erroneous in that it took the place of much more pertinent teaching and
planning: how best to try to escape when detected.

Unfortunately the Franks were by no means the only ones who, out 26
of anxiety, became unable to contemplate their true situation and with it
to plan accordingly. Anxiety, and the wish to counteract it by clinging to
each other, and to reduce its sting by continuing as much as possible
with their usual way of life incapacitated many, particularly when survival plans required changing radically old ways of living that they cherished, and which had become their only source of satisfaction.

My young relative, for example, was unable to persuade other mem- 27
bers of his family to go with him when he left the small town where he
had lived with them. Three times, at tremendous risk to himself, he returned to plead with his relatives, pointing out first the growing persecution of the Jews, and later the fact that transport to the gas chambers had
already begun. He could not convince these Jews to leave their homes
and break up their families to go singly into hiding.

As their desperation mounted, they clung more determinedly to 28
their old living arrangements and to each other, became less able to consider giving up the possessions they had accumulated through hard work
over a lifetime. The more severely their freedom to act was reduced, and
what little they were still permitted to do restricted by insensible and degrading regulations imposed by the Nazis, the more did they become
unable to contemplate independent action. Their life energies drained
out of them, sapped by their ever-greater anxiety. The less they found
strength in themselves, the more they held on to the little that was left of
what had given them security in the past — their old surroundings, their
customary way of life, their possessions — all these seemed to give their

lives some permanency, offer some symbols of security. Only what had once been symbols of security now endangered life, since they were excuses for avoiding change. On each successive visit the young man found his relatives more incapacitated, less willing or able to take his advice, more frozen into inactivity, and with it further along the way to the crematoria where, in fact, they all died.

Levin renders a detailed account of the desperate but fruitless efforts 29 made by small Jewish groups determined to survive to try to save the rest. She tells how messengers were "sent into the provinces to warn Jews that deportation meant death, but their warnings were ignored because most Jews refused to contemplate their own annihiliation."[2] I believe the reason for such refusal has to be found in their inability to take action. If we are certain that we are helpless to protect ourselves against the danger of destruction, we cannot contemplate it. We can consider the danger only as long as we believe there are ways to protect ourselves, to fight back, to escape. If we are convinced none of this is possible for us, then there is no point in thinking about the danger; on the contrary, it is best to refuse to do so.

As a prisoner in Buchenwald, I talked to hundreds of German Jew- 30 ish prisoners who were brought there as part of the huge pogrom in the wake of the murder of vom Rath in the fall of 1938. I asked them why they had not left Germany, given the utterly degrading conditions they had been subjected to. Their answer was: How could we leave? It would have meant giving up our homes, our work, our sources of income. Having been deprived by Nazi persecution and degradation of much of their self-respect, they had become unable to give up what still gave them a semblance of it: their earthly belongings. But instead of using possessions, they became captivated by them, and this possession by earthly goods became the fatal mask for their possession by anxiety, fear, and denial.

How the investment of personal property with one's life energy 31 could make people die bit by bit was illustrated throughout the Nazi persecution of the Jews. At the time of the first boycott of Jewish stores, the chief external goal of the Nazis was to acquire the possessions of the Jews. They even let Jews take some things out of the country at that time if they would leave the bulk of their property behind. For a long time the intention of the Nazis, and the goal of their first discriminatory laws, was to force undesirable minorities, including Jews, into emigration.

Although the extermination policy was in line with the inner logic 32 of Nazi racial ideology, one may wonder whether the idea that millions of Jews (and other foreign nationals) could be submitted to extermina-

---

[2]Nora Levin, *The Holocaust* (New York: Thomas Y. Crowell, 1968).

tion did not partially result from seeing the degree of degradation Jews accepted without fighting back. When no violent resistance occurred, persecution of the Jews worsened, slow step by slow step.

Many Jews who on the invasion of Poland were able to survey their 33 situation and draw the right conclusions survived the Second World War. As the Germans approached, they left everything behind and fled to Russia, much as they distrusted and disliked the Soviet system. But there, while badly treated, they could at least survive. Those who stayed on in Poland believing they could go on with life-as-before sealed their fate. Thus in the deepest sense the walk to the gas chamber was only the last consequence of these Jews' inability to comprehend what was in store; it was the final step of surrender to the death instinct, which might also be called the principle of inertia. The first step was taken long before arrival at the death camp.

We can find a dramatic demonstration of how far the surrender to 34 inertia can be carried, and the wish not to know because knowing would create unbearable anxiety, in an experience of Olga Lengyel.[3] She reports that although she and her fellow prisoners lived just a few hundred yards from the crematoria and the gas chambers and knew what they were for, most prisoners denied knowledge of them for months. If they had grasped their true situation, it might have helped them save either the lives they themselves were fated to lose, or the lives of others.

When Mrs. Lengyel's fellow prisoners were selected to be sent to the 35 gas chambers, they did not try to break away from the group, as she successfully did. Worse, the first time she tried to escape the gas chambers, some of the other selected prisoners told the supervisors that she was trying to get away. Mrs. Lengyel desperately asks the question: How was it possible that people denied the existence of the gas chambers when all day long they saw the crematoria burning and smelled the odor of burning flesh? Why did they prefer ignoring the exterminations to fighting for their very own lives? She can offer no explanation, only the observation that they resented anyone who tried to save himself from the common fate, because they lacked enough courage to risk action themselves. I believe they did it because they had given up their will to live and permitted their death tendencies to engulf them. As a result, such prisoners were in the thrall of the murdering SS not only physically but also psychologically, while this was not true for those prisoners who still had a grip on life.

Some prisoners even began to serve their executioners, to help speed 36 the death of their own kind. Then things had progressed beyond simple inertia to the death instinct running rampant. Those who tried to serve

---

[3]Olga Lengyel, *Five Chimneys: The Story of Auschwitz* (Chicago: Ziff-Davis, 1947).

their executioners in what were once their civilian capacities were merely continuing life as usual and thereby opening the door to their death.

For example, Mrs. Lengyel speaks of Dr. Mengele, SS physician at 37 Auschwitz, as a typical example of the "business as usual" attitude that enabled some prisoners, and certainly the SS, to retain whatever balance they could despite what they were doing. She describes how Dr. Mengele took all correct medical precautions during childbirth, rigorously observing all aseptic principles, cutting the umbilical cord with greatest care, etc. But only half an hour later he sent mother and infant to be burned in the crematorium.

Having made his choice, Dr. Mengele and others like him had to 38 delude themselves to be able to live with themselves and their experience. Only one personal document on the subject has come to my attention, that of Dr. Nyiszli, a prisoner serving as "research physician" at Auschwitz.⁴ How Dr. Nyiszli deluded himself can be seen, for example, in the way he repeatedly refers to himself as working in Auschwitz as a physician, although he worked as the assistant of a criminal murderer. He speaks of the Institute for Race, Biological, and Anthropological Investigation as "one of the most qualified medical centers of the Third Reich," although it was devoted to proving falsehoods. That Nyiszli was a doctor didn't alter the fact that he — like any of the prisoner foremen who served the SS better than some SS were willing to serve it — was a participant in the crimes of the SS. How could he do it and live with himself?

The answer is: by taking pride in his professional skills, irrespective 39 of the purpose they served. Dr. Nyiszli and Dr. Mengele were only two among hundreds of other — and far more prominent — physicians who participated in the Nazis' murderous pseudo-scientific human experiments. It was the peculiar pride of these men in their professional skill and knowledge, without regard for moral implications, that made them so dangerous. Although the concentration camps and crematoria are no longer here, this kind of pride still remains with us; it is characteristic of a modern society in which fascination with technical competence has dulled concern for human feelings. Auschwitz is gone, but so long as this attitude persists, we shall not be safe from cruel indifference to life at the core.

I have met many Jews as well as gentile anti-Nazis, similar to the ac- 40 tivist group in Hungary described earlier, who survived in Nazi Germany and in the occupied countries. These people realized that when a world goes to pieces and inhumanity reigns supreme, man cannot go on living his private life as he was wont to do, and would like to do; he cannot, as

---

⁴Miklos Nyiszli, *Auschwitz: A Doctor's Eyewitness Account* (New York: Frederick Fell, 1960).

the loving head of a family, keep the family living together peacefully, undisturbed by the surrounding world; nor can he continue to take pride in his profession or possessions, when either will deprive him of his humanity, if not also of his life. In such times, one must radically reevaluate all of what one has done, believed in, and stood for in order to know how to act. In short, one has to take a stand on the new reality — a firm stand, not one of retirement into an even more private world.

If today, Negroes in Africa march against the guns of a police that 41 defends *apartheid* — even if hundreds of dissenters are shot down and tens of thousands rounded up in camps — their fight will sooner or later assure them of a chance for liberty and equality. Millions of the Jews of Europe who did not or could not escape in time or go underground as many thousands did, could at least have died fighting as some did in the Warsaw ghetto at the end, instead of passively waiting to be rounded up for their own extermination.

## Discussion Questions

1. Summarize the three psychological mechanisms with which people confronted the knowledge of the concentration camps. Which of these three, according to Bettelheim, accounts for the universal admiration of Anne Frank's diary? What danger does Bettelheim see in this admiration?
2. Bettelheim suggests that the Franks had other choices than remaining in hiding and trying to preserve their gentle family life. What were those choices? Why does Bettelheim think they would have been superior to the choices the Franks made? How does he use the example of his distant relatives in Hungray to prove his point?
3. What lesson does Bettelheim draw from the story of Marga Minco?
4. What is Bettelheim's criticism of Anne's conclusion in the movie and stage versions of her life story: "In spite of everything, I still believe that people are really good at heart." In what way does this statement relieve us?
5. What did Bettelheim's conversations with fellow victims in Buchenwald reveal about the reasons for their failure to try to escape? How does Olga Lengyel's experience confirm Bettelheim's point?
6. How does Bettelheim account for the ability of prisoners who assisted the Nazis to live with themselves?
7. What comparison does Bettelheim make between the Jews of Europe during the Nazi period and blacks in South Africa today? How does this comparison reinforce his thesis?

## Writing Suggestions

1. If you are familiar with *The Diary of a Young Girl* in any of its versions — book, play, or movie — give your own response to it. Did you admire Anne

Frank? Do you agree or disagree with Bettelheim's claim that admiration for her and her family is based on unrealistic assumptions about the way people should behave in life-threatening circumstances?

2. Bettelheim refers to the prisoners who assisted the Nazis in the concentration camps as men who took pride in "their professional skill and knowledge, without regard for moral implications." Are there such people among us today? If so, choose an example and write an essay describing their activities and arguing that they are dangerous for the reasons Bettelheim gives.

# *Where College Fails Us*

## CAROLINE BIRD

Caroline Bird, a former editor and teacher, argues against the popular assumption that college confers benefits on all who attend. She offers detailed objections to some of college's most oft-cited advantages and urges high school graduates to consider whether a college education is worth the investment in time, expense, dependency, and future returns.

The case *for* college has been accepted without question for more 1 than a generation. All high school graduates ought to go, says Conventional Wisdom and statistical evidence, because college will help them earn more money, become ''better'' people, and learn to be more responsible citizens than those who don't go.

But college has never been able to work its magic for everyone. And 2 now that close to half our high school graduates are attending, those who don't fit the pattern are becoming more numerous, and more obvious. College graduates are selling shoes and driving taxis; college students sabotage each other's experiments and forge letters of recommendation in the intense competition for admission to graduate school. Others find no stimulation in their studies, and drop out — often encouraged by college administrators.

Some observers say the fault is with the young people themselves — 3 they are spoiled, stoned, overindulged, and expecting too much. But that's mass character assassination, and doesn't explain all campus unhappiness. Others blame the state of the world, and they are partly right. We've been told that young people have to go to college because our economy can't absorb an army of untrained eighteen-year-olds. But disillusioned graduates are learning that it can no longer absorb an army of trained twenty-two-year-olds, either.

Some adventuresome educators and campus watchers have openly 4 begun to suggest that college may not be the best, the proper, the only place for every young person after the completion of high school. We may have been looking at all those surveys and statistics upside down, it seems, and through the rosy glow of our own remembered college experiences. Perhaps college doesn't make people intelligent, ambitious, happy, liberal, or quick to learn new things — maybe it's just the other way around, and intelligent, ambitious, happy, liberal, and quick-learning people are merely the ones who have been attracted to college in the first place. And perhaps all those successful college graduates would have been successful whether they had gone to college or not. This is heresy to those of us who have been brought up to believe that if a little schooling is good, more has to be much better. But contrary evidence is beginning to mount up.

The unhappiness and discontent of young people is nothing new, 5 and problems of adolescence are always painfully intense. But while traveling around the country, speaking at colleges, and interviewing students at all kinds of schools — large and small, public and private — I was overwhelmed by the prevailing sadness. It was as visible on campuses in California as in Nebraska and Massachusetts. Too many young people are in college reluctantly, because everyone told them they ought to go, and there didn't seem to be anything better to do. Their elders sell them college because it's good for them. Some never learn to like it, and talk about their time in school as if it were a sentence to be served.

Students tell us the same thing college counselors tell us — they go 6 because of pressure from parents and teachers, and stay because it seems to be an alternative to a far worse fate. It's "better" than the Army or a dead-end job, and it has to be pretty bad before it's any worse than staying at home.

College graduates say that they don't want to work "just" for the 7 money: They want work that matters. They want to help people and save the world. But the numbers are stacked against them. Not only are there not enough jobs in world-saving fields, but in the current slowdown it has become evident that there never were, and probably never will be, enough jobs requiring higher education to go around.

Students who tell their advisers they want to help people, for exam- 8 ple, are often directed to psychology. This year the Department of Labor estimates that there will be 4,300 new jobs for psychologists, while colleges will award 58,430 bachelor's degrees in psychology.

Sociology has become a favorite major on socially conscious cam- 9 puses, but graduates find that social reform is hardly a paying occupation. Male sociologists from the University of Wisconsin reported as gainfully employed a year after graduation included a legal assistant, sports editor, truck unloader, Peace Corps worker, publications director, and a stockboy — but no sociologist per se. The highest paid worked for the post office.

Publishing, writing, and journalism are presumably the vocational 10 goal of a large proportion of the 104,000 majors in Communications and Letters expected to graduate in 1975. The outlook for them is grim. All of the daily newspapers in the country combined are expected to hire a total of 2,600 reporters this year. Radio and television stations may hire a total of 500 announcers, most of them in local radio stations. Nonpublishing organizations will need 1,100 technical writers, and public-relations activities another 4,400. Even if new graduates could get all these jobs (they can't, of course), over 90,000 of them will have to find something less glamorous to do.

Other fields most popular with college graduates are also pathetically small. Only 1,900 foresters a year will be needed during this decade, although schools of forestry are expected to continue graduating twice that many. Some will get sub-professional jobs as forestry aides. Schools of architecture are expected to turn out twice as many as will be needed, and while all sorts of people want to design things, the Department of Labor forecasts that there will be jobs for only 400 new industrial designers a year. As for anthropologists, only 400 will be needed every year in the 1970s to take care of all the college courses, public-health research, community surveys, museums, and all the archaeological digs on every continent. (For these jobs graduate work in anthropology is required.)

Many popular occupations may seem to be growing fast without necessarily offering employment to very many. "Recreation work" is always cited as an expanding field, but it will need relatively few workers who require more special training than life guards. "Urban planning" has exploded in the media, so the U.S. Department of Labor doubled its estimate of the number of jobs to be filled every year in the 1970s — to a big, fat 800. A mere 200 oceanographers a year will be able to do all the exploring of "inner space" — and all that exciting underwater diving you see demonstrated on television — for the entire decade of the 1970s.

Whatever college graduates *want* to do, most of them are going to wind up doing what *there is* to do. During the next few years, according to the Labor Department, the biggest demand will be for stenographers and secretaries, followed by retail-trade salesworkers, hospital attendants, bookkeepers, building custodians, registered nurses, foremen, kindergarten and elementary-school teachers, receptionists, cooks, cosmetologists, private-household workers, manufacturing inspectors, and industrial machinery repairmen. These are the jobs which will eventually absorb the surplus archaeologists, urban planners, oceanographers, sociologists, editors, and college professors.

Vocationalism is the new look on campus because of the discouraging job market faced by the generalists. Students have been opting for medicine and law in droves. If all those who check "doctor" as their career goal succeed in getting their MDs, we'll immediately have ten times the target ratio of doctors for the population of the United States. Law

11

12

13

14

schools are already graduating twice as many new lawyers every year as the Department of Labor thinks we will need, and the oversupply grows annually.

Specialists often find themselves at the mercy of shifts in demand, 15 and the narrower the vocational training, the more risky the long-term prospects. Engineers are the classic example of the "Yo-Yo" effect in supply and demand. Today's shortage is apt to produce a big crop of engineering graduates after the need has crested, and teachers face the same squeeze.

Worse than that, when the specialists turn up for work, they often 16 find that they have learned a lot of things in classrooms that they will never use, that they will have to learn a lot of things on the job that they were never taught, and that most of what they have learned is less likely to "come in handy later" than to fade from memory. One disillusioned architecture student, who had already designed and built houses, said, "It's the degree you need, not everything you learn getting it."

A diploma saves the employer the cost of screening candidates and 17 gives him a predictable product: He can assume that those who have survived the four-year ordeal have learned how to manage themselves. They have learned how to budget their time, meet deadlines, set priorities, cope with impersonal authority, follow instructions, and stick with a task that may be tiresome without direct supervision.

The employer is also betting that it will be cheaper and easier to 18 train the college graduate because he has demonstrated his ability to learn. But if the diploma serves only to identify those who are talented in the art of schoolwork, it becomes, in the words of Harvard's Christopher Jencks, "a hell of an expensive aptitude test." It is unfair to the candidates because they themselves must bear the cost of the screening — the cost of college. Candidates without the funds, the academic temperament, or the patience for the four-year obstacle race are ruled out, no matter how well they may perform on the job. But if "everyone" has a diploma, employers will have to find another way to choose employees, and it will become an empty credential.

(Screening by diploma may in fact already be illegal. The 1971 rul- 19 ing of the Supreme Court in *Griggs* v. *Duke Power Co.* contended that an employer cannot demand a qualification which systemcially excludes an entire class of applicants, unless that qualification reliably predicts success on the job. The requiring of a high school diploma was outlawed in the *Griss* case, and this could extend to a college diploma.)

The bill for four years at an Ivy League college is currently climbing 20 toward $25,000; at a state university, a degree will cost the student and his family about $10,000 (with taxpayers making up the difference).

Not many families can afford these sums, and when they look for fi- 21
nancial aid, they discover that someone else will decide how much they
will actually have to pay. The College Scholarship Service, which establishes a family's degree of need for most colleges, is guided by noble
principles: uniformity of sacrifice, need rather than merit. But families
vary in their willingness to ''sacrifice'' as much as the bureaucracy of the
CSS thinks they ought to. This is particularly true of middle-income parents, whose children account for the bulk of the country's college students. Some have begun to rebel against this attempt to enforce the
same values and priorities on all. ''In some families, a college education
competes with a second car, a color television, or a trip to Europe — and
it's possible that college may lose,'' one financial-aid officer recently
told me.

Quite so. College is worth more to some middle-income families 22
than to others. It is chilling to consider the undercurrent of resentment
that families who ''give up everything'' must feel toward their college-
age children, or the burden of guilt children must bear every time they
goof off or receive less than top grades in their courses.

The decline in return for a college degree within the last generation 23
has been substantial. In the 1950s, a Princeton student could pay his expenses for the school year — eating club and all — on less than $3,000.
When he graduated, he entered a job market which provided a comfortable margin over the earnings of his agemates who had not been to college. To be precise, a freshman entering Princeton in 1956, the earliest
year for which the Census has attempted to project lifetime earnings,
could expect to realize a 12.5 percent return on his investment. A
freshman entering in 1972, with the cost nearing $6,000 annually, could
expect to realize only 9.3 percent, less than might be available in the
money market. This calculation was made with the help of a banker and
his computer, comparing college as an investment in future earnings
with other investments available in the booming money market of 1974,
and concluded that in strictly financial terms, college is not always the
best investment a young person can make.

I postulated a young man (the figures are different with a young 24
woman, but the principle is the same) whose rich uncle would give him,
in cash, the total cost of four years at Princeton — $34,181. (The total in-
cludes what the young man would earn if he went to work instead of to
college right after high school.) If he did not spend the money on Princeton, but put it in the savings bank at 7.5 percent interest compounded
daily, he would have, at retirement age sixty-four, more than five times
as much as the $199,000 extra he could expect to earn between twenty-
two and sixty as a college man rather than a mere high school graduate.
And with all that money accumulating in the bank, he could invest in

349

something with a higher return than a diploma. At age twenty-eight, when his nest egg had reached $73,113, he could buy a liquor store, which would return him well over 20 percent on his investment, as long as he was willing to mind the store. He might get a bit fidgety sitting there, but he'd have to be dim-witted to lose money on a liquor store, and right now we're talking only about dollars.

If the young man went to a public college rather than Princeton, the 25 investment would be lower, and the payoff higher, of course, because other people — the taxpayers — put up part of the capital for him. But the difference in return between an investment in public and private colleges is minimized because the biggest part of the the investment in either case is the money a student might earn if he went to work, not to college — in economic terms, his "foregone income." That he bears himself.

Rates of return and dollar signs on education are a fascinating brain 26 teaser, and, obviously, there is a certain unreality to the game. But the same unreality extends to the traditional calculations that have always been used to convince taxpayers that college is a worthwhile investment.

The ultimate defense of college has always been that while it may 27 not teach you anything vocationally useful, it will somehow make you a better person, able to do anything better, and those who make it through the process are initiated into the "fellowship of educated men and women." In a study intended to probe what graduates seven years out of college thought their colleges should have done for them, the Carnegie Commission found that most alumni expected the "development of my abilities to think and express myself." But if such respected educational psychologists as Bruner and Piaget are right, specific learning skills have to be acquired very early in life, perhaps even before formal schooling begins.

So, when pressed, liberal-arts defenders speak instead about some- 28 thing more encompassing, and more elusive. "College changed me inside," one graduate told us fervently. The authors of a Carnegie Commission report, who obviously struggled for a definition, concluded that one of the common threads in the perceptions of a liberal education is that it provides "an integrated view of the world which can serve as an inner guide." More simply, alumni say that college should have "helped me to formulate the values and goals of my life."

In theory, a student is taught to develop these values and goals him- 29 self, but in practice, it doesn't work quite that way. All but the wayward and the saintly take their sense of the good, the true, and the beautiful from the people around them. When we speak of students acquiring

"values" in college, we often mean that they will acquire the values —
and sometimes that means only the tastes — of their professors. The values of professors may be "higher" than many students will encounter
elsewhere, but they may not be relevant to situations in which students
find themselves in college and later.

Of all the forms in which ideas are disseminated, the college profes- 30
sor lecturing a class is the slowest and most expensive. You don't have to
go to college to read the great books or learn about the great ideas of
Western Man. Today you can find them everywhere — in paperbacks, in
the public libraries, in museums, in public lectures, in adult-education
courses, in abridged, summarized, or adapted form in magazines, films,
and television. The problem is no longer one of access to broadening
ideas; the problem is the other way around: how to choose among the
many courses of action proposed to us, how to edit the stimulations that
pour into our eyes and ears every waking hour. A college experience that
piles option an option and stimulation on stimulation merely adds to the
contemporary nightmare.

What students and graduates say that they did learn on campus 31
comes under the heading of personal, rather than intellectual, development. Again and again I was told that the real value of college is learning
to get along with others, to practice social skills, to "sort out my head,"
and these have nothing to do with curriculum.

For whatever impact the academic experience used to have on col- 32
lege students, the sheer size of many undergraduate classes in the 1970s
dilutes faculty-student dialogue, and, more often than not, they are
taught by teachers who were hired when colleges were faced with a shortage of qualified instructors, during their years of expansion and when
the big rise in academic pay attracted the mediocre and the less than
dedicated.

On the social side, colleges are withdrawing from responsibility for 33
feeding, housing, policing, and protecting students at a time when the
environment of college may be the most important service it could render. College officials are reluctant to "intervene" in the personal lives of
the students. They no longer expect to take over from parents, but often
insist that students — who have, most often, never lived away from home
before — take full adult responsibility for their plans, achievements, and
behavior.

Most college students do not live in the plush, comfortable country- 34
club-like surroundings their parents envisage, or, in some cases, remember. Open dorms, particularly when they are coeducational, are noisy,
usually overcrowded, and often messy. Some students desert the institutional "zoos" (their own word for dorms) and move into run-down,

351

overpriced apartments. Bulletin boards in student centers are littered with notices of apartments to share and the drift of conversation suggests that a lot of money is dissipated in scrounging for food and shelter.

Taxpayers now provide more than half of the astronomical sums 35 that are spent on higher education. But less than half of today's high school graduates go on, raising a new question of equity: Is it fair to make all the taxpayers pay for the minority who actually go to college? We decided long ago that it is fair for childless adults to pay school taxes because everyone, parents and nonparents alike, profits by a literate population. Does the same reasoning hold true for state-supported higher education? There is no conclusive evidence on either side.

Young people cannot be expected to go to college for the general 36 good of mankind. They may be more altruistic than their elders, but no great numbers are going to spend four years at hard intellectual labor, let alone tens of thousands of family dollars, for "the advancement of human capability in society at large," one of the many purposes invoked by the Carnegie Commission report. Nor do any considerable number of them want to go to college to beat the Russians to Jupiter, improve the national defense, increase the Gross National Product, lower the crime rate, improve automobile safety, or create a market for the arts — all of which have been suggested at one time or other as benefits taxpayers get for supporting higher education.

One sociologist said that you don't have to have a reason for going 37 to college because it's an institution. His definition of an institution is something everyone subscribed to without question. The burden of proof is not on why you should go to college, but why anyone thinks there might be a reason for not going. The implication — and some educators express it quite frankly — is that an eighteen-year-old high school graduate is still too young and confused to know what he wants to do, let alone what is good for him.

Mother knows best, in others words. 38

It had always been comfortable for students to believe that authori- 39 ties, like Mother, or outside specialists, like educators, could determine what was best for them. However, specialists and authorities no longer enjoy the credibility former generations accorded them. Patients talk back to doctors and are not struck suddenly dead. Clients question the lawyer's bills and sometimes get them reduced. It is no longer self-evident that all adolescents must study a fixed curriculum that was constructed at a time when all educated men could agree on precisely what it was that made them educated.

The same with college. If high school graduates don't want to con- 40 tinue their education, or don't want to continue it right away, they may perceive more clearly than their elders that college is not for them.

College is an ideal place for those young adults who love learning 41 for its own sake, who would rather read than eat, and who like nothing better than writing research papers. But they are a minority, even at the prestigious colleges, which recruit and attract the intellectually oriented.

The rest of our high school graduates need to look at college more 42 closely and critically, to examine it as a consumer product, and decide if the cost in dollars, in time, in continued dependency, and in future returns, is worth the very large investment each student — and his family — must make.

## Discussion Questions

1.  What three reasons does Bird cite as the ones most often given for going to college? Does she offer adequate objections to all three? Which is treated most elaborately? Why do you think she has been less attentive to the other reasons?
2.  Spell out as precisely as possible the problems that Bird is trying to solve. What solutions does she offer? Do they seem practical? Helpful? Why or why not?
3.  This article appeared in 1975. Are her data about employment and college expenses still relevant? If they are not, does this fact change her argument in any way?
4.  What are the "real" reasons, as Bird sees them, that millions of students are attending college? Has your own experience confirmed the truth of her observations?
5.  Summarize the reasons for Bird's doubts about tax support for college education. Do you think they are valid?

## Writing Suggestions

1.  Write an essay telling to what extent college has so far satisfied or failed to satisfy your expectations. (You should limit your discussion to one or two important topics.) Begin by setting out what your expectations were, whether vague or specific. Be as honest as you can; try to avoid clichés. Then provide evidence to support your claim that college has satisfied or disappointed.
2.  Elaborate on one of the ostensible reasons for college: ". . . college will help them [students] . . . learn to be more responsible citizens than those who don't go." How true is that? Think of the qualities that make for re-

sponsible citizenship; then write an argument that a college education can or cannot help to develop these qualities.

3. Interview a few employers in your community. Ask them if they prefer to hire college graduates and why or why not. Use this information to support or refute Bird's and Christopher Jencks's contention that college is only "a hell of an expensive aptitude test."

# It's Failure, Not Success

## ELLEN GOODMAN

The author objects to any definition of success that "eliminates value judgments and edits out moral questions." Real success, she argues, is not just feeling good about yourself; it's feeling good because you've changed your behavior to make life more comfortable for those around you.

I knew a man who went into therapy about three years ago because, as he put it, he couldn't live with himself any longer. I didn't blame him. The guy was a bigot, a tyrant and a creep.

In any case, I ran into him again after he'd finished therapy. He was still a bigot, a tyrant and a creep, *but* . . . he had learned to live with himself.

Now, I suppose this was an accomplishment of sorts. I mean, nobody else could live with him. But it seems to me that there are an awful lot of people running around and writing around these days encouraging us to feel good about what we should feel terrible about, and to accept in ourselves what we should change.

The only thing they seem to disapprove of is disapproval. The only judgment they make is against being judgmental, and they assure us that we have nothing to feel guilty about except guilt itself. It seems to me that they are all intent on proving that I'm OK and You're OK, when in fact, I may be perfectly dreadful and you may be unforgivably dreary, and it may be — gasp! — *wrong*.

What brings on my sudden attack of judgmentitis is success, or rather, *Success!* — the latest in a series of exclamation-point books all concerned with How to Make it.

In this one, Michael Korda is writing a recipe book for success. Like the other authors, he leapfrogs right over the "Shoulds" and into the "Hows." He eliminates value judgments and edits out moral questions as if he were Fanny Farmer and the subject was the making of a blueberry pie.

It's not that I have any reason to doubt Mr. Korda's advice on the way to achieve success. It may very well be that successful men wear handkerchiefs stuffed neatly in their breast pockets, and that successful single women should carry suitcases to the office on Fridays whether or not they are going away for the weekend.

He may be realistic when he says that "successful people generally  8
have very low expectations of others." And he may be only slightly cynical when he writes: "One of the best ways to ensure success is to develop expensive tastes or marry someone who has them."

And he may be helpful with his handy hints on how to sit next to  9
someone you are about to overpower.

But he simply finesses the issues of right and wrong — silly words,  10
embarrassing words that have been excised like warts from the shiny surface of the new how-to books. To Korda, guilt is not a prod, but an enemy that he slays on page four. Right off the bat, he tells the would-be successful reader that:

— It's OK to be greedy.

— It's OK to look out for Number One.

— It's OK to be Machiavellian (if you can get away with it).

— It's OK to recognize that honesty is not always the best policy (provided you don't go around saying so).

— And it's always OK to be rich.

Well, in fact, it's not OK. It's not OK to be greedy, Machiavellian,  11
dishonest. It's not always OK to be rich. There is a qualitative difference between succeeding by making napalm or by making penicillin. There is a difference between climbing the ladder of success, and macheteing a path to the top.

Only someone with the moral perspective of a mushroom could as-  12
sure us that this was all OK. It seems to me that most Americans harbor ambivalence toward success, not for neurotic reasons, but out of a realistic perception of what it demands.

Success is expensive in terms of time and energy and altered behav-  13
ior — the sort of behavior he describes in the grossest of terms: "If you can undermine your boss and replace him, fine, do so, but never express anything but respect and loyalty for him while you're doing it."

This author — whose *Power!* topped the best-seller list last year — is  14
intent on helping rid us of that ambivalence which is a signal from our conscience. He is like the other "Win!" "Me First!" writers, who try to make us comfortable when we should be uncomfortable.

They are all Doctor Feelgoods, offering us placebo prescriptions in-  15
stead of strong medicine. They give us a way to live with ourselves, perhaps, but not a way to live with each other. They teach us a whole lot more about "Failure!" than about success.

## Discussion Questions

1. Describe the popular attitude to which Goodman objects. Explain her critical comment, "The only judgment they make is against being judgmental."
2. Summarize her principal objection to Michael Korda's "recipe book for success."
3. How does Goodman herself feel about success?
4. What does she mean when she claims that the success advocated by Korda is really failure, not success?

## Writing Suggestions

1. Are guilt and shame always destructive, as a "Doctor Feelgood" might claim? Or can they serve a useful purpose? Write about an occasion when such feelings led to a constructive result.
2. Write about the experience of someone you know or have heard about who achieved success at the sacrifice of certain moral values. Or choose someone who achieved success without sacrificing his or her values. Use Goodman's definitions in your discussion.

# A Proposal
# to Abolish Grading

## PAUL GOODMAN

Now almost twenty years old, this essay still enjoys a wide circulation. In it Paul Goodman, a college professor and writer whose views were popular among students in the 1960s, makes a radical proposal to do away with one of the sacred institutions of higher learning. His assumptions about the negative relationship between grading and the purposes of education are clearly stated.

Let half a dozen of the prestigious Universities — Chicago, Stanford, the Ivy League — abolish grading, and use testing only and entirely for pedagogic purposes as teachers see fit. 1

Anyone who knows the frantic temper of the present schools will 2 understand the transvaluation of values that would be effected by this modest innovation. For most of the students, the competitive grade has come to be the essence. The naïve teacher points to the beauty of the subject and the ingenuity of the research; the shrewd student asks if he is responsible for that on the final exam.

Let me at once dispose of an objection whose unanimity is quite fascinating. I think that the great majority of professors agree that grading 3 hinders teaching and creates a bad spirit, going as far as cheating and plagiarizing. I have before me the collection of essays, *Examining in Harvard College*, and this is the consensus. It is uniformly asserted, however, that the grading is inevitable; for how else will the graduate schools, the foundations, the corporations *know* whom to accept, reward, hire? How will the talent scouts know whom to tap?

By testing the applicants, of course, according to the specific task- 4 requirements of the inducting institution, just as applicants for the Civil Service or for licenses in medicine, law, and architecture are tested. Why should Harvard professors do the testing *for* corporations and graduate schools?

The objection is ludicrous. Dean Whitla, of the Harvard Office of 5 Tests, points out that the scholastic-aptitude and achievement tests used for *admission* to Harvard are a super-excellent index for all-around Harvard performance, better than high-school grades or particular Harvard course-grades. Presumably, these college-entrance tests are tailored for what Harvard and similar institutions want. By the same logic, would not an employer do far better to apply his own job-aptitude test rather than to rely on the vagaries of Harvard section-men? Indeed, I doubt that many employers bother to look at such grades; they are more likely to be interested merely in the fact of a Harvard diploma, whatever that connotes to them. The grades have most of their weight with the graduate schools — here, as elsewhere, the system runs mainly for its own sake.

It is really necessary to remind our academics of the ancient history 6 of Examination. In the medieval university, the whole point of the gruelling trial of the candidate was whether or not to accept him as a peer. His disputation and lecture for the Master's was just that, a master-piece to enter the guild. It was not to make comparative evaluations. It was not to weed out and select for an extra-mural licensor or employer. It was certainly not to pit one young fellow against another in an ugly competition. My philosophic impression is that the medievals thought they knew what a good job of work was and that we are competitive because we do not know. But the more status is achieved by largely irrelevant competitive evaluation, the less will we ever know.

(Of course, our American examinations never did have this purely 7 guild orientation, just as our faculties have rarely had absolute autonomy; the examining was to satisfy Overseers, Elders, distant Regents — and they as paternal superiors have always doted on giving grades, rather than accepting peers. But I submit that this set-up itself makes it impossible for the student to *become* a master, to *have* grown up, and to commence on his own. He will always be making A or B for some overseer. And in the present atmosphere, he will always be climbing on his friend's neck.)

Perhaps the chief objectors to abolishing grading would be the students and their parents. The parents should be simply disregarded; their anxiety has done enough damage already. For the students, it seems to me that a primary duty of the university is to deprive them of their props, their dependence on extrinsic valuation and motivation, and to force them to confront the difficult enterprise itself and finally lose themselves in it.

A miserable effect of grading is to nullify the various uses of testing. 9 Testing, for both student and teacher, is a means of structuring, and also of finding out what is blank or wrong and what has been assimilated and can be taken for granted. Review — including high-pressure review — is a means of bringing together the fragments, so that there are flashes of synoptic insight.

There are several good reasons for testing, and kinds of test. But if 10 the aim is to discover weakness, what is the point of down-grading and punishing it, and thereby inviting the student to conceal his weakness, by faking and bulling, if not cheating? The natural conclusion of synthesis is the insight itself, not a grade for having had it. For the important purpose of placement, if one can establish in the student the belief that one is testing *not* to grade and make invidious comparisons but for his own advantage, the student should normally seek his own level, where he is challenged and yet capable, rather than trying to get by. If the student dares to accept himself as he is, a teacher's grade is a crude instrument compared with a student's self-awareness. But it is rare in our universities that students are encouraged to notice objectively their vast confusion. Unlike Socrates, our teachers rely on power-drives rather than shame and ingenuous idealism.

Many students are lazy, so teachers try to goad or threaten them by    11 grading. In the long run this must do more harm than good. Laziness is a character-defense. It may be a way of avoiding learning, in order to protect the conceit that one is already perfect (deeper, the despair that one *never* can be). It may be a way of avoiding just the risk of failing and being down-graded. Sometimes it is a way of politely saying, "I won't." But since it is the authoritarian grown-up demands that have created such attitudes in the first place, why repeat the trauma? There comes a time when we must treat people as adult, laziness and all. It is one thing courageously to fire a do-nothing out of your class; it is quite another thing to evaluate him with a lordly F.

Most important of all, it is often obvious that balking in doing the    12 work, especially among bright young people who get to great universities, means exactly what it says: The work does not suit me, not this subject, or not at this time, or not in this school, or not in school altogether. The student might not be bookish; he might be school-tired; perhaps his development ought now to take another direction. Yet unfortunately, if such a student is intelligent and is not sure of himself, he *can* be bullied into passing, and this obscures everything. My hunch is that I am describing a common situation. What a grim waste of young life and teacherly effort! Such a student will retain nothing of what he has "passed" in. Sometimes he must get mononucleosis to tell his story and be believed.

And ironically, the converse is also probably commonly true. A student    13 flunks and is mechanically weeded out, who is really ready and eager to learn in a scholastic setting, but he has not quite caught on. A good teacher can recognize the situation, but the computer wreaks its will.


## Discussion Questions

1. Why do you think Goodman calls on "half a dozen of the prestigious Universities" intead of all universities to abolish grading?

2. Where does the author reveal the purposes of his proposal?
3. Most professors, Goodman argues, think that grading hinders teaching. Why, then, do they continue to give grades? How does Goodman reply to their objections?
4. What does Goodman think the real purpose of testing should be? How does grading "nullify the various uses of testing"?

## Writing Suggestions

1. Do you agree that grading prevents you from learning? If so, write an essay in which you support Goodman's thesis by reporting what your own experience has been.
2. If you disagree with Goodman, write an essay that outlines the benefits of grading.
3. Is there a way better than grading to evaluate the work of students — a way that would achieve the goals of education Goodman values? Suggest a method and explain why it would be superior to grading.

# Stereotype Truth

## WILLIAM B. HELMREICH

William Helmreich, professor of sociology at the City University of New York, takes issue with the popular notion that stereotypes are always the result of ignorance and hostility. He offers evidence that some of our stereotypes about ethnic groups are rooted in history and cultural experience.

"Stereotype" is a dirty word among some intellectuals and others  1
who feel that, when used to describe members of a race, religion, or nationality, it indicates prejudices. Perhaps it is time we changed our thinking.

How have particular groups come to be identified with certain  2
traits? Puerto Ricans are not thought of as grasping in business but Jews are. Blacks sometimes are categorized as musically inclined but the Chinese are not. We have the "fighting Irish," "stupid Poles," "clannish Italians," "stolid Swedes." Where did these ideas originate? How true are they?

Such sterotypes usually stem from the historical experiences of the  3
group itself and the experiences of those with whom the group has had contact. Although stereotypes are often highly inaccurate, a good many have quite a bit of truth to them. Rather than deny their validity, we should make a greater effort at understanding and appreciating them. Let's take some examples.

Are Hispanics apt to be warmer and more emotional than members  4
of other groups? There seems to be almost universal agreement on the validity of this stereotype among professionals and lay people who work with Hispanics. Latin American politics, for example, are known for warmth of personal relationships and are based more on mutual trust than on written agreements. The pattern is similar in business relationships but its clearest expression can be found in the family.

The anthropologist Oscar Lewis often observed that Hispanic fami-  5
lies he studied had warm, emotional ties, especially between mother and child. Psychiatrists have pointed out that Hispanic mothers kiss and cuddle infants more than Anglo mothers, and remain intensely involved with their children throughout their lives.

Researchers have attributed such behavior to the extended-family  6
structure common among Hispanics. As a result, the child learns to re-

gard a greater number of people with warmth and affection. Others note that historically Hispanics have come from societies where the individual was born into a social and economic system that remained fixed throughout his life. They therefore tended to place more importance on personal qualities to make distinctions among those with whom they lived.

Are Jews better businessmen than others? This is impossible to 7 prove. Yet there is enough evidence present to suggest that they indeed might have an edge in this area. For one thing, Jews have been in business for centuries. Forbidden to own land by the Roman Catholic Church and denied entry into the craft guilds during medieval times, Jews were forced to turn to moneylending to survive.

The Jewish religion and, in particular, the Talmud, with its empha- 8 sis on abstract thinking, also has played a role. From childhood on, the stress was on sharpening the mind, and when economic opportunities arose the Jew was able to apply his intellectual acumen to that sphere as well. After all, interest, futures, options, stocks, and, most importantly, money itself, were also abstractions. Yet another factor was that lacking a homeland for centuries, never certain when persecution might strike, Jews came to see money as the only means of survival, something with which to buy protection or acquire certain rights.

Are blacks more musically gifted than others? Certainly music was a 9 central feature of their African heritage, which had hunting songs, drinking songs, work songs, funeral songs, etc. Music was integral to the black churches founded in this country. It was in them that African exiles were able to fully express themselves as they prayed, rocked, shouted, sang, and danced.

When white society's fascination with blacks reached unprece- 10 dented heights during the Harlem renaissance in the 1920's, music became a way in which blacks could move up the socio-economic ladder. This meant, of course, that black parents were more likely to encourage their children as soon as they demonstrated any abilities in this area. Whatever the reasons, probably no other group in the United States has contributed as much to music, song, and dance.

In my race-relations courses at City College, I caution students not 11 to generalize, and to judge each person on his or her own merits. Obviously other nationalities also possess in varying degrees the characteristics I have discussed here. Moreover, there are many blacks who do not have any discernible musical talent, Jews who lack ''business sense,'' as well as cold and unresponsive Hispanics. Still, there are such things as tendencies and traits, positive and negative, that are rooted in a group's history and culture. Ignoring or minimizing them can be as bad as exaggerating them.

## Discussion Questions

1. Helmreich has written this article to correct a common misconception. What is it?
2. Summarize some of the familiar stereotypes cited by Helmreich.
3. What, according to the author, is the origin of stereotypes?
4. How does the author explain the stereotypes of Hispanics? Jews? Blacks?
5. How does Helmreich talk about stereotypes to his classes?

## Writing Suggestions

1. Choose another stereotype, describe it, suggest the reasons for its origin and persistence, and evaluate its accuracy. Examples include dumb jocks, Latin lovers, southern hospitality, Jewish mothers, American tourists, greedy businessmen, cheerleaders, beauty pageant contestants, rock musicians.
2. Describe an experience of your own with a stereotype, and tell what meaning it had for you. What did it teach you about stereotyping?

# Test-Tube Babies: Solution or Problem?

## RUTH HUBBARD

Ruth Hubbard, professor of biology at Harvard University, objects to test-tube babies on several grounds. She believes not only that the medical procedures they require are risky but that important social and ethical problems have been overlooked in the push toward this new technology.

In vitro fertilization of human eggs and the implantation of early embryos into women's wombs are new biotechnologies that may enable some women to bear children who have hitherto been unable to do so. In that sense, it may solve their particular infertility problems. On the other hand, this technology poses unpredictable hazards since it intervenes in the process of fertilization, in the first cell divisions of the fertilized egg, and in the implantation of the embryo into the uterus. At present we have no way to assess in what ways and to what extent these interventions may affect the women or the babies they acquire by this procedure. Since the use of the technology is only just beginning, the financial and technical investments it represents are still modest. It is therefore important that we, as a society, seriously consider the wisdom of implementing and developing it further.

According to present estimates, about 10 million Americans are infertile by the definition that they have tried for at least a year to achieve pregnancy without conceiving or carrying a pregnancy to a live birth. In about a third of infertile couples, the incapacity rests with the woman only, and for about a third of these women the problem is localized in the fallopian tubes (the organs that normally propel an egg from the ovary to the uterus or womb). These short, delicate tubes are easily blocked by infection or disease. Nowadays the most common causes of blocked tubes are inflammations of the uterine lining brought on by IUDs, pelvic inflammatory disease, or gonorrhea. Once blocked, the tubes are difficult to reopen or replace, and doctors presently claim only a one-in-three success rate in correcting the problem. Thus, of the 10 million infertile people in the country, about 600 thousand (or 6 per cent) could perhaps be helped to pregnancy by in vitro fertilization. (These numbers are from Barbara Eck Menning's *Infertility: A Guide for the Childless Couple*, Prentice-Hall, 1977. Ms. Menning is executive director of Resolve, a national, nonprofit counseling service for infertile couples located in Belmont, Mass.)

Louise Brown, born in England in July, 1978, is the first person    3
claimed to have been conceived in vitro. Since then, two other babies
conceived outside the mother are said to have been born — one in England, the other in India. In none of these cases have the procedures by
which the eggs were obtained from the woman's ovary, fertilized, stored
until implanatation, and finally implanted in her uterus been described
in any detail. However, we can deduce the procedures from animal experimentation and the brief published accounts about the three babies.

The woman who is a candidate for in vitro fertilization has her hor-    4
mone levels monitored to determine when she is about to ovulate. She is
then admitted to the hospital and the egg is collected in the following
way: a small cut is made in her abdomen; a metal tube containing an op-
tical arrangement that allows the surgeon to see the ovaries and a narrow-
bore tube (called a micropipette) are inserted through the cut; and the
egg is removed shortly before it would normally be shed from the ovary.
The woman is ready to go home within a day, at most.

When the procedure was first developed, women were sometimes    5
given hormones to make them "superovulate" — produce more than
one egg (the usual number for most women). But we do not know
whether this happened with the mothers of of the three "test-tube" babies that have been born. Incidentally, this superovulation reportedly is
no longer induced, partly because some people believe it is too risky.

After the egg has been isolated, it is put into a solution that keeps it    6
alive and nourishes it, and is mixed with sperm. Once fertilized, it is allowed to go through a few cell divisions and so begin its embryonic development — the still-mysterious process by which a fertilized egg becomes a baby. The embryo is then picked up with another fine tube,
inserted through the woman's cervix, and flushed into the uterus.

If the uterus is not at the proper stage to allow for implantation (ap-    7
proximately 17 to 23 days after the onset of each menstruation) when the
embryo is ready to be implanted, the embryo must be frozen and stored
until the time is right in a subsequent menstrual cycle. Again, we do not
know whether the embryos were frozen and stored prior to implantation
with the two British babies; we are told that the Indian one was.

In sum, then, there is a need, and there is a technology said to meet    8
that need. But as a woman, a feminist, and a biologist, I am opposed to
using it and developing it further.


## HEALTH RISKS

As a society, we do not have a very good track record in anticipating    9
the problems that can arise from technological interventions in compli-

cated biological systems. Our physical models are too simpleminded and have led to many unforeseen problems in the areas of pest control, waste disposal, and other aspects of what is usually referred to as the ecological crisis.

In reproductive biology, the nature of the many interacting pro- 10 cesses is poorly understood. We are in no position to enumerate or describe the many reactions that must occur at just the right times during the early stages of embryonic development when the fertilized egg begins to divide into increasing numbers of cells, implants itself in the uterus, and establishes the pattern for the different organ systems that will allow it to develop into a normal fetus and baby.

The safety of this in vitro procedure cannot be established in animal 11 experiments because the details and requirements of normal embryonic development are different for different kinds of animals. Nor are the criteria of "normalcy" the same for animals and for people. The guinea pigs of the research and implementation of in vitro fertilization will be:

— the women who donate their eggs,
— the women who lend their wombs (who, of course, need not be the same as the egg-donors; rent-a-wombs clearly are an option), and
— the children who are produced.

The greatest ethical and practical questions arise with regard to the 12 children. They cannot consent to be produced, and we cannot know what hazards their production entails until enough have lived out their lives to allow for statistical analysis of their medical histories.

This example shows the inadequacy of our scientific models because 13 it is not obvious how to provide "controls," in the usual scientific sense of the term, for the first generation of "test-tube" individuals; they will be viewed as "special" at every critical juncture in their lives. When I ask myself whether I would want to be a "test-tube person," I know that I would not like to have to add *those* self-doubts to my more ordinary repertory of insecurities.

A concrete example of a misjudgment with an unfortunate outcome 14 that could not be predicted was the administration of the chemical thalidomide, a "harmless tranquilizer" touted as a godsend and prescribed to pregnant women, which resulted in the births of thousands of armless and legless babies. Yet there the damage was visible at birth and the practice could be stopped, though not until after it had caused great misery. But take the case of the hormone DES (diethyl stilbesterol), which was prescribed for pregnant women in the mistaken (though at the time honest) belief that it could prevent miscarriages. Some 15 years passed before many of the daughters of these women developed an unusual form of vaginal cancer. Both these chemicals produced otherwise rare diseases, so the damage was easy to detect and its causes could be sought. Had the chemicals produced more common symptoms, it would have been much more difficult to detect the damage and to pinpoint which drugs were harmful.

The important point is that both thalidomide and DES changed the 15 environment in which these babies developed — in ways that could not have been foreseen and that we still do not understand. This happened because we know very little about how embryos develop. How then can we claim to know that the many chemical and mechanical manipulations of eggs, sperms, and embryos that take place during in vitro fertilization and implantation are harmless?

## A WOMAN'S RIGHT?

The push toward this technology reinforces the view, all too preva- 16 lent in our society, that women's lives are unfulfilled, or indeed worthless, unless we bear children. I understand the wish to have children, though I also know many people — women and men — who lead happy and fulfilled lives without them. But even if one urgently wants a child, why must it be biologically one's own? It is not worth opening the hornet's nest of reproductive technology for the privilege of having one's child derive from one's own egg or sperm. Foster and adoptive parents are much needed for the world's homeless children. Why not try to change the American and international practices that make it difficult for people who want children to be brought together with children who need parents?

Advocates of this new technology argue that every woman has a 17 right to bear a child and that the technology will extend this right to a group previously denied it. It is important to examine this argument and to ask in what sense women have a "right" to bear children. In our culture, many women are taught from childhood that we must do without lots of things we want — electric trains, baseball mitts, perhaps later an expensive education or a well-paying job. We are also taught to submit to all sorts of social restrictions and physical dangers — we cannot go out alone at night, we allow ourselves to be made self-conscious at the corner drugstore and to be molested by strangers or bosses or family members without punching them as our brothers might do. We are led to believe that we must put up with all this — and without grousing — because as women we have something beside which everything else pales, something that will make up for everything: we can have babies! To grow up paying all the way and then to be denied that child *is* a promise unful-filled; that's cheating.

But I would argue that to promise children to women by means of 18 an untested technology — that is being tested only as it is used on them and their babies — is adding yet another wrong to the burdens of our so-cialization. Take the women whose fallopian tubes have been damaged by an infection provoked by faulty IUDs. They are now led to believe that problems caused by one risky, though medically approved and ad-ministered, technology can be relieved by another, much more invasive and hazardous technology.

I am also concerned about the extremely complicated nature of the 19 technology. It involves many steps, is hard to demystify, and requires highly skilled professionals. There is no way to put control over this tech-nology into the hands of the women who are going to be exposed to it. On the contrary, it will make women and their babies more dependent than ever upon a high-technology, super-professionalized medical sys-tem. The women and their babies must be monitored from before con-ception until birth, and the children will have to be observed all their lives. Furthermore, the pregnancy-monitoring technologies themselves involve hazard. From the start, women are locked into subservience to the medical establishment in a way that I find impossible to interpret as an increase in reproductive freedom, rights, or choices.

## HEALTH PRIORITIES

The final issue — and a major one — is that this technology is ex- 20 pensive. It requires prolonged experimentation, sophisticated profes-sionals, and costly equipment. It will distort our health priorities and funnel scarce resources into a questionable effort. The case of the Indian baby is a stark illustration, for in that country, where many children are dying from the effects of malnutrition and poor people have been forc-ibly sterilized, expensive technologies are being pioneered to enable a relatively small number of well-to-do people to have their own babies.

In the United States, as well, many people have less-than-adequate 21 access to such essential health resources as decent jobs, food and housing, and medical care when they need it. And here, too, poor women have been and are still being forcibly sterilized and otherwise coerced into *not* having babies, while women who can pay high prices will become guinea pigs in the risky technology of in vitro fertilization.

In vitro fertilization is expensive and unnecessary in comparison 22 with many pressing social needs, including those of children who need homes. We must find better and less risky solutions for women who want to parent but cannot bear children of their own.

## Discussion Questions

1. Hubbard offers a long introduction before she states her thesis. What kind of information does the introduction include? Is it necessary? Where does she state her thesis?
2. Why, according to Hubbard, is the procedure risky? Where do the greatest problems arise?
3. What is the purpose of the thalidomide and DES examples? Are they effective?
4. How would Hubbard solve the problem of childlessness for those who want children? Does her solution seem reasonable?
5. What burdens of socialization must women bear? How does Hubbard establish a relationship between those burdens and the ''right'' to bear children?
6. What are her principal objections to the technology of in vitro fertilization? Which of them might derive from her definition of herself as a feminist?

## Writing Suggestions

1. Which of Hubbard's arguments against test-tube babies do you find most persuasive? Which do you find weakest? Explain your choices.
2. Hubbard thinks that some reasons for wanting children are less defensible than others. Discuss why couples today have fewer children than their grandparents. Are some of these reasons less ''admirable'' than others?

# I Have a Dream

## MARTIN LUTHER KING, JR.

This speech was delivered on August 28, 1963, at a demonstration in Washington by more than 200,000 people demanding jobs and civil rights for blacks. The speaker, Martin Luther King, Jr., an ordained minister, was the leader of the nonviolent civil rights movement and won the Nobel Peace Prize in 1964. This oration, an oft-quoted example of the inspirational style, has become a classic of the genre.

Five score years ago, a great American, in whose symbolic shadow 1
we stand, signed the Emancipation Proclamation. This momentous decree came as a great beacon light of hope to millions of Negro slaves who had been seared in the flames of withering injustice. It came as a joyous daybreak to end the long night of captivity.

But one hundred years later, we must face the tragic fact that the 2
Negro is still not free. One hundred years later, the life of the Negro is still sadly crippled by the manacles of segregation and the chains of discrimination. One hundred years later, the Negro lives on a lonely island of poverty in the midst of a vast ocean of material prosperity. One hundred years later, the Negro is still languishing in the corners of American society and finds himself an exile in his own land. So we have come here today to dramatize an appalling condition.

In a sense we have come to our nation's capital to cash a check. 3
When the architects of our republic wrote the magnificent words of the Constitution and the Declaration of Independence, they were signing a promissory note to which every American was to fall heir. This note was a promise that all men would be guaranteed the unalienable rights of life, liberty, and the pursuit of happiness.

It is obvious today that America has defaulted on this promissory 4
note insofar as her citizens of color are concerned. Instead of honoring this sacred obligation, America has given the Negro people a bad check; a check which has come back marked "insufficient funds." But we refuse to believe that the bank of justice is bankrupt. We refuse to believe that there are insufficient funds in the great vaults of opportunity of this nation. So we have come to cash this check — a check that will give us upon demand the riches of freedom and the security of justice. We have also come to this hallowed spot to remind America of the fierce urgency of *now*. This is no time to engage in the luxury of cooling off or

to take the tranquilizing drugs of gradualism. *Now* is the time to make real the promises of Democracy. *Now* is the time to rise from the dark and desolate valley of segregation to the sunlit path of racial justice. *Now* is the time to open the doors of opportunity to all of God's children. *Now* is the time to lift our nation from the quicksands of racial injustice to the solid rock of brotherhood.

It would be fatal for the nation to overlook the urgency of the mo- 5 ment and to underestimate the determination of the Negro. This sweltering summer of the Negro's legitimate discontent will not pass until there is an invigorating autumn of freedom and equality. 1963 is not an end, but a beginning. Those who hope that the Negro needed to blow off steam and will now be content will have a rude awakening if the nation returns to business as usual. There will be neither rest nor tranquillity in America until the Negro is granted his citizenship rights. The whirlwinds of revolt will continue to shake the foundations of our nation until the bright day of justice emerges.

But there is something that I must say to my people who stand on 6 the warm threshold which leads into the palace of justice. In the process of gaining our rightful place we must not be guilty of wrongful deeds. Let us not seek to satisfy our thirst for freedom by drinking from the cup of bitterness and hatred. We must forever conduct our struggle on the high plane of dignity and discipline. We must not allow our creative protest to degenerate into physical violence. Again and again we must rise to the majestic heights of meeting physical force with soul force. The marvelous new militancy which has engulfed the Negro community must not lead us to a distrust of all white people, for many of our white brothers, as evidenced by their presence here today, have come to realize that their destiny is tied up with our destiny and their freedom is inextricably bound to our freedom. We cannot walk alone.

And as we walk, we must make the pledge that we shall march 7 ahead. We cannot turn back. There are those who are asking the devotees of civil rights, "When will you be satisfied?" We can never be satisfied as long as the Negro is the victim of the unspeakable horrors of police brutality. We can never be satisfied as long as our bodies, heavy with the fatigue of travel, cannot gain lodging in the motels of the highways and the hotels of the cities. We cannot be satisfied as long as the Negro's basic mobility is from a smaller ghetto to a larger one. We can never be satisfied as long as a Negro in Mississippi cannot vote and a Negro in New York believes he has nothing for which to vote. No, no, we are not satisfied, and we will not be satisfied until justice rolls down like waters and righteousness like a mighty stream.

I am not unmindful that some of you have come here out of great 8 trials and tribulations. Some of you have come fresh from narrow jail cells. Some of you have come from areas where your quest for freedom left you battered by the storms of persecution and staggered by the winds of police brutality. You have been the veterans of creative suffering. Continue to work with the faith that unearned suffering is redemptive.

Go back to Mississippi, go back to Alabama, go back to South Carolina, go back to Georgia, go back to Louisiana, go back to the slums and ghettos of our northern cities, knowing that somehow this situation can and will be changed. Let us not wallow in the valley of despair. 9

I say to you today, my friends, that in spite of the difficulties and frustrations of the moment I still have a dream. It is a dream deeply rooted in the American dream. 10

I have a dream that one day this nation will rise up and live out the true meaning of its creed: "We hold these truths to be self-evident; that all men are created equal." 11

I have a dream that one day on the red hills of Georgia the sons of former slaves and the sons of former slaveowners will be able to sit down together at the table of brotherhood. 12

I have a dream that one day even the state of Mississippi, a desert state sweltering with the heat of injustice and oppression, will be transformed into an oasis of freedom and justice. 13

I have a dream that my four little children will one day live in a nation where they will not be judged by the color of their skin but by the content of their character. 14

I have a dream today. 15

I have a dream that one day the state of Alabama, whose governor's lips are presently dripping with the words of interposition and nullification, will be transformed into a situation where little black boys and black girls will be able to join hands with little white boys and white girls and walk together as sisters and brothers. 16

I have a dream today. 17

I have a dream that one day every valley shall be exalted, every hill and mountain shall be made low, the rough places will be made plain, and the crooked places will be made straight, and the glory of the Lord shall be revealed, and all flesh shall see it together. 18

This is our hope. This is the faith with which I return to the South. With this faith we will be able to hew out of the mountain of despair a stone of hope. With this faith we will be able to transform the jangling discords of our nation into a beautiful symphony of brotherhood. With this faith we will be able to work together, to pray together, to struggle together, to go to jail together, to stand up for freedom together, knowing that we will be free one day. 19

This will be the day when all of God's children will be able to sing 20
with new meaning

> My country, 'tis of thee,
> Sweet land of liberty,
>   Of thee I sing:
> Land where my fathers died,
> Land of the pilgrims' pride,
> From every mountain-side
>   Let freedom ring.

And if America is to be a great nation this must become true. So let 21
freedom ring from the prodigious hilltops of New Hampshire. Let freedom ring from the mighty mountains of New York. Let freedom ring
from the heightening Alleghenies of Pennsylvania!

Let freedom ring from the snowcapped Rockies of Colorado! 22

Let freedom ring from the curvaceous peaks of California! 23

But not only that; let freedom ring from Stone Mountain of 24
Georgia!

Let freedom ring from Lookout Mountain of Tennessee! 25

Let freedom ring from every hill and molehill of Mississippi. From 26
every mountainside, let freedom ring.

When we let freedom ring, when we let it ring from every village 27
and every hamlet, from every state and every city, we will be able to
speed up that day when all of God's children, black men and white men,
Jews and Gentiles, Protestants and Catholics, will be able to join hands
and sing in the words of the old Negro spiritual, "Free at last! free at
last! thank God almighty, we are free at last!"

## Discussion Questions

1. King's style alternates between the abstract and the concrete, between the
   grandiloquent and the simple, with abundant use of metaphors. Find examples of these qualities. Are all the stylistic strategies equally effective?
   Explain your answer.
2. What specific injustices suffered by black people does King mention? Why
   does he interrupt his series of "Let freedom ring" imperatives at the end
   with the statement, "But not only that"?
3. What values does the speech stress? Would these values be equally appealing to both blacks and whites? Why or why not?
4. More than twenty years later, how much of King's indictment of conditions
   remains true? Mention specific changes or lack of changes. If conditions
   have improved, does that make his speech less meaningful today?

## Writing Suggestions

1.  Using the same material as the original, rewrite this speech for an audience that is not impressed with the inspirational style. Think carefully about the changes in language you would make to persuade this audience that, despite your dispassionate treatment, injustices exist and should be rectified.
2.  Choose another highly emotional subject — for example, women's rights, child pornography, nuclear power — and write an inspirational speech or advertisement urging your audience to change their views. Be passionate, but try to avoid sentimentality or corniness. (You may want to look at other examples of the inspirational or hortatory style in a collection of speeches, among them speeches made in favor of the abolition of slavery and women's suffrage, declarations of war, and inaugural addresses.)

# Homosexuality:
# Tolerance Versus Approval

## JOHN LEO

In this essay John Leo, associate editor of *Time* magazine, argues that "the best public policy toward homosexuals is no
public policy at all." He questions some of the "respectable"
assumptions underlying disapproval of homosexuality but concludes that tolerance need not mean approval.

*Homosexuality is . . . (check one): (1) unnatural and perverse, (2) a*    1
*simple sexual preference, (3) a result of childhood trauma, (4) learned*
*behavior, morally neutral, (5) a problem of genes or hormones, (6) a pri-*
*vate matter that is none of the public's business.*

As answers to this question would prove, the nation has never been    2
so confused on the subject of homosexuality as now.

In general, there has been a marked growth of tolerance. In the    3
1960s, when an aide to President Johnson was arrested for committing a
homosexual act, he was expected to resign in disgrace — and did. This
year (1979) a Congressman who apologized for trying to buy sex from a
teen-age boy won his party's support, and re-election. Homosexual publishing is booming, and gays now receive far more sympathetic coverage
in the media. Gay bars and bathhouses operate unmolested in large
communities and small. Police who were once notorious for harassing homosexuals are now likely to be found playing good-will softball games
with gays. Although sodomy laws are still on the books in many states,
there is clearly little will to enforce them. The recent attempt to pass
major punitive legislation against gays — California's Proposition 6 —
was soundly defeated.

At the same time, there is a strong reaction against the homosexual    4
rights movement. Polls show resistance to homosexuals as schoolteachers,
and to laws that seem to enshrine homosexuals as a specially protected
minority. Still, now that homosexuals, and their opponents, are pressing
for various laws, many Americans are questioning their own gut feeling
that homosexuality is wrong. Many are downright ashamed or guilty
about this aversion. Is their feeling merely instinct and prejudice? Or are
there valid, respectable reasons for distaste for homosexuality and its
public claims?

The most basic opposition to homosexuality seems to arise from reli-    5 gion. In the Judaeo-Christian tradition, homosexual acts are considered sinful. Leviticus calls homosexuality "an abomination," and St. Paul condemns the practice three times. Homosexuals and their allies in the churches argue that these proscriptions are culture-bound and no longer apply. One argument is that the ancient Hebrews associated homosexuality with the competing Canaanite religion and with the vengeance of conquering armies, which routinely sodomized the vanquished as a gesture of contempt. Some Christians suggest that St. Paul was attacking loveless sexuality and a refusal by heterosexuals to procreate. Another argument, received with some incredulity by conservative church members, is that Jesus Christ would have endorsed homosexual mating if he had been culturally able to envision Christians incapable of being attracted to the opposite sex.

What about other cultures? The only worldwide survey of sexual behavior, published in 1951 by Psychologist Frank Beach and Anthropologist Clellan Ford, found that 49 out of 76 societies approved some form of homosexuality. Yet this approval extended only to sharply limited expressions of homosexuality, such as ritual acts, puberty rites and youthful premarital affairs. Beach and Ford found no society where predominant or exclusive homosexuality was affirmed. 6

Even cultures and people not religiously oriented can object to homosexuality on broadly moral grounds. True, Kinsey considered bisexuality natural. Most researchers think that homosexuality, like heterosexuality, is learned behavior, the product of subtle interaction between a child and the significant people around the child. This argument now carries such weight in the academic world that researchers seem reluctant to investigate the origins of homosexuality without also investigating the origins of heterosexuality. 7

The main problem with this position is that heterosexuality requires no complicated explanation. Even though most heterosexual acts do not lead to reproduction, sex between a man and woman has an obvious biological function. Homosexuality has no such function, and cannot ever have it. The push of evolution and the survival of human culture are geared to heterosexual mating. 8

Another reason for opposing homosexuality — and one long considered very liberal — is that it represents a sickness, or at least some form of biological or emotional disorder. Evidence to date casts doubt on the theory that homosexuality is biologically based. Freud, who believed that homosexuality was the fruit of early psychic stress, considered it to be a developmental arrest rather than an illness. As he wrote to the mother of an American homosexual, "It is assuredly no advantage, but it is nothing to be ashamed of, no vice, no degradation; it cannot be classified as an illness." Freudians have spun off dozens of theories of homo- 9

sexuality, many of them focusing on mother fixation in males and a fear
of aggression from other males.

In the hands of his successors Freud's view hardened into the theory   10
that homosexuality was pathological. But the rise of the Gay Liberation
movement and the decline of popular support for the theories of psycho-
analysis have seriously eroded the hard line Freudian view. Militant gays
have been strikingly successful in portraying Freudianism as a kind of
conservative priestcraft devoted to enforcing the heterosexual status quo.
When the gay rights movement demanded that the American Psychiatric
Association remove the "sick" label from homosexuals, the association
was in no mood to disagree. First, the homosexual lobby had demonstrated, in the words of one Freudian, "that there is a large ambulatory
population of homosexuals out there who do not need psychiatric help."
And second, the lobbyists argued, with heavy effect, that the "sick" label is the linchpin of society's oppression of homosexuals.

In a highly political compromise, the A.P.A. adopted a statement   11
declaring that "homosexuality, *per se*, cannot be classified as a mental
disorder." The operative term, *per se*, left homosexuals free to think
that they had been declared "normal" and traditional psychiatrists free
to think that homosexuality, though not a disorder itself, was, or could
be, a symptom of underlying problems. To compound the confusion,
the association felt that it had to list homosexuality somewhere, so it created a new diagnostic category, "sexual orientation disturbance," for
homosexuals dissatisfied with their sexuality. This diagnosis can only be
applied with the patient's consent. It is a bit like dermatologists voting
to ordain that acne is indeed a skin blemish, but only if the acne sufferer
thinks it is. Though the A.P.A. vote seems to have pushed a great many
therapists toward a more benign view of homosexuality, a strong body of
psychiatric opinion still insistently holds that homosexuality reflects psychic disturbance. Last year an informal poll of 2,500 psychiatrists showed
that a majority believed that homosexuals are sick.

Personality tests comparing heterosexuals and homosexuals have not   12
been of much help in resolving the confusion. Seven recent studies of
lesbians and straight women, for instance, conclude, variously, that: lesbians are not more neurotic but prone to anxiety; more neurotic; more
depressed; less depressed; not more neurotic; not necessarily more neurotic; and less neurotic. The recent Kinsey Institute study of homosexuals, published as the book *Homosexualities*, reported that a minority of
gays are indeed deeply disturbed, but that the majority function about
as well as heterosexuals.

In the welter of conflicting studies, researchers tend to agree on at   13
least one point: homosexuals report more problems with their parents —

unloving attitudes by at least one parent and parental conflict — than comparable groups of heterosexuals. This finding has been consistent among researchers who find homosexuals sick and those who find them well. Psychologists Seymour Fisher and Roger P. Greenberg, in their book *The Scientific Credibility of Freud's Theories and Therapy*, debunk much of Freud, but conclude that he was right about the fathers of male homosexuals. "In study after study," they write, "this father emerges as unfriendly, threatening or difficult to associate with."

Another area of agreement in the studies: there seem to be many 14 more male than female homosexuals. Kinsey estimated that there are two to three times as many males, and, though the actual figures are obviously unknowable, later researchers have roughly agreed. This evidence points away from the theory that homosexuality is a random variation (which ought to be randomly distributed by sex) and toward the theory that it is heavily related to special problems of male development, which appears to be more complicated and disaster-prone than that of the female. In this view, homosexuality is one of many unconscious strategies chosen by some children under great pressure, primarily pressure created by parents. It is, in short, nothing to despise, nothing to celebrate.

Many people disapprove of homosexuality because of the assump- 15 tion, long popular among some historians, that is is a sign of decadence and because of the fear of "contagion." About this, the evidence is, at best, mixed. The first point depends on what one means by decadence. The open, even glaring display of homosexuality may be seen simply as another sign of generally relaxed rules, which apply to heterosexual behavior as well. As for the "seduction of the innocent," there is little evidence that homosexual teachers, for example, are any more a threat to young pupils than heterosexual teachers. In most children, sexual orientation — the "learned" behavior that the psychologists talk about — is fixed early in life, probably by age five. In the rare cases when that orientation is not set until school age, it is doubtful that a homosexual teacher will have much impact. In fact, children raised by homosexual parents almost always grow up heterosexual. On the other hand, common sense observation shows that in many fields homosexuals do function as admired role models, and that growing social acceptance allows potential homosexuals to follow their bent rather than trying to suppress it.

In sum, there are plenty of "respectable," valid reasons, including 16 reasons of taste, for opposing homosexuality. That is very different from trying to justify the persecution or oppression of homosexuals, for which there is no case at all. The trouble, however, is that for most heterosexuals the issue is not tolerance but social approval — the difference between placards that read I'M PROUD OF MY GAY SON and I'M PROUD MY SON IS GAY. Every oppressed group seeks a positive image, and some gays argue that homosexuals will never be truly free until society produces a positive image of homosexuality. That is precisely what the majority of Americans are unwilling to grant, however much they regret the past oppressions of homosexuals.

Many people who do not consider homosexuality either sinful or 17 sick are still not prepared to say that it is merely a matter of preference, just as good as — if not better than — other forms of sexual behavior. This question of social approval lurks behind the debate over gay teachers. Many parents believe that if current laws dictate the hiring of gay teachers, future ones may require that homosexuality and heterosexuality be discussed in sex education classes as equally desirable choices. Richard Emery, a civil liberties lawyer in Manhattan, suggests just that. Gay Activist Bruce Voeller says he believes that parents who try to push their children toward heterosexuality are guilty of an unjustified use of "straight power." This is understandable minority-group politics. And it is just as understandable if parents reply that this argument is absurd, and that they want to spare their children the kind of shocks and pressures that seem to be involved in homosexualty.

The same kind of fear is operating in the debate over gay rights 18 laws. Though polls show increasing tolerance of homosexuality, opposition to laws that might be read as endorsements of homosexuality or special treatment for gays is clearly rising. As if to clinch the point that Americans are leaning in both directions at once, homosexual activists report that when rights laws are defeated, as they were in Miami, discrimination against homosexuals declines.

Homosexuals counter that increased tolerance is not enough, that 19 the nation owes them protective laws like those passed in favor of blacks and women. A good many liberals have bought this argument, partly out of feelings of guilt over past cruelties to homosexuals. But it is possible to doubt that homosexuals are a class of citizens entitled to such legislation. The government's function is not to guarantee jobs or apartments for every disaffected group in society but only to step in where systematic or massive discrimination requires it. That is clearly not the case with homosexuals, who, unlike blacks and women, are already well integrated into the economy. Homosexuals ("We are everywhere") claim that they represent 10% of every profession — police, fire fighters, teachers, surgeons, even the psychiatrists who voted on the mental health of homosexuals.

The homosexual complaint is a claim that homosexuals should not 20 have their private behavior judged when it enters the public arena. No group in America enjoys that protection under the law. "It's a life-style question," said one opponent of a gay rights law in Eugene, Ore. "We've never seen legislation passed to protect a life-style." Simple-minded prejudice is, of course, a standard feature of many hiring decisions. But, in a free society, employers and landlords are granted considerable latitude in taking into account all publicly known aspects of an applicant's character and behavior.

The problem is that laws passed for blacks and women are not cur- 21 rently viewed as rare exceptions to the general rule that employers and landlords can hire or rent to whom they please. Instead, such laws have come to be regarded as a basis for extending the same legal guarantees to a wide array of other aggrieved groups. The handicapped, for instance, have been included as protected persons in much legialtion. Alcoholics may be next. In fact, a professor has sued Brooklyn College on grounds that he was let go because of alcoholism. The Government has entered the suit on the professor's side, arguing that alcoholics should be considered handicapped persons under the 1973 Rehabilitation Act. If he wins the suit, it will be illegal for federally assisted colleges to prefer teetotaling teachers over alcoholics. Enough. The Government has better things to do than proliferate categories of unfireable citizens. Like Masons, millenarians and est graduates, homosexuals must take their chances in the marketplace, just as everyone else does.

It is true that America has a great deal to be ashamed of in its treat- 22 ment of homosexual citizens. It owes them fairness, but not the kinds of legislation sought by gay groups. In their franker moments, homosexual activists refer to gay rights laws as educational efforts and many heterosexuals have no wish to be part of such efforts. The best policy toward homosexuals is no public policy at all — no sodomy laws, no special interventions pro or con. On matters of consensual adult sex, the law is, or should be, blind.

## Discussion Questions

1. What are the three major reasons Leo gives for public disapproval of homosexuality? What kinds of evidence does he provide to support or refute the validity of these reasons? Does Leo's treatment seem to reflect a belief that some reasons are stronger than others? Explain your answer.
2. How does the author distinguish between the demand for protective laws for homosexuals and the demand for protective laws for blacks and women?
3. What dangers does Leo see in extending legal guarantees to a "wide array of other aggrieved groups"?

## Writing Suggestions

1. Do you agree with Leo that homosexuals are less entitled to protective legislation than blacks and women? If not, write an essay arguing that they are justified in asking for such laws.
2. A sex education course in a Florida junior high school teaches that homosexuality is an acceptable alternative to heterosexuality. Do you think this choice should be suggested to junior high school students? Justify your answer by explaining the values that support it.

# The Case for Torture

## MICHAEL LEVIN

Michael Levin, professor of philosophy at the City College of
New York, makes an unusual argument in favor of a practice
almost universally condemned. Under certain conditions, he
says, torture is not only permissible but "morally mandatory."
His hypothetical examples test the reader's own principles of
right and wrong and willingness to act on those principles.

It is generally assumed that torture is impermissible, a throwback to    1
a more brutal age. Enlightened societies reject it outright, and regimes
suspected of using it risk the wrath of the United States.

I believe this attitude is unwise. There are situations in which tor-    2
ture is not merely permissible but morally mandatory. Moreover, these
situations are moving from the realm of imagination to fact.

Suppose a terrorist has hidden an atomic bomb on Manhattan Is-    3
land which will detonate at noon on July 4 unless . . . (here follow the
usual demands for money and release of his friends from jail). Suppose,
further, that he is caught at 10 a.m. of the fateful day, but — preferring
death to failure — won't disclose where the bomb is. What do we do? If
we follow due process — wait for his lawyer, arraign him — millions of
people will die. If the only way to save those lives is to subject the terrorist to the most excruciating possible pain, what grounds can there be for
not doing so? I suggest there are none. In any case, I ask you to face the
question with an open mind.

Torturing the terrorist is unconstitutional? Probably. But millions    4
of lives surely outweigh constitutionality. Torture is barbaric? Mass murder is far more barbaric. Indeed, letting millions of innocents die in deference to one who flaunts his guilt is moral cowardice, an unwillingness
to dirty one's hands. If *you* caught the terrorist, could you sleep nights
knowing that millions died because you couldn't bring yourself to apply
the electrodes?

Once you concede that torture is justified in extreme cases, you have    5
admitted that the decision to use torture is a matter of balancing innocent lives against the means needed to save them. You must now face
more realistic cases involving more modest numbers. Someone plants a
bomb on a jumbo jet. He alone can disarm it, and his demands cannot
be met (or if they can, we refuse to set a precedent by yielding to his
threats). Surely we can, we must, do anything to the extortionist to save

the passengers. How can we tell 300, or 100, or 10 people who never asked to be put in danger, "I'm sorry, you'll have to die in agony, we just couldn't bring ourselves to . . ."

Here are the results of an informal poll about a third, hypothetical, 6 case. Suppose a terrorist group kidnapped a newborn baby from a hospital. I asked four mothers if they would approve of torturing kidnappers if that were necessary to get their own newborns back. All said yes, the most "liberal" adding that she would administer it herself.

I am not advocating torture as punishment. Punishment is ad- 7 dressed to deeds irrevocably past. Rather, I am advocating torture as an acceptable measure for preventing future evils. So understood, it is far less objectionable than many extant punishments. Opponents of the death penalty, for example, are forever insisting that executing a murderer will not bring back his victim (as if the purpose of capital punishment were supposed to be resurrection, not deterrence or retribution). But torture, in the cases described, is intended not to bring anyone back but to keep innocents from being dispatched. The most powerful argument against using torture as a punishment or to secure confessions is that such practices disregard the rights of the individual. Well, if the individual is all that important — and he is — it is correspondingly important to protect the rights of individuals threatened by terrorists. If life is so valuable that it must never be taken, the lives of the innocents must be saved even at the price of hurting the one who endangers them.

Better precedents for torture are assassination and pre-emptive at- 8 tack. No Allied leader would have flinched at assassinating Hitler, had that been possible. (The Allies did assassinate Heydrich.) Americans would be angered to learn that Roosevelt could have had Hitler killed in 1943 — thereby shortening the war and saving millions of lives — but refused on moral grounds. Similarly, if nation A learns that nation B is about to launch an unprovoked attack, A has a right to save itself by destroying B's military capability first. In the same way, if the police can by torture save those who would otherwise die at the hands of kidnappers or terrorists, they must.

There is an important difference between terrorists and their victims 9 that should mute talk of the terrorists' "rights." The terrorist's victims are at risk unintentionally, not having asked to be endangered. But the terrorist knowingly initiated his actions. Unlike his victims, he volunteered for the risks of his deed. By threatening to kill for profit or idealism, he renounces civilized standards, and he can have no complaint if civilization tries to thwart him by whatever means necessary.

Just as torture is justified only to save lives (not extort confessions or 10 recantations), it is justifiably administered only to those *known* to hold innocent lives in their hands. Ah, but how can the authorities ever be sure they have the right malefactor? Isn't there a danger of error and abuse? Won't We turn into Them?

Questions like these are disingenuous in a world in which terrorists 11 proclaim themselves and perform for television. The name of their game is public recognition. After all, you can't very well intimidate a government into releasing your freedom fighters unless you announce that it is your group that has seized its embassy. "Clear guilt" is difficult to define, but when 40 million people see a group of masked gunmen seize an airplane on the evening news, there is not much question about who the perpetrators are. There will be hard cases where the situation is murkier. Nonetheless, a line demarcating the legitimate use of torture can be drawn. Torture only the obviously guilty, and only for the sake of saving innocents, and the line between Us and Them will remain clear.

There is little danger that the Western democracies will lose their 12 way if they choose to inflict pain as one way of preserving order. Paralysis in the face of evil is the greater danger. Some day soon a terrorist will threaten tens of thousands of lives, and torture will be the only way to save them. We had better start thinking about this.

## Discussion Questions

1. What is Levin's thesis? What specific moral justification does he provide?
2. How does he try to convince us that the situations he describes are "moving from the realm of imagination to fact"? Are his hypothetical examples effective? What answer does Levin expect to his question, "Could you sleep nights knowing that millions died because you couldn't bring yourself to apply the electrodes?" How does the expected answer advance his argument?
3. What distinction does Levin make between his case for torture and torture as punishment?
4. What analogy does he make with assassination and preemptive attacks? Is it persuasive?
5. What answer does Levin give to the objection that torture violates an individual's rights?
6. If we become torturers of terrorists, are we then as guilty of evil as the terrorists? How does Levin answer this question?

## Writing Suggestions

1. Levin claims that torture in certain situations is "morally mandatory." If you disagree, argue that torture — or assassination of a tryant or a preemp-

tive attack against an enemy — is wrong. Make clear the moral principles on which you base your argument.

2. If you agree with Levin, use further examples to show how the course of history might have been changed for the benefit of humankind if torture or assassination had been carried out — or might be changed if torture or assassination were to be carried out now.

3. Choose another activity universally regarded as evil, and argue that it can have beneficial consequences in certain circumstances.

# The Indispensable Opposition

## WALTER LIPPMANN

This famous essay by Walter Lippmann, author, editor, and columnist, makes a point about free speech that is too often ignored — that opposing views must be heard, not because "everyone has a 'right' to say what he pleases," but because free speech is "a system for finding the truth." Listening to the views of others, whether we like them or not, is indispensable to the preservation of liberty.

Were they pressed hard enough, most men would probably confess that political freedom — that is to say, the right to speak freely and to act in opposition — is a noble ideal rather than a practical necessity. As the case for freedom is generally put today, the argument lends itself to this feeling. It is made to appear that, whereas each man claims his freedom as a matter of right, the freedom he accords to other men is a matter of toleration. Thus, the defense of freedom of opinion tends to rest not on its substantial, beneficial, and indispensable consequences, but on a somewhat eccentric, a rather vaguely benevolent, attachment to an abstraction.

It is all very well to say with Voltaire, "I wholly disapprove of what you say, but will defend to the death your right to say it," but as a matter of fact most men will not defend to the death the rights of other men: if they disapprove sufficiently what other men say, they will somehow suppress those men if they can.

So, if this is the best that can be said for liberty of opinion, that a man must tolerate his opponents because everyone has a "right" to say what he pleases, then we shall find that liberty of opinion is a luxury, safe only in pleasant times when men can be tolerant because they are not deeply and vitally concerned.

Yet actually, as a matter of historic fact, there is a much stronger foundation for the great constitutional right of freedom of speech, and as a matter of practical human experience there is a much more compelling reason for cultivating the habits of free men. We take, it seems to me, a naively self-righteous view when we argue as if the right of our opponents to speak were something that we protect because we are magnanimous, noble, and unselfish. The compelling reason why, if liberty of opinion did not exist, we should have to invent it, why it will eventually have to be restored in all civilized countries where it is now suppressed, is that we must protect the right of our opponents to speak because we must hear what they have to say.

We miss the whole point when we imagine that we tolerate the freedom of our political opponents as we tolerate a howling baby next door, as we put up with the blasts from our neighbor's radio because we are too peaceable to heave a brick through the window. If this were all there is to freedom of opinion, that we are too goodnatured or too timid to do anything about our opponents and our critics except to let them talk, it would be difficult to say whether we are tolerant because we are magnanimous or because we are lazy, because we have strong principles or because we lack serious convictions, whether we have the hospitality of an inquiring mind or the indifference of an empty mind. And so, if we truly wish to understand why freedom is necessary in a civilized society, we must begin by realizing that, because freedom of discussion improves our own opinions, the liberties of other men are our own vital necessity.

We are much closer to the essence of the matter, not when we quote Voltaire, but when we go to the doctor and pay him to ask us the most embarrassing questions and to prescribe the most disagreeable diet. When we pay the doctor to exercise complete freedom of speech about the cause and cure of our stomachache, we do not look upon ourselves as tolerant and magnanimous, and worthy to be admired by ourselves. We have enough common sense to know that if we threaten to put the doctor in jail because we do not like the diagnosis and the prescription it will be unpleasant for the doctor, to be sure, but equally unpleasant for our own stomachache. That is why even the most ferocious dictator would rather be treated by a doctor who was free to think and speak the truth than by his own Minister of Propaganda. For there is a point, the point at which things really matter, where the freedom of others is no longer a question of their right but of our own need.

The point at which we recognize this need is much higher in some men than in others. The totalitarian rulers think they do not need the freedom of an opposition: they exile, imprison, or shoot their opponents. We have concluded on the basis of practical experience, which goes back to Magna Carta and beyond, that we need the opposition. We pay the opposition salaries out of the public treasury.

In so far as the usual apology for freedom of speech ignores this experience, it becomes abstract and eccentric rather than concrete and human. The emphasis is generally put on the right to speak, as if all that mattered were that the doctor should be free to go out into the park and explain to the vacant air why I have a stomachache. Surely that is a miserable caricature of the great civic right which men have bled and died for. What really matters is that the doctor should tell *me* what ails me, that I should listen to him; that if I do not like what he says I should be free to call in another doctor; and that then the first doctor should have to listen to the second doctor; and that out of all the speaking and listening, the give-and-take of opinions, the truth should be arrived at.

This is the creative principle of freedom of speech, not that it is a 9 system for the tolerating of error, but that it is a system for finding the truth. It may not produce the truth, or the whole truth all the time, or often, or in some cases ever. But if the truth can be found, there is no other system which will normally and habitually find so much truth. Until we have thoroughly understood this principle, we shall not know why we must value our liberty, or how we can protect and develop it.

Let us apply this principle to the system of public speech in a totali- 10 tarian state. We may, without any serious falsification, picture a condition of affairs in which the mass of the people are being addressed through one broadcasting system by one man and his chosen subordinates. The orators speak. The audience listens but cannot and dare not speak back. It is a system of one-way communication; the opinions of the rulers are broadcast outwardly to the mass of the people. But nothing comes back to the rulers from the people except the cheers; nothing returns in the way of knowledge of forgotten facts, hidden feelings, neglected truths, and practical suggestions.

But even a dictator cannot govern by his own one-way inspiration 11 alone. In practice, therefore, the totalitarian rulers get back the reports of the secret police and of their party henchmen down among the crowd. If these reports are competent, the rulers may manage to remain in touch with public sentiment. Yet that is not enough to know what the audience feels. The rulers have also to make great decisions that have enormous consequences, and here their system provides virtually no help from the give-and-take of opinion in the nation. So they must either rely on their own intuition, which cannot be permanently and continually inspired, or, if they are intelligent despots, encourage their trusted advisers and their technicians to speak and debate freely in their presence.

On the walls of the houses of Italian peasants one may see inscribed 12 in large letters the legend, "Mussolini is always right." But if that legend is taken serously by Italian ambassadors, by the Italian General Staff, and by the Ministry of Finance, then all one can say is heaven help Mussolini, heaven help Italy, and the new Emperor of Ethiopia.[1]

For at some point, even in a totalitarian state, it is indispensable 13 that there should exist the freedom of opinion which causes opposing opinions to be debated. As time goes on, that is less and less easy under a despotism; critical discussion disappears as the internal opposition is liq-

---

[1]Benito Mussolini was dictator of Italy, which he led into World War II, at the time this essay was written. — ED.

uidated in favor of men who think and feel alike. That is why the early successes of despots, of Napoleon I and of Napoleon III, have usually been followed by an irreparable mistake. For in listening only to his yes men — the others being in exile or in concentration camps, or terrified — the despot shuts himself off from the truth that no man can dispense with.

We know all this well enough when we contemplate the dictatorships. But when we try to picture our own system, by way of contrast, what picture do we have in our minds? It is, is it not, that anyone may stand up on his own soapbox and say anything he pleases, like the individuals in Kipling's poem[2] who sit each in his separate star and draw the Thing as they see it for the God of Things as they are. Kipling, perhaps, could do this, since he was a poet. But the ordinary mortal isolated on his separate star will have an hallucination, and a citizenry declaiming from separate soapboxes will poison the air with hot and nonsensical confusion. | 14

If the democratic alternative to the totalitarian one-way broadcasts is a row of separate soapboxes, then I submit that the alternative is unworkable, is unreasonable, and is humanly unattractive. It is above all a false alternative. It is not true that liberty has developed among civilized men when anyone is free to set up a soapbox, is free to hire a hall where he may expound his opinions to those who are willing to listen. On the contrary, freedom of speech is established to achieve its essential purpose only when different opinions are expounded in the same hall to the same audience. | 15

For, while the right to talk may be the beginning of freedom, the necessity of listening is what makes the right important. Even in Russia and Germany a man may still stand in an open field and speak his mind. What matters is not the utterance of opinions. What matters is the confrontation of opinions in debate. No man can care profoundly that every fool should say what he likes. Nothing has been accomplished if the wisest man proclaims his wisdom in the middle of the Sahara Desert. This is the shadow. We have the substance of liberty when the fool is compelled to listen to the wise man and learn; when the wise man is compelled to take account of the fool, and to instruct him; when the wise man can increase his wisdom by hearing the judgment of his peers. | 16

That is why civilized men must cherish liberty — as a means of promoting the discovery of truth. So we must not fix our whole attention on the right of anyone to hire his own hall, to rent his own broadcasting station, to distribute his own pamphlets. These rights are incidental; and though they must be preserved, they can be preserved only by regarding | 17

---

[2] "L'Envoi." — ED.

them as incidental, as auxiliary to the substance of liberty that must be cherished and cultivated.

Freedom of speech is best conceived, therefore, by having in mind  18 the picture of a place like the American Congress, an assembly where opposing views are represented, where ideas are not merely uttered but debated, or the British Parliament, where men who are free to speak are also compelled to answer. We may picture the true condition of freedom as existing in a place like a court of law, where witnesses testify and are cross-examined, where the lawyer argues against the opposing lawyer before the same judge and in the presence of one jury. We may picture freedom as existing in a forum where the speaker must respond to questions; in a gathering of scientists where the data, the hypothesis, and the conclusion are submitted to men competent to judge them; in a reputable newspaper which not only will publish the opinions of those who disagree but will re-examine its own opinion in the light of what they say.

Thus the essence of freedom of opinion is not in mere toleration as  19 such, but in the debate which toleration provides: it is not in the venting of opinion, but in the confrontation of opinion. That this is the practical substance can readily be understood when we remember how differently we feel and act about the censorship and regulation of opinion purveyed by different media of communication. We find then that, in so far as the medium makes difficult the confrontation of opinion in debate, we are driven towards censorship and regulation.

There is, for example, the whispering campaign, the circulation of  20 anonymous rumors by men who cannot be compelled to prove what they say. They put the utmost strain on our tolerance, and there are few who do not rejoice when the anonymous slanderer is caught, exposed, and punished. At a higher level there is the moving picture, a most powerful medium for conveying ideas, but a medium which does not permit debate. A moving picture cannot be answered effectively by another moving picture; in all free countries there is some censorship of the movies, and there would be more if the producers did not recognize their limitations by avoiding political controversy. There is then the radio. Here debate is difficult: it is not easy to make sure that the speaker is being answered in the presence of the same audience. Inevitably, there is some regulation of the radio.

When we reach the newspaper press, the opportunity for debate is  21 so considerable that discontent cannot grow to the point where under normal conditions there is any disposition to regulate the press. But when newspapers abuse their power by injuring people who have no means of replying, a disposition to regulate the press appears. When we arrive at Congress we find that, because the membership of the House is so large, full debate is impracticable. So there are restrictive rules. On the other hand, in the Senate, where the conditions of full debate exist, there is almost absolute freedom of speech.

This shows us that the preservation and development of freedom of 22 opinion are not only a matter of adhering to abstract legal rights, but also, and very urgently, a matter of organizing and arranging sufficient debate. Once we have a firm hold on the central principle, there are many practical conclusions to be drawn. We then realize that the defense of freedom of opinion consists primarily in perfecting the opportunity for an adequate give-and-take of opinion; it consists also in regulating the freedom of those revolutionists who cannot or will not permit or maintain debate when it does not suit their purposes.

We must insist that free oratory is only the beginning of free 23 speech; it is not the end, but a means to an end. The end is to find the truth. The practical justification of civil liberty is not that self-expression is one of the rights of man. It is that the examination of opinion is one of the necessities of man. For experience tells us that it is only when free- dom of opinion becomes the compulsion to debate that the seed which our fathers planted has produced its fruit. When that is understood, freedom will be cherished not because it is a vent for our opinions but because it is the surest method of correcting them.

The unexamined life, said Socrates, is unfit to be lived by man. This 24 is the virtue of liberty, and the ground on which we may best justify our belief in it, that it tolerates error in order to serve the truth. When men are brought face to face with their opponents, forced to listen and learn and mend their ideas, they cease to be children and savages and begin to live like civilized men. Then only is freedom a reality, when men may voice their opinions because they must examine their opinions.

The only reason for dwelling on all this is that if we are to preserve 25 democracy we must understand its principles. And the principle which distinguishes it from all other forms of government is that in a democ- racy the opposition not only is tolerated as constitutional but must be maintained because it is in fact indispensable.

The democratic system cannot be operated without effective opposi- 26 tion. For, in making the great experiment of governing people by con- sent rather than by coercion, it is not sufficient that the party in power should have a majority. It is just as necessary that the party in power should never outrage the minority. That means that it must listen to the minority and be moved by the criticisms of the minority. That means that its measures must take account of the minority's objections, and that in administering measures it must remember that the minority may become the majority.

The opposition is indispensable. A good statesman, like any other 27 sensible human being, always learns more from his opponents than from his fervent supporters. For his supporters will push him to disaster unless his opponents show him where the dangers are. So if he is wise he will often pray to be delivered from his friends, because they will ruin him. But, though it hurts, he ought also to pray never to be left without opponents; for they keep him on the path of reason and good sense.

The national unity of a free people depends upon a sufficiently even 28 balance of political power to make it impracticable for the administration to be arbitrary and for the opposition to be revolutionary and irreconcilable. Where that balance no longer exists, democracy perishes. For unless all the citizens of a state are forced by circumstances to compromise, unless they feel that they can affect policy but that no one can wholly dominate it, unless by habit and necessity they have to give and take, freedom cannot be maintained.

## Discussion Questions

1. What is Lippmann's criticism of free speech based on toleration? Why does he call this view, expressed by Voltaire, an abstraction?
2. Summarize in your own words Lippmann's thesis — what he calls "a much stronger foundation for the great constitutional right of freedom of speech." Point out the different places in the essay where he states this thesis explicitly.
3. What hypothetical examples does Lippmann use to support his claim? Are they persuasive?
4. What dangers does Lippmann foresee for dictatorships in which one-way communication is practiced? Does he think that these dangers are possible in a democracy?

## Writing Suggestions

1. In recent years some members of university audiences have prevented speakers with opposing views from being heard. Select an example, real or hypothetical, of speakers espousing views that are considered racist, sexist, or militaristic by some members of the audience. Write an essay arguing for or against the necessity to listen to such speakers. Make clear the assumptions or general principles on which you base your argument.
2. Do you agree with Lippmann that being brought face to face with those who hold opposing views and being forced to listen to them helps us mature and begin to live like civilized people rather than like children or savages? If so, choose an episode from your own life when open debate caused you to make a change for the better. Analyze in detail the way you arrived at the "truth."

# The Penalty of Death

## H. L. MENCKEN

Although H. L. Mencken's essay in favor of capital punishment
was written almost fifty years ago, the issues remain essentially
the same. After rejecting two of the most familiar arguments
against capital punishment, Mencken, a newspaper reporter,
editor, and columnist known for his cynicism, rests his own case
on a knowledge of human nature and especially the desire for
*katharsis*, "a healthy letting off of steam."

Of the arguments against capital punishment that issue from uplift- 1
ers, two are commonly heard most often, to wit:

1. That hanging a man (or frying him or gassing him) is a dreadful
   business, degrading to those who have to do it and revolting to
   those who have to witness it.
2. That it is useless, for it does not deter others from the same crime.

The first of these arguments, it seems to me, is plainly too weak to 2
need serious refutation. All it says, in brief, is that the work of the hangman is unpleasant. Granted. But suppose it is? It may be quite necessary
to society for all that. There are, indeed, many other jobs that are unpleasant, and yet no one thinks of abolishing them — that of the
plumber, that of the soldier, that of the garbage-man, that of the priest
hearing confessions, that of the sand-hog, and so on. Moreover, what evidence is there that any actual hangman complains of his work? I have
heard none. On the contrary, I have known many who delighted in their
ancient art, and practiced it proudly.

In the second argument of the abolitionists there is rather more 3
force, but even here, I believe, the ground under them is shaky. Their
fundamental error consists in assuming that the whole aim of punishing
criminals is to deter other (potential) criminals — that we hang or elec-
trocute A simply in order to so alarm B that he will not kill C. This, I believe, is an assumption which confuses a part with the whole. Deterrence, obviously, is *one* of the aims of punishment, but it is surely not
the only one. On the contrary, there are at least a half dozen, and some
are probably quite as important. At least one of them, practically considered, is *more* important. Commonly, it is described as revenge, but revenge is really not the word for it. I borrow a better term from the late
Aristotle: *katharsis*. *Katharsis*, so used, means a salubrious discharge of

emotions, a healthy letting off of steam. A school-boy, disliking his teacher, deposits a tack upon the pedagogical chair; the teacher jumps and the boy laughs. This is *katharsis*. What I contend is that one of the prime objects of all judicial punishments is to afford the same grateful relief (*a*) to the immediate victims of the criminal punished, and (*b*) to the general body of moral and timorous men.

These persons, and particularly the first group, are concerned only    4
indirectly with deterring other criminals. The thing they crave primarily is the satisfaction of seeing the criminal actually before them suffer as he made them suffer. What they want is the peace of mind that goes with the feeling that accounts are squared. Until they get that satisfaction they are in a state of emotional tension, and hence unhappy. The instant they get it they are comfortable. I do not argue that this yearning is no-ble; I simply argue that it is almost universal among human beings. In the face of injuries that are unimportant and can be borne without dam-age it may yield to higher impulses; that is to say, it may yield to what is called Christian charity. But when the injury is serious Christianity is ad-journed, and even saints reach for their sidearms. It is plainly asking too much of human nature to expect it to conquer so natural an impulse. A keeps a store and has a bookkeeper, B. B steals $700, employs it in play-ing at dice or bingo, and is cleaned out. What is A to do? Let B go? If he does so he will be unable to sleep at night. The sense of injury, of injus-tice, of frustration will haunt him like pruritus. So he turns B over to the police, and they hustle B to prison. Thereafter A can sleep. More, he has pleasant dreams. He pictures B chained to the wall of a dungeon a hun-dred feet underground, devoured by rats and scorpions. It is so agreeable that it makes him forget his $700. He has got his *katharsis*.

The same thing precisely takes place on a larger scale when there is a    5
crime which destroys a whole community's sense of security. Every law-abiding citizen feels menaced and frustrated until the criminals have been struck down — until the communal capacity to get even with them, and more than even, has been dramatically demonstrated. Here, mani-festly, the business of deterring others is no more than an afterthought. The main thing is to destroy the concrete scoundrels whose act has alarmed everyone, and thus made everyone unhappy. Until they are brought to book that unhappiness continues; when the law has been exe-cuted upon them there is a sigh of relief. In other words, there is *ka-tharsis*.

I know of no public demand for the death penalty for ordinary    6
crimes, even for ordinary homicides. Its infliction would shock all men of normal decency of feeling. But for crimes involving the deliberate and inexcusable taking of human life, by men openly defiant of all civilized order — for such crimes it seems, to nine men out of ten, a just and

proper punishment. Any lesser penalty leaves them feeling that the criminal has got the better of society — that he is free to add insult to injury by laughing. That feeling can be dissipated only by a recourse to *katharsis*, the invention of the aforesaid Aristotle. It is more effectively and economically achieved, as human nature now is, by wafting the criminal to realms of bliss.

The real object to capital punishment doesn't lie against the actual extermination of the condemned, but against our brutal American habit of putting it off so long. After all, every one of us must die soon or late, and a murderer, it must be assumed, is one who makes that sad fact the cornerstone of his metaphysic. But it is one thing to die, and quite another thing to lie for long months and even years under the shadow of death. No sane man would choose such a finish. All of us, despite the Prayer Book, long for a swift and unexpected end. Unhappily, a murderer, under the irrational American system, is tortured for what, to him, must seem a whole series of eternities. For months on end he sits in prison while his lawyers carry on their idiotic buffoonery with writs, injunctions, mandamuses, and appeals. In order to get his money (or that of his friends) they have to feed him with hope. Now and then, by the imbecility of a judge or some trick of juridic science, they actually justify it. But let us say that, his money all gone, they finally throw up their hands. Their client is now ready for the rope or the chair. But he must still wait for months before it fetches him.

That wait, I believe, is horribly cruel. I have seen more than one man sitting in the death-house, and I don't want to see any more. Worse, it is wholly useless. Why should he wait at all? Why not hang him the day after the last court dissipates his last hope? Why torture him as not even cannibals would torture their victims? The common answer is that he must have time to make his peace with God. But how long does that take? It may be accomplished, I believe, in two hours quite as comfortably as in two years. There are, indeed, no temporal limitations upon God. He could forgive a whole herd of murderers in a millionth of a second. More, it has been done.

## Discussion Questions

1. How does Mencken dispose of the two most often heard objections to capital punishment?
2. What does he think is the most important reason for supporting capital punishment? How does he define *katharsis*? Do Mencken's rather cynical examples seem appropriate to his thesis?
3. What "real" objection to capital punishment does Mencken take seri-

ously? Do the conditions he describes still exist? How important do you think they are as an objection to capital punishment?

4.  In the last paragraph Mencken asks, "Why torture him as not even cannibals would torture their victims?" Does this seem consistent with what he has said earlier about the satisfaction of "seeing the criminal . . . suffer"?

## Writing Suggestions

1.  If you agree with Mencken that the death penalty is an appropriate punishment for premeditated homicide, choose an issue he has dealt with briefly or one he has neglected and develop it as part of your argument in favor of capital punishment.
2.  Do you think that Mencken has successfully demolished the important arguments against capital punishment? If not, pick out an issue you think Mencken has overlooked or failed to answer satisfactorily and develop it as part of an argument against capital punishment.
3.  If you are against capital punishment, write an essay proposing substitute punishments that might satisy those who are in favor of it.

# Politics and
# the English Language

**GEORGE ORWELL**

This essay, written after World War II, develops George Orwell's claim that careless and dishonest use of language contributes to careless and dishonest thought and political corruption. Political language, he argues, is "largely the defense of the indefensible." But Orwell, novelist, critic, and political satirist best known for his book *1984*, believes that bad language habits can be reversed, and he lists rules for getting rid of some of the most offensive.

Most people who bother with the matter at all would admit that the 1
English language is in a bad way, but it is generally assumed that we cannot by conscious action do anything about it. Our civilization is decadent and our language — so the argument runs — must inevitably share in the general collapse. It follows that any struggle against the abuse of language is a sentimental archaism, like preferring candles to electric light or hansom cabs to aeroplanes. Underneath this lies the half-conscious belief that language is a natural growth and not an instrument which we shape for our own purposes.

Now, it is clear that the decline of a language must ultimately have 2
political and economic causes: it is not due simply to the bad influence of this or that individual writer. But an effect can become a cause, reinforcing the original cause and producing the same effect in an intensified form, and so on indefinitely. A man may take to drink because he feels himself to be a failure, and then fail all the more completely because he drinks. It is rather the same thing that is happening to the English language. It becomes ugly and inaccurate because our thoughts are foolish, but the slovenliness of our language makes it easier for us to have foolish thoughts. The point is that the process is reversible. Modern English, especially written English, is full of bad habits which spread by imitation and which can be avoided if one is willing to take the necessary trouble. If one gets rid of these habits one can think more clearly, and to think clearly is a necessary first step towards political regeneration: so that the fight against bad English is not frivolous and is not the exclusive concern of professional writers. I will come back to this presently, and I hope that by that time the meaning of what I have said here will have become

clearer. Meanwhile, here are five specimens of the English language as it is now habitually written.

These five passages have not been picked out because they are especially bad—I could have quoted far worse if I had chosen—but because they illustrate various of the mental vices from which we now suffer. They are a little below the average, but are fairly representative samples. I number them so that I can refer back to them when necessary:

(1) I am not, indeed, sure whether it is not true to say that the Milton who once seemed not unlike a seventeenth-century Shelley had not become out of an experience ever more bitter in each year, more alien [sic] to the founder of that Jesuit sect which nothing could induce him to tolerate.

Professor Harold Laski (Essay in *Freedom of Expression*).

(2) Above all, we cannot play ducks and drakes with a native battery of idioms which prescribes such egregious collocations of vocables as the Basic *put up with* for *tolerate* or *put at a loss* for *bewilder*.

Professor Lancelot Hogben (*Interglossa*).

(3) On the one side we have the free personality: by definition it is not neurotic, for it has neither conflict nor dream. Its desires, such as they are, are transparent, for they are just what institutional approval keeps in the forefront of consciousness; another institutional pattern would alter their number and intensity; there is little in them that is natural, irreducible, or culturally dangerous. But *on the other side*, the social bond itself is nothing but the mutual reflection of these self-secure integrities. Recall the definition of love. Is not this the very picture of a small academic? Where is there a place in this hall of mirrors for either personality or fraternity?

Essay on psychology in *Politics* (New York).

(4) All the "best people" from the gentlemen's clubs, and all the frantic fascist captains, united in common hatred of Socialism and bestial horror of the rising tide of the mass revolutionary movement, have turned to acts of provocation, to foul incendiarism, to medieval legends of poisoned wells, to legalize their own destruction of proletarian organizations, and rouse the agitated petty-bourgeoisie to chauvinistic fervor on behalf of the fight against the revolutionary way out of the crisis.

Communist pamphlet.

(5) If a new spirit *is* to be infused into this old country, there is one thorny and contentious reform which must be tackled, and that is the humanization and galvanization of the B.B.C. Timidity here will bespeak cancer and atrophy of the soul. The heart of Britain may be sound and of strong beat, for instance, but the British lion's roar at present is like that of Bottom in Shakespeare's *Midsummer Night's Dream*—as gentle as any sucking dove. A virile new Britain cannot continue indefinitely to be traduced in the eyes or rather ears, of the world by the effete languors of Langham Place, brazenly masquerading as "standard English." When the

Voice of Britain is heard at nine o'clock, better far and infinitely less ludicrous to hear aitches honestly dropped than the present priggish, inflated,
inhibited, school-ma'amish arch braying of blameless bashful mewing
maidens!

Letter in *Tribune*.

Each of these passages has faults of its own, but, quite apart from 4
avoidable ugliness, two qualities are common to all of them. The first is
staleness of imagery: the other is lack of precision. The writer either has a
meaning and cannot express it, or he inadvertently says something else,
or he is almost indifferent as to whether his words mean anything or not.
The mixture of vagueness and sheer incompetence is the most marked
characteristic of modern English prose, and especially of any kind of political writing. As soon as certain topics are raised, the concrete melts into
the abstract and no one seems to think of turns of speech that are not
hackneyed: prose consists less and less of *words* chosen for the sake of
their meaning, and more and more of *phrases* tacked together like the
sections of a prefabricated hen-house. I list below, with notes and examples, various of the tricks by means of which the work of prose-construc-
tion is habitually dodged:

*Dying Metaphors.* A newly invented metaphor assists thought by 5
evoking a visual image, while on the other hand a metaphor which is
technically "dead" (e.g., *iron resolution*) has in effect reverted to being
an ordinary word and can generally be used without loss of vividness. But
in between these two classes there is a huge dump of worn-out metaphors which have lost all evocative power and are merely used because
they save people the trouble of inventing phrases for themselves. Examples are: *Ring the changes on, take up the cudgels for, toe the line, ride
roughshod over, stand shoulder to shoulder with, play into the hands of,
no axe to grind, grist to the mill, fishing in troubled waters, rift within
the lute, on the order of the day, Achilles' heel, swan song, hotbed.*
Many of these are used without knowledge of their meaning (what is a
"rift," for instance?), and incompatible metaphors are frequently
mixed, a sure sign that the writer is not interested in what he is saying.
Some metaphors now current have been twisted out of their original
meaning without those who use them even being aware of the fact. For
example, *toe the line* is sometimes written *tow the line*. Another example is *the hammer and the anvil*, now always used with the implication
that the anvil gets the worst of it. In real life it is always the anvil that
breaks the hammer, never the other way about: a writer who stopped to
think what he was saying would be aware of this, and would avoid per-
verting the original phrase.

*Operators or Verbal False Limbs.* These save the trouble of picking 6
out appropriate verbs and nouns, and at the same time pad each sentence with extra syllables which give it an appearance of symmetry. Characteristic phrases are: *render inoperative, militate against, make contact
with, be subjected to, give rise to, give grounds for, have the effect of,
play a leading part (role) in, make itself felt, take effect, exhibit a tendency to, serve the purpose of,* etc., etc. The keynote is the elimination of
simple verbs. Instead of being a single word, such as *break, stop, spoil,
mend, kill,* a verb becomes a *phrase,* made up of a noun or adjective
tacked on to some general-purpose verb such as *prove, serve, form, play,
render.* In addition, the passive voice is wherever possible used in preference to the active, and noun constructions are used instead of gerunds
(*by examination of* instead of *by examining*). The range of verbs is further cut down by means of the *-ize* and *de-* formation, and the banal
statements are given an appearance of profundity by means of the *not
un-* formation. Simple conjunctions and prepositions are replaced by
such phrases as *with respect to, having regard to, the fact that, by dint
of, in view of, in the interests of, on the hypothesis that*; and the ends of
sentences are saved from anticlimax by such resounding commonplaces
as *greatly to be desired, cannot be left out of account, a development to
be expected in the near future, deserving of serious consideration,
brought to a satisfactory conclusion,* and so on and so forth.

*Pretentious Diction.* Words like *phenomenon, element, individual* 7
(as noun), *objective, categorical, effective, virtual, basic, primary, promote, constitute, exhibit, exploit, utilize, eliminate, liquidate,* are used
to dress up simple statements and give an air of scientific impartiality to
biased judgments. Adjectives like *epoch-making, epic, historic, unforgettable, triumphant, age-old, inevitable, inexorable, veritable,* are used
to dignify the sordid processes of international politics, while writing
that aims at glorifying war usually takes on an archaic color, its characteristic words being: *realm, throne, chariot, mailed fist, trident, sword,
shield, buckler, banner, jackboot, clarion.* Foreign words and expressions
such as *cul de sac, ancien régime, deus ex machina, mutatis mutandis,
status quo, gleichshaltung, weltanschauung,* are used to give an air of
culture and elegance. Except for the useful abbreviations *i.e., e.g.,* and
*etc.,* there is no real need for any of the hundreds of foreign phrases now
current in English. Bad writers, and especially scientific, political and sociological writers, are nearly always haunted by the notion that Latin or
Greek words are grander than Saxon ones, and unnecessary words like *expedite, ameliorate, predict, extraneous, deracinated, clandestine, subaqueous* and hundreds of others constantly gain ground from their An

glo-Saxon opposite numbers.[1] The jargon peculiar to Marxist writing (*hyena, hangman, cannibal, petty bourgeois, these gentry, lackey, flunkey, mad dog, White Guard*, etc.) consists largely of words and phrases translated from Russian, German or French; but the normal way of coining a new word is to use a Latin or Greek root with the appropriate affix and, where necessary, the *-ize* formation. It is often easier to make up words of this kind (*deregionalize, impermissible, extramarital, nonfragmentatory* and so forth) than to think up the English words that will cover one's meaning. The result, in general, is an increase in slovenliness and vagueness.

*Meaningless Words*. In certain kinds of writing, particularly in art criticism and literary criticism, it is normal to come across long passages which are almost completely lacking in meaning.[2] Words like *romantic, plastic, values, human, dead, sentimental, natural, vitality*, as used in art criticism, are strictly meaningless in the sense that they not only do not point to any discoverable object, but are hardly ever expected to do so by the reader. When one critic writes, "The outstanding feature of Mr. X's work is its living quality," while another writes, "The immediately striking thing about Mr. X's work is its peculiar deadness," the reader accepts this as a simple difference of opinion. If words like *black* and *white* were involved, instead of the jargon words *dead* and *living*, he would see at once that language was being used in an improper way. Many political words are similarly abused. The word *Fascism* has now no meaning except in so far as it signifies "something not desirable." The words *democracy, socialism, freedom, patriotic, realistic, justice*, have each of them several different meanings which cannot be reconciled with one another. In the case of a word like *democracy*, not only is there no agreed definition, but the attempt to make one is resisted from all sides. It is almost universally felt that when we call a country democratic we are praising it: consequently the defenders of every kind of regime claim that it is a democracy, and fear that they might have to stop using the

---

[1]An interesting illustration of this is the way in which the English flower names which were in use till very recently are being ousted by Greek ones, *snapdragon* becoming *antirrhinum*, *forget-me-not* becoming *myosotis*, etc. It is hard to see any practical reason for this change of fashion: it is probably due to an instinctive turning-away from the more homely word and a vague feeling that the Greek word is scientific.

[2]Example: "Comfort's catholicity of perception and image, strangely Whitmanesque in range, almost the exact opposite in aesthetic compulsion, continues to evoke that trembling atmospheric accumulative hinting at a cruel, an inexorably serene timelessness . . . Wrey Gardiner scores by aiming at simple bull's-eyes with precision. Only they are not so simple, and through this contented sadness runs more than the surface bitter-sweet of resignation." (*Poetry Quarterly*.)

word if it were tied down to any one meaning. Words of this kind are often used in a consciously dishonest way. That is, the person who uses
them has his own private definition, but allows his hearer to think he
means something quite different. Statements like *Marshal Pétain was a
true patriot, The Soviet Press is the freest in the world, The Catholic
Church is opposed to persecution*, are almost always made with intent to
deceive. Other words used in variable meanings, in most cases more or
less dishonestly, are: *class, totalitarian, science, progressive, reactionary,
bourgeois, equality*.

Now that I have made this catalogue of swindles and perversions, let 9
me give another example of the kind of writing that they lead to. This
time it must of its nature be an imaginary one. I am going to translate a
passage of good English into modern English of the worst sort. Here is a
well-known verse from *Ecclesiastes*:

> I returned and saw under the sun, that the race is not to the swift, nor
> the battle to the strong, neither yet bread to the wise, nor yet riches to men
> of understanding, nor yet favor to men of skill; but time and chance hap-
> peneth to them all.

Here it is in modern English:

> Objective consideration of contemporary phenomena compels the
> conclusion that success or failure in competitive activities exhibits no tend-
> ency to be commensurate with innate capacity, but that a considerable ele-
> ment of the unpredictable must invariably be taken into account.

This is a parody, but not a very gross one. Exhibit (3), above, for in- 10
stance, contains several patches of the same kind of English. It will be
seen that I have not made a full translation. The beginning and ending
of the sentence follow the original meaning fairly closely, but in the middle the concrete illustrations — race, battle, bread — dissolve into the
vague phrase "success or failure in competitive activities." This had to
be so, because no modern writer of the kind I am discussing — no one capable of using phrases like "objective consideration of contemporary
phenomena" — would ever tabulate his thoughts in that precise and detailed way. The whole tendency of modern prose is away from concrete-
ness. Now analyze these two sentences a little more closely. The first contains forty-nine words but only sixty syllables, and all its words are those
of everyday life. The second contains thirty-eight words of ninety syllables: eighteen of its words are from Latin roots, and one from Greek. The
first sentence contains six vivid images, and only one phrase ("time and
chance") that could be called vague. The second contains not a single
fresh, arresting phrase, and in spite of its ninety syllables it gives only a

shortened version of the meaning contained in the first. Yet without a doubt it is the second kind of sentence that is gaining ground in modern English. I do not want to exaggerate. This kind of writing is not yet universal, and outcrops of simplicity will occur here and there in the worst-written page. Still, if you or I were told to write a few lines on the uncertainty of human fortunes, we should probably come much nearer to my imaginary sentence than to the one from *Ecclesiastes*.

As I have tried to show, modern writing at its worst does not consist   11
in picking out words for the sake of their meaning and inventing images in order to make the meaning clearer. It consists in gumming together long strips of words which have already been set in order by someone else, and making the **results** presentable by sheer humbug. The attraction of this way of writing is that it is easy. It is easier — even quicker once you have the habit — to say *In my opinion it is a not unjustifiable assumption that* than to say *I think*. If you use ready-made phrases, you not only don't have to hunt about for words; you also don't have to bother with the rhythms of your sentences, since these phrases are generally so arranged as to be more or less euphonious. When you are composing in a hurry — when you are dictating to a stenographer, for instance, or making a public speech — it is natural to fall into a pretentious, Latinized style. Tags like a *consideration which we should do well to bear in mind* or *a conclusion to which all of us would readily assent* will save many a sentence from coming down with a bump. By using stale metaphors, similes and idioms, you save much mental effort, at the cost of leaving your meaning vauge, not only for your reader but for yourself. This is the significance of mixed metaphors. The sole aim of a metaphor is to call up a visual image. When these images clash — as in *The Fascist octopus has sung its swan song, the jackboot is thrown into the melting pot* — it can be taken as certain that the writer is not seeing a mental image of the objects he is naming; in other words he is not really thinking. Look again at the examples I gave at the beginning of this essay. Professor Laski (1) uses five negatives in fifty-three words. One of these is superfluous, making nonsense of the whole passage, and in addition there is the slip *alien* for akin, making further nonsense, and several avoidable pieces of clumsiness which increase the general vagueness. Professor Hogben (2) plays ducks and drakes with a battery which is able to write prescriptions, and, while disapproving of the every-day phrase *put up with*, is unwilling to look *egregious* up in the dictionary and see what it means. (3), if one takes an uncharitable attitude towards it, is simply meaningless: probably one could work out its intended meaning by reading the whole of the article in which it occurs. In (4), the writer knows more or less what he wants to say, but an accumulation of stale phrases chokes him like tea leaves blocking a sink. In (5), words and

meaning have almost parted company. People who write in this manner usually have a general emotional meaning — they dislike one thing and want to express solidarity with another — but they are not interested in the detail of what they are saying. A scrupulous writer, in every sentence that he writes, will ask himself at least four questions, thus: What am I trying to say? What words will express it? What image or idiom will make it clearer? Is this image fresh enough to have an effect? And he will probably ask himself two more: Could I put it more shortly? Have I said anything that is avoidably ugly? But you are not obliged to go to all this trouble. You can shirk it by simply throwing your mind open and letting the ready-made phrases come crowding in. They will construct your sentences for you — even think your thoughts for you, to a certain extent — and at need they will perform the important service of partially concealing your meaning even from yourself. It is at this point that the special connection between politics and the debasement of language becomes clear.

In our time it is broadly true that political writing is bad writing. 12 Where it is not true, it will generally be found that the writer is some kind of rebel, expressing his private opinions and not a "party line." Orthodoxy, of whatever color, seems to demand a lifeless, imitative style. The political dialects to be found in pamphlets, leading articles, manifestos, White Papers and the speeches of under-secretaries do, of course, vary from party to party, but they are all alike in that one almost never finds in them a fresh, vivid, home-made turn of speech. When one watches some tired hack on the platform mechanically repeating the familiar phrases — *bestial atrocities, iron heel, bloodstained tyranny, free peoples of the world, stand shoulder to shoulder* — one often has a curious feeling that one is not watching a live human being but some kind of dummy; a feeling which suddenly becomes stronger at moments when the light catches the speaker's spectacles and turns them into blank discs which seem to have no eyes behind them. And this is not altogether fanciful. A speaker who uses that kind of phraseology has gone some distance towards turning himself into a machine. The appropriate noises are coming out of his larynx, but his brain is not involved as it would be if he were choosing his words for himself. If the speech he is making is one that he is accustomed to make over and over again, he may be almost unconscious of what he is saying, as one is when one utters the responses in church. And this reduced state of consciousness, if not indispensable, is at any rate favorable to political conformity.

In our time, political speech and writing are largely the defense of 13 the indefensible. Things like the continuance of British rule in India, the Russian purges and deportations, the dropping of the atom bombs on Japan, can indeed be defended, but only by arguments which are too brutal for most people to face, and which do not square with the professed aims of political parties. Thus political language has to consist largely of euphemism, question-begging and sheer cloudy vagueness. Defenseless villages are bombarded from the air, the inhabitants driven out into the countryside, the cattle machine-gunned, the huts set on fire with incendiary bullets: this is called *pacification*. Millions of peasants are robbed of their farms and sent trudging along the roads with no more than they can carry; this is called *transfer of population* or *rectification of frontiers*. People are imprisoned for years without trial, or shot in the back of the neck or sent to die of scurvy in Arctic lumber camps: this is called *elimination of unreliable elements*. Such phraseology is needed if one wants to name things without calling up mental pictures of them. Consider for instance some comfortable English professor defending Russian totalitarianism. He cannot say outright, "I believe in killing off your opponents when you can get good results by doing so." Probably, therefore, he will say something like this:

> While freely conceding that the Soviet régime exhibits certain features which the humanitarian may be inclined to deplore, we must, I think, agree that a certain curtailment of the right to political opposition is an unavoidable concomitant of transitional periods, and that the rigors which the Russian people have been called upon to undergo have been amply justified in the sphere of concrete achievement.

The inflated style is itself a kind of euphemism. A mass of Latin   14
words fall upon the facts like soft snow, blurring the outlines and covering up all the details. The great enemy of clear language is insincerity. When there is a gap between one's real and one's declared aims, one turns as it were instinctively to long words and exhausted idioms, like a cuttlefish squirting out ink. In our age there is no such thing as "keeping out of politics." All issues are political issues, and politics itself is a mass of lies, evasions, folly, hatred and schizophrenia. When the general atmosphere is bad, language must suffer. I should expect to find — this is a guess which I have not sufficient knowledge to verify — that the German, Russian and Italian languages have all deteriorated in the last ten or fifteen years, as a result of dictatorship.

But if thought corrupts language, language can also corrupt   15
thought. A bad usage can spread by tradition and imitation, even among people who should and do know better. The debased language that I have been discussing is in some ways very convenient. Phrases like *a not unjustifiable assumption, leaves much to be desired, would serve no good purpose, a consideration which we should do well to bear in mind*, are a continuous temptation, a packet of aspirins always at one's elbow. Look back through this essay, and for certain you will find that I have again and again committed the very faults I am protesting against.

By this morning's post I have received a pamphlet dealing with conditions in Germany. The author tells me that he "felt impelled" to write it. I open it at random, and here is almost the first sentence that I see: "(The Allies) have an opportunity not only of achieving a radical transformation of Germany's social and political structure in such a way as to avoid a nationalistic reaction in Germany itself, but at the same time of laying the foundations of a co-operative and unified Europe." You see, he "feels impelled" to write—feels, presumably, that he has something new to say—and yet his words, like cavalry horses answering the bugle, group themselves automatically into the familiar dreary pattern. This invasion of one's mind by ready-made phrases (*lay the foundations, achieve a radical transformation*) can only be prevented if one is constantly on guard against them, and every such phrase anaesthetizes a portion of one's brain.

I said earlier that the decadence of our language is probably curable. 16 Those who deny this would argue, if they produced an argument at all, that language merely reflects existing social conditions, and that we cannot influence its development by any direct tinkering with words and constructions. So far as the general tone or spirit of a language goes, this may be true, but it is not true in detail. Silly words and expressions have often disappeared, not through any evolutionary process but owing to the conscious action of a minority. Two recent examples were *explore every avenue* and *leave no stone unturned*, which were killed by the jeers of a few journalists. There is a long list of flyblown metaphors which could similarly be got rid of if enough people would interest themselves in the job; and it should also be possible to laugh the *not un-* formation out of existence,[3] to reduce the amount of Latin and Greek in the average sentence, to drive out foreign phrases and strayed scientific words, and, in general, to make pretentiousness unfashionable. But all these are minor points. The defense of the English language implies more than this, and perhaps it is best to start by saying what it does *not* imply.

To begin with it has nothing to do with archaism, with the salvag- 17 ing of obsolete words and turns of speech, or with the setting up of a "standard English" which must never be departed from. On the contrary, it is especially concerned with the scrapping of every word or idiom which has outworn its usefulness. It has nothing to do with correct grammar and syntax, which are of no importance so long as one makes one's meaning clear, or with the avoidance of Americanisms, or with having what is called a "good prose style." On the other hand it is not concerned with fake simplicity and the attempt to make written English col-

---

[3] One can cure oneself of the *not un-* formation by memorizing this sentence: *A not unblack dog was chasing a not unsmall rabbit across a not ungreen field.*

**407**

loquial. Nor does it even imply in every case preferring the Saxon word to the Latin one, though it does imply using the fewest and shortest words that will cover one's meaning. What is above all needed is to let the meaning choose the word, and not the other way about. In prose, the worst thing one can do with words is to surrender to them. When you think of a concrete object, you think wordlessly, and then, if you want to describe the thing you have been visualizing you probably hunt about till you find the exact words that seem to fit. When you think of something abstract you are more inclined to use words from the start, and unless you make a conscious effort to prevent it, the existing dialect will come rushing in and do the job for you, at the expense of blurring or even changing your meaning. Probably it is better to put off using words as long as possible and get one's meaning as clear as one can through pictures or sensations. Afterwards one can choose — not simply *accept* — the phrases that will best cover the meaning, and then switch round and decide what impression one's words are likely to make on another person. This last effort of the mind cuts out all stale or mixed images, all prefabricated phrases, needless repetitions, and humbug and vagueness generally. But one can often be in doubt about the effect of a word or a phrase, and one needs rules that one can rely on when instinct fails. I think the following rules will cover most cases:

(i) Never use a metaphor, simile or other figure of speech which you are used to seeing in print.

(ii) Never use a long word where a short one will do.

(iii) If it is possible to cut a word out, always cut it out.

(iv) Never use the passive where you can use the active.

(v) Never use a foreign phrase, a scientific word or a jargon word if you can think of an everyday English equivalent.

(vi) Break any of these rules sooner than say anything outright barbarous.

These rules sound elementary, and so they are, but they demand a deep change in attitude in anyone who has grown used to writing in the style now fashionable. One could keep all of them and still write bad English, but one could not write the kind of stuff that I quoted in those five specimens at the beginning of this article.

I have not here been considering the literary use of language, but merely language as an instrument for expressing and not for concealing or preventing thought. Stuart Chase and others have come near to claiming that all abstract words are meaningless, and have used this as a pretext for advocating a kind of political quietism. Since you don't know what Fascism is, how can you struggle against Fascism? One need not swallow such absurdities as this, but one ought to recognize that the 18 present political chaos is connected with the decay of language, and that one can probably bring about some improvement by starting at the verbal end. If you simplify your English, you are freed from the worst follies of orthodoxy. You cannot speak any of the necessary dialects, and when you make a stupid remark its stupidity will be obvious, even to yourself. Political language — and with variations this is true of all political parties, from Conservatives to Anarchists — is designed to make lies sound truthful and murder respectable, and to give an appearance of solidity to pure wind. One cannot change this all in a moment, but one can at least change one's own habits, and from time to time one can even, if one jeers loudly enough, send some worn-out and useless phrase — some *jackboot, Achilles' heel, hotbed, melting pot, acid test, veritable inferno* or other lump of verbal refuse — into the dustbin where it belongs.

## Discussion Questions

1. Orwell disagrees with a common assumption about language. What is it? Where in the essay does he attack this assumption directly?
2. What faults do his five samples of bad language have in common? Pick out examples of these faults in each passage.
3. What "tricks" for avoiding good prose does Orwell list? Do you think that some are more dangerous or misleading than others? Explain the reasons for your answer.
4. What different reasons does Orwell suggest for the slovenliness of much political writing and speaking? What examples does he give to support these reasons? Are they persuasive?
5. How does Orwell propose that we get rid of our bad language habits? Do you think his recommendations are realistic? Can the teaching of writing in school assist in the remedy?
6. Why does Orwell urge the reader to "look back through this essay" to find "the very faults I am protesting against"? Can you, in fact, find any?

## Writing Suggestions

1. Choose a speech or an editorial whose meaning seems to be obscured by pretentious diction, meaningless words, euphemism, or "sheer cloudy vagueness." Point out the real meaning of the piece. If you think that its purpose is deceptive, expose the unpleasant truth that the author is concealing. Use Orwell's device, giving concrete meaning to any abstractions. (One source of speeches is a publication called *Vital Speeches of the Day*. Another is the *New York Times*, which often prints in full, or excerpts major portions of, speeches by leading figures in public life.)

2. Orwell's essay appeared before the widespread use of television. Do you think that TV makes it harder for politicians to be dishonest? Choose a particular public event — a war, rioting in the streets, a terrorist activity, a campaign stop — and argue either for or against the claim that televised coverage makes it harder for a politician to engage in "sheer cloudy vagueness." Or does it make no difference at all? Be specific in your use of evidence.

# The War of the Woods

## NOEL PERRIN

Noel Perrin, essayist and professor of English at Dartmouth, finds that those who use the woods for sport in winter split sharply between snowmobilers and cross-country skiers. Their preferences reflect not only class divisions but the different ways that city people and country people use their energies when they are relaxing.

American sports are notoriously hard to divide along class lines. I mean more than the obvious fact that rich and poor rub shoulders at baseball games, or that a carload of Cornell professors may turn up at a grubby boxing match, having driven four hours to get there. I mean that even where myth says there's a distinction, it won't stand up under examination. Myth says, for example, that people with yachts are upperclass and people with motorboats aren't. No so. The board of directors of any large corporation is likely to contain some old poop who owns a yacht and another old poop who is commodore of a power squadron. Sometimes it's even the same old poop at different stages of his career. Similarly, one lower-income family on the Maine coast is likely enough to own both a little motorboat and a little sailboat.

There is one exception to all this camaraderie. At least there is in New England. The two winter sports of snowmobiling and cross-country skiing split along class lines so sharply that if I were a sociologist engaged in classifying some little town in Massachusetts or Vermont, I wouldn't even bother to study residence patterns or sexual habits. I'd just wait for winter. Then I'd hang around in the woods and see who came humping by on skis and who roared past on a snow machine. I could divide that town in one day, provided snow conditions were good.

*Why* cross-country skiing and snowmobiling reflect class lines so perfectly is not easy to figure out. Certainly it is not a conscious act of group loyalty. No one says, "Hm, I run the town dump, so I'd better get a snow machine," or "Well, I *was* a Wellesley drop-out; I need some knickers and a pair of Finnish touring skis."

It is tempting to think it must have something to do with instant gratification versus patience and discipline. After all, what is supposed to characterize middle-class behavior is the ability to defer pleasure. Give a lower-class type a thousand dollars, and he blows it in three days, the theory goes; whereas if you give a middle-class person the thousand, he invests it at 18 percent. Then six months later he blows the interest. (Unless he's *really* committed to bourgeois values, in which case he waits 35 years.)

But that won't wash. It's true enough that you can leap on a snow-    5
mobile as a total novice and vroom right off, while the technique of cross-country takes some acquiring. But it's also true that the snowmobiler may be a devoted pool player as well, and he devoted plenty of time to learning *that*. Or he may have put in hundreds or even thousands of hours practicing basketball throws, punting technique, you name it, all in hope of future glory. Some other principle is at work.

Could it be the well-known theory of compensation? This says that    6
the poor, leading relatively powerless lives, make up for it as much as they can by owning powerful machines. The more menial your job, the greater your desire to spend your spare time scaring the wits out of people with your huge motorcycle. Or dominating the woods with your speedy snowmobile.

No, that won't wash, either. *All* classes in American like powerful    7
machinery. People with very unmenial jobs still get very excited about Mercedes-Benzes, and like to dominate the fast lanes of highways. The really rich go in for private jets. We need a third principle.

I suspect, though I can't prove it, that the true cause is that both    8
snowmobiling and cross-country skiing started as rural sports. And to the rural mind the key difference is that one is a great deal more work than the other.

A countryman's life consists basically of an endless amount of physi-    9
cal activity. You get up early in the morning in order to do the "chores": feeding livestock, milking, cleaning the barn, and so on. As soon as chores are finished, you go off to fix fences. As soon as that's done, you climb on the tractor and start mowing rowen. Since it's just one of the givens that you are going to be tired every night, you never waste a movement if you can help it. It is for this reason that summer people are sometimes amazed and even scornful to see a native who is cutting wood throw his chain saw in a truck and drive 300 yards back into the woods to where he is working. *They* would have walked, carrying the saw, saving gas, observing the beauties of nature. They are environmentalists; he's a clod. Actually, he's just saving a little extra energy for splitting wood.

It is this Principle of the Conservation of Energy, I think, that origi-    10
nally determined who rode snowmobiles and who put on the cross-countries. In the old days, rural people simply didn't go out much in the winter — except to bring in wood and do chores. They could have; they had surplus time and energy. The work of a farm is lightest in the winter. But the principle is deeply ingrained, and their instinctive preference was to

hang around the house being bored, if necessary, rather than go out and do a lot of hard slogging through the snow in search of something as ephemeral as mere pleasure. (It is for the same reason that midwestern grain farmers, who are richer and don't have chores, tend to go to Florida in the winter. Florida is essentially the big house around which they hang, until it's time for spring planting.)

Then snowmobiles came along — ski-doos, they were first called in 11 New England, after the original Canadian make. Every person in the country perked up his or her head. I put in ''her'' because ski-doos were especially appealing to rural wives. All spring, summer, and fall they were used to working as hard in the house (and sometimes the barn, too) as their husbands did out in the fields and woods. With so much cooking to do, lots of them became pretty hefty women.

Now suddenly here was an effortless way to go out in the winter — 12 and not only that, but riding on the same machine with their husbands. A second honeymoon! The two of them could revisit, traveling at high speed up the mountainsides, places they once picnicked when they were carefree courting youngsters. I know one elderly farm couple in Vermont, avid snowmobilers, who particularly like to visit his old work sites. Fifty years ago they were just married and didn't have a cent. He would be out chopping cordwood for two dollars a cord. She would walk all the way out to where he was to bring him his dinner (which is what country people eat for lunch). Now they whoosh out by snowmobile and recall old times.

But, of course, rural people are not the only ones who live in the 13 country. There are also large numbers of urbanites. There are the summer people, the young college graduates who have joined the counterculture and moved here for good, the people with year-round second homes. Their working lives have been very different — mostly cooped up in offices. If they're tired at night, it's from too much mental tension. Their bodies cry out for use. So their principle has been that when you have free time, you try to find a way to use up energy as rapidly as possible. (This is the only conceivable explanation for jogging.)

Consequently, they tend to see the countryside as a sort of enor- 14 mous gymnasium, just as midwestern farmers see Florida as an enormous living room. They naturally opt for skis. And their Principle of Hard Play, like the countryman's conservation of energy principle, applies even when the original conditions don't. The young back-to-the landers aren't cooped up in offices; they're out logging with horses or spading up a two-acre garden. But come the first big snow, they wouldn't dream of going out on a machine. Childhood conditioning is too strong. They load a little backpack with gorp, snap on their skis, and go out to spend even more energy.

I have been in an especially good position to observe all this, be- 15
cause I happen to be right in the middle. I am one of perhaps ten people
in my part of Vermont who are both snowmobilers and cross-country skiers. I really like both sports. This reflects a deep division in my whole
life. Half the time I am a middle-class teacher at Dartmouth, and the
other half I am a working-class farmer. I mow fields on contract to summer people, sell wood and stack it for the customers, know what it's like
to be a servant. ("That's not where I told you to stack it," the buyer says
coldly. "Move the pile behind the garage.") I am so deeply into rurality
that my own childhood conditioning has almost been overcome.

There's just enough left, though, so that I understand very well why 16
cross-country skiers despise snowmobilers. Sometimes when I'm out on
skis I do myself. Yes, snow machines are noisy. Smelly, too — fouling the
crisp winter air with their exhausts. Yes, it's annoying to spend two
hours skiing to some remote and peaceful ridge, alone or with a silent
friend, and to think you are utterly away from everything — when suddenly a herd of nine snowmobilers roars up right behind you and thun-
ders on over the ridge, all but throwing beer cans at you as they pass.
Yes, sometimes they do environmental damage without either knowing
or caring. And, yes, it can just about wreck a weekend if some neighbor's
nine-year-old child spends most of the daylight hours going monoto-
nously around and around one field, wasting gas, forever gunning the
engine, doing something very close to profaning the Sabbath. In such
moods I reflect quite gleefully that as fuel prices continue to rise, snow
machines may just up and vanish. In New England, at least, they are already in decline. Ten years ago there were 26,654 registered in Vermont.
Five years ago, still building: 34,715. Now the number has shrunk to
22,107.

But when it's my own daughter out circling our back pasture, I feel 17
quite differently. I admire the skill with which she takes sharp turns on a
steep hillside and the daring of her jumps. I love to see her shining eyes
as she comes in from the kind of morning she wouldn't dream of spending on skis.

And when I go out myself, which is usually with a few farmer 18
friends, there are two things I understand. One is the sheer pleasure of
hurtling headlong across the landscape and winding up in places one
might otherwise never have reached in a lifetime — a cliff top two towns
away, say, known to no one but the snowmobilers and the occasional
hawk or owl. The skiers think we don't notice nature because we're too
busy steering our machines. What they don't realize is that we're usually
going somewhere — a farther place than *they're* likely to get — and when
we reach it, we stop and dismount. Then we see everything, especially
the views, since we go up a lot of hills. We know their landscape better

than they do, as a rule. (A lot of skiers just shuffle around golf courses, anyway — jogging with flaps on their feet.)

The other thing I understand is just how infuriating the middle 19 class is, with its assumptions of moral superiority. They used to say that we country people kept coal in our bathtubs. (If you have a stove right near the bathroom, it can be a handy place, too.) Then they criticized us for having TV sets when we were poor, and for buying expensive cars on time. They didn't stop to reflect that if *we* didn't buy on time, *they* wouldn't be getting 18 percent on their money. They need our installment payments to run their economy.

And now they scorn us for our snow machines. They're the ones 20 who are aggressive, not we. If some of them are up here in the winter, they'll call the police in a minute if we go across a corner of "their" land — even if, and perhaps especially if, it was land they bought from one of us about two years ago. They're the ones who pointedly avert their faces when we pass — do all but hold their noses. We're willing to share the outdoors with them, but they'd like to abolish us. (Though the ones that dare to venture off the golf courses and their little pre-arranged routes seem surprisingly often to take advantage of the trails we've packed down. Then they're outraged if one of us happens to come along our own trail that we made, while they are using it. They think they own that, too.)

I know what they say. They say we are perfectly welcome to be out- 21 doors, but we should all learn to ski cross-country ourselves — including Aunt Etty, who is 68, weighs 185, and has varicose veins. Maybe it would be better for Aunt Etty if she were only 38, weighed 125, and skied like an angel. But she's not an angel, she's a fat old lady who still works hard (she cleaned your house last week, skier), and this is the only way she'll ever be out here, and she loves it.

## Discussion Questions

1. The author uses a familiar organizational pattern — setting out explanations which he will refute before giving what he thinks is the right reason. Which reasons does he think are the wrong ones for explaining the differences between snowmobilers and cross-country skiers?
2. Where does Perrin state what he considers the main reason for the distinction? How does he support his idea?
3. How does Perrin explain the fact that city people who now live in the country use skis instead of snowmobiles?
4. Summarize Perrin's objections to snowmobiles. Considering that he supports snowmobiles, is recognition of their disadvantages a good argumentative strategy? Why or why not?

5. How does the author use his own experience to advance his claim?
6. In supporting the snowmobilers, Perrin makes an implicit appeal to several values that he believes his readers will share. What are they? Do they strengthen his argument?

## Writing Suggestions

1. Choose a couple of summer sports that seem to be differentiated along class or other (for instance, generational) lines. Write an essay that explains the differences and makes a judgment about the values they reflect.
2. If you are a city person and have spent some time in the country, or vice versa, write an essay telling whether or not you behave differently in the new environment. Try to explain the reasons for your behavior, whether it is the same or different.

# Socrates to His Accusers

## PLATO

Plato (427?–347 B.C.), a pupil of Socrates, the celebrated Greek philosopher and teacher, wrote a number of dialogues representing the discussions between Socrates and his pupils. In the monologue that follows, Plato reports what Socrates is alleged to have said to the Athenian lawmakers who condemned him to death for leading his pupils to question Athenian institutions. Socrates committed suicide by swallowing poisonous hemlock.

Not much time will be gained, O Athenians, in return for the evil 1
name which you will get from the detractors of the city, who will say that
you killed Socrates, a wise man; for they will call me wise even though I
am not wise when they want to reproach you. If you had waited a little
while, your desire would have been fulfilled in the course of nature. For I
am far advanced in years, as you may perceive, and not far from death. I
am speaking now only to those of you who have condemned me to
death. And I have another thing to say to them: You think that I was
convicted through deficiency of words — I mean, that if I had thought fit
to leave nothing undone, nothing unsaid, I might have gained an ac-
quittal. Not so; the deficiency which led to my conviction was not of
words — certainly not. But I had not the boldness or impudence of inclination to address you as you would have liked me to address you, weep-
ing and wailing and lamenting, and saying and doing many things
which you have been accustomed to hear from others, and which, as I
say, are unworthy of me. But I thought that I ought not to do anything
common or mean in the hour of danger: nor do I now repent of the manner of my defence, and I would rather die having spoken after my manner, than speak in your manner and live. For neither in war nor yet at law
ought any man to use every way of escaping death. For often in battle
there is no doubt that if a man will throw away his arms, and fall on his
knees before his pursuers, he may escape death; and in other dangers
there are other ways of escaping death, if a man is willing to say and do
anything. The difficulty, my friends, is not in avoiding death, but in
avoiding unrighteousness; for that runs faster than death. I am old and
move slowly, and the slower runner has overtaken me, and my accusers
are keen and quick, and the faster runner, who is unrighteousness, has
overtaken them. And now I depart hence condemned by you to suffer

the penalty of death, and they, too, go their ways condemned by the truth to suffer the penalty of villainy and wrong; and I must abide by my award — let them abide by theirs. I suppose that these things may be regarded as fated — and I think that they are well.

And now, O men who have condemned me, I would fain prophesy 2 to you; for I am about to die, and that is the hour in which men are gifted with prophetic power. And I prophesy to you who are my murderers, that immediately after my death punishment far heavier than you have inflicted on me will surely await you. Me you have killed because you wanted to escape the accuser, and not to give an account of your lives. But that will not be as you suppose: far otherwise. For I say that there will be more accusers of you than there are now; accusers whom hitherto I have restrained: and as they are younger they will be more severe with you, and you will be more offended at them. For if you think that by killing men you can avoid the accuser censuring your lives, you are mistaken; that is not a way of escape which is either possible or honorable; the easiest and noblest way is not to be crushing others, but to be improving yourselves. This is the prophecy which I utter before my departure, to the judges who have condemned me.

Friends, who would have acquitted me, I would like also to talk 3 with you about this thing which has happened, while the magistrates are busy, and before I go to the place at which I must die. Stay then awhile, for we may as well talk with one another while there is time. You are my friends, and I should like to show you the meaning of this event which has happened to me. O my judges — for you I may truly call judges — I should like to tell you of a wonderful circumstance. Hitherto the familiar oracle within me has constantly been in the habit of opposing me even about trifles, if I was going to make a slip or error about anything; and now as you see there has come upon me that which may be thought, and is generally believed to be, the last and worst evil. But the oracle made no sign of opposition, either as I was leaving my house and going out in the morning, or when I was going up into this court, or while I was speaking, at anything which I was going to say; and yet I have often been stopped in the middle of a speech; but now in nothing I either said or did touching this matter has the oracle opposed me. What do I take to be the explanation of this? I will tell you. I regard this as a proof that what has happened to me is a good, and that those of us who think that death is an evil are in error. This is a great proof to me of what I am saying, for the customary sign would surely have opposed me had I been going to evil and not to good.

Let us reflect in another way, and we shall see that there is great rea- 4 son to hope that death is a good, for one of two things: either death is a state of nothingness and utter unconsciousness, or, as men say, there is a change and migration of the soul from this world to another. Now if you suppose that there is no consciousness, but a sleep like the sleep of him who is undisturbed even by the sight of dreams, death will be an unspeakable gain. For if a person were to select the night in which his sleep was undisturbed even by dreams, and were to compare with this the other days and nights of his life, and then were to tell us how many days and nights he had passed in the course of his life better and more pleasantly than this one, I think that any man, I will not say a private man, but even the great king, will not find many such days or nights, when compared with the others. Now if death is like this, I say that to die, is gain; for eternity is then only a single night. But if death is the journey to another place, and there, as men say, all the dead are, what good, O my friends and judges, can be greater than this? If indeed when the pilgrim arrives in the world below, he is delivered from the professors of justice in this world, and finds the true judges who are said to give judgment there, Minos and Rhadamanthus and Æacus and Triptolemus, and other sons of God who were righteous in their own life, that pilgrimage will be worth making. What would not a man give if he might converse with Orpheus and Musæus and Hesiod and Homer? Nay, if this be true, let me die again and again. I, too, shall have a wonderful interest in a place where I can converse with Palamedes, and Ajax the son of Telamon, and other heroes of old, who have suffered death through an unjust judgment; and there will be no small pleasure, as I think, in comparing my own sufferings with theirs. Above all, I shall be able to continue my search into true and false knowledge; as in this world, so also in that; I shall find out who is wise, and who pretends to be wise, and is not. What would not a man give, O judges, to be able to examine the leader of the great Trojan expedition; or Odysseus or Sisyphus, or numberless others, men and women too! What infinite delight would there be in conversing with them and asking them questions! For in that world they do not put a man to death for this; certainly not. For besides being happier in that world than in this, they will be immortal, if what is said is true.

Wherefore, O judges, be of good cheer about death, and know this 5 of a truth — that no evil can happen to a good man, either in life or after death. He and his are not neglected by the gods; nor has my own approaching end happened by mere chance. But I see clearly that to die and be released was better for me; and therefore the oracle gave no sign. For which reason also, I am not angry with my accusers, or my condemners; they have done me no harm, although neither of them meant to do me any good; and for this I may gently blame them.

Still I have a favor to ask of them. When my sons are grown up, I 6 would ask you, O my friends, to punish them; and I would have you trouble them, as I have troubled you, if they seem to care about riches, or anything, more than about virtue; or if they pretend to be something when they are really nothing — then reprove them, as I have reproved you, for not caring about that for which they ought to care, and thinking that they are something when they are really nothing. And if you do this, I and my sons will have received justice at your hands.

The hour of departure has arrived, and we go our ways — I to die, and you to live. Which is better, God only knows.  7

## Discussion Questions

1. In the first paragraph, Socrates explains his failure to plead for his life. What does this explanation tell us about his character?
2. What does Socrates prophesy in paragraph 2? Does he think that his death will put an end to the "corruption" of the young or lead to escape from censure for the accusers? Why or why not?
3. How does Socrates assure himself that the sentence of death is not evil? What does this suggest about his religious beliefs?
4. What possibilities does Socrates outline as reasons to hope that death is a good? He uses analogy as an argumentative strategy. Is it effective?
5. What favor does Socrates ask of his friends? How does this favor confirm our previous views of his character and values?

## Writing Suggestions

1. Socrates was condemned as a subversive teacher. How far should teachers be allowed to go in encouraging their pupils to question institutions of the state? Think of extreme cases, such as teachers who might be Nazis or Communists. Write either a defense or a refutation of the teacher's right to teach anything he or she believes to be true.
2. Write an apology or a defense of someone you think has been wrongly condemned (a politician, an entertainer, a sports figure, a historic victim, someone on campus).

# A Modest Proposal

## JONATHAN SWIFT

This essay is acknowledged by almost all critics to be the most powerful example of irony in the English language. (*Irony* means saying one thing but meaning another.) Jonathan Swift, prolific satirist and dean of St. Patrick's Cathedral in Dublin, was moved to write it in protest against the terrible poverty in which the Irish were forced to live under British rule. Notice that the essay is organized according to one of the patterns outlined in the Appendix of this book — presenting the stock issues. First, Swift establishes the need for a change, then he offers his proposal and, finally, he lists its advantages.

1   It is a melancholy object to those who talk through this great town[1] or travel in the country, when they see the streets, the roads, and cabin doors, crowded with beggars of the female sex, followed by three, four, or six children, all in rags and importuning every passenger for an alms. These mothers, instead of being able to work for their honest livelihood, are forced to employ all their time in strolling to beg sustenance for their helpless infants, who, as they grow up, either turn thieves for want of work, or leave their dear native country to fight for the Pretender in Spain, or sell themselves to the Barbados.[2]

2   I think it is agreed by all parties that this prodigious number of children in the arms, or on the backs, or at the heels of their mothers, and frequently of their fathers, is in the present deplorable state of the kingdom a very great additional grievance; and therefore whoever could find out a fair, cheap, and easy method of making these children sound, useful members of the commonwealth would deserve so well of the public as to have his statue set up for a preserver of the nation.

3   But my intention is very far from being confined to provide only for the children of professed beggars; it is of a much greater extent, and shall take in the whole number of infants at a certain age who are born of parents in effect as little able to support them as those who demand our charity in the streets.

---

[1]Dublin. — ED.

[2]The Pretender was James Stuart, who was exiled in Spain. Many Irishmen had joined an army attempting to return him to the English throne in 1718. Others had become indentured servants, agreeing to work for a set number of years in the Barbados or other British colonies in exchange for their transportation out of Ireland. — ED.

As to my own part, having turned my thoughts for many years upon ₄ this important subject, and maturely weighed the several schemes of other projectors,[3] I have always found them grossly mistaken in their computation. It is true, a child just dropped from its dam may be supported by her milk for a solar year, with little other nourishment; at most not above the value of two shillings, which the mother may certainly get, or the value in scraps, by her lawful occupation of begging; and it is exactly at one year that I propose to provide for them in such a manner as instead of being a charge upon their parents or the parish, or wanting food and raiment for the rest of their lives, they shall on the contrary contribute to the feeding, and partly to the clothing, of many thousands.

There is likewise another great advantage in my scheme, that it will ₅ prevent those voluntary abortions, and that horrid practice of women murdering their bastard children, alas, too frequent among us, sacrificing the poor innocent babes, I doubt, more to avoid the expense than the shame, which would move tears and pity in the most savage and inhuman breast.

The number of souls in this kingdom being usually reckoned one ₆ million and a half, of these I calculate there may be about two hundred thousand couples whose wives are breeders; from which number I subtract thirty thousand couples who are able to maintain their own children, although I apprehend there cannot be so many under the present distress of the kingdom; but this being granted, there will remain an hundred and seventy thousand breeders. I again subtract fifty thousand for those women who miscarry, or whose children die by accident or disease within the year. There only remain an hundred and twenty thousand children of poor parents annually born. The question therefore is, how this number shall be reared and provided for, which, as I have already said, under the present situation of affairs, is utterly impossible by all the methods hitherto proposed. For we can neither employ them in handicraft or agriculture; we neither build houses (I mean in the country) nor cultivate land. They can very seldom pick up a livelihood by stealing till they arrive at six years old, except where they are of towardly parts;[4] although I confess they learn the rudiments much earlier, during which time they can however be looked upon only as probationers, as I have been informed by a principal gentleman in the country of Cavan, who protested to me that he never knew above one or two instances under the age of six, even in a part of the kingdom so renowned for the quickest proficiency in that art.

---

[3]Planners. —.ED.
[4]Innate talents. — ED.

I am assured by our merchants that a boy or a girl before twelve 7
years old is no salable commodity; and even when they come to this age
they will not yield above three pounds, or three pounds and a half a
crown at most on the Exchange; which cannot turn to account either to
the parents or the kingdom, the charge of nutriment and rags having
been at least four times that value.

I shall now therefore humbly propose my own thoughts, which I 8
hope will not be liable to the least objection.

I have been assured by a very knowing American of my acquaint- 9
ance in London, that a young healthy child well nursed is at a year old a
most delicious, nourishing, and wholesome food, whether stewed,
roasted, baked, or boiled; and I make no doubt that it will equally serve
in a fricassee or a ragout.[5]

I do therefore humbly offer it to public consideration that of the 10
hundred and twenty thousand children, already computed, twenty thousand may be reserved for breed, whereof only one fourth part to be
males, which is more than we allow to sheep, black cattle, or swine; and
my reason is that these children are seldom the fruits of marriage, a circumstance not much regarded by our savages, therefore one male will be
sufficient to serve four females. That the remaining hundred thousand
may at a year old be offered in sale to the persons of quality and fortune
through the kingdom, always advising the mother to let them suck plen-
tifully in the last month, so as to render them plump and fat for a good
table. A child will make two dishes at an entertainment for friends; and
when the family dines alone, the fore or hind quarter will make a reasonable dish, and seasoned with a little pepper or salt will be very good
boiled on the fourth day, especially in winter.

I have reckoned upon a medium that a child just born will weigh 11
twelve pounds, and in a solar year if tolerably nursed increaseth to
twenty-eight pounds.

I grant this food will be somewhat dear, and therefore very proper 12
for landlords, who, as they have already devoured most of the parents,
seem to have the best title to the children.

Infant's flesh will be in season throughout the year, but more plen- 13
tiful in March, and a little before and after. For we are told by a grave
author, an eminent French physician,[6] that fish being a prolific diet,
there are more children born in Roman Catholic countries about nine
months after Lent than at any other season; therefore, reckoning a year
after Lent, the markets will be more glutted than usual, because the

---

[5]Stew. — ED.

[6]A reference to Swift's favorite French writer, François Rabelais, who was actually a
broad satirist known for his coarse humor. — ED.

number of popish infants is at least three to one in this kingdom; and therefore it will have one other collateral advantage, by lessening the number of Papists among us.

I have already computed the charge of nursing a beggar's child (in 14 which list I reckon all cottagers, laborers, and four-fifths of the farmers) to be about two shillings per annum, rags included; and I believe no gentleman would repine to give ten shillings for the carcass of a good fat child, which, as I have said, will make four dishes of excellent nutritive meat, when he hath only some particular friend or his own family to dine with him. Thus the squire will learn to be a good landlord, and grow popular among the tenants; the mother will have eight shillings net profit, and be fit for work till she produces another child.

Those who are more thrifty (as I must confess the times require) may 15 flay the carcass; the skin of which artificially[7] dressed will make admirable gloves for ladies, and summer boots for fine gentlemen.

As to our city of Dublin, shambles[8] may be appointed for this pur- 16 pose in the most convenient parts of it, and butchers we may be assured will not be wanting; although I rather recommend buying the children alive, and dressing them hot from the knife as we do roasting pigs.

A very worthy person, a true lover of his country, and whose virtues 17 I highly esteem, was lately pleased in discoursing on this matter to offer a refinement upon my scheme. He said that many gentlemen of his kingdom, having of late destroyed their deer, he conceived that the want of venison might be well supplied by the bodies of young lads and maidens, not exceeding fourteen years of age nor under twelve, so great a number of both sexes in every county being now ready to starve for want of work and service; and these to be disposed of by their parents, if alive, or otherwise by their nearest relations. But with due deference to so excellent a friend and so deserving a patriot, I cannot be altogether in his sentiments; for as to the males, my American acquaintance assured me from frequent experience that their flesh was generally tough and lean, like that of our schoolboys, by continual exercise, and their taste disagreeable; and to fatten them would not answer the charge. Then as to the females, it would, I think with humble submission, be a loss to the public, because they soon would become breeders themselves; and besides, it is not improbable that some scrupulous people might be apt to censure such a practice (although indeed very unjustly) as a little bordering upon cruelty; which, I confess, hath always been with me the strongest objection against any project, how well soever intended.

But in order to justify my friend, he confessed that this expedient 18

---

[7]With art or craft. — ED.

[8]Butcher shops or slaughterhouses. — ED.

was put into his head by the famous Psalmanazar,[9] a native of the island Formosa, who came from thence to London above twenty years ago, and in conversation told my friend that in his country when any young person happened to be put to death, the executioner sold the carcass to persons of quality as a prime dainty; and that in his time the body of a plump girl of fifteen, who was crucified for an attempt to poison the emperor, was sold to his Imperial Majesty's prime minister of state, and other great mandarins of the court, in joints from the gibbet, at four hundred crowns. Neither indeed can I deny that if the same use were made of several plump young girls in this town, who without one single groat to their fortunes cannot stir abroad without a chair, and appear at the playhouse and assemblies in foreign fineries which they never will pay for, the kingdom would not be the worse.

Some persons of a desponding spirit are in great concern about that 19 vast number of poor people who are aged, diseased, or maimed, and I have been desired to employ my thoughts what course may be taken to ease the nation of so grievous an encumbrance. But I am not in the least pain upon that matter, because it is very well known that they are every day dying and rotting by cold and famine, and filth and vermin, as fast as can be reasonably expected. And as to the younger laborers, they are now in almost as hopeful a condition. They cannot get work, and consequently pine away for want of nourishment to a degree that if any time they are accidentally hired to common labor, they have not strength to perform it; and thus the country and themselves are happily delivered from the evils to come.

I have too long digressed, and therefore shall return to my subject. I 20 think the advantages by the proposal which I have made are obvious and many, as well as of the highest importance.

For first, as I have already observed, it would greatly lessen the 21 number of Papists, with whom we are yearly overrun, being the principal breeders of the nation as well as our most dangerous enemies; and who stay at home on purpose to deliver the kingdom to the Pretender, hoping to take their advantage by the absence of so many good Protestants, who have chosen rather to leave their country than to stay at home and pay tithes against their conscience to an Episcopal curate.

Secondly, the poorer tenants will have something valuable of their 22 own, which by law may be made liable to distress,[10] and help to pay their landlord's rent, their corn and cattle being already seized and money a thing unknown.

---

[9]Georges Psalmanazar was a Frenchman who pretended to be Japanese and wrote an entirely imaginary *Description of the Isle Formosa*. He had become well known in gullible London society. — ED.

[10]Subject to possession by lenders. — ED.

Thirdly, whereas the maintenance of an hundred thousand chil- 23
dren, from two years old and upwards, cannot be computed at less than
ten shillings a piece per annum, the nation's stock will be thereby increased fifty thousand pounds per annum, besides the profit of a new
dish introduced to the tables of all gentlemen of fortune in the kingdom
who have any refinement in taste. And the money will circulate among
ourselves, the goods being entirely of our own growth and manufacture.

Fourthly, the constant breeders, besides the gain of eight shillings 24
sterling per annum by the sale of their children, will be rid of the charge
of maintaining them after the first year.

Fifthly, this food would likewise bring great custom to taverns, 25
where the vintners will certainly be so prudent as to procure the best receipts for dressing it to perfection, and consequently have their houses
frequented by all the fine gentlemen, who justly value themselves upon
their knowledge in good eating; and a skillful cook, who understands
how to oblige his guests, will contrive to make it as expensive as they
please.

Sixthly, this would be a great inducement to marriage, which all 26
wise nations have either encouraged by rewards or enforced by laws and
penalties. It would increase the care and tenderness of mothers toward
their children, when they were sure of a settlement for life to the poor
babes, provided in some sort by the public, to their annual profit instead
of expense. We should see an honest emulation among the married
women, which of them could bring the fattest child to the market. Men
would become as fond of their wives during the time of their pregnancy
as they are now of their mares in foal, their cows in calf, or sows when
they are ready to farrow; nor offer to beat or kick them (as is too frequent
a practice) for fear of a miscarriage.

Many other advantages might be enumerated. For instance, the ad- 27
dition of some thousand carcasses in our exportation of barreled beef,
the propagation of swine's flesh, and improvements in the art of making
good bacon, so much wanted among us by the great destruction of pigs,
too frequent at our tables, which are no way comparable in taste or mag-
nificence to a well-grown, fat, yearling child, which roasted whole will
make a considerable figure at a lord mayor's feast or any other public entertainment. But this and many others I omit, being studious of brevity.

Supposing that one thousand families in this city would be constant 28
customers for infants' flesh, besides others who might have it at merry
meetings, particularly weddings and christenings, I compute that Dublin would take off annually about twenty thousand carcasses, and the rest
of the kingdom (where probably they will be sold somewhat cheaper) the
remaining eighty thousand.

I can think of no one objection that will possibly be raised against 29 this proposal, unless it should be urged that the number of people will be thereby much lessened in the kingdom. This I freely own, and it was indeed one principal design in offering it to the world. I desire the reader will observe, that I calculate my remedy for this one individual kingdom of Ireland and for no other that ever was, is, or I think ever can be upon earth. Therefore let no man talk to me of other expedients: of taxing our absentees at five shillings a pound: of using neither clothes nor household furniture except what is of our own growth and manufacture: of utterly rejecting the materials and instruments that promote foreign luxury: of curing the expensiveness of pride, vanity, idleness, and gaming in our women: of introducing a vein of parsimony, prudence, and temperance: of learning to love our country, in the want of which we differ even from Laplanders and the inhabitants of Topinamboo:[11] of quitting our animosities and factions, nor acting any longer like the Jews, who were murdering one another at the very moment their city was taken:[12] of being a little cautious not to sell our country and conscience for nothing: of teaching landlords to have at least one degree of mercy toward their tenants: lastly, of putting a spirit of honesty, industry, and skill into our shopkeepers; who, if a resolution could now be taken to buy only our native goods, would immediately unite to cheat and exact upon us in the price, the measure, and the goodness, nor could ever yet be brought to make one fair proposal of just dealing, though often and earnestly invited to it.

Therefore I repeat, let no man talk to me of these and the like expedients, till he hath at least some glimpse of hope that there will ever be some hearty and sincere attempt to put them in practice.    30

But as to myself, having been wearied out for many years with offering vain, idle, visionary thoughts, and at length utterly despairing of success, I fortunately fell upon this proposal, which, as it is wholly new, so it hath something solid and real, of no expense and little trouble, full in our own power, and whereby we can incur no danger in disobliging England. For this kind of commodity will not bear exportation, the flesh being of too tender a consistence to admit a long continuance in salt, although perhaps I could name a country which would be glad to eat up our whole nation without it.    31

After all, I am not so violently bent upon my own opinion as to reject any offer proposed by wise men, which shall be found equally innocent, cheap, easy, and effectual. But before something of that kind shall be advanced in contradiction to my scheme, and offering a better, I de-    32

---

[11]District of Brazil inhabited by primitive natives. —ED.

[12]During the Roman siege of Jerusalem (70 A.D.), prominent Jews were charged with collaborating with the enemy and put to death. —ED.

sire the author or authors will be pleased maturely to consider two points. First, as things now stand, how they will be able to find food and raiment for an hundred thousand useless mouths and backs. And secondly, there being a round million of creatures in human figure throughout this kingdom, whose sole subsistence put into a common stock would leave them in debt two millions of pounds sterling, adding those who are beggars by profession to the bulk of farmers, cottagers, and laborers, with their wives and children who are beggars in effect; I desire those politicians who dislike my overture, and may perhaps be so bold to attempt an answer, that they will first ask the parents of these mortals whether they would not at this day think it a great happiness to have been sold for food at a year old in this manner I prescribe, and thereby have avoided such a perpetual scene of misfortunes as they have since gone through by the oppression of landlords, the impossibility of paying rent without money or trade, the want of common sustenance, with neither house nor clothes to cover them from the inclemencies of the weather, and the most inevitable prospect of entailing the like or greater miseries upon their breed forever.

I profess, in the sincerity of my heart, that I have not the least per- 33 sonal interest in endeavoring to promote this necessary work, having no other motive than the public good of my country, by advancing our trade, providing for infants, relieving the poor, and giving some pleasure to the rich. I have no children by which I can propose to get a single penny; the youngest being nine years old, and my wife past childbearing.

## Discussion Questions

1. What implicit assumption about the treatment of the Irish underlies Swift's proposal? Do expressions such as ''just dropped from its dam'' and ''whose wives are breeders'' give the reader a clue?
2. In this essay Swift assumes a persona; that is, for the purposes of the proposal he makes, he pretends to be a different person. Describe the characteristics of that person. Point out the places in the essay that reveal them.
3. In several places, however, Swift reveals himself, the outraged witness of English cruelty and indifference. Note the language that seems to reflect his own feelings.
4. Throughout the essay Swift recites lists of facts, many of them in the form of statistics. How do these facts contribute to the persuasiveness of his argument? How do they affect the reader?
5. What social practices and attitudes of both the Irish and the English does Swift condemn?

6. Does Swift offer any solutions for the problems he attacks? How do you know?
7. When this essay first appeared in 1729, some readers took it seriously and accused Swift of monstrous cruelty. Can you think of reasons why these readers failed to recognize the ironic intent?

## Writing Suggestions

1. Try an ironical essay of your own. Choose a subject that clearly lends itself to such treatment. As Swift did, use logic and restraint in your language.
2. Choose a problem for which you think you have a solution. Defend your solution by using the stock issues as your pattern of organization.

# The Health-Care System

## LEWIS THOMAS

Lewis Thomas, chancellor of the Memorial Sloan-Kettering Cancer Center, wonders why Americans have become obsessed with fears about their health at a time when the national health has never been better. Such fears, he thinks, will make any health-care system unworkable.

The health-care system of this country is a staggering enterprise, in any sense of the adjective. Whatever the failures of distribution and lack of coordination, it is the gigantic scale and scope of the total collective effort that first catches the breath, and its cost. The dollar figures are almost beyond grasping. They vary from year to year, always upward, ranging from something like $10 billion in 1950 to an estimated $140 billion in 1978, with much more to come in the years just ahead, whenever a national health-insurance program is installed. The official guess is that we are now investing a round 8 percent of the GNP in Health; it could soon rise to 10 or 12 percent. 1

Those are the official numbers, and only for the dollars that flow in an authorized way — for hospital charges, physician's fees, prescribed drugs, insurance premiums, the construction of facilities, research, and the like. 2

But these dollars are only part of it. Why limit the estimates to the strictly professional costs? There is another huge marketplace, in which vast sums are exchanged for items designed for the improvement of Health. 3

The television and radio industry, no small part of the national economy, feeds on Health, or, more precisely, on disease, for a large part of its sustenance. Not just the primarily medical dramas and the illness or surgical episodes threaded through many of the nonmedical stories, in which the central human dilemma is illness; almost all the commercial announcements, in an average evening, are pitches for items to restore failed health: things for stomach gas, constipation, headaches, nervousness, sleeplessness or sleepiness, arthritis, anemia, disquiet, and the despair of malodorousness, sweat, yellowed teeth, dandruff, furuncles, piles. The food industry plays the role of surrogate physician, advertising breakfast cereals as though they were tonics, vitamins, restoratives; they are now out-hawked by the specialized Health-food industry itself, with 4 its nonpolluted, organic, "naturally" vitalizing products. Chewing gum is sold as a tooth cleanser. Vitamins have taken the place of prayer.

The publishing industry, hardcover, paperbacks, magazines, and 5 all, seems to be kept alive by Health, new techniques for achieving mental health, cures for arthritis, and diets mostly for the improvement of everything.

The transformation of our environment has itself become an im- 6 mense industry, costing rather more than the moon, in aid of Health. Pollution is supposed to be primarily a medical problem; when the television weatherman tells whether New York's air is "acceptable" or not that day, he is talking about human lungs, he believes. Pollutants which may be impairing photosynthesis by algae in the world's oceans, or destroying all the life in topsoil, or killing all the birds are being worried about lest they cause cancer in us, for heaven's sake.

Tennis has become more than the national sport; it is a rigorous dis- 7 cipline, a form of collective physiotherapy. Jogging is done by swarms of people, out onto the streets each day in underpants, moving in a stolid sort of rapid trudge, hoping by this to stay alive. Bicycles are cures. Meditation may be good for the soul but it is even better for the blood pressure.

As a people, we have become obsessed with Health. 8

There is something fundamentally, radically unhealthy about all 9 this. We do not seem to be seeking more exuberance in living as much as staving off failure, putting off dying. We have lost all confidence in the human body.

The new consensus is that we are badly designed, intrinsically falli- 10 ble, vulnerable to a host of hostile influences inside and around us, and only precariously alive. We live in danger of falling apart at any moment, and are therefore always in need of surveillance and propping up. Without the professional attention of a health-care system, we would fall in our tracks.

This is a new way of looking at things, and perhaps it can only be 11 accounted for as a manifestation of spontaneous, undirected, societal *propaganda*. We keep telling each other this sort of thing, and back it comes on television or in the weekly newsmagazines, confirming all the fears, instructing us, as in the usual final paragraph of the personal-advice columns in the daily paper, to "seek professional help." Get a checkup. Go on a diet. Meditate. Jog. Have some surgery. Take two tablets, with water. *Spring* water. If pain persists, if anomie persists, if boredom persists, see your doctor.

It is extraordinary that we have just now become convinced of our 12 bad health, our constant jeopardy of disease and death, at the very time when the facts should be telling us the opposite. In a more rational world, you'd think we would be staging bicentennial ceremonies for the celebration of our general good shape. In the year 1976, out of a population of around 220 million, only 1.9 million died, or just under 1 percent, not at all a discouraging record once you accept the fact of mortality itself. The life expectancy for the whole population rose to seventy-two years, the longest stretch ever achieved in this country. Despite the persisting roster of still-unsolved major diseases — cancer, heart disease, stroke, arthritis, and the rest — most of us have a clear, unimpeded run at a longer and healthier lifetime than could have been foreseen by any earlier generation. The illnesses that plague us the most, when you count up the numbers in the U.S. Vital Statistics reports, are respiratory and gastrointestinal infections, which are, by and large, transient, reversible affairs needing not much more than Grandmother's advice for getting through safely. Thanks in great part to the improved sanitary engineering, nutrition, and housing of the past century, and in real but less part to contemporary immunization and antibiotics, we are free of the great infectious diseases, especially tuberculosis and lobar pneumonia, which used to cut us down long before our time. We are even beginning to make progress in our understanding of the mechanisms underlying the chronic illnesses still with us, and sooner or later, depending on the quality and energy of biomedical research, we will learn to cope effectively with most of these, maybe all. We will still age away and die, but the aging, and even the dying, can become a healthy process. On balance, we ought to be more pleased with ourselves than we are, and more optimistic for the future.

The trouble is, we are being taken in by the propaganda, and it is 13 bad not only for the spirit of society; it will make any health-care system, no matter how large and efficient, unworkable. If people are educated to believe that they are fundamentally fragile, always on the verge of mortal disease, perpetually in the need of support by health-care professionals at every side, always dependent on an imagined discipline of "preventive" medicine, there can be no limit to the numbers of doctors' offices, clinics, and hospitals required to meet the demand. In the end, we would all become doctors, spending our days screening each other for disease.

We are, in real life, a reasonably healthy people. Far from being in- 14 eptly put together, we are amazingly tough, durable organisms, full of health, ready for most contingencies. The new danger to our well-being, if we continue to listen to all the talk, is in becoming a nation of healthy hypochrondriacs, living gingerly, worrying ourselves half to death.

And we do not have time for this sort of thing anymore, nor can we 15 afford such a distraction from our other, considerably more urgent problems. Indeed, we should be worrying that our preoccupation with personal health may be a symptom of copping out, an excuse for running upstairs to recline on a couch, sniffing the air for contaminants, spraying the room with deodorants, while just outside, the whole of society is coming undone.

## Discussion Questions

1. Almost half Thomas's essay is devoted to proving the immense cost of the health-care system. What factors, according to him, contribute to this cost? Is all the evidence equally convincing?
2. Why does the author consider our obsession with health "radically unhealthy"?
3. How does Thomas account for this "new way of looking at things"?
4. How does he support his claim that Americans are in "general good shape"?
5. What relationship does Thomas see between our fears about our health and the efficiency of a health-care system?
6. Does he suggest more productive worries than those about our health?

## Writing Suggestions

1. Select one or more of the sources of health information mentioned by Thomas and write an essay in which you (1) elaborate on the information provided; (2) analyze the method of presentation; and (3) evaluate the soundness of the information.
2. Do you agree that sports and exercise consciousness indicates that we have "lost all confidence in the human body"? If you disagree, offer what you think are the real reasons for the appeal of tennis, jogging, and other athletic activities.

# Drugs

## GORE VIDAL

Gore Vidal, a novelist, essayist, and twice candidate for Congress, argues that a solution to drug and alcohol addiction is possible. "Simply make all drugs available and sell them at cost." Vidal bases his prescription, which many people find shocking, on a moral principle — that adults in a free society should be permitted to do what they want with their own lives.

It is possible to stop most drug addiction in the United States within 1 a very short time. Simply make all drugs available and sell them at cost. Label each drug with a precise description of what effect — good and bad — the drug will have on the taker. This will require heroic honesty. Don't say that marijuana is addictive or dangerous when it is neither, as millions of people know — unlike "speed," which kills most unpleasantly, or heroin, which is addictive and difficult to kick.

For the record, I have tried — once — almost every drug and liked 2 none, disproving the popular Fu Manchu theory that a single whiff of opium will enslave the mind. Nevertheless many drugs are bad for certain people to take and they should be told why in a sensible way.

Along with exhortation and warning, it might be good for our citizens to recall (or learn for the first time) that the United States was the 3 creation of men who believed that each man has the right to do what he wants with his own life as long as he does not interfere with his neighbor's pursuit of happiness (that his neighbor's idea of happiness is persecuting others does confuse matters a bit).

This is a startling notion to the current generation of Americans. 4 They reflect a system of public education which has made the Bill of Rights, literally, unacceptable to a majority of high school graduates (see the annual Purdue reports) who now form the "silent majority" — a phrase which that underestimated wit Richard Nixon took from Homer who used it to describe the dead.

Now one can hear the warning rumble begin: if everyone is allowed 5 to take drugs everyone will and the GNP will decrease, the Commies will stop us from making everyone free, and we shall end up a race of zombies, passively murmuring "groovy" to one another. Alarming thought. Yet it seems most unlikely that any reasonably sane person will become a drug addict if he knows in advance what addiction is going to be like.

Is everyone reasonably sane? Some people will always become drug 6 addicts just as some people will always become alcoholics, and it is just

434

too bad. Every man, however, has the power (and should have the legal right) to kill himself if he chooses. But since most men don't, they won't be mainliners either. Nevertheless, forbidding people things they like or think they might enjoy only makes them want those things all the more. This psychological insight is, for some mysterious reason, perennially denied our governors.

It is a lucky thing for the American moralist that our country has always existed in a kind of time-vacuum: we have no public memory of anything that happened before last Tuesday. No one in Washington today recalls what happened during the years alcohol was forbidden to the people by a Congress that thought it had a divine mission to stamp out Demon Rum — launching, in the process, the greatest crime wave in the country's history, causing thousands of deaths from bad alcohol, and creating a general (and persisting) contempt among the citizenry for the laws of the United States. 7

The same thing is happening today. But the government has learned nothing from past attempts at prohibition, not to mention repression. 8

Last year when the supply of Mexican marijuana was slightly curtailed by the Feds, the pushers got the kids hooked on heroin and deaths increased dramatically, particularly in New York. Whose fault? Evil men like the Mafiosi? Permissive Dr. Spock? Wild-eyed Dr. Leary? No. 9

The Goverment of the United States was responsible for those deaths. The bureaucratic machine has a vested interest in playing cops and robbers. Both the Bureau of Narcotics and the Mafia want strong laws against the sale and use of drugs because if drugs are sold at cost there would be no money in it for anyone. 10

If there was no money in it for the Mafia, there would be no friendly playground pushers, and addicts would not commit crimes to pay for the next fix. Finally, if there was no money in it, the Bureau of Narcotics would wither away, something they are not about to do without a struggle. 11

Will anything sensible be done? Of course not. The American people are as devoted to the idea of sin and its punishment as they are to making money — and fighting drugs is nearly as big a business as pushing them. Since the combination of sin and money is irresistible (particularly to the professional politician), the situation will only grow worse. 12

## Discussion Questions

1. What is Vidal's solution for the drug problem?
2. Why does he tell the reader that he has tried almost every drug?
3. What moral reason does Vidal give to justify legalization of marijuana?

4. How does he answer the objection that his solution will unleash a drug epidemic?
5. What proof does Vidal offer that government attempts to control drug use have been failures? In what way, according to Vidal, is the government of the United States to blame for deaths from drug abuse?
6. Why will Americans probably refuse to legalize marijuana?

## Writing Suggestions

1. Write a paper arguing against the free use of saccharin, Valium, laetrile (a medically unproven cancer cure), or any other substance.
2. Do you think that a high school teacher who admits to smoking marijuana regularly should be dismissed? Explain your reasons.
3. Suppose a younger sister or brother — junior high school age — asked your advice about whether to begin smoking marijuana. What would your answer be?

# *Appendix: Writing an Argumentative Essay*

The person who understands how arguments are constructed has an important advantage in today's world. Television commercials, political speeches, newspaper editorials, and magazine advertisements, as well as many communications between individuals, all draw on the principles we have examined in the preceding chapters. By now you should be fairly adept at picking out claims, support, and warrants (explicit or un-stated) in these presentations. The next step is to apply your skills to writing an argument of your own. The process of using what you have learned will enhance your ability to analyze critically the marketing efforts with which we are all bombarded every day. Mastering the writing of arguments also gives you a valuable tool for communicating with other people in school, on the job, and even at home.

In this appendix we will move through the various stages involved in creating an argumentative essay: choosing a topic, researching the idea, organizing material, writing, and revising. We will consider also the more general question of how to use the principles already discussed to persuade a real audience. You may be tempted to assume that the primary audience for your paper is your instructor. In fact, ultimately your most important audience is yourself. The more carefully you follow the guidelines here, and the more thought you give to your work at each point, the better you will be able to utilize the art of argument after this course is over.

## FINDING AN APPROPRIATE TOPIC

An old British recipe for jugged hare is said to begin, "First, catch your hare." To write an argumentative essay, you first must choose your topic. This is a relatively easy task for someone writing an argument as part of his or her job — a lawyer defending a client, for example, or an advertising executive presenting a campaign. For a student, however, it can be daunting. Which of the many ideas in the world worth debating would make a good subject?

Several guidelines can help you evaluate the possibilities. Perhaps your assignment limits your choices. If you have been asked to write a research paper, you obviously must find a topic on which research is available. If your assignment is more open ended, you need a topic that is worth the time and effort you expect to invest in it. In either case, your subject should be one that interests you. It may be one on which you already hold a strong opinion, or it may be one you're curious about and might not otherwise bother to investigate. Don't feel you have to write about what you know — very often finding out what you don't know will turn out to be more satisfying. You should, however, choose a subject that is familiar enough for you to argue about it without fearing you're in over your head.

### Invention Strategies

As a starting point, think of conversations you've had in the past few days or weeks that have involved defending a position. Is there some current political issue you're concerned about? Some dispute with friends that would make a valid essay topic? One of the best sources is controversies in the media. Keep your project in mind as you watch TV, read, or listen to the radio. You may even run into a potential subject in your course reading assignments or classroom discussions. Fortunately for the would-be essay writer, nearly every human activity includes its share of disagreement.

As you consider possible topics, write them down. One that looks unlikely at first glance may suggest others or may have more appeal when you come back to it later. Further, simply putting words on paper has a way of stimulating the thought processes involved in writing. Even if your ideas are tentative, the act of converting them into phrases or sentences can often help in developing them.

### Evaluating Possible Topics

Besides interesting you, your topic must interest your audience. Who is the audience? For a lawyer it is usually a judge or jury; for a columnist, anyone he or she can persuade to read a newspaper. For the student writer, the audience is to some extent hypothetical. You should assume that your essay is directed at readers who are reasonably intelligent and well informed, but who have no specific knowledge of the subject. It may be useful to imagine you are writing for a local or school publication — this may be the case if your essay turns out well.

Be sure, too, that you choose a topic with two sides. The purpose of an argument is to defend or refute a thesis, which means the thesis must be debatable. In evaluating a subject that looks promising, ask yourself: Can a case be made for the opposing view? If not, you have no workable ground for building your own case.

Finally, check the scope of your thesis. Consider how long your essay will be, and whether you can do justice to your topic in that amount of space. For example, suppose you want to argue in favor of worldwide nuclear disarmament. Is this a thesis you can support persuasively in a short paper? One way to find out is by listing the potential issues or points about which arguers might disagree. "The future of the world is in danger as long as nuclear weapons exist." Obviously this statement is too general. You would have to specify what you mean by the future of the world (the continuation of human life? of all life? of the earth itself?) and exactly how nuclear weapons endanger it before the claim would hold up. You could narrow it down: "Human beings are error-prone; therefore as long as nuclear weapons exist there is the chance that a large number of people will be killed accidentally." Though this statement is more specific, and includes an important warrant, it still depends on other unstated warrants: that one human being (or a small group) is in the position to discharge a nuclear weapon capable of killing a large number of people; that such a weapon could, in fact, be discharged by mistake given current safety systems. Can you expect to show sufficient evidence for these assumptions in the space available to you?

By now it should be apparent that arguing in favor of nuclear disarmament is too broad an undertaking. A more workable approach might be to defend or refute one of the disarmament proposals under consideration by the U.S. Congress, or to show that nuclear weapons pose some specific danger (such as long-term water pollution) that is sufficient reason to strive for disarmament.

Can a thesis be too narrow? Certainly. If this is true of the one you have chosen, you probably realized it when you asked yourself whether the topic was debatable. If you can prove your point convincingly in a paragraph, or even a page, you need a broader or more two-sided thesis.

At this preliminary stage, don't worry if you don't know exactly how to word your thesis. It's useful to write down a few possible phrasings to be sure your topic is one you can work with, but you need not be precise. The information you unearth as you do research will help you to formulate your ideas. Also, stating a thesis in final terms is premature until you know the organization and tone of your essay.

## To This Point

Let's assume you have surveyed a range of possible topics and chosen one that provides you with a suitable thesis for your essay. Before you go on, check your thesis against the following questions:

1. Is this topic one that will interest both me and my audience?
2. Do I know enough about it to have a rough idea what ideas to use in supporting it, and how to go about finding evidence to back them up?
3. Is the topic debatable?
4. Is my thesis appropriate in scope for an essay of this length?

## RESEARCHING THE IDEA

Once you have decided what to write about, you're ready to lay the foundations for your essay. Undoubtedly you already have some ideas of claims and evidence you can use to support your thesis. In addition to your own reasons for believing in the position you plan to defend, these include the pros or cons you raised when you evaluated your topic. If you have not already done so, write down these points. They will provide a good place to start research.

## Preparing an Initial Outline

An outline, like an accounting system or a computer program, is a practical device for organizing information. Nearly every elementary and high school student learns how to make an outline. Once past high school, however, outlines are much more often recommended than used. What will you gain if you outline your argument? Time. The minutes you spend organizing your subject at the outset generally save at least double the time later, when you have few minutes to spare.

Your preliminary outline establishes an order of priority for your argument. Which supporting points are issues to be defended, which are warrants, and which are evidence? Which supporting points are most persuasive? By constructing a map of your territory, you can identify the research routes that are likely to be most productive. You can also pinpoint any gaps in your reasoning.

List each issue as a main heading in your outline. Next, write below it any relevant support (or sources of support) that you are aware of. Then reexamine the list and consider which issues appear likely to offer the strongest support for your argument. You should number these in order of importance.

At this point, your outline probably consists mostly of issues that support your claim. The primary purpose of research is to gather support to back up these statements. If your research is thorough, it will also point you toward additional ideas. (Most reports of data include conclusions that may become claims in your argument.) Warrants, on the other hand, you will usually have to uncover for yourself.

If you are uncertain of the difference between claims, warrants, and support, look back at Chapters 2, 5, and 4, respectively.

## Secondary and Primary Sources

Because the success of any argument depends in large part on the quantity and quality of the support behind it, research can be crucial. There are two general ways to gather support. The first is to find data provided by scholars and investigators who have studied the subject and reported their findings in books, magazines, and newspapers. In some cases reports present arguments of their own; in others, they are purely factual. The Census Bureau, for example, compiles statistical data on the population of the United States. These statistics can then be used by sociologists and demographers to interpret population trends and make predictions, or by an essayist who needs to know the nation's current population. Usually the best place to find this type of information, known as *secondary sources*, is the library.

The other way of gathering support is to do your own data collecting from primary sources. A *primary source* is raw information not already compiled or interpreted. It is most useful when your topic relates to a local issue, one involving your school or town, for example. If you wanted to investigate a nuclear facility in your area, you could check public records (try the town hall) and conduct interviews with local officials, employees of the facility, and other experts. You may also be able to draw on your own experience.

**441**

## General Guidelines for Research

Whichever type of source you are working with, the following guidelines will help you keep your research on track:

1. Focus your investigation on building your argument, not merely collecting information about the topic. Do follow any promising leads that turn up from the sources you consult, but don't be diverted into general reading that has no direct bearing on your thesis.

2. Look for at least two pieces of evidence to support each claim you make. If you cannot find sufficient evidence, you may need to revise or abandon the claim.

3. Use a variety of sources: not only different publications but information drawn from different fields.

4. Be sure your sources are authoritative. We have already pointed out elsewhere the necessity for examining the credentials of sources. Although it may be difficult or impossible for those outside the field to conclude that one authority is more trustworthy than another, some guidelines are available. Articles and essays in scholarly journals are probably more authoritative than articles in college newspapers. Authors whose credentials include many publications and years of study at reputable institutions are probably more reliable than newspaper columnists and the so-called man in the street. However, we can judge reliability much more easily if we are dealing with facts and inferences than with values and emotions.

5. Don't let your sources' opinions outweigh your own. Your essay should demonstrate that the thesis and ideas you present are yours, arrived at after careful reflection and supported by research. The thesis need not be original, but your paper should be more than a collection of quotations or a report of the facts and opinions you have been reading. It should be clear to the reader that the quotations and other materials support *your* claim and that *you* have been responsible for finding and emphasizing the important issues, for examining the data, and for choosing between strong and weak opinions.

## Using the Library

Let's turn now to an example of a real assignment requiring library research. Suppose that you have chosen to defend the following thesis: *Adopted persons should be entitled to see their birth records and trace the origins of their adoptions.* In many states adoption records are sealed, and adoptees have no access to any information about their natural parents or the circumstances of their adoption. Recently some adoptees have brought suit against the government and adoption agencies in an effort to force disclosure of the records. How can you most effectively use the library to research this topic?

You can begin by consulting the listings under "Adoption" in the card catalog of the library, the *Readers' Guide to Periodical Literature*, and the *New York Times Index*. If you are in doubt about how to locate material, ask the reference librarian to help you. Read first to acquire general familiarity with the subject. Make sure that you are covering both sides of the question — arguments both for and against the rights of adoptees to their birth records — as well as facts and opinions from a variety of sources. In investigating this subject, you will encounter data from historians, philosophers, psychologists, sociologists, and social workers; their varied points of view will contribute to the strength of your claim.

As you read, look for what seem to be the major issues. They will probably be repeated by all or most of your sources. For this claim the major issues may be summarized as follows: (1) the fundamental right of people to know their origins; (2) the psychological harm to adoptees who are prevented from knowing them. On the other side, these issues will emerge: (1) the dangers of revelation to the relationship between adopted children and their adoptive parents; (2) the legal problems resulting from discovery. The latter, of course, are the issues you will have to refute. Your note taking should begin to emphasize these important issues.

Write down questions as they occur to you. Why are adoption records sealed? Do all states seal them? What happens when adoptees sue for the right to see their records? Is there a constitutional right to know one's origins? What are the consequences of knowing and being deprived of the right to know?

### Keeping Your Research Organized

Your preliminary outline provides guideposts for your research. You will need to revise it as you go along to make room for new claims and evidence, and for the questions that come up as you read. Rather than try to fit each new piece of information into your outline, you can use the numbering and/or lettering system in your outline to cross-reference your notebook or file cards.

Insofar as possible, keep all material related to the same claim in the same place. You might do this by making a separate pile of file cards for each claim and its supports and questions, or by reserving several pages in your notebook for information bearing on each claim.

Once you are satisfied that you have defended all the issues that will appear in your essay, you should be able to determine what kind of organization will be most effective for your argument. If you choose a cause-effect arrangement, you will try to prove that the sealing of documents has been the *cause* of distressing damage. If you choose a comparison-contrast development, you will contrast two or more situations to prove that the consequences of open access to records are preferable to the consequences of secrecy. Whatever the approach, your outline should reflect it. As you take notes, refer to your outline frequently to ensure that you are acquiring sufficient data to support all the points you intend to use.

How do you know when you have done enough research? If you have kept your outline updated, you have a visual record of your progress. Check this against the guidelines on page 442: Is each claim backed by at least two pieces of support? Do your sources represent a range of authors and of types of data? If a large proportion of your support comes from one book, or if most of your references are to newspaper articles, you probably need to keep working. On the other hand, if your notes cite five different authorities making essentially the same point, you may have collected more data than you need. It can be useful to point out that more than one authority holds a given view and to make notes of examples that are notably different from one another. But it is not necessary to take down all the passages or examples expressing the same idea.

Following your outline closely will prevent you from recording material that is interesting but not relevant. If you aren't sure whether you will want to use a certain piece of information later, don't copy the whole passage. Instead, make a note for future reference so that you can find it again if you need it. For example:

> Adoptees' self-perception related to their views about their home life. Tables on page 168 in Appendix. Triseliotis, *In Search of Origins*.

Taking too many notes is, however, preferable to taking too few, a problem that will force you to go back to the library for the missing information. For the ideas and quotations in your notes, you should always take down enough information to enable you to find the references again as quickly as possible.

## Quoting and Paraphrasing

You may want to quote one or two passages from your sources if they express an idea in words more effective than your own. In this particular project, you would come across expressions of strong emotion by both adoptees and their adoptive parents worth quoting in full. The following passage, which reveals the desolate feelings of one adoptee who could not discover her biological parents, is an example of such a quotation.

> I feel I am a person not in my own right. I feel I have lived a lie . . . I stand before the mirror and ask, "Who am I? Who do I belong to?" There are times when I wish I had not been born. . . . I feel I need a whole new life, as if everything had been a deception. Soon after I found I was adopted I realised that adopted people are a race apart. When I told my fiancé his reaction was, "I do not know what my mother and father will feel." . . . When my boy was born and my mother-in-law visited me in hospital she exclaimed: "Thank God he has taken from our side of the family." I know what she was getting at and it hurt.[1]

For a thesis that pertains less directly to people's emotions, it is preferable to restrict quotations to four or five lines at most. Remember that the purpose of your essay is to express your own views about the topic. Lengthy quoting may shift the emphasis away from your argument to your sources' views.

If you find a point you want to refer to directly but would prefer not to quote, you can paraphrase, or reword it. Paraphrasing, like quoting, should be used with discrimination. It is most useful when the material from your source is too long for your essay or in a style markedly different from your own. The following extract is an example:

> There was a general reluctance among adoptive parents to reveal or share information about the child's original genealogy and also how he came to be adopted. Though this attitude, as well as the reluctance to reveal the adoptive situation at all, had some cultural sanction in certain parts of the country, in most other cases information was deliberately withheld because of the parents' fears and anxieties. The adoptees interpreted their parents' failure to share with them as reflecting a lack of trust and precariously built relationships. Many regretted the fact that "telling" about adoption and gradually sharing information was not used as an opportunity to develop and cement relationships.[2]

This paragraph is too long to include in a brief research paper (six to ten pages). The idea, however, can be summarized — that is, shortened and translated into your own language:

> Adoptive parents often failed to reveal the truth to their children because of their own fears and anxieties. But the adoptees interpreted this failure as a lack of trust in their relationship. They felt that the truth might have brought them closer to their adoptive parents.

---

[1] John Triseliotis, *In Search of Origins* (Boston: Beacon Press, 1975), p. 87.
[2] Ibid., p. 156.

## Giving Credit to Your Sources

You know, of course, that the exact words of a source may not be quoted without credit. Ideas and conclusions that are not your own also must be attributed to the original source. A paraphrase such as the one above, for example, should be introduced with a phrase identifying the author and indicating that this is his or her view. A reference also should be included at the end of your paper noting the author, the full name of the publication, and the page number.

Giving credit to the sources you use serves two important purposes: It reflects your own honesty and seriousness as a researcher, and it enables the reader to find the source of the reference and read further, sometimes to verify that the source has been correctly used. Your source citations should be complete enough to accomplish both of these aims. As you take notes, and as you write your essay, keep a full record of the documents and authors you have consulted (including page numbers). If the authors you cite are scholarly investigators, write down their full professional identifications. ''Doctor'' or ''Professor'' may not be enough to help you find the source again or to convince a reader that your evidence is trustworthy.

Other books to which your instructor can direct you will give you explicit information about the accepted form for footnotes and bibliography. You may be able simply to follow the forms used by one or more of your sources, if their footnotes and bibliographies include the same range of publications (newspapers, magazines, books by single and multiple authors, collections of essays) as your own research. However, because there is more than one style for footnotes and bibliography, make sure the one you are using is acceptable to your instructor or institution.

## Using Primary Sources

If your essay is on a topic that requires firsthand rather than library research, your needs will be somewhat different. Let's examine an assignment calling for research about a local problem. In this case you can go directly to primary sources without consulting books and journals. You may have one or two purposes in mind: You may want to establish the fact that a problem exists (because you think that not all members of the community are aware of it); having determined that the problem is real, you may want to propose a solution.

Suppose you decide to investigate the food services on campus, about which you have heard numerous complaints. After talking informally with students about their reactions to the food in the dining commons, the coffee shops, the snack bars, and elsewhere, you might distribute a questionnaire to a selected group to get information about the specific grounds for complaint — nutritional value, cost, variety, quantity of food, quality of service. Eliciting useful information from a questionnaire is not, however, as simple as it seems, and you should probably consult a sociologist or psychologist on campus to find the most reliable sample of students and the most appropriate questions for your particular study.

You will also, of course, want to ask questions of those in charge of the food service to discover their view of the problem. If they agree with the students that the service is unsatisfactory, perhaps they can offer reasons that they consider beyond their control. Or they may disagree and point out the injustice of the students' complaints.

The answers to these questions might then lead you to interview university officials and to consult records about food purchases and budgets, if they are accessible. And even an investigation into a local problem can benefit from library research and a look at journal articles about the ways other schools have solved, or failed to solve, the same problems.

### To This Point

Before you leave the library or your primary sources for your typewriter, check to make sure your research is complete.

1. Does your working outline show any gaps in your argument?
2. Have you found adequate data to support your claim?
3. Have you identified the warrants linking your claim with data and ensured that these warrants too are adequately documented?
4. If you intend to quote or paraphrase sources in your essay, do your notes include exact copies of all statements you may want to use and complete references?
5. Have you answered all the relevant questions that have come up during your research?
6. Do you have enough information both on your sources and the format for footnotes and bibliography to document your paper?

## ORGANIZING YOUR ESSAY

The next phase in writing an argument is to organize the results of your thinking and research into a logical and persuasive form. Possibly the process of reading about your topic, answering questions, amassing evidence, and revising your outline has suggested an approach. If not, you should look closely at your outline now, recalling your purposes when you began your investigation, and develop a strategy for using the information you have gathered to achieve those purposes.

The first point to establish is what type of thesis you plan to present. Is your intention to make readers aware of some problem? To offer a solution to a problem? To defend a position? To refute a position held by others? The way you organize your material will depend to a great extent on your goal. With that goal in mind, look over your outline and reevaluate the relative importance of your issues. Which ones are most convincing? Which are backed up by the strongest support? Which ones relate to facts, and which concern values?

## Case Study: Coed Bathrooms

To see how we raise and evaluate issues in a specific context, let's look at a controversy that surfaced recently at a large university. Students living in coed dorms elected to retain their coed bathrooms. The university administration, however, withdrew its approval, in part because of growing protests from parents and alumni.

The students raised these issues:

1. The rights of students to choose their living arrangements
2. The absence of coercion on those who did not wish to participate
3. The increase in civility between the sexes as a result of sharing accommodations
4. The practicality of coed bathrooms, which preclude the necessity for members of one sex to travel to a one-sex bathroom on another floor
5. The success of the experiment so far

On the other side, the administration introduced the following issues:

1. The role of the university *in loco parentis*
2. The necessity for the administration to retain the goodwill of parents and alumni
3. The dissatisfaction of some students with the arrangement
4. The inability of immature students to respect the rights of others and resist the temptation of sexual activity

Now let's analyze these issues, comparing their strengths and weaknesses.

1. It was clear that not all the issues in this dispute were equally important. The arguers decided, therefore, to give greater emphasis to the

issues that were most likely to be ultimately persuasive to their audiences and less attention to those that were difficult to prove or narrower in their appeal. The issue of convenience, for example, seemed a minor point. How much cost is imposed in being required to walk up or down a flight of stairs?

2. It was also clear that, as in several of the other cases we have examined, the support consisted of both factual data and appeals to values. In regard to the factual data, each side reported evidence to prove that

a. The experiment was or was not a success
b. Civility had or had not increased
c. The majority of students did or did not favor the plan
d. Coercion had or had not been applied

The factual data were important. If the administration could prove that the interests of some students had been injured, then the student case for coed bathrooms would be weakened.

But let us assume that the factual claims either were settled or remained in abeyance. We now turn our attention to a second set of issues, a contest over the values to be served.

3. Both sides claimed adherence to the highest principles of university life. Here the issues, while no easier to resolve, offered greater opportunity for serious and fruitful discussion.

The first question to be resolved was that of democratic control. The students asserted, ''We should be permitted to have coed bathrooms because we can prove that the majority of us want them.'' The students hoped that the university community would agree with the implied analogy: that the university community should resemble a political democracy and that students should have full rights as citizens of that community. (This is an argument also made in regard to other areas of university life.)

The university denied that it was a democracy in which students had equal rights and insisted that it should not be. They offered their own analogical proof: Students are not permitted to hire their own teachers or to choose their manner of instruction, their courses of study, their grades, or the rules of admission. The university, they insisted, represented a different kind of community, like a home, in which the experienced are required to lead and instruct the inexperienced.

Students responded by pointing out that coed bathrooms or any other aspect of their living arrangements were areas in which *they* were experts and that freedom to choose living arrangements was not to be confused with a demand for equal participation in academic matters. Moreover, it was also true that in recent years the verdict had increasingly been rendered in favor of rights of special groups as against those of institutions. Students' rights have been among those that have benefited from the movement toward freedom of choice.

4. The second issue was related to the first but introduced a practical consideration, namely, the well-being of the university. The administration argued that more important than the wishes of the students in this essentially minor dispute was the necessity for retaining the support and goodwill of parents and alumni, who are ultimately responsible for the very existence of the university.

The students agreed that this support was necessary but felt that parents and alumni could be persuaded to consider the good reasons in the students' argument. Some students were inclined to carry the argument over goals even further. They insisted that if the university could maintain its existence only at the cost of sacrificing principles of democracy and freedom, then perhaps the university had forfeited its right to exist.

In making our way through this debate, we have summarized a procedure for tackling the issues in any controversial problem.

1.  Raise the relevant issues and arrange them in order of importance because you plan to devote more time and space to issues you regard as crucial.
2.  Produce the strongest evidence you can to support your factual claims, knowing that the opposing side or critical readers may try to produce conflicting evidence.
3.  Defend your value claims by finding support in the fundamental principles with which most people in a democracy would agree.
4.  Argue with yourself. Try to foresee what kinds of refutation are possible. Try to anticipate and meet the opposing arguments.

### Arranging Material Persuasively

With these four points in mind, let us look at various ways of organizing an argumentative essay. It would be foolish to decide in advance how many paragraphs an essay ought to have; however, you can and should choose a general strategy before you begin writing. If your thesis is a declarative one, presenting an opinion or recommending some course of action, you may choose simply to state your main idea and then defend it. If your thesis argues against an opposing view, you probably will want to mention that view and then refute it. Both these organizations introduce the thesis in the first or second paragraph (called the *thesis paragraph*). A third possibility is to start by establishing that a problem exists and then introduce your thesis as the solution; this method can be called *presenting the stock issues*. Although these three approaches sometimes overlap in practice, examining each one individually can help you structure your essay. Let's take a look at each arrangement.

## DEFENDING THE MAIN IDEA

All forms of organization will require you to defend your main idea, but one way of doing this is simple and direct. Early in the paper state the main idea that you will defend throughout your argument. You can also indicate here the two or three points you intend to develop in support of your claim; or you can raise these later as they come up. Your thesis is that widespread vegetarianism would solve a number of problems. You could phrase it this way: "If the majority of people in this country adopted a vegetarian diet, we would see improvements in the economy, in the health of our people, and in moral sensitivity." You would then develop each of the three claims in your list with appropriate data and warrants. Notice that the thesis statement in the first (thesis) paragraph has already outlined your organizational pattern.

Defending the main idea is effective for factual claims and also for policy claims, in which you urge the adoption of a certain policy and give the reasons for its adoption. It is most appropriate when your thesis is straightforward and can be readily supported by direct statements.

## REFUTING THE OPPOSING VIEW

Many of the arguments you will write are responses to other arguments with which you disagree. In these essays, begin with a brief summary of the view you intend to refute. For example:

> Victorian morality has come to serve as a foil for any kind of social "liberation." We think of Victorian society as an unfettered patriarchy in which women were molded into passive and obedient servants, and everyone's sexual appetite was suppressed to the point of neurosis.[3]

You can probably guess that the author will now undertake to prove that this notion is false. (The title of the article from which this passage is taken, "Victorian Savvy," is also a giveaway.)

## PRESENTING THE STOCK ISSUES

Presenting the stock issues, or stating the problem before the solution, is a type of organization borrowed from traditional debate format.

---

[3] William Tucker, "Victorian Savvy," *New York Times*, June 26, 1983, sec. 4, p. 21.

It works for policy claims when an audience must be convinced that a need exists for changing the status quo (present conditions) and for introducing plans to solve the problem. You begin by establishing that a problem exists (need). You then propose a solution (plan), which is your thesis. Finally, you show the reasons for adopting the plan (advantages). These three elements — need, plan, and advantages — are the so-called stock issues.

For example, suppose you wanted to argue that measures for reducing acid rain should be introduced at once. You would first have to establish a need for such measures by defining the problem and providing evidence of damage. Then you would produce your thesis, a means for improving conditions. Finally you would suggest the benefits that would follow from implementation of your plan. Notice that in this organization your thesis paragraph usually falls well into your essay, although it may also appear at the beginning.

## Ordering Claims for Emphasis

Whichever way you choose to work, you should revise your outline to reflect the order in which you intend to present your thesis and supporting ideas. Not only the placement of your thesis paragraph but the arrangement of your ideas will determine what points in your essay receive the most emphasis.

Suppose your purpose is to convince the reader that cigarette smoking is a bad habit. You might decide to concentrate on three unpleasant attributes of cigarette smoking: (1) it is unhealthy; (2) it is dirty; (3) it is expensive. Obviously, these are not equally important as possible deterrents. You would no doubt consider the first reason, accompanied by evidence to prove the relationship between cigarette smoking and cancer, heart disease, emphysema, and other diseases, the most compelling. This issue, therefore, should be given greater emphasis than the others.

There are several ways to achieve emphasis. One is to make the explicit statement that you, the writer, consider a certain issue the most important.

> Finally, and *most importantly*, human culture is often able to neutralize or reverse what might otherwise be genetically advantageous consequences of selfish behavior.[4]

---

[4]Peter Singer, *The Expanding Circle* (New York: New American Library, 1982), p. 171.

This quotation also reveals a second way—placing the material to be emphasized in an emphatic position, first or last in the essay. The end position, however, is generally the more emphatic.

A third way to achieve emphasis is to elaborate on the material to be emphasized, treating it at greater length, offering more data and reasons for it than you give for the other issues.

## Considering Scope and Audience

With a working outline in hand that indicates the order of your thesis and claims, you are almost ready to begin turning your notes into prose. First, however, it is useful to review the limits on your essay to be sure your writing time will be used to the best possible advantage.

The first limit involves scope. As mentioned earlier, your thesis should introduce a claim that can be adequately supported in the space available to you. If your research has opened up more aspects than you anticipated, you may want to narrow your thesis to one major subtopic. Or you could emphasize only the most persuasive arguments for your position (assuming these are sufficient to make your case) and omit the others. In a brief essay (three to four pages), three issues are probably all you have room to develop. On the other hand, if you suspect your thesis can be proved in one or two pages, look for ways to expand it. What additional issues might be brought in to bolster your argument? Alternatively, is there a larger issue for which your thesis could become a supporting idea?

Other limits on your essay are imposed by the need to make your points in a way that will be persuasive to an audience. The style and tone you choose depend not only on the nature of the subject, but also on how you can best convince readers that you are a credible source. *Style* in this context refers to the physical elements of your prose — simple versus complex sentences, active versus passive verbs, metaphors, analogies, and other literary devices. *Tone* is the approach you take to your topic — solemn or humorous, detached or sympathetic. Style and tone together compose your voice as a writer.

Many students assume that a writer's voice is inborn, like a singer's. In fact, a writer (like a singer) typically adapts his or her voice to the material and the audience. Perhaps the easiest way to appreciate this is to think of two or three works by the same author that are written in different voices. For example, compare Woody Allen's essay "My Speech to the Graduates" (p. 169) with his films *Annie Hall* or *Interiors*. Or compare the speeches of two different characters in the same story, novel, or film. Every writer has individual talents and inclinations that appear in most or all of his or her work. A good writer, however, is able to amplify some stylistic elements and diminish others, and to change tone, by choice.

It is usually appropriate in a short paper to choose an expository style, which emphasizes the elements of your argument rather than your personality. You may want to appeal to your readers' emotions as well as their intellects, but keep in mind that sympathy is most effectively gained when it is supported by believable evidence. If you press your point stridently, your audience is likely to be suspicious rather than receptive. If you sprinkle your prose with jokes or metaphors, you may diminish your credibility by detracting from the substance of your case. Both humor and analogy can be useful tools, but they should be used with discretion.

You can discover some helpful pointers on essay style by reading the editorials in newspapers such as the *New York Times*, the *Washington Post*, or the *Wall Street Journal*. These authors are typically addressing a mixed audience comparable to the hypothetical readers of your own essay. Though their approaches vary, each writer is attempting to portray himself or herself as an objective analyst whose argument deserves careful attention.

Again, remember your goals. You are trying to persuade your audience of something; an argument is, by its nature, directed at people who do not initially agree with its thesis. Therefore, your voice as well as the claims you make must be convincing.

## To This Point

The organizing steps that come between research and writing are often neglected. Careful planning at this stage, however, can save much time and effort later. As you prepare to start writing, you should be able to answer the following questions:

1. Is the purpose of my essay to persuade readers to accept a potentially controversial idea, to refute someone else's position, or to propose a solution to a problem?
2. Have I decided on an organization that is likely to accomplish this purpose?
3. Does my outline arrange my thesis and issues in an appropriate order to emphasize the most important issues?
4. Does my outline show an argument whose scope suits the needs of this essay?
5. What questions of style and tone do I need to keep in mind as I write to ensure that my argument will be persuasive?

# WRITING

## Beginning Your Essay

Having found a claim you can defend and the voice you will adopt toward your audience, you must now think about how to begin. An introduction to your subject should be more than just the first paragraph of your essay. It should invite the reader to give attention to what you have to say. It should also point you in the direction you will take in developing your argument. You may want to begin the actual writing of your essay with the thesis paragraph. It is useful to consider the whole paragraph rather than simply the thesis statement for two reasons. First, not all theses are effectively expressed in a single sentence. Second, the rest of the paragraph will be closely tied to your statement of the main idea. You may show why you have chosen this topic or why your audience will benefit from reading your essay. You may introduce your warrant, qualify your claim, and in other ways prepare for the body of your argument. Readers will perceive the whole paragraph as a unit, so it makes sense to approach it that way.

Consider first the kind of argument you intend to present. Does your essay make a factual claim? Does it address values? Does it recommend a policy or action? Is it a rebuttal of some current policy or belief? The answers to these questions will influence the way you introduce the subject.

If your thesis makes a factual claim, you may be able to summarize it in one or two opening sentences. "Whether we like it or not, money is obsolete. The currency of today is not paper or coin, but plastic." Refutations are easy to introduce in a brief statement: "Contrary to popular views on the subject, the institution of marriage is as sound today as it was a generation ago."

A thesis that defends a value is usually best preceded by an explanatory introduction. "Some wars are morally defensible" is a thesis that can be stated as a simple declarative opening sentence. However, readers who disagree may not read any farther than the first line. Someone defending this claim is likely to be more persuasive if he or she first gives an example of a situation in which war is or was preferable to peace, or presents the thesis less directly.

One way to keep such a thesis from alienating the audience is to phrase it as a question. "Are all wars morally indefensible?" Still better would be to prepare for the question:

> Few if any of us favor war as a solution to international problems. We are too vividly aware of the human suffering imposed by armed conflict, as well as the political and financial turmoil that inevitably result. Yet can we honestly agree that no war is ever morally defensible?

Notice that this paragraph gains appeal from use of the first person. The author implies that he or she shares the readers' feelings but has good reasons for believing those feelings are not sufficient grounds for condemning all wars. Even if readers are skeptical, the conciliatory phrasing of the thesis should encourage them to continue reading.

For any subject that is highly controversial or emotionally charged, especially one that strongly condemns an existing situation or belief, you may sometimes want to express your indignation directly. Of course, you must be sure that your indignation can be justified. The author of the following introduction, a physician and writer, openly admits that he is about to make a case that may offend readers.

> Is there any polite way to introduce today's subject? I'm afraid not. It must be said plainly that the media have done about as sorry and dishonest a job of covering health news as is humanly possible, and that when the media do not fail from bias and mendacity, they fail from ignorance and laziness.[5]

If your thesis advocates a policy or makes a recommendation, it may be a good idea, as in a value claim, to provide a short background. The following paragraph introduces an argument favoring relaxation of controls in high schools.

> "Free the New York City 275,000" read a button worn by many young New Yorkers some years ago. The number was roughly the total of students enrolled in the City's high schools.
>
> The condition of un-freedom which it described was not, however, unique to the schools of one city. According to the Carnegie Commission's comprehensive study of American public education, *Crisis in the Classroom*, public schools across the country share a common characteristic, namely, "preoccupation with order and control." The result is that students find themselves the victims of "oppressive and petty rules which give their schools a repressive, almost prison-like atmosphere."[6]

There are also other ways to introduce your subject. One is to begin with an appropriate quotation.

> "Reading makes a full man, conversation makes a ready man, and writing makes an exact man." So Francis Bacon told us around 1600. Recently I have been wondering how Bacon's formula might apply to present-day college students.[7]

[5] Michael Halberstam, "TV's Unhealthy Approach to Health News," *TV Guide*, September 20–26, 1980, p. 24.

[6] Alan Levine and Eve Carey, *The Rights of Students* (New York: Avon Books, 1977), p. 11.

[7] William Aiken, "The Conversation on Campus Today Is, Uh . . .", *Wall Street Journal*, May 4, 1982, p. 18.

Or you may begin with an anecdote. In the following introduction to an article about the relation between cancer and mental attitude, the author recounts a personal experience.

> Shortly after I moved to California, a new acquaintance sat in my San Francisco living room drinking rose-hip tea and chainsmoking. Like so many residents of the Golden West, Cecil was "into" all things healthy, from jogging to *shiatsu* massage to kelp. Tobacco didn't seem to fit, but he told me confidently that there was no contradiction. "It all has to do with energy," he said. "Unless you have a lot of negative energy about smoking cigarettes, there's no way they can hurt you; you won't get cancer."[8]

Finally, you may introduce yourself as the author of the claim.

> I wish to argue an unpopular cause: the cause of the old, free elective system in the academic world, or the untrammeled right of the undergraduate to make his own mistakes.[9]

> My subject is the world of Hamlet. I do not of course mean Denmark, except as Denmark is given a body by the play; and I do not mean Elizabethan England, though this is necessarily close behind the scenes. I mean simply the imaginative environment that the play asks us to enter when we read it or go to see it.[10]

You should, however, use such introductions with care. They suggest an authority about the subject that you shouldn't attempt to assume unless you can demonstrate you are entitled to it.

## Some Guidelines for Good Essay Writing

In general, the writer of an argument follows the same rules that govern any form of expository writing. Your style should be clear and readable, your organization logical, your ideas connected by transitional phrases or sentences, your paragraphs coherent. The main difference between an argument and other essays, as noted earlier, is the need to persuade an audience to adopt a belief or take an action. You should assume your readers will be critical rather than neutral or sympathetic. Therefore, you must be equally critical of your own work. Any apparent gap in reasoning or ambiguity in presentation is likely to weaken the argument.

---

[8]Joel Guerin, "Cancer and the Mind," *Harvard Magazine*, November–December 1978, p. 11.

[9]Howard Mumford Jones, "Undergraduates on Apron Strings," *Atlantic Monthly*, October 1955, p. 45.

[10]Maynard Mack, "The World of Hamlet," *Yale Review*, June 1952, p. 502.

For the rest of this section we will concentrate on constructing a successful essay. In the following section we will turn to revising, the writer's insurance policy against flaws in style and structure.

As you read the essays in this book and elsewhere, you will discover that good style in argumentative writing shares several characteristics:

— Variety in sentence structure: a mixture of both long and short sentences, different sentence beginnings

— Rich but standard vocabulary: avoidance of specialized terms unless they are fully explained, word choice appropriate to a thoughtful argument

— Use of details and examples to illustrate and clarify abstract terms, principles, and generalizations

You should take care to avoid the following:

— Unnecessary repetition: making the same point without new data or interpretation

— Exaggeration or stridency, which can create suspicion of your fairness and powers of observation

— Short paragraphs of one or two sentences, which are common in advertising and newspaper writing to get the reader's attention but are inappropriate in a thoughtful essay

In addition to these stylistic principles, seven general points are worth keeping in mind:

1. Although *you*, like *I*, should be used judiciously, it can be found even in the treatment of weighty subjects. Here is an example from an essay by the distinguished British mathematician and philosopher, Bertrand Russell.

> Suppose you are a scientific pioneer and you make some discovery of great scientific importance and suppose you say to yourself, "I am afraid this discovery will do harm": you know that other people are likely to make the same discovery if they are allowed suitable opportunities for research; you must therefore, if you do not wish the discovery to become public, either discourage your sort of research or control publication by a board of censors.[11]

Don't be afraid to use *you* or *I* when they are useful to emphasize the presence of the person making the argument.

---

[11] "Science and Human Life," in *What is Science?* edited by James R. Newman (New York: Simon and Schuster, 1955), p. 12.

2. Don't pad. This point should be obvious; the word *pad* suggests the addition of unnecessary material. Many writers find it tempting, however, to enlarge a discussion even when they have little more to say. It is never wise to introduce more words into an essay that has already made its point. If the essay turns out to be shorter than you had hoped, it may mean that you have not sufficiently developed the subject or that the subject was less substantial than you thought when you selected it. Padding, which is easy to detect in its repetition and sentences empty of content, weakens the writer's credibility.

3. For any absolute generalization—a statement containing words such as *all* or *every*—consider the possibility that there may be at least one example that will weaken the generalization. Such a precaution means that you won't have to backtrack and admit that your generalization is not, after all, universal. A student who was arguing against capital punishment for the reason that all killing was wrong suddenly paused in her presentation and added, "On the other hand, if given the chance, I'd probably have been willing to kill Hitler." This admission meant that she recognized important exceptions to her rule and that she would have to qualify her generalization in some significant way.

4. When offering an explanation, especially one that is complicated or extraordinary, look first for a cause that is easier to accept, one that doesn't strain credibility. (In Chapter 7, we called attention to this principle.) For example, a few years ago a great many people were bemused by reports about the mysterious Bermuda Triangle, which had apparently swallowed up ships and planes since the mid–nineteenth century. The forces at work were variously described as space-time warps, UFOs that transported earthlings to other planets, and sea monsters seeking revenge. But a careful investigation revealed familiar, natural causes. A reasonable person interested in the truth would have searched for more conventional explanations before accepting the bizarre stories of extraterrestrial creatures. He or she would also exercise caution when confronted by conspiracy theories that try to account for controversial political events, such as the assassination of President John Kennedy.

5. Check carefully for questionable warrants. Your outline should specify your warrants. When necessary, these should be included in your essay to link claims with support. Many an argument has failed because it depended on an unstated warrant with which the reader did not agree. If you were arguing for a physical education requirement at your school, you might make a good case for all the physical and psychological benefits of such a requirement. But you would certainly need to introduce and develop the warrant on which your claim was based—that it is the proper function of a college or university to provide the benefits of a physical education. Many readers would agree that physical education is

valuable, but they might question the assumption that an academic institution should introduce a nonintellectual enterprise into the curriculum. At any point where you draw a controversial or tenuous conclusion, be sure your reasoning is clear and logical.

6. Avoid conclusions that are merely summaries. Summaries may be needed in long technical papers, but in brief arguments they create endings that are without force or interest. In the closing paragraph you should find a new idea that emerges naturally from the development of the whole argument.

7. Strive for a paper that is unified, coherent, and emphatic where appropriate. A *unified* essay stays focused on its goal and aims each claim, warrant, and piece of evidence toward that goal. Extraneous information or unsupported claims impair unity. *Coherence* means that all ideas are fully explained and adequately connected by transitions. To ensure coherence, give especially close attention to the beginnings and ends of your paragraphs: Is each new concept introduced in a way that shows it following naturally from the one that preceded it? *Emphasis*, as we have mentioned, is a function partly of structure and partly of language. Your most important claims should be placed where they are certain of receiving the reader's attention: key sentences at the beginning or end of a paragraph, key paragraphs at the beginning or end of your essay. Sentence structure also can be used for emphasis. If you have used several long, complex sentences, you can emphasize a significant point by stating it briefly and simply. You can also create emphasis with verbal flags, such as ''The primary issue to consider . . .'' or ''Finally, we cannot ignore . . .''

All clear expository prose will exhibit the qualities of unity, coherence, and emphasis. But the success of an argumentative essay is especially dependent on them because the reader may have to follow a line of reasoning that is both complicated and unfamiliar. Moreover, an essay that is unified, coherent, and properly emphatic will be more readable, the first requisite of an effective argument.

## REVISING

The final stage in writing an argumentative essay is revising. The first step is to read through what you have written for mistakes. Next, check your work against the guidelines listed under ''Organizing Your Essay'' and ''Writing.'' Have you omitted any of the claims, warrants, or supporting evidence on your outline? Is each paragraph coherent in itself? Do your paragraphs work together to create a coherent essay? All the elements of the argument — the issues raised, the underlying assumptions, and the supporting material — should contribute to the development of the claim in your thesis statement. Any material which is interesting but irrelevant to that claim should be cut. Finally, does your essay reach a clear conclusion that reinforces your thesis?

Be sure, too, that the style and tone of your paper are appropriate for the topic and the audience. If you were an outside reader, would you find this essay informative and persuasive? Remember that people choose to read an argument because they want the answer to a troubling question or the solution to a recurrent problem. Besides stating your thesis in a way that invites the reader to join you in your investigation, you must retain your audience's interest through a discussion that may be unfamiliar or contrary to their convictions. The outstanding qualities of argumentative prose style, therefore, are clarity and readability.

Style is obviously harder to evaluate in your own writing than organization. Your outline provides a map against which to check the structure of your paper. Clarity and readability, by comparison, are somewhat abstract qualities. Two procedures may be helpful. The first is to read two or three (or more) essays by other authors whose style you admire and then turn back to your own. Awkward spots in your prose are easier to see if you get away from it and tune in to someone else's perspective than if you simply keep rereading your own writing.

The second method is to read aloud. If you have never tried it, you are likely to be surprised at how valuable this can be. Again, start with someone else's work that you feel is clearly written. You may need to practice before arriving at a smooth rhythmic delivery that satisfies you. And you must listen to what you are reading. Your objective is to absorb the patterns of English structure that characterize the clearest, most readable prose. Then read your own paper aloud and listen to the construction of your sentences. Are they also clear and readable? Do they say what you want them to say? How would they sound to a reader? According to one theory, you can learn the rhythm and phrasing of a language as you learn the rhythm and phrasing of a melody. And you will often *hear* a mistake or a clumsy construction in your writing although it has escaped your eye in proofreading.

## MANUSCRIPT PREPARATION AND DOCUMENTATION

In preparing your final draft, follow whatever guidelines your instructor has provided or consult a handbook or other guide for specific advice on format and documentation. Usually the manuscript should be typed double spaced, on 8½" × 11", 20-pound, white typing paper, with margins of 1" to 1½" on all sides. Each paragraph should be indented five spaces. Correct your mistakes with white correction fluid or, if there are only a few, cross them out and neatly write the correction above the line. Number each page in the upper right corner. Proofread the finished paper carefully for mistakes in spelling, grammar, and punctuation.

If you wish to include headings, they should be placed and worded to alert the reader to main points or important changes in subject. Do not use headings to convey any of the content of your argument; that is the function of the text. Each heading should be typed on a separate line, either starting at the left margin or centered, and capitalized or underlined for emphasis.

As you write, include a source citation for each quotation or piece of information taken from another writer's work. Your instructor may suggest a form for these citations. The most common forms are (1) traditional footnotes, in which a footnote number follows the cited passage and the source information is provided in a note either at the foot of the page or, more often, at the end of the paper; or (2) the 1984 Modern Language Association (MLA) style or the American Psychological Association (APA) style, both of which provide, in slightly different forms, an abbreviated citation (author's last name, page number, and — in APA — the date) in parentheses in the text. Whichever format you follow, include at the end of your paper a bibliography that lists alphabetically by author the works you have cited. Your instructor may also ask you to include all the sources you consulted in researching your essay, whether or not they are actually cited in your paper. Your bibliography can be typed single spaced.

Your essay should be preceded by a title page. If your instructor has not specified a form, give the title of your paper, your instructor's name, and the date.

## IN CONCLUSION

A successful argumentative essay meets the following criteria:

1. It presents a thesis that is of interest to both the writer and the audience, is debatable, and can be defended in the amount of space available.
2. Each statement offered in support of the thesis is backed up with enough evidence to give it credibility. Data cited in the essay come from a variety of sources. All quotations and direct references to primary or secondary sources are fully documented.
3. The warrants linking claims with support are either specified or im-

plicit in the author's data and line of reasoning. No claim should depend on an unstated warrant with which skeptical readers might disagree.

4. The thesis is clearly presented and adequately introduced in a thesis paragraph, which indicates the purpose of the essay.

5. Supporting statements and data are organized in a way that builds the argument, emphasizes the author's main ideas, and justifies the essay's conclusions.

6. All possible opposing arguments are anticipated and refuted.

7. The essay is written in a style and tone appropriate to the topic and the intended audience. The author's prose is clear and readable.

8. The manuscript is clean, carefully proofed, and typed in an acceptable format.

ACKNOWLEDGMENTS

(Continued from page iv)

American Enterprise Institute, "Affirmative Action: The Answer to Discrimination?" from the A.E.I. Roundtable, 1976.

Jim Bates, "U.S. Immigration Policy." This article first appeared in the November/December 1981 issue of *The Humanist* and is reprinted by permission.

Bruno Bettelheim, "The Ignored Lesson of Anne Frank." From *Surviving and Other Essays* by Bruno Bettelheim. Copyright © 1979 by Bruno Bettelheim and Trude Bettelheim as Trustees. Reprinted by permission of Alfred A. Knopf, Inc.

Caroline Bird, "Where College Fails Us." From *Signature*, 1975.

Brigid Brophy, "The Rights of Animals." From *Don't Never Forget: Collected Views and Reviews* by Brigid Brophy (1966). Reprinted by permission of the author.

Leo Buscaglia, "Say 'I Love You' Today." Reprinted by permission of the author.

Wayne A. Cornelius, "When the Door Is Closed to Illegal Aliens, Who Pays?" Copyright © 1977 by The New York Times Company. Reprinted by permission.

Norman Cousins, "The Right to Die." © 1975 Saturday Review Magazine Co. Reprinted by permission.

Nora Ephron, "Deep Throat." From *Crazy Salad: Some Things about Women* by Nora Ephron. Copyright © 1973 by Nora Ephron. Reprinted by permission of Alfred A. Knopf, Inc.

Willard Gaylin, "Still, a Person Owns Himself." Copyright © 1982 by The New York Times Company. Reprinted by permission.

Howard Glickstein, "Discrimination in Higher Education." From *Reverse Discrimination*, Barry R. Gross, editor. Reprinted by permission of Prometheus Books.

Ellen Goodman, "It's Failure, Not Success." From *Close to Home* by Ellen Goodman. Copyright © 1979 by The Washington Post Company. Reprinted by permission of Simon & Schuster, Inc.

Paul Goodman, "A Proposal to Abolish Grading." Reprinted from *Compulsory Mis-Education* by Paul Goodman. Copyright 1964, by permission of the publisher, Horizon Press, New York.

Walter Goodman, "What Is a Civil Libertarian to Do When Pornography Becomes So Bold?" Copyright © 1976 by The New York Times Company. Reprinted by permission.

Meg Greenfield, "Creating a 'Learning Society.'" Copyright 1983 by Newsweek, Inc. All rights reserved. Reprinted by permission.

Garrett Hardin, "Smokescreens and Evasions." From *Naked Emperors — Essays of a Taboo-Stalker* by Garrett Hardin. Copyright © 1982 by William Kaufmann, Inc., Los Altos, CA. Reprinted with permission, all rights reserved.

William B. Helmreich, "Stereotype Truth." Copyright © 1981 by The New York Times Company. Reprinted by permission.

Sidney Hook, "Discrimination, Color Blindness, and the Quota System." From *Reverse Discrimination*, Barry R. Gross, editor. Reprinted by permission of Prometheus Books.

Ruth Hubbard, "Test-Tube Babies: Solution or Problem?" From March/April 1980 issue of *Technology Review*. Copyright 1980. Reprinted with permission from *Technology Review*.

Jesse Jackson, "Why Blacks Need Affirmative Action." From September/October 1978 issue of *Regulation*. Reprinted by permission.

Susan Jacoby, "Hers." Copyright © 1978 by Susan Jacoby. Reprinted by permission of the author.

Martin Luther King, Jr., "I Have a Dream." Copyright © 1963 by Martin Luther King, Jr. Reprinted by permission of Joan Daves.

Irving Kristol, "Pornography and Censorship." From *Reflections of a Neoconservative: Looking Back, Looking Ahead* by Irving Kristol. © 1983 by Basic Books, Inc., Publishers. Reprinted by permission of the publisher.

William M. Lamers, Jr., M.D., "Funerals Are Good for People." Copyright © and published by Medical Economics Company, Inc., at Oradell, NJ. By permission.

Richard D. Lamm, "America Needs Fewer Immigrants." Copyright © 1981 by The New York Times Company. Reprinted by permission.

Franklin Lavin, "Registration Drive." From *The Washington Monthly*, April 1983. Reprinted with permission from *The Washington Monthly*. Copyright by The Washington Monthly Co., Washington, DC.

John Leo, "Homosexuality: Tolerance Versus Approval." Copyright 1979 Time Inc. All rights reserved. Reprinted by permission from *Time*.

Michael Levin, "The Case for Torture." Copyright 1982 by Newsweek, Inc. All rights reserved, reprinted by permission.

Michael Levin, "How to Tell Bad from Worse." Copyright 1981 by Newsweek, Inc. All rights reserved, reprinted by permission.

Michael Levin, "The Springsteening of Disarmament." Copyright © 1982 by The New York Times Company. Reprinted by permission.

Carolyn Lewis, "My Unprodigal Sons." Copyright 1982 by Newsweek, Inc. All rights reserved, reprinted by permission.

Walter Lippmann, "The Indispensable Opposition." Copyright 1939 by The Atlantic Monthly Company. Used with permission of the President and Fellows of Harvard College.

Daniel C. Maguire, "Who Should Decide?" From *Death by Choice* by Daniel C. Maguire. Copyright © 1973, 1974 by Daniel C. Maguire. Reprinted by permission of Doubleday & Company, Inc.

Bruce Powell Majors, "Gun Control: Historically Ineffective, Imprudent, and Coercive." Reprinted from the July 13 and July 29, 1981, issues of *The Northwest Current* by permission of the author.

H. L. Mencken, "The Penalty of Death." Copyright 1926 by Alfred A. Knopf, Inc. Renewed 1954 by H. L. Mencken. Reprinted from *A Mencken Chrestomathy* by H. L. Mencken by permission of the publisher.

Jan Morris, "Down, Down on America." Copyright © 1983 by The New York Times Company. Reprinted by permission.

Lynn Morrison and Gerald S. Levey, "Lab Animals' Use." Copyright © 1983 by The New York Times Company. Reprinted by permission.

Jacob Neusner, "The Speech the Graduates Didn't Hear." Copyright © 1983 by Jacob Neusner. Reprinted from *The Daily Herald*, June 12, 1983. Used by permission of the author.

The New York Times Company, "View from Two Sides on How to Vault the Color Bar." Copyright © 1981 by The New York Times Company. Reprinted by permission. Letters to the Editor Copyright © 1981, 1982 by The New York Times Company.

Timothy Noah, "Monkey Business." From the June 2, 1982, issue of *The New Republic*. Reprinted by permission.

Andrew Oldenquist, "On Belonging to Tribes." Copyright 1982 by Newsweek, Inc. All rights reserved, reprinted by permission.

George Orwell, "Politics and the English Language." Copyright 1946 by Sonia Brownell Orwell, renewed 1974 by Sonia Orwell. "A Hanging" copyright 1950 by Sonia Orwell, renewed 1978 by Sonia Pitt-Rivers. Both selections reprinted from *Shooting an Elephant and Other Essays* by George Orwell. Reprinted by permission of Harcourt Brace Jovanovich, Inc., the estate of the late Sonia Brownell Orwell, and Martin Secker & Warburg, Ltd.

Noel Perrin, "The War of the Woods." Reprinted from the December 1982 issue of *Yankee* by permission of the author.

James Rachels, M.D., "Active and Passive Euthanasia." Reprinted by permission of the *New England Journal of Medicine*, Vol. 292, pp. 78–80, 1975.

Albert Rosenfeld, "Animal Rights Versus Human Health." Reprinted from the June issue of *Science '81* by permission of *Science '84* Magazine, © the American Association for the Advancement of Science.

Jane Rule, "Pornography Is a Social Disease." Copyright © 1984 by Jane Rule. Reprinted by permission of the author.

Jeffrey St. John, "E.R.A. Could Swamp Courts: Women's Lib Amendment Not Simple Legal Formula." Reprinted from the May 9, 1972, issue of *The Columbus Dispatch* by permission of Copley News Service.

Peter Singer, "Animal Liberation." Reprinted from the April 15, 1973, issue of *The New York Review of Books* by permission of the author.

Roger Sipher, "So That Nobody Has to Go to School If They Don't Want To." Copyright © 1977 by The New York Times Company. Reprinted by permission.

Thomas Sowell, "Dissenting from Liberal Orthodoxy." From American Enterprise Institute reprint no. 59, 1976. Reprinted by permission of the American Enterprise Institute.

Gloria Steinem, "The Real Linda Lovelace." From *Outrageous Acts and Everyday Rebellions* by Gloria Steinem. Copyright © 1983 by Gloria Steinem. Reprinted by permission of Holt, Rinehart and Winston, Publishers.

Richard Stengel, "No More MoonJune: Love's Out." Copyright © 1979 by The New York Times Company. Reprinted by permission.

Lewis Thomas, "The Health-Care System." From *The Medusa and the Snail* by Lewis Thomas. Copyright © 1975 by Lewis Thomas. Originally published in the *New England Journal of Medicine*. Reprinted by permission of Viking Penguin Inc.

Frank Trippett, "A Red Light for Scofflaws." Copyright © 1983 Time Inc. All rights reserved. Reprinted by permission from *Time*.

Gore Vidal, "Drugs: A Case for Legalizing Marijuana." Copyright © 1970 by Gore Vidal. Reprinted by permission of William Morris Agency, Inc., on behalf of the author.

Wilcomb E. Washburn, "Quotas Are Tough If All Are Minorities." Reprinted by permission of *The Wall Street Journal* © Dow Jones & Company, Inc., 1984. All rights reserved.

George F. Will, "Lotteries Cheat, Corrupt the People." © 1984, Washington Post Writers Group. Reprinted with permission.

# Glossary and
# Index of Terms

**Abstract:**　expressing a quality apart from a specific object or event; contrasted with *concrete*　*140–144*

**Argument:**　a process of reasoning and advancing proof about issues on which conflicting views may be held; a statement or statements providing support for a claim　*3–23*

**Audience:**　the people who will hear or read an argument　*13*

**Authority:**　a respectable, reliable source of evidence　*27, 86–90*

**Claim:**　the conclusion of an argument; what the arguer is trying to prove　*10–11, 24–53*

**Cliché:**　a worn-out expression or idea, no longer capable of producing a visual image or provoking thought about a subject　*148–150*

**Concrete:**　characterizing a real thing or experience; contrasted with *abstract*　*140–144*

**Connotation:**　the emotional overtones that attach to a word through long usage, in contrast to its explicit, literal meaning　*134–136*

**Credibility:**　the audience's belief in the arguer's trustworthiness; see also *ethos*　*13–17, 86–89*

**Data:**　see *evidence*

**Two wrongs make a right:** diverting attention from the issue by introducing a new point *187–188*

**Induction:** reasoning by which we arrive at a general statement on the basis of the observation of particulars *174–175*

**Inference:** an interpretation of the facts *28–29*

**Motivational appeal:** an attempt to reach an audience by recognizing their needs and values and how these contribute to their decision making *11, 90–96*

**Need:** anything, whether psychological or physiological, required for the survival and welfare of a human being *91–93*

**Picturesque language:** words that produce images in the minds of the audience *138–140*

**Policy:** a course of action recommended or taken to solve a problem or guide decisions *11, 38–40*

**Qualifier:** a restriction placed on the claim to indicate that it may not always be true as stated *26, 109*

**Reservation:** a restriction placed on the warrant to indicate that unless certain conditions are met, the warrant may not establish a connection between the support and the claim *109*

**Slanting:** selecting facts or words with connotations that favor the arguer's bias and discredit alternatives *136–138*

**Slogan:** an attention-getting expression used largely in politics or advertising to promote support of a cause or product without giving adequate proof *150–154*

**Style:** choices in words and sentence structure that make a writer's language distinctive *457–458*

**Support:** any material that serves to prove an issue or claim; in addition to evidence, it includes appeals to the needs and values of the audience *11, 75–96*

**Thesis:** the main idea of an essay *438–440*

**Values:** conceptions or ideas that act as standards for judging what is right or wrong, worthwhile or worthless, beautiful or ugly, good or bad *10, 31–34, 94–96*

**Warrant:** a general principle or assumption that establishes a connection between the support and the claim *11–12, 108–119*

# Index to Authors
# and Titles